The Biblical
85

Space and Time in the
Religious Life of the Near East

Space and Time
in the Religious Life
of the Near East

Nicolas Wyatt

Sheffield
Academic Press
www.SheffieldAcademicPress.com

Copyright © 2001 Sheffield Academic Press

Published by
Sheffield Academic Press Ltd
Mansion House
19 Kingfield Road
Sheffield S11 9AS
England
www.SheffieldAcademicPress.com

Printed on acid-free paper in Great Britain
by Bookcraft Ltd
Midsomer Norton, Bath

British Library Cataloguing-in-Publication Data

A catalogue record for this book is available
from the British Library

ISBN 1-84127-288-4

For David, Simon and Geoffrey

'Mercy!' cried Gandalf. 'If the giving of information is to be the cure of your inquisitiveness, I shall spend all the rest of my days in answering you. What more do you want to know?'

'The names of all the stars, and of all living things, and the whole history of Middle-earth and Over-heaven and of the Sundering Seas,' laughed Pippin.

J. R. R. Tolkien, The Lord of the Rings

CONTENTS

This book began life as a compilation of texts for students in a new course resulting from the revision of degree structures at New College, in the University of Edinburgh. The theme of the entire course was 'Space and Time in World Religions' (covering the religions of the ancient Near East, India, and Africa, Islam and Christianity). My own brief was to cover religions in the ancient Near East, which I interpreted as incorporating the longest lived of the ancient Near Eastern religions, ancient 'Israelite' religion, which survives in its latest historical forms as Judaism and Christianity. This is the channel through which many of the ancient memes were transmitted into the religiosity of today. This will explain a bias that will become evident to readers, in so far as these parameters have controlled much of the initial choice of material. In some cases (especially at §3 as an excursus) I have even included some early Christian examples of motifs, to illustrate continuity in the conflict myth. But in attempting to turn it into a book of wider use, which I hope will be of more general interest both to Religious Studies and Theology (Biblical Studies) students, I have broadened the range of treatment with the addition of further materials, though remaining roughly within the original parameters. This volume will therefore attempt a thematic and selective, though by no means a complete, coverage of ancient Near Eastern religion. If I be accused of neglecting some issues, e.g. ethics, I readily concede the omission, but justify myself on the basis of bringing a volume of tolerable length to my readers. Besides, those who make such accusations may prefer not to read my views on the subject, if they expect a bit of Jusaeo-Christian triumphalism.

As a source book addressed primarily to students, it behoves me to offer explanations of obscurities, to cross-refer on a significant scale, in short, to provide as much help to the reader as possible, though not, I hope, at the expense of an adequate exposition of modes of thought at first sight very far removed from our own. The original lectures to which the source book provided a supplement were also accompanied by a two-page handout to each lecture, providing an outline of the theme. It has seemed worthwhile to incorporate some of this material as introductory to each section, for which I had already written introductions. While I have removed excessive repetition, any teacher will know that some repetition is crucial to what you want to communicate: First you tell your auditors what you are going to say; then you say it; and finally you tell them what you have said. This may seem excessively indulgent on my part, but as cognoscenti will recall, 'What I tell you three times is true!', as the Bellman observed in *The Hunting of the Snark*. As a lecture course, this material was also illustrated with a considerable number of slides. This dimension is now unfortunately missing (and would in any event have entailed considerable additional commentary).

Much of this material is taken from published versions (not always the most recent, for a number of subjective reasons, often no more than stylistic, though I have endeavoured to take some account of accuracy). Unattributed translations are my own.

I am very conscious that many areas are underexploited, as I observed above, and that the choice of location of certain passages is at times seemingly rather quixotic. Thus §3 deals with large numbers of myths that would equally well be at home in §8. The reason is of course that the theme of water as a cosmic symbol controls the matter. And yet I have not been wholly consistent, and nor shall I lose much sleep over pedantic issues of this sort. Many passages could equally be placed in different sections, to illustrate different themes: any categorization will at times be at times a strait-jacket on materials that defy narrow definition. One of the satisfying features of Religious Studies is the constant discovery of things resistant to classification.

A number of people have given me feedback as this volume comes to term. Among these I should thank in particular Robert Allan, Vicki Clifford, Sara Gross, Abraham Kovacs, and Susan Sanders of New College, and other old friends (that is, friends of long standing), notably Graeme Auld, Margaret Barker, Peter Hayman, David Reimer and Wilfred Watson. Robert Allan was also of great help with various editorial matters, and I wish to acknowledge the University of Edinburgh for funding the costs of this. As usual, my debt to my wife Betty cannot be adequately expressed.

N. Wyatt
New College
Edinburgh
August 2001

Acknowledgments

The author wishes to thank the following publishers for permission to use materials as outlined, where they remain in copyright:

Allen and Unwin (Harper-Collins),
C. Blacker and M. Loewe, *Ancient Cosmologies* (1975), for §2(19);
M. Loewe and C. Blacker, *Divination and Oracles* (1981), for §§11(34, 35, 36, 37, 38, 39, 41);

The American Philosophical Association,
S. N. Kramer, *Sumerian Mythology* (1944), for §§2(12), 4(4);

Aris and Phillips,
R. O. Faulkner, *The Ancient Egyptian Coffin Texts* (1973-8), for §2(26), 11(42);

E. J. Brill,
W. Hallo (ed.), *The Context of Scripture* (1999-), for §§3(19, 20, 21); 8(6); 12(5);

Vetus Testamentum (Zatelli) for §10(9);

British Museum Publications,
R. O. Faulkner, *The Ancient Egyptian Book of the Dead* (1985), for §§2(22); 4(3); 5(3); 6(6); 7(1, 2); 9(7, 8); 11(43, 44, 45);

Chicago University Press,
J. H. Breasted, *Ancient Records of Egypt* (1906), for §§2(28); 6(1, 26); 7(4, 5, 6, 7); 8(4); 11(9, 10); 11(25); 12(2);

T. and T. Clark,
M. Maher, *The Aramaic Bible* 1B (1992), for 5(13);

Doubleday,
J. H. Charlesworth (ed.), *The Old Testament Pseudepigrapha* (1983), for §§7(20, 21);

Eisenbrauns,
W. Horowitz, *Mesopotamian Cosmic Geography* (1998), for §2(24);

Harvard University Press,
F. J. Miller, *Ovid, Metamorphoses* (1956), for §4(13, 14);

Helsinki University Press,
I. Starr, *Queries to the Sun-god: Divination and Politics in Sargonid Assyria* (1990), for 11(6);
S. Parpola, *Assyrian Prophecies* (1997), for §§11(7, 8);

Hodder and Stoughton (Hodder Headline),
S. G. F. Brandon, *Creation Legends of the Ancient Near East* (1963) for §§2(3, 4, 5);

Methuen,
S. Morenz, *Egyptian Religion* (1973), for §4(15);

Thomas Nelson,
R. Patai, *Man and Temple* (1948), for §6(28, 33);

Oxford Centre for Hebrew and Jewish Studies,

Journal of Jewish Studies (1998), for §9(6).

Oxford University Press,
S. Dalley, *Myths from Mesopotamia* (1991), for §§2(9, 10, 13, 14, 36, 37), 4(5, 6); 7(14); 9(1, 2);
R. O. Faulkner, *The Ancient Egyptian Pyramid Texts* (1969), for §§2(27), 4(3); 5(2); 6(6); 7(1, 2, 9); 8(1);

Penguin Books,
W. B. Emery, *Archaic Egypt* (1961), for §12(1);

Princeton University Press,
J. B. Pritchard (ed.), *Ancient Near Eastern Texts Relating to the Old Testament* (1969³), for §§2(2, 6, 7, 8, 23, 25, 29); 3(13, 23); 4(17); 5(1, 4); 7(3, 10, 12); 8(3, 5, 7, 8); 10(1, 2, 5); 11(1, 2, 3, 25, 26, 31, 33); 12(10, 15);

Routledge,
E. Kuhrt, *The Ancient Near East* (1995), for §12(9);

Scholars Press,
S. B. Parker, *The Pre-biblical Narrative Tradition* (1989), for §(11(20);
J-J. Glassner, *Mesopotamian Chronicles* (2001), for §§12(6, 7, 8);
W. J. Murnane, *Texts from the Amarna Period* (1995), §§7(11); 12(3);

Sheffield Academic Press,
M. E. J. Richardson, *Hammurabi's Laws* (2000), for §3(22);
N. Wyatt, *Religious Texts from Ugarit* (1998), for §§3(4), 4(2a, 18, 19, 20, 21); 5(5, 6); 6(2, 3, 15); 7(16, 17); 8(9); 9(3); 10(3, 10); 11(17, 40);

SCM Press,
W. Beyerlin, *Near Eastern Religious Texts relating to the Old Testament* (1978), for §11(5, 18, 19, 21);

SPCK,
H. Ringgren, *Religions of the Ancient Near East* (1973), for §§10(6, 7).

University of California Press,
M. Lichtheim, *Ancient Egyptian Literature*, 3 volumes (1976), for §8(2).

AARSR	American Academy of Religion Studies in Religion
AB	*Anchor Bible*
ABD	*Anchor Bible Dictionary* (Freedman)
AfO	*Archiv für Orientforschung*
AHES	*Archive for History of Exact Sciences*
ALASP	Abhandlungen zur Literatur Alt-Syrien-Palästinas
AnBib	Analecta Biblica
ANET	*Ancient Near Eastern Texts relating to the Old Testament* (Pritchard)
AOAT	Alte Orient und Altes Testament
ARE	*Ancient Records of Egypt* 5 volumes (ed. J. H. Breasted, Chicago: Chicago University Press 1906)
AuOr	*Aula Orientalis*
AuOrS	*Aula Orientalis* Supplementa
AUS	American University Studies
BASOR	*Bulletin of the American Schools of Oriental Research*
BD	*Book of the Dead* (Faulkner, *The Ancient Egyptian Book of the Dead*)
BHS	*Biblia Hebraica Stuttgartensia*)K. Elliger and W. Rudolph (eds), Deutsche Bibelgesellschaft, Stuttgart, 1984)
BiOr	Biblica et Orientalia
BS	The Biblical Seminar
BZAW	Beihefte zur *Zeitschrift für die alttestamentliche Wissenschaft*
BZNW	Beihefte zur *Zeitschrift für die neutestamentliche Wissenschaft*
CA	*Current Anthropology*
CBQ	*Catholic Biblical Quarterly*
CBQMS	Catholic Biblical Quarterly Monograph Series
CR: BS	*Currents in Research: Biblical Studies*
CS	*The Context of Scripture* 3 volumes (HALLO)
CT	*Coffin Text* (R. O. Faulkner, *The ancient Egyptian Coffin Texts* 3 volumes, Warminster: Aris and Phillips 1973-8)
DDD	*Dictionary of Deities and Demons in the Bible* (eds K. van der Toorn *et al.*, Leiden: Brill 1995. Second edition 1999)
ERE	*Encyclopaedia of Religion and Ethics* ed. J. Hastings (Edinburgh: T. and T. Clark)
ESHM	European Seminar in Historical Methodology
FCB	Fuentes de la Ciencia Biblica
GR	*The Geographical Review*
HALOT	*Hebrew and Aramaic Lexicon of the Old Testament* 5 volumes (L. Koehler and W. Baumgartner eds, Leiden: Brill, 1994-2000. ET by M. E. J. Richardson).
HR	*History of Religion*
HSMP	Harvard Semitic Museum Publications
HSS	Harvard Semitic Studies
HUCA	*Hebrew Union College Annual*
ICC	International Critical Commentary
JAOS	*Journal of the American Oriental Society*
JEOL	*Jaarbericht Ex Oriente Lux*

JJS	*Journal of Jewish Studies*
JNES	*Journal of Near Eastern Studies*
JRAS	*Journal of the Royal Asiatic Society*
JSS	*Journal of Semitic Studies*
LS	*A Greek-English Lexicon* (H. G. Liddell and R. Scott, eds, Oxford: Clarendon 1940⁹)
MG	*Miscellanea Gregoriana*
MÄS	Münchner ägyptologische Studien
OBO	Orbis Biblicus et Orientalis
OTP	*Old Testament Pseudepigrapha* (Charlesworth)
PÄ	Probleme der Ägyptologie
PT	*Pyramid Text* (Faulkner, *The ancient Egyptian Pyramid Texts*)
RSPT	*Royal Society Philosophical Transactions*
SAA	State Archives of Assyria
SBE	Sacred Books of the East
SBLDS	Society of Biblical Literature Dissertation Series
SBT	Studies in Biblical Theology
SCL	Slather Classical Lectures
SFSHJ	South Florida Studies in the History of Judaism
SHCANE	Studies in the history and culture of the ancient Near East
SJOT	*Scandinavian Journal of the Old Testament*
ST	*Studia Theologica*
STS	Semitic Texts and Studies
UBL	Ugaritisch-Biblische Literatur
UCOP	University of Cambridge Oriental Publications
UUÅ	*Uppsala Universitets Årskrift*
UF	*Ugarit-Forschungen*
VT	*Vetus Testamentum*
WMANT	Wissenschaftliche Monographien zum Alten und Neuen Testament
ZAW	*Zeitschrift für die Alttestamentliche Wissenschaft*
ZNW	*Zeitschrift für die Neutestamentliche Wissenschaft*

*	refers to an introductory paragraph (e.g. *11.2.1)
§	refers to a text cited (e.g. §3(5))

INTRODUCTION

Two common themes by which religious traditions may usefully be explored are space and time. All religions have much to say on both topics, even if often only indirectly, because religion as a human experience is concerned to deal with the problems of space and time as these affect people's everyday lives and future destinies, both in terms of the natural flow and extent of these aspects of experience, and above all as matters taken into consciousness (and indeed the subconscious) and turned this way and that as expressing problems to be overcome, and providing the symbolic means for so doing.

Expressed in another way, it is the developing capacity to measure space and time which is one of the fundamental roots of human culture, and religion is that complex of cognitive and ritual forms which integrate this into consciousness, and validate ('sacralize') the common perception. It is this idea of 'the common perception', of the common paradigm, which explains why calendar changes have often been regarded as a threat to a community, and thus resisted. The paradigm is to be defended against all 'heresies'!

Similarly, Galileo's discoveries posed a profound threat to the paradigm of the geocentric universe, still maintained as 'the common perception' at the time in Christendom; and revision of the calendar in 1753-4 led to mobs in Bristol lamenting the loss of eleven days from their lives[1].

The issues raised in our discussion are essentially existential problems, faced by all people as conscious beings, such as how did the world begin? How will it end? Where do we come from? Where are we going? What lies above the sky? What lies below the earth? What happens when we come to the edge or end of the world? Why does orientation matter, both of individuals, and also of buildings, particularly temples and tombs, but also ordinary dwelling places, and agglomerates of buildings, such as villages and towns? Why do we think of height and depth in considering human hierarchies and divine realms? Why do we attribute to the gods much the same kind of social, spatial and temporal life as our own? Merely to pose the question in these forms illustrates the ubiquity of such metaphors. These became 'institutional problems', in so far as human groups, working with a group dynamic transcending individuality for the common good, addressed them and found collective solutions. The striking feature of these solutions, when viewed across the spectrum of a number of societies, as here, is the degree to which they resulted from the

---

[1]   Richards 1998, 255.

application of common strategies, with the fundamental identities of purpose far outweighing the differences in detail. And while such a statement may well raise hackles in some circles, as in Biblical Studies, where a number of scholars have drawn attention to its sense of unique identity, and more importantly, to *their* sense of its unique identity, coupled with a profound suspicion of all comparative work, which has characterized it from its inception, it will seem almost a commonplace among students of Religious Studies or Anthropology, where human universals are recognized in every local variation.

In this volume, we shall examine ideas of space and time as held explicitly or implicitly in the religions of the ancient Near East, in addition to some further aspects of religious life, in so far as the metaphors throw light on them. This designation covers the so-called 'Fertile Crescent', the river valleys of the Nile in Egypt, the Jordan and Orontes in Syria, and of the Tigris and Euphrates in Iraq (ancient 'Mesopotamia'), together with the land bridge joining them, that is Palestine, Syria and Turkey. It was in this region that cities first developed in Western Asia, paralleled by similar developments in Pakistan (the 'Indus Valley culture') and China. Greece will also feature to some extent, in as much as it was on the edge of the area under consideration, and heir to many oriental traditions.

As the 'Neolithic revolution' progressed from the tenth millennium BCE, with its slow transition from a hunter-gatherer to an agricultural lifestyle, people became increasingly sedentary, and from villages grew cities, and from small territories surrounding the villages grew kingdoms and then empires. Egypt was first unified under a common rule in about 3150-3100 BCE, the beginning of the so-called Pharaonic Age. Mesopotamia followed with the rise of Agade in the south, then of Babylon, in the latter part of the third millennium BCE, with Assyria and Elam following.

The history of the region over a long period of time is exceedingly complex. While local histories can be written, they should not really be treated in isolation from one another, since economic and political forces linked them from early times, and as will become evident, the ideas, beliefs, practices and social structures we encounter are not a random set of disconnected elements, but local developments of shared experience, and a complex network of interlocking symbols and values, often influenced in one area by political pressures from another. This became the more sophisticated with the passage of time, so that, for instance, many compositions in the Hebrew Bible (the 'Old Testament') may be seen as a reworking of older forms found in the surrounding regions. The clearest example of this is the Flood Story (*Genesis* 6-8, §4(8)) which clearly owes a considerable debt to Babylonian tradition, expressed in the *Gilgamesh* story (§4(6)) and *Atrahasis* (§4(5)), yet develops its own insights.

It is very easy so to classify and give an account of religions that a coherent structure appears to be deceptively simple. This often leads to the caricaturing of traditions with which one is only partially familiar (or at any rate other people's). Most religions are infinitely complex, preserving for later ages ideas which have long since become outmoded, and preserving alongside 'orthodoxy' many undercurrents of heterodoxy. Indeed, the orthodoxy of one generation may be the heresy of another, and if concerns for precise, orthodox belief are not required in a tradition, the possible variations and permutations are limitless. Any degree of orthodoxy is to some extent a function of central social and political control. And as anyone specializing in the study of this area of scholarship will entirely appreciate, many ideological (and thus religious) matters are not to be separated from a political matrix.

We may further observe that to speak of the 'religions' of the ancient Near East can be seriously misleading. The very use of the term 'religion' to denote a disparate complex of beliefs and practices, so that 'my religion' is to be distinguished from 'your religion', is really a modern perception[2]. We cannot speak of 'Egyptian religion' in the singular, because the phenomenon we call 'religion', for which the Egyptians had no specific

---

[2] The term 'religion' is usually explained on the basis of Cicero's famous etymology (*De Natura Deorum* ii 28), *religio* being derived from *relego* II, the third conjugation verb meaning 'to gather together'; or this is rejected in favour of taking it to be related to the first conjugation verb *religare*, 'to bind'. I have never found either of these convincing, since the former smacks of folk-etymology rather than serious philology, and we should expect **relegio*, while the latter not only amounts to the same thing in semantic terms, but begs the question in supposing that a noun in *-io* is likely to be formed on the basis of a verbal formation in *-are* (this in any case provides rather for *religatio*, and cf. also the n. *ligo-ligonis* [not *ligio*]). A more convincing link, in my view, is to be seen with *relinquo* ('to leave'), *religio* being an abstract formation on the supine stem *relictum*. Cf. *relatio* from *relatum* (*refero*). Thus 'religion' is essentially 'tradition' ('that which is left, survives or remains'), and its performance and beliefs are the perpetuation of traditional performances and beliefs. The emphasis here is on memory and its enormous importance for social identity and survival. Memory played a huge part in the survival of the construction and preservation of the texts gathered in this volume. See also **1.3.2, 1.8.2, 3. The best overall *definition* of religion remains that of Ambrose Bierce: 'Religion, n. A daughter of Hope and Fear, explaining to Ignorance the nature of the Unknowable'. Any attempt at an academic definition will merely enter a morass of disagreements, and certainly cannot be brief.

term, was variously conceived in the different groups making up Egyptian society. The royal family and priesthoods of the great temples practised one kind of religion, centring on the person of the divine king, while other forms were found among the different social and regional groupings of society, and in addition foreign groups, such as slaves, temporary residents, diplomats and merchants, all brought their own beliefs and practices with them. What we nowadays call 'Egyptian religion' was all of these together (though of some we know very little), and in the nature of dynamic, social phenomena, they were constantly interacting and changing, so that the 'religion' of say the eighteenth dynasty might be very different from that of the nineteenth. The same is true, not only of the broad cultural groupings of the region at every stage of history, but can also be demonstrated even for individual cities, such as Ugarit, where it is increasingly recognized that we see not one religion, but a number[3]. The same is also true of Israel, where generations of scholars have conventionally written of 'Israelite religion' as though it were entirely unitary, with a number of manifestations written off as 'false religion', or 'dissident religion'. A recent study (Zevit 2001) now writes of 'Israelite religions', allowing, rather late in the day, the authenticity of each form.

The present selection will appear to be complex on other grounds, that we are covering all the cultures of the so-called ancient Near East, over a three-thousand-year period, from the origins of writing down to the birth of Christianity. Is it fair to treat them together? Ideally we would devote an entire volume to each one. But beneath the evident differences between them, lie undercurrents of similarity of type (e.g. all practised sacrifice[4], all began with polytheism as the normal way of perceiving the divine order, all shared similar techniques for addressing the future, or matters of pastoral theology, and so on), and we can say that each grew out of ancient forms of ritual designed to construct and manage a world of meaning for human life. Thus, the 'sub-text' of religions apparently quite dissimilar is a basic similarity of deep structure. Recognition of this enriches our understanding of each tradition, as the insights gained by the

---

[3]   Thus van der Toorn 1996, 153-82 dealt specifically with family religion, Brody 1998 treated the religion of seafarers, and del Olmo 1999 that of the royal cultus and temple priesthoods.

[4]   Christianity claimed that God himself had provided the final sacrifice (Jesus), a theme paralleled in Judaism with the Aqedah (the 'binding' of Isaac narrated in *Genesis* 22:1-18, §5(14)), and both probably influenced by the Phoenician myth Eusebius described (§12(9) n. 5 below).

examination of one enable us to discern hitherto unsuspected aspects of others.

Another feature of the material selected and discussed here is its insistent richness in referential terms. Imposing the twelve-part pattern I have used (generated initially by the need to give lecture topics) seems at times to have become something of a strait-jacket. A number of texts could readily be cited as prime examples in more than one section, indeed, a few are; in addition, I have not stinted in the cross-referencing of materials, to show how every category of thought actually sheds light on every other. This is indeed a seamless robe, as we should come to expect of the infinite flexibility and creativity of the human mind, and it is mainly for purposes of intellectual coherence that we deliberately impose boundaries which may serve an immediate purpose, and yet become restrictive if imposed too rigorously. We see a similar phenomenon in the distinction of disciplines in our academic institutions. This may have been convenient to get to grips with vastly expanding knowledge, and suits our administrators. Yet every academic who makes a serious stab at any research finds himself or herself up against invisible barriers which must be broken down. Of course, the danger in being seen to break down barriers can lead to the charge that one has overemphasized the similarities, and underestimated the differences. This is considered a particular problem in Theological Studies, and in particular in Biblical Studies, when the kind of comparisons I make here are advocated as a means of illuminating a biblical text by reference to outside sources[5]. I have attempted to deal with this issue at greater length in Wyatt 2001a.

This is not the place to deal in any detail with the difficult questions of the origin of religion and its ultimate significance (often treated in terms of its 'truth', on which see below). But it is an issue I have always had in mind in teaching ancient Near Eastern religions, and a few comments may be helpful, because I think that these are important questions, and because they have in part determined my choice of materials and their juxtaposition. Readers must be satisfied with a pointer to some of the recent publications which have, in my view, usefully advanced discussion. In view of confessional perceptions which colour people's views in the matter, a number of observations should be made.

Firstly, to describe something as religious does not immediately put it in a privileged category. This often happens in Religious Studies, for instance, and sometimes in a double fashion, as when 'theology' (that is, usually, Christian, or biblical, theology) is declared to be *sui generis*, and everything

---

[5]   The classic essay on the subject is Frankfort 1951.

else irrelevant; or when religion (any religion) is declared to be *sui generis*, and any qualification in other terms is attacked as reductionism in a disparaging sense.   There are pathologies as well as good points in all religions[6]. As well as serving as powerful drivers in the advance of culture and the betterment of the human lot, they have been directly responsible for some of the most horrible episodes in human history, and some have practised or still practise low-level terrorism on their adherents. It may be a disagreeable surprise to some to realize that such charges are to be laid at the door, primarily, of those religions which have been regarded as most successful, or as most advanced (namely Judaism, Christianity and Islam, though Hinduism and Shinto are not exempt).   True, barbarities were always practised throughout human history, and always had a religious tinge, such as the extermination of entire peoples as fulfilment of obligations to gods (§§12(10)), or the sacrifices of prisoners of war.

Secondly, any definition of religion which cannot be applied universally, giving an adequate account of Christianity, for example, along with all other religious manifestations, cannot be an adequate definition.   An appeal to history, so that Christianity is seen as the ultimate development and fulfilment of the prior history of all religions[7], is manifestly inadequate. Not only does Islam make precisely the same claim, but the main Asiatic systems such as the various schools of Hinduism and Buddhism have their own histories of ever-greater refinement, and if they do not make the claim explicitly, they certainly do so implicitly. But such a quest, for the ultimate religion, while a natural enough human enquiry, as people seek a way to follow (and notice the spatial metaphor, which occurs in many traditions!) cannot really be advanced as an academic explanation, even if it often is. For it introduces into the discussion the old chestnut 'truth', as though a religious claim somehow has a unique status which is immune from disproof. This really will not do, as it merely opens the door to gullibility.   And in practice, no one talks of religious

---

[6]   J. Z. Smith 1999 has achieved a remarkable insight into the symbolic forces at work in the Jonestown tragedy, by comparison with the *Bacchae* of Euripides. (It is particularly relevant to the present volume because its concern for space, and the invasion of others' space.) But this does not redeem what was still a tragedy and waste of human life. But the *Bacchae* explored a similar pathology. The crusades, Jewish pogroms or the inquisition are surely to be seen as altogether negative experiences within the history of Christendom. Explanation is not justification.

[7]   See Eilberg-Schwartz 1990, ix.

truth in general, but 'my religious truth', which is limited to the speaker's own religion, thus falling foul of the principle of universalism[8].

In the course the preparation of this volume, I came across an interesting paper by Flanagan. I found the following passage of particular relevance to the present work:

> Many recent critics writing on the history of ideas and science have been impressed by the fact that until the age of 4 to 6 or 7 years of age, children seem not to distinguish sharply between space and time. Contrary to adult impressions, the ability to differentiate spatial and temporal orders is an acquired skill... The skill needed in order to exist and survive in a real world of moving objects and passing time is not innate in humans or the world around them. Newton thought that it is;
>
> Einstein hypothesized — against common sense — that it is not.[9]

The practice of religion played a large part in the process by which these cultural constructs were shaped and experienced. Ancient religions were rather concerned primarily with the management of this world, contrary to many studies in religion, which emphasize their otherworldly, transcendental and even eschatological concern, as though their purpose was (I shall limit myself to the past) always to provide a means of escape from the material world. The common view just described is certainly how many religions today are perhaps to be categorized (though with qualifications), and we can see the progress of such emphases, usually triggered by social and political crisis, such as the collapse of empires and the deportation of peoples, in the history of every culture. But whether the 'otherworldly' assessment was ever true of religions in the early urban period (from the Early Bronze to the Iron Age, *ca* 3000-500 BCE in the Near East) is debatable. It certainly remains undocumented. It seems to me that a far better way of categorizing these early forms was as systems of social management, part of the software, as it were, of the increasingly complex organization of people as economic development led to population growth, and the consequent division of societies into specialized groups. Those in power, naturally, were those who first learnt, or even invented, time consciousness in terms of the construction of

---

8   The tendency to make exclusive truth-claims is a pity, because it immediately invites and evokes invidious comparisons, claims and counter-claims. No religion should be regarded as having a monopoly of 'truth'. There is no cognitive 'truth' in religious claims. They are subjective, symbolic and poetic accounts of individuals' and individual cultures' engagement with life, which become common property by virtue of their utility, like all memes, and are entirely valid so long as one remains within the believing community.

9   Flanagan 1995, 72.

calendars, and space management in terms not merely of 'national' territory, but perhaps more importantly of hierarchical territory, or sacred territory. All such developments must have taken place over centuries, if not millennia, going back, ultimately, to the Neolithic period[10] and the earliest sedentarization.

The dates cited in this book are generally those given in Kuhrt 1995. Ancient chronology is often provisional, and various schemes are given, often setting Egyptian dates for some periods in parallel columns to acknowledge variations. James 1991 and Rohl 1995 both represent attempts at a reconsideration of the data, with a proposed omission of at least 250 years from the dates given for the second millennium, and have received a predictably cautious, at times hostile, and sometimes even vitriolic response. The jury is still out.

---

[10]   It was in the Neolithic that the first transformation of ancient religiosity into the basic forms of all subsequent religiosity first developed. Cf. Cauvin 1994.

Chapter 1

ORIENTATION AND THE LOCATION OF THE SELF

We examine here the vocabularies of a number of languages spoken in the ancient world, with particular reference to terms for the cardinal points and their metaphorical uses. When the history of words is examined, they frequently reveal interesting things quite unsuspected of the derivative terms. The vocabulary to be discussed here lies at the very roots of the human perception of space and time, in so far as this finds expression in language.

Suggested Reading:

D'Aquili and Newberg 1998; Wyatt 1996a.

1.1 Introduction

1.1.1 The tables that follow in the present chapter are a development into other languages of the results of an enquiry I originally made into orientation in Ugaritic thought, with Hebrew usage provided as a control on account of its philological similarities (Wyatt 1996a). It appears from the evidence given here that the claims I made for two languages and their respective cultural contexts are valid for several more, thus reflecting what looks increasingly like a universal human experience.

1.1.2 Time is handled quite uniquely by the human species *Homo Sapiens*, and perhaps by its immediate hominid forebears, such as *Homo Neanderthalensis* and *Homo Erectus*, though there is no certainty about how far we can theorize with these older forms[1]. What is increasingly clear, as noted in the introduction, is that notions of time and space are culturally learned. They are not simple 'givens' of our biological constitution. The fact that we can trace conceptions through language, as illustrated by the tables, is eloquent testimony to their linguistic, and therefore *a priori* cultural, origins. People (*Homo Sapiens*) *know* that they are mortal, and that time corrupts all that they hold dear. Yet there is a universal conviction that there is some essence, a 'soul' or 'self', that can withstand

---

[1] The recognition that a rock discovered at Berekhat Ram in the Golan in 1986 shows evidence of deliberate and systematic technical treatment (carving and scratching) and probably represents an attempt at representation of the human form in Acheulian culture, to be dated to *ca* 200,000 years ago, completely overturns the last twenty years of work in palaeoanthropology. See Marshak 1996, 1997. For we now have evidence that *Homo Erectus* may have had some capacity in symbolizing, a skill hitherto supposed to be restricted (perhaps to *Homo Neanderthalensis* and) to *Homo Sapiens*. The kind of symbolic activity represented in the selections in the present book therefore has a far longer prehistory than previously thought possible.

such corruption.   Even if it be regarded as purely egotistical as an individual conviction, it is maintained as a social conviction, for without such hope, society would die.

1.1.3   What if there were some way of 'overcoming time', of neutralizing its effects, of becoming immortal?   This *emotional* response to time was paralleled by a *practical* response to time.   With the gradual rise of agriculture in the Neolithic period (from *ca* 10000 BCE in the Near East) it became increasingly important to be able to determine the time for sowing the grain, or in Egypt for predicting the time of the regular inundation, to ensure that people could harness its synchrony with the growing season of vegetation.   The accompanying slow rise of urbanism (more food leading to larger population and more complex social organization) also increasingly required some agreed measure of time for bureaucratic and military purposes.

1.1.4   This practical concern was accompanied, or even driven, by an equally important ritual concern with the measurement and management of time, which had much older roots.   Sets of thirty in scratches or dots on sticks and bones in Palaeolithic cultures indicate that the phases of the moon were possibly recognized by the early hunters of Australasia and Europe, some 50-30,000 years ago.   All ancient cultures developed complex calendars (with varying degrees of error) and one indicator of the development of culture is the gradual refinement of the calendar to its present state of very high precision and atomic clocks (see Richards 1998). A powerful means of guaranteeing that the calendar (however imperfect) was strictly observed was to measure time's passage with regular or periodic rituals, the emotional stimulation no doubt reinforcing a sense of the rhythmic flow of time.   At the same time rituals had the added benefit of reinforcing all other kinds of social value, guaranteeing increasing power to kings and priesthoods.

1.1.5   The ancient Near Eastern evidence will appear on the surface to be far removed from the religion of indigenous and traditional forms of tribal and small-scale societies round the world.   There is however one important factor linking them all, and this is that the shamanistic practices so well evidenced in these latter contexts also played a part in the original rise of urban culture.   Priests and kings 'entered heaven', 'conversed with the gods', 'brought divine commands down to earth', and so on[2].

---

[2]   See §§7(12-26).

1.2 The Tables

1.2.1 The following tables give the vocabulary of orientation in a number of languages, cited mostly from the ancient Near Eastern world. These reveal an important psychological constant, in spite of variations in practice, in the experience and classification of space and time.

There are three different classes of vocabulary (reading columns down the page):
i) Homuncular/Religious;
ii) Cosmological/Solar;
iii) Topographic/economic.
These represent three ways of determining orientation, with reference to
i) the self (one's own body);
ii) celestial measurements (primarily the sun);
iii) geographical measurements, using local landmarks such as rivers or mountains.

The oldest of these is certainly the first (though it evidently takes its basic positioning from the sun, as the vocabulary shows). It is also the most subjective one (and so is validated emotionally).

1.2.2 Self-centredness may seem 'selfish' in the moral sense, but is the necessarily irreducible basis for all experience. We have to start from our own self-awareness, and even if it is conditioned by our social context (i.e., it is a 'social construction of reality'[3]) then society itself is in part a function of innumerable individual experiences. Much that follows in cosmology and ritual may be seen to have its roots in this starting point.

1.3 Orientation i): the East

1.3.1 In most cultures orientation means just what it says: it means turning one's face towards the rising sun (Latin *oriens*). Much that follows is dependent on this. Even when a different 'orientation' is observed, as for instance in Egypt, the same psychological and world-structuring process is at work.

1.3.2 Let us start from Hebrew and Ugaritic. The word *qedem* (= *qadmu*) means three things, probably in this order of development: i) 'face'; ii) 'East'; iii) 'past'. The order of development can be seen from the primary meaning of the term ('face') which was then aligned on the East-West axis, and was subsequently used metaphorically to refer to time. Thus *we face*

---

3   Berger and Luckmann 1971.

the past[4].   This is crucial to much human, and especially religious experience and practice.   We 'see' the past, which thus provides us, through memory and narrative, with accounts of how we came to be where we are.   Such accounts are often called 'myth'.   Even our modern forms of history are mythical in so far as we see 'teachings' in our reflexion on the past.

1.4   Orientation ii): the West

As we face East, it follows that the West is behind us.   This is borne out by the vocabulary.   In the same way as before, and with the same semantic expansion, the word *'aḫar* (= *aḫru*) means 'back', 'West' and 'future'.   It is worth considering what this must mean in terms of the human consciousness of time.   The future lies behind us, unseen, unknown and unknowable.   Awareness that there is a future will generate apprehension or fear of what may happen, and perhaps encourage the development of means to predict or control it.

1.5   Orientation iii): the South

This is of necessity on the right side.   For evolutionary and neurological reasons, resulting in the way the two hemispheres of the brain process different functions, the right side is associated with security, well-being and the morally 'right'.   Its geographical direction is a metaphorical extension of the body-term.

1.6   Orientation iv) the North

On the other hand (!), the left, which is towards the north, represents 'sinister' (Latin *sinister* = 'left hand') and dangerous things and functions, including where the gods dwell, for they are dangerous powers.   Its geographical direction is again a metaphorical extension of the body-term.

1.7   What this means for Personal Experience

The beauty of all this is that we can *all* be aware of it.   The experience of 'facing the past' is not alien to us.   We speak of 'turning our back on the past', 'putting it behind us', as striking metaphors precisely because they deliberately reverse a more normal, unspoken and altogether archaic

---

4   Tuan 1977, 35 fig. 2 has a different schema.   The vocabulary of the tables in the present volume (§§1(1-9) argues against his perception of orientation, at least for the ancient world.

experience. In our 'mind's eye', we can *only* see the past with any clarity. We have to 'face up to what we have done'.[5]

In what follows, I speak of *my* experience, since I am the subject of all I say. But you, reader, can also think of it all in the first person. For these are human universals.

1.8 The Flow of Time

1.8.1   I stand on a line[6] going from east to west, from past to future. I am moving along this line, backwards. The past recedes, and every moment I experience is already a *past experience*. The more remote it is, the more difficult it is to remember, but at the same time, those long-lost things that I do remember are important. Since I live in a community, I remember not just my own experiences, but those of the community, reported down the generations in oral tradition. This tends to become sacred, for tradition records those events which validate and authenticate the community's sense of identity.

1.8.2   With a community tradition, memory can transcend death. We can 'remember' things we never experienced, vicariously, listening to our parents or the tribal elders, or rehearsing the community's oral tradition[7].

---

[5]   Of course we have largely broken free from this apparently fixed structure, and there is no doubt that the ancients were also emancipated from it. The secondary vocabularies for orientation (columns 2 and 3 in the tables) do not presuppose it. But there is no escaping the fact that column 1 *does* presuppose it. And the symbolic significance of this in terms of religious cosmologies which shape our thinking and experience still remains with us. It requires no great stretch of the imagination to enter into the archaic mode. One area of experience in which we still *do* look into the past is astronomical observation. Everything we see in the night sky is from the past. The light of many stars and galaxies has taken millions of years to reach us.

[6]   Disputes over whether it is a straight line, a one-way line, or distinctions are to be made between 'historical' straight-line time as allegedly experienced by Israel in contrast to cyclical views entertained by all Israel's 'pagan' neighbours (thus for example G. E. Wright 1950, 1952) are misdirected. Indeed, the cyclicity itself, commonly attributed to Mesopotamian thought, is seriously questioned by Lambert 1976, 172-3, as well as being alleged of Israel by J. B. Curtis 1963. The basic experience outlined above appears to be universal, and is certainly supported by the vocabularies in the tables. The broader issues are dealt with in §12 and the Epilogue.

[7]   Cf. the concept of 'prosthetic memory' proposed by Landsberg 1995.

There are limits to this, unless it is transformed by the ever-repeated memory into epic and myth, by which time it will have lost its historical anchorage.

1.8.3 But imagine the quantum leap in a community's capacity to 'remember' through narrative when it can commit the tradition to writing. Suddenly the remote past, far beyond narrative memory, can be brought up in the mind: stories of battles long ago, of the rise and fall of empires, of how we came to live here and own this territory, or why we wander, lost and rejected, in lands not our own.   An important feature to remember in speaking in these terms is the enormous power generated by language. Words had a life of their own. Names were an essential part of a person. Erase the name, as in Egyptian rituals (§§8(5), 11(16)), and the consequence was 'his name is not; he is not!' The power and authority of language, whether divine, royal, or merely individual utterance, was not to be lightly ignored. As we shall see, much of the holding together of this fragile edifice depends on words, and their agreed authority. Consign them to writing, and we see the beginning of the idea of the immutability of the utterance: 'the moving finger writes…'.[8]

1.9   the Extent and Management of Space

1.9.1 Still passing through me as subject, is a line at right angles to the time-line. This goes from North to South. We have seen how the hands have from remote times had a universal symbolic value: South is good; North is bad (or, more neutrally: south, the right hand, is safe; north, the left hand, is dangerous). This, as an axis always interacting with the time line, may be experienced as a moral one. Between them these two axes encompass all my experience, past (remembered), present (which is fleeting) and future (unknown), and the whole moral gamut as it interacts with all activities remembered and reexperienced.

1.9.2 And since orientation is an establishment of a fixed position in space, it serves as a control of space. Things nearby are important, either because they are my territory, my possessions, my family (we speak of relatives and friends as 'near'). Things or people that are more distant are

---

[8]   Not too much should be made of the initial impact of writing upon general memory among the common people before the rise of libraries (e.g. that of the Assyrian king Ashurbanipal), except where specialists (scribes, poets, priests) started to use it widely as a tool. It is our huge dependence on the scattered written remains from the ancient world which makes us prone to overestimate their importance in antiquity.

of less consequence. A gradation can be observed: something is valued in direct proportion to proximity. This idea can be turned metaphorically to a vast range of experiences, structures and values[9].

1.9.3 Conceptions of territory, and the construction of cities, palaces and temples all presuppose common metaphorical applications of the human body and our experience of it onto the external world.

1.10   Practical Effects

1.10.1 We shall also see that the axes drawn through me (or collectively, ourselves) as subject contain and define most experiences and processes in religion.

1.10.2 On the temporal axis, the remote past is where mythic events 'happened', providing patterns for present belief and behaviour. Rituals reactualize ('représent') the mythic realities now. Mythic time is said to be 'the eternal present', because it determines the present. In so far as it can be tapped into through ritual and experience, we may even say that religion is perceived as having the capacity to reverse the flow of time, to annul its destructive potential.   But it also provides patterns for interpreting and indeed shaping the unknown future, which can be determined, influenced or discerned through appropriate ritual and technical procedures (§11).

1.10.3 On the moral-spatial axis, proximity to the self as 'centre' implies reality, commonly expressed as holiness. This term works particularly well in English, because it contains the unifying principle of the self as one. But of course it translates a variety of ancient terms whose meaning was often separation (e.g. √*qdš*) or dedication (√*ḥrm*). Temples, homes for the gods modelled on human houses, are places of 'reality' and therefore sacredness. Distance from the self means a progressive approach to the 'end of the world', where reality breaks down. Paradoxically, however, these polarities are often related in cultic activity, which may in some circumstances appear to be the process of reconciliation of contradictions and opposites, though in others it is precisely the maintenance of differences in the face of tendencies to the dissolution of categories.

---

9   Mol 1976, 1-2.

1.11   **Other Dimensions**

1.11.1   In addition to the two horizontal axes we have discussed, and their concomitant world-construction, there lies another dimension altogether, a third, intersecting them: the vertical axis, up and down. It points to the transcendent and infernal dimensions. Lying outside the spatio-temporal plane (because men cannot generally fly), it represents other potentialities. The movement upwards was particularly important in the ancient world in articulating the power believed to accrue to gods, and to those special men (it was generally men, and not women, who featured in this aspect) who were believed either by special qualities of their own (charisma), or *ex officio* by virtue of their royal or priestly status, to be able to enter heaven. The movement downwards was universally associated with death, and the common lot of all men (and women) who were not able to evade its gravitational pull. But this simple opposition was in reality more complex, for heaven unleashed destructive powers, expressed for example in flood stories, while the underworld, with its springs, was the source of the renewal of the earth and the replenishment of life. The ocean (§§3, 4), both surrounding the earth in horizontal terms and overarching and underlying it in vertical terms, symbolized all potentialities, of life and death.

1.11.2   This other vertical dimension is to be seen as the probable source, and certainly the locus, of developing ideas concerning *post-mortem* felicity or judgment, giving rise, gradually, to the eschatologies of contemporary religion. We can see it rather well in the Hebrew terminology for travel to Egypt. Egypt serves as a symbolic location in many biblical passages, as a cipher for exile, a 'land of the dead'. Consequently, one always 'goes down (*yārad*) to Egypt', as though entering the underworld (Wyatt 1990a). The supreme sacrifice, the burnt offering, or holocaust, is in Hebrew *ʿōlâ*, 'a going up'.

1.11.3   A further aspect of the language just mentioned comes out with particular clarity in biblical thought. In the Bible, we find that human beings are made of two substances, the divine breath (if you like, air from above) and clay (earth from below). This is explicit in §2(18). The two come together (merge) in the birth of a person (the person in *Genesis* 2 is initially androgynous, but is then split into male and female). When a person dies, there is a separation of these constituent parts. The air, or divine breath, returns upwards, and the clay (or 'dust') returns downwards. This may be discerned in such passages as *Job* 10:9, 27:3 and 32:8 (breath), and 27:3, 33:4 (earth), describing the constituent parts, and 34:14-5 describing their separation at death. We thus have an interesting reversal of the symbolism operating at the macrocosmic level, where the separation of the two is the first point of cosmic organization (§§2(15)), and cosmic dissolution is expressed in terms of their coming together again (§§4(8)). This is perhaps spelt out most clearly in biblical thought, but is an undercurrent in other forms. The blood (of Kingu) used in the creation of Mesopotamian men (§2(14)) is analogous to air, because being divine blood, it belongs to the heavenly realm.

1.12   Inner Space

There is, of course, strictly nothing which we can call 'inner space'. Our heads are solid. Yet we appear to experience it. Jaynes wrote that 'conscious mind is a spatial analog of the world and mental acts are analogs of bodily acts' (Jaynes 1976, 66; cf. Hall 1966). That is, in our mental processing of experience, and construction of a conscious world, we use external spatiality as a metaphor for the construction of an inner one. Unable to control external space, we find ourselves in full control of our inner space. We construct it as we will, though we are not entirely in control, subject as we are to genetic predispositions and experiences (the old 'nature and nurture' dilemma). We use the props provided by these experiences to shape a world in conformity with the cultural context in which we find ourselves. This allows us to catalogue experience in acceptable ways, thus reinforcing our adherence in the social matrix, which in turn reinforces our sense of 'ontological worth', of true being. Within human history, that complex of experiences and processes which most cements the individual within society, and society within its historical and geographical context (that is, having territory and history) is the stuff of religion. Its essentially symbolic nature is a necessity brought about by the half-way house inhabited by humanity. Berger remarked of our species that 'biologically deprived of a man-world, he constructs a human world. This world, of course, is culture.' (Berger 1973, 16) One of the most powerful tools in this constructive process has been religion.

TABLES OF THE VOCABULARY OF ORIENTATION

§1(1) Ugaritic

	TERM	MEANING
	i) Homuncular/Religious	
EAST	*qdm*	'face', 'in front'
WEST	*aḫr*	'behind'
NORTH		
SOUTH		
	ii) Cosmological/Solar	
EAST	*ṣat*	'coming out'
WEST	*ʿrb* (*ṣba*)	'going in' ('joining'?)
NORTH	*šmal*	'left'
SOUTH	*ymn*	'right'
	iii) Topographic/economic	
EAST		
WEST		
NORTH	(cf. *ṣpn*)	
SOUTH		

§1(2) Hebrew

	TERM	MEANING
i) Homuncular/Religious		
EAST	*qedem* *qadmōnî*	'face' 'in front'
WEST	*'aḥar, 'aḥ ᵃrôn*	'behind'
NORTH	*sᵉmôl*	'left'
SOUTH	*yāmîn, tēmān*	'right'
ii) Cosmological/Solar		
EAST	*mizraḥ* *mōṣā'*	'shining' 'coming out'
WEST	*maᶜᵃrāb* *mābō'*	'going in', 'coming in'
NORTH		
SOUTH		
iii) Topographic/economic		
EAST		
WEST	*yām*	'sea'
NORTH	*ṣāpôn*	(cf. Ugaritic *ṣpn*)
SOUTH	*negeb* *dārôm*	'sahel' (original sense unclear)

§1(3) Arabic

	TERM	MEANING
	i) Homuncular/Religious	
EAST	qadam, qidm, qidam	'precede' 'past', 'antiquity'
WEST	dabūr	'west wind' (√'turn one's back')
NORTH	šamāl, šimal	'north (wind)' 'left'
SOUTH	yaman, yamin	'south' 'right hand'
	Cosmological/Solar	
EAST		
WEST	majrib	'west' (√ws ʿrb)
NORTH		
SOUTH		
	Topographic/economic	
EAST		
WEST		
NORTH		
SOUTH		

§1(4) Akkadian

	TERM	MEANING
i) Homuncular/Religious		
EAST	*aqdamātum* *qudmu* *pānānu* *maḫru*	'front, east' 'front', 'past' 'face', 'past' 'face', 'past'
WEST	*aḫarātum* *aḫru* *emnu* √*imnum* *warkātu* (— Sumerian egir)	'back, west' 'future' 'west' ('right hand') 'future', 'behind'
NORTH	*yamīna* *šumêlu*	'left hand, north' 'left'
SOUTH	*sim'al* [*imittum* (√*imnum*	'right hand, south' 'right (hand)'] = WS *ymn*)
ii) Cosmological/Solar		
EAST	*ṣitum* *ṣīt šamšim*	'coming out' 'sunrise'
WEST	*erēbu*	'going in (of sun)'
NORTH		
SOUTH		
iii) Topographic/economic		
EAST	*šadû*	'mountain' 'steppe' 'east wind'
WEST	*amurru*	'west', 'west land'
NORTH	*elû* *ištānu*	'upstream' 'north', 'north land'
SOUTH	*šūtu* *šaplitum*	south wind lower' *šaplu* = 'downstream'

§1(5) Sumerian

	TERM	MEANING
	i) Homuncular/Religious	
EAST	NIM	
WEST	[e g i r	'future', 'behind'] (no spatial sense)
NORTH	GÚB.NU	'left hand'
SOUTH	ZI.DA	'right hand'
	ii) Cosmological/Solar	
EAST		
WEST		
NORTH		
SOUTH		
	Topographic/economic	
EAST		
WEST	MAR.TU (= Akkadian *amurru*)	'west'
NORTH	AN.TA (= Akkadian *elû*)	'upstream'
SOUTH	KI.TA (= Akkadian *šaplu*)	'downstream'

§1(6) Greek

	TERM	MEANING
i) Homuncular/Religious		
EAST	√πρω- πρωϊ πρωτος	'early' 'first' 'earliest'
WEST	[ἀχερων √WS *aḥr*] ἐσχατος (LXX)	[= Styx] 'last'
NORTH	ἀριστερος	'left (hand)'
SOUTH	δεξια	'right (hand)'
ii) Cosmological/Solar		
EAST	ἀνατολη (√ἀνατελλω)	'rising'
WEST	δυσμη √δυω	'setting'
NORTH		
SOUTH		
iii) Topographic/economic		
EAST		
WEST	θαλασσα (LXX)	'sea'
NORTH	βορεας, βορρας	'north wind'
SOUTH	νοτος	'south wind'

§1(7) Latin

	TERM	MEANING
i) Homuncular/Religious		
EAST	*principium* (*Genesis* 2:8 VG)	'head' 'beginning'
WEST		
NORTH	*sinister*	'left'
SOUTH	*dexter*	'right'
ii) Cosmological/Solar		
EAST	*oriens*	'rising'
WEST	*occidens, occasus*	'setting'
NORTH	*aquilo*	'north wind'
SOUTH	*meridies*	'mid-day'
iii) Topographic/economic		
EAST		
WEST		
NORTH		
SOUTH	*auster* √Gk αὐω? *australis*	'south wind' ('dryer') 'southern'

§1(8) Egyptian

	TERM	MEANING
i) Homuncular/Religious		
EAST	*i3bt* *i3bty*	'east, left side eastern, left'
WEST	*imnt* *imn* √Sem. *ymn*	'west, right hand' 'western, right side'
NORTH	*mḥt* cf. *mḥ3* cf. *m-ḥt* *pḥw*	'north', 'back of head' 'behind', 'future' 'back, end, last'
SOUTH	*ḥntiw* *ḥnt* *ḥntw*	'southern' 'past', 'face', 'in front' 'sail south', 'upstream' 'before, earlier'
ii) Cosmological/Solar		
EAST	*wbn*	'rise' (sun)
WEST	*ḥtp*	'set' (sun), 'be at rest', 'be propitiated', 'appease'
NORTH		
SOUTH		
iii) Topographic/economic		
EAST		
WEST		
NORTH	*ḥdi*	'sail north, downstream'
SOUTH	*rsw*	'south'

Egyptian 'orientation' is different (cf. The Sanskrit 'anomaly' below), though its psychological principles remain constant. The organization of the body in space we call orientation is based simply on facing the most prominent feature of the outside world impinging on consciousness, viz., in most contexts, the rising sun. In an important strand of Egyptian thought the most significant feature was the flow of the Nile. The Egyptians faced upstream, towards the south. The vocabulary items listed above (col. 1) fit the familiar body alignment, but with the south replacing the east. From this flow conceptions of time in relation to the body, so that the future is still behind the subject.

On the other hand, in one aspect, that of journeying from birth to death (and on to rebirth), an east-west temporal alignment *is* followed. Thus the east represents the past and the west the future, as in the other systems above. The passage of the sun reiterates this idea on a daily basis. But this cosmological orientation is not represented in the common vocabulary (above). However, the term for 'west', *imnt*, while probably strictly related etymologically to the Semitic *ymn*, 'right hand', may also be construed as 'unseen' (cf. the divine name Amun, *imn*, 'the Unseen one'). The dead are called *imntyw*, as in the title of Osiris *ḫnty imntyw*, 'Foremost of the Westerners', where the latter part may also allow, by paronomasia, the sense 'the unseen ones', which would correspond to the invisibility of the future in the other systems listed.

In an interesting discussion of the Egyptian vocabulary, Takács (1999, 36-7) drew attention to two features: firstly the ambiguity of some Egyptian terminology, whose directional reference obvious depended on dialect (and therefore local social affiliation), and secondly, that *imn* may be related (by way of metathesis) to Egyptian *wnm*, 'eat', being therefore the 'eating hand'. The right hand remains the 'eating hand', And the left the 'toilet hand', in many cultures today. Cf. English 'cack-handed', where 'cack' and its Indo-European cognates (cf. Greek κακος, 'evil'!) means 'faeces'. The term 'khaki' says it all!

§1(9) Sanskrit

	TERM	MEANING
	i) Homuncular/Religious	
EAST	*pūrva*	'east', 'in front of', 'preceding', 'first', 'primaeval' (but not 'face')
	paurastya	'situated in front, foremost, eastern (people)'
	prāci	'east'
	√*prāñc*	'being in front, facing, east, former, previous'
WEST	*pratīcī*	'westward, behind, future'
	paśca	'westward', 'behind, later'
	carama	'western, last'
	apara	'hinder, later, following, western'
NORTH	*uttara*	'north', 'left'
SOUTH	*dakṣiṇa*	'southern', 'of the right hand', 'dextrous' (cog. Lat. *dexter*)
	ii) Cosmological/Solar	
EAST	*udaya*	sunrise
WEST	*asta* (in compounds)	mythical mountain where sun set
NORTH	*udīcī* √*udañc*	'north' ('go up')
SOUTH	*avāñc*	'south' ('go down')
	iii) Topographic/economic	
EAST		
WEST		
NORTH	*kaubera* √*Kubera*	'northern' (K. god of north)
SOUTH		

The Sanskrit vocabulary is spectacularly out of keeping with the cosmology of the cardinal points in theology, as reflected in the iconography of the *caturmukhaliṅga*:

West	Brahmā	Creation of the World	Time Past
North	Viṣṇu	Sustenance of the World	Time Present
South	Śiva	Destruction of the World	Time Future
East	Mahādeva	Transcendence	Eternity
[Zenith	Īśāna	Ineffability	Quintessence of above][1]

1   the non-Vedic tradition works on the principle of five elements and dimensions, not four.

I have given examples here from languages beyond the confines of the ancient Near East, to indicate that the same principle operates on a wide front, and perhaps universally. We would expect this, in any case, if religion and religious experience has the same neurological foundations in all human experience. Some religions become forward-looking in their fuller development, with an increasing concern for eschatology; this is probably true of Judaism, Christianity and Islam. But they do not lose touch with the old ways: the past continues to be projected into the future.

Another interesting orientational complex is the one observed in the architectural form of the gothic cathedrals of mediaeval Europe. The scheme here may be represented as follows:

East: origins and ultimate destiny, expressed in the notion of 'eternity' and transcendence;

North: the past, expressed in the imagery of the Old Testament, usually with a predictive bias (prophets foretelling Christ);

South: the present, expressed in the imagery of the New Testament, specifically the life of Christ;

West: the future, expressed in the imagery of the Last Judgment.

See Wyatt 1996a for discussion of the biological and psychological foundations of the human sense of space and time, as reflected in the vocabulary given here.

Chapter 2

Mythic Shapings of the World

For millennia, human societies have asked questions concerning the origin of the world about them, and of the shape and relationship of its various parts. Since human experience is based largely on awareness and memory of its own actions, which gradually allowed ideas of causation to develop, it is natural that narratives concerning the origin of everything should attribute action and causation to human-like beings (gods), and explore the various types of human activity as the means by which the world began. These were not competing scientific explanations: they were rather complementary poetic ones. Such narratives exhibit that most important distinguishing trait of humans: the capacity to generate and use symbols (also nowadays identified as 'memes').

Suggested Reading:
Blacker and Loewe 1975; Blackmore 1999; Brandon 1963; Clifford 1994; Fleming 2000; Frankfort 1949; Guthrie 1993; Huxley 1997; Jaynes 1976; Keel 1978, 15-77; Simkins 1997, 121-44; Stadelmann 1970; Wyatt 1996b, 19-115; id. 2001c.

2.1 Introduction

To be systematic, we need to deal with the various sub-divisions of cosmology under separate headings. This we shall do in later chapters. Our task in this chapter is to see the most general principles of the structuring of the world. We begin with the subjective experience of the world already discussed. Two principles control the results of experience, common sense and the principle of anthropomorphism. We may also usefully distinguish *processes* (how things come about: §§I-V) and *structures* (their form: §§VI-VIII).

2.2 Processes: Cosmogony

2.2.1 Cosmogony is the origin of the world. Cosmogonic myths are creation stories, and thus say something about perceptions of time and its beginning. These commonly fall into the following categories, all metaphors modelled on human activities:

i) Sexual generation. Examples of this are Atum's creation in Heliopolis and Ptah's in Memphis;

ii) Technology: the deity is a potter or a metal-worker, as Amun, Khnum, or Yahweh;

iii) Conflict: a great primaeval battle takes place, and the victor makes the world out of the vanquished; thus Marduk, Elohim (= Yahweh). (See in particular the texts in §3 for this theme);

iv)   Speech: a divine word is sufficient to create things. Thus Ptah,
Elohim (= Yahweh).

2.2.2   What are the roots of such Language? A feature of all these
accounts is the universal principle that supernatural beings — gods and
goddesses — are the subjects of all the actions. But their behaviour is that
of ordinary people, raised to a heroic level. They are thus metaphors of
human world-construction. Guthrie 1993 shows how anthropomorphism
is a basic human tendency, and an important strategy in survival. The
oddest human tendencies, like being religious, all have powerful genetic
components, driven further by the 'genes' of culture, called 'memes'. See
Blackmore 1999, for a good account of their role in cultural evolution.

2.2.3   Within the scope of cosmogony we need to distinguish the making
of humans. It is inevitable that humans should form the centre of human
consciousness, and consequently of the human world (cf. §1 *passim*). This
biological imperative is given cultural (and thus religious) sanction by
making the construction of humans the culmination of divine creative
activity. Where a motive is expressed, it is so in terms of the service of the
gods (that is, in cultic practice). See particularly §§2(11-12, 14, 18) and §8(7).
Thus the human practice of ritual was justified as fulfilling divine
purposes. Rituals were patterns of everyday tasks, done on the gods'
behalf.

2.3   Structures: Cosmology

2.3.1   Cosmology is the ordering, or mental construction, of the world[1].
We have seen the subjective basis for all experience, which produces a
ready-made means of organizing space and time, of orientating oneself
individually or communally with reference to the external world.

2.3.2   This provides a framework within which one may learn to give
structure and meaning to that world. This happens in all societies, and has
two aspects. The first is the pragmatic one of learning to tell the time, in

---

[1]   In modern astronomy, 'cosmology' is the preferred term for both aspects, the
creation of the world (here 'cosmogony', or process) and the structure (here
'cosmology' or structure).   The differentiation implied here in distinct
vocabulary is probably more helpful in Religious Studies. We might further
refine the distinction by noting that myths, in their narrative manifestation,
often tell how something such as the world came into being (as an aspect of
the cosmogonic process, however extended), while cosmology is represented
rather in the general presuppositions of the mind (the 'mythic mind', Wyatt
2001a).

the large-scale sense of recognizing the regular phases of the moon, the length of the solar year, and the flow of tides and seasons. Becoming aware of what variations occurred was crucial for the rise of organized complex social life, such as was lived in the villages, then the cities, then the countries and then the great empires of the ancient world. The organization of space at all these levels was also vital to the smooth running of a community on any scale. In practical terms this might be called secular, but it was never entirely separated from the sacred in the ancient world, and ritual was the means by which both space and time were organized and harnessed to a community's use.

2.3.3 The second aspect was the one in which religion impinged on all these realities, sanctioning some forms of behaviour, forbidding others, and providing the mythical and ritual structures which validated human life, and gave it 'meaning'. We look at a number of typical ancient Near Eastern cosmologies, and in each case have selected passages which describe boundaries. These allow demarcation and differentiation, part of the human need to categorize. Boundaries are important metaphors of the constraints cultural life imposes on people. A nice example is the significance of dietary laws in *Leviticus* 16, as explained by Douglas 1970.

2.4 Forms

2.4.1 Texts §§2(19-23) describe the actual *shape* of the world, as imagined. The salient feature, common to all accounts, is the geocentric universe. This generally lies as a flat plate lying horizontally at the centre of a great sphere. Outside this sphere, above, below, and around (for Greece see §§2(30-4)), lies the 'cosmic ocean'. The whole world is thus contained in a womb-like structure. See §2(41). Egypt in addition had celestial and infernal Niles mirroring the earthly Nile (§§2(25-29)).

2.4.2 There are a number of 'layers' to this sphere, spheres within spheres, up to seven in number: §§2(19, 23), Mesopotamia; §§2(20-1) Israel; §2(22) Egypt. These can be echoed in the construction of temples: cf. Ugarit §6(3) and Edfu. This metaphor is maintained right down into mediaeval thought. Where did the idea originate? Probably in the recognition of 'seven planets' (§2(42)), a spatial conception in turn perhaps determined by temporal concerns (such as the fourfold division of the lunar month, giving seven whole days to each quarter).

2.5 Boundaries

These are implicit in the structures, and are crucial in the life of people, as they move spatially and temporally. Graphic accounts of the dangerous barriers of the underworld are found at §2(22), Egypt, and §2(23), Mesopotamia. The celestial boundary (symbolized spatially in temples by the holy of holies) is treated in §§6, 7.

2.6   Mapping

One of the most extraordinary breakthroughs of mental evolution which probably resulted from settlement and the invention of writing, was the capacity to use 'mind-space' to construct an ideal form of real territory. See *1.12. This gave rise to abstract, two-dimensional representations in miniature of the real world.   As an example of this we consider a Babylonian world map (§2(24)) dating from *ca* 700 BCE. This is the earliest known map of the whole world (earlier local maps are known, generally fairly realistic), though Herodotus, writing somewhat later, described similar Greek maps, perhaps reflecting a similar construction. The basic conception persisted into the Middle Ages[2].

2.7   Time

The gradual flow of the seasons was obviously recognized by ancient hunter-gatherers.   They also, from Upper Palaeolithic times, were probably aware of lunar cycles. The growth of agriculture, herding and settled life in communities necessitated more detailed organization, and some early examples (§§2(38-40)) show the same basic structures, though they differed in detail. We shall see the importance of time-measurement in the observance of periodic festivals.

2.8   Sevens

Seven evidently serves as a frequent spatio-temporal metaphor. Probably deriving from lunations and their measurement (into quarters), it was 'found' to have celestial correspondences ('seven planets': §2(42)). These planets all circled round a geocentric universe, having a profound influence on its processes, for those with the wisdom to understand. The

---

[2]   Cf. the following: Bagrow 1964, pl. A (Arabic *Mappa Mundi* by al-Istakhri, 10th century), pl. B (Matthew Paris map of Britain, *ca* 1250), pl. D (*Mappa Mundi*, Genoa, 1457); Camille 1996, fig. 28 (Earth, at the centre of planetary-influence rings/spheres, 14th century Book of Hours), fig. 38 (*Mappa Mundi* from a 12th century Psalter), fig. 65 (the circle of time in a square frame: the wheel of ten ages of man, Psalter of Robert de Lisle); Woodward 1987, pl. 3 (Muslim *Mappa Mundi* copied in 1154 from al-Idrisi's map), pl. 7 (MS of the Cosmographie de Pomponius Mela), pl. 9 (Mozarabic Beatus MS *Mappa Mundi*, 10th century), pl. 11 (square diagrammatic *Mappa Mundi*, German, 9th century), etc.

temporal and spatial correspondence discerned here was no doubt seen as self-confirming.

I   Egypt: local Cosmogony Traditions

We have a number of cosmogonic traditions, originating in the chief temples of the main cities of Egypt. Every temple claimed to be built on the *ben*-stone (on which see §§2(2, 5), 5(1-3) below). This was the first dry land to appear from the primordial ocean (*nw*, deified as the god Nu), and was comparable in its symbolism to sacred mountains and omphaloi found in other traditions (see §§5(5-15)). To be at the centre of the world was an implicit claim of absolute reality, and of absolute age, from creation itself. Such claims for a temple, and the cosmogonic claims made in the present examples for its deity, were a powerful statement of the prestige of the city in question. In a pre-philosophical world, it amounted to an absolute truth claim. Egypt appears to have tolerated a number of such 'truth claims' (if that is the right way to characterize them), which may seem mutually exclusive to us, but which were rather complementary in Egyptian thought. This complementary nature was perhaps enhanced by the variety of means used to create, as distinguished here. In some examples, different methods are used in a complementary fashion (e.g. masturbation and spitting in §2(1), sex and speech in §2(2, 7), showing perhaps that the idea was to suggest how things were formed by analogy, rather than making literal statements.

The figures used to express the creation in narrative form were inevitably drawn from human experience. From where could metaphors and symbols originate if not from experience? So the great creative acts with which human beings were familiar, sexual reproduction, various forms of 'making' by technological means, speech (very powerful in creating a 'human' world) and war, which enlarged territory, and thus 'created' space.

2(1)   Heliopolis: Sex

I (Atum) became united with my members. They came forth from my very self after I had played the husband with my fist. The seed which fell from my hand I spat out from my mouth as Shu, I expectorated as Tefnut. I became three gods from one god...

(P. Nes-Min)

Atum was the sun-god of Heliopolis, who then became the setting sun in the enlarged triad Khepri-Ra-Atum (the sun at its rising, zenith and setting). Here he is seen as androgynous, a common feature of creation gods (cf. §2(2)). The masturbation image is a striking, and perhaps rather disconcerting one, but is found among a number of Egyptian gods (Amun, Amenapet, Atum, and Min); it is also found in India (Prajāpati), and may be the means by which the West Semitic god El begot two daughters, whom he then married to beget other gods, with an echo in *Psalm* 8 (see Wyatt 1994).

Shu was the air-god (air separating sky, Nut, from earth, Geb: see §2(41)).

Tefnut was the goddess of mists and clouds.

2(2)   Memphis: (Sex and) Giving Birth

> He [Ptah] is indeed Ta-Tenen[1], who brought forth[2] the gods,
> for everything comes forth from him...

(ANET 5: the Shabako Stone)

1   Ta-Tenen (*t3 tnn*) means 'the Rising Earth'. Ptah, the chief god of Memphis, perhaps originating as the craftsman-god of the Tura limestone quarries, is here identified with an ancient earth-deity, the very embodiment of the concept of the primordial, and is androgynous. Cf. the motif of the *ben*-stone below, and the further Memphite tradition at §2(7).

2   Sc. as a mother giving birth, the feminine aspect of the androgynous deity.

2(3)   Hermopolis: an Egg i)

Thoth was the ibis-god of Hermopolis. For the intimate relationship of Thoth with Ra, and Thoth as creator, see Boylan 1922, 58-82 and 107-23.

O egg of the water (Thoth), source of the earth, product of the Ogdoad[1], great in heaven and great in the underworld, dweller in the thicket, chief of the Isle of the Lake of the Two Knives, I came forth with thee from thy nest.

(Brandon 1963, 44: Harris Magical Papyrus R vi 10-2)

1   The Ogdoad was a group of eight gods: at Hermopolis they were Nun and Naunet (the primordial abyss), Huh and Hauhet (infinity), Kuk and Kauket (darkness), and Amun and Amaunet (invisibility). The second of each pair was the consort of the first, and the set constituted the 'primaeval gods' or 'Urgötter', who constructed the earth, and gave it their characteristics. With Thoth, they formed the Ennead (group of nine gods) of Hermopolis. Enneads were found in most of the main temples of Egypt, though the constituent members varied, as indeed did their number. An Ennead is an ideal figure (as it were 3 × 3, or plurality pluralized) and indicates all possible divine forms, paradoxically seen as unitary in nature. Note that in this passage the Ogdoad (themselves emanations from Thoth) collectively lay the first egg. Thus the primordial god is self-regenerating, a common motif with the creator-gods of Egypt.

2(4)   Hermopolis: an Egg ii)

Thou (Ra[1]) art ascended on high, coming forth from the secret egg, as the child of the Ogdoad.

(Brandon 1963, 45: Cairo ostracon)

1   Notice that here and in the next passage it is Ra rather than Thoth who is the author of the egg, an example of the solarization of various cults that took place in Egypt.

2(5) Hermopolis: an Egg iii)

Thy habitation, at the beginning, was the hillock of Hermopolis[1]. Thou (Ra[2]) didst touch the earth in the Isle of the Two Knives. Thou didst raise thyself from the waters, out of the secret egg, with Amaunet[3] in attendance.

(Brandon 1963, 45)

1   The idea of the 'primordial hill' (the *ben*-stone) here is to be compared with such passages as §§2(2) and 5(1-3).

2   Cf. §2(4) n. 1.

3   Amaunet was the female counterpart and consort of Amun at Hermopolis, where the pair were the final members of the Ogdoad, emanations of Thoth.

Thoth, god of Hermopolis, appeared in two forms, as the ibis (god of wisdom and law, scribe and thus recorder of legal decisions) and as the baboon (measurer of time, space, weight, etc.). His consort was variously Maat (*m3't*, 'truth, justice') and Seshat, goddess of writing.

2(6) Thebes: Various Elements Including 'Making'

Thebes grew to national importance with the rise of the Middle Kingdom, from *ca* 2040 BCE, when local dynasts reunited Egypt following its fragmentation during the first intermediate period (*ca* 2260-2040 BCE). Its local god Amun, seemingly of Hermopolitan origin, merged with Montu, the war-god of Armant, Min, the ithyphallic god of Coptos, and Ra of Heliopolis. He appears in various forms in iconography, as a goose (laying the primordial egg, cf. §§2(3-5)), a ram, a man, an ithyphallic man or a serpent (the last two forms are Amenapet, 'Amun of Luxor', the self-regenerating form).

1   Thou (Amun-Ra)[1] art the Sole One, who made all that is,
        the Solitary One[2], who made what exists,
    from whose eyes mankind came forth,
        and upon whose mouth the gods came into being.
5   He who made herbage for the cattle,
        and the fruit trees for mankind;
    who made that on which the fish in the river may live,
        and the bird soaring in the sky.
    He who gives life to that which is in the egg,
10   gives life to the son of the slug,
        and makes that on which gnats may live...[3]

(*ANET* 366: Hymn to Amun-Ra)

1   Amun (*imn*, 'invisible'), later fused with Ra ('sun') as Amun-Ra, was the chief god of Thebes.

2   The expression 'the Solitary One' implies that Amun-Ra was conceptualized monotheistically. But such language, commonly found in hymnody, is rather 'henotheism' (the treatment of a deity as though monotheistically conceived), and not only is such language used of several of the senior deities, but these same deities evidently coexist with others in the same texts. The kinds of concern which inform modern views of monotheism (and are commonly supposed to be the Bible's concern) do not really help in understanding the present situation. It is perhaps more helpful to think of the gods as poetic, metaphorical figures, who could be recombined at will, now treated in isolation, now merging with others to achieve a particular ideological or theological effect.

Henotheistic language of this kind was particularly prevalent in the New Kingdom following the Amarna period, during which Akhenaten (Amenhotpe IV) had promoted the cult of the (visible) sun-disc, in antagonism to the cult of the invisible sun ('Amun', *imn*, means 'invisible').

3   The final tricolon gives a charming account of the divine concern for the lowliest life-forms. It would be wrong to read a sentimental eco-consciousness into this, but it does give an insight into the Egyptian view that the whole of nature was the outworking of the divine will.

2(7)   Memphis : Speech

In many ways, not least in its use of speech as the medium for creation, this is the most sophisticated cosmogonic account from the ancient Near East, anticipating the account of *Genesis* I by perhaps 300 years or so. According to the tradition outlined in the preamble, this is a copy of an old account from the Old Kingdom, before 2260 BCE, which would make its theology all the more remarkable. However, scholars generally treat this claim with scepticism. The Shabako Stone, from which §2(2) also comes, is in the British Museum. It ended up as a millstone, so that much of the middle of the inscription is worn away.

The mighty great one is Ptah, who transmitted life to all gods, as well as to their Kas[1], through this heart, by which Horus became Ptah, and through this tongue, by which Thoth became Ptah... His Ennead is before him in the form of teeth and lips... which pronounced the name of everything, from which Shu and Nut came forth... Thus all the gods were formed, and his Ennead was completed. Indeed, all the divine order really came into being through what the heart thought and what the tongue commanded... Thus were made all crafts, the action of the arms, the movement of the legs, and the activity of every member, in conformity with this command which the heart thought, which came forth from the tongue... He is indeed Ta-Tenen, who brought forth the gods, for everything came forth from him... And so Ptah was satisfied[2], after he had made everything, as well as all the divine order. He had formed the gods, he had made cities, he had founded nomes...

(*ANET* 5: the Shabako Stone)

1   Ka (*k3*) is the power of a deity to act (*k3* having the sense of 'power'), as it
        were his or her 'divine spirit'. It appears to be independent of the substance of
        the god, and is conventionally transmitted to the king by the divine embrace
        shown in many reliefs. Thus royal power, as divine, was also characterized by
        the Ka.

2   That is, Ptah was pleased, like God in *Genesis* 1. The created order is good, as
        conforming to the divine intention.

This important text, the continuation of §2(2) (see the Shabako Stone in the British
Museum) provides a close parallel to the cosmogony of *Genesis* 1 (§§2(15, 17), 3(6)).
Ptah here creates all things by his divine utterance. Horus (who is also the king) is the
heart, that is the mind and will of Ptah, a grandiose view of monarchy! Thoth, the god
of wisdom, is the agency of the divine utterance by Ptah's tongue, articulated through
his teeth and lips, the Ennead of Memphis. In this figure, the entire godhead
collaborates in the utterance of the divine word, which creates by naming, for the
name is the identity. Cf. Spieser 2000 on the autonomy of royal names as divine
beings.

Note the typically Egyptian way of happily identifying gods, particularly when, as here,
it is a major deity of whom more or less universal claims are being made, and he
absorbs other deities as hypostases of his various activities. This is always a dynamic
process, appropriate to each moment, rather than a once-for-all historical
development.

2(8)   An Egyptian Creation Tradition from el-Berseh
(*ca* 2000 BCE): Making

Inscriptions on coffins from el-Berseh dating to the Middle Kingdom. Mortuary
inscriptions provide a large proportion of our information about Egyptian theology.
Their function was frequently to identify the deceased with such and such a deity as a
means of counteracting the destructive forces of darkness and avoiding annihilation.
The *Coffin Texts* (Faulkner 1973-8) are part of a long liturgical and literary tradition that
can be traced back to the *Pyramid Texts*, and forward to the *Book of the Dead* (§9(5)).

The All-Lord (= Ra) says in the presence of those stilled from tumult on
the journey to the court[1]: 'Pray, be prosperous in peace! I repeat for you
four good deeds, which my own heart did for me in the midst of the
serpent-coil, in order to still evil. I did four good deeds within the portal
of the horizon[2].
I made the four winds that every man might breathe thereof like his fellow
in his time.
                            That is one deed thereof.
I made the great inundation that the poor man might have rights therein
like the great man.
                            That is one deed thereof[3].
I made every man like his fellow. I did not command that they do evil,
but it was their hearts which violated what I said[4].

That is one deed thereof.

I made their hearts to cease from forgetting the West, in order that divine offerings might be given to the gods of the nomes.

That is one deed thereof.

I brought into being the four gods from my sweat[5], while men are the tears of my eye[6].

(*ANET* 7-8: *CT* 1130)

1   The allusion is to the law-court. From the earliest literary allusions (the *Pyramid Texts*, on 5th and 6th dynasty pyramid walls) it is evident that common people expected a *post-mortem* judgment (the king alone being exempt). While by the time of the *Book of the Dead*, in the New Kingdom, Osiris was regarded as judge of the dead, it had earlier been Ra who fulfilled this role, as in the present inscription. Cf. Brandon 1967.

2   The term *akhet* (*3ḥt*) means 'horizon' (where the sky and earth meet), 'place where the dead go', or as here, 'the shrine of a god'. The theme of the term is liminality, where two different orders of reality meet. See §§7(1-11) below.

3   Civil rights for all! It is evident that ancient religions cannot be simply dismissed as 'immoral', as so often done by Christian or Jewish apologists. The 'great inundation' here denotes the annual flooding of the Nile valley, which brings new silt deposits to enrich the soil.

4   Note the element of theodicy: evil is attributed to human inclination, the deity being exempt from responsibility. A similar idea is found in the Shabako stone, where Ptah creates in men the possibilities for good or evil. The Jewish doctrine of the two 'yetzers' (*yᵉṣārîm*, 'inclinations') was similar, and may have been influenced by Egyptian thought.

5   This plays on the similarity between the terms for 'four', *fdw*, and that for 'sweat', *fdt*. The 'four gods' here are probably the gods of the cardinal points. In *the Book of the Dead* they guard the deceased's body-organs and guarantee their future regeneration.

6   This plays on the similarity between the terms for 'tear', *rmt*, and for 'man, people', *rmt*.

     These last two word-plays are typical of many ancient theologies. It tells us something about the power of the uttered word, which was believed to contribute to the reification of things. Cf. Adam naming the animals in *Genesis* 2:19.

These Egyptian passages illustrate an important principle: *any* shrine fulfils the role of 'world-centre' in its active use in the cult. In the above cases §§2(1-7), the major temples in Egypt (particularly from a political point of view: each was a powerful regional centre, and had, with the exception of Memphis, a new royal foundation, formerly been an important shrine of a pre-dynastic kingdom) all claim to be the place where the first land (sacralized as the '*ben*-stone': see note to §5(2)) emerged from the primaeval flood (*Nw* or *Nwn*). This and analogues in other traditions are also presupposed in accounts of the foundation or restoration of temples (cf. §§6(1, 26, 27, 28), 8(7)).

II   Mesopotamia: local Cosmogony Traditions

2(9)   Babylon: the Conflict of Marduk and Tiamat

This passage is from the Babylonian 'epic of creation', called in Akkadian *Enuma Eliš* from its opening words 'When on high…'. It narrates the early processes of creation, in which Apsu and Tiamat, respectively fresh waters (male) and salt waters (female) beget the early generations of the gods. When they plot to kill their children, because they are causing a disturbance, Apsu is killed. But none of the gods dares confront the furious Tiamat, until Marduk volunteers. His price is kingship of the gods. When this is granted, he goes into battle with Tiamat.   To the name Tiamat (variously *Ti'āmatu(m)*, *tāmtum*, *têmtum*) cf. Hebrew *t^ehôm* in *Genesis* 1, §§2(15), 3(6), where the divine personality has been emptied from the conception. We resume treatment of the *Chaoskampf* (Chaos-conflict) theme at §§3(1-16).

1   Tiamat screamed aloud in a passion,
      her lower parts shook together from the depths.
   She recited the incantation, and kept casting her spell.
      Meanwhile the gods of battle were sharpening their weapons.
5   Face to face they came, Tiamat and Marduk, sage of the gods[1].
      they engaged in combat,
      they closed for battle.
   The Lord spread out his net and made it encircle her,
      to her face he dispatched the *imhullu*-wind, which had been
         behind:
10   Tiamat opened her mouth to swallow it,
      and he forced in the *imhullu*-wind.
      so that she could not close her lips.
   Fierce winds distended her belly;
      her insides were constipated and she stretched her mouth
         wide.
15   He shot an arrow which pierced her belly,
      split her down the middle and slit her heart,
      vanquished her and extinguished her life.
   He threw down her corpse and stood on top of her.[2]

                              (Dalley 1989, 253: *Enuma Elish* iv 89-104, adapted)

1   Wisdom is one of the essential qualities of kingship.

2   To this gesture cf. §6(16) and n. 1.

This tradition (on which see also §2(10)) is a glorification of the chief god of Babylon, Marduk.   It ends with a recitation of his fifty cult titles, and was narrated at the Babylonian *Akitû* festival (§10(5)).   The narrative is a mixture of genres, now theogony, now cosmogony (§2(10)), now hymn. To this theogonic section cf. Hesiod's *Theogony* (Evelyn-White 1914, 78-155; M. L. West 1966, id. 1988, 3-33).

2(10) Marduk Constructs the World:
Division of the Vanquished Deity

The actual making of the world fits into the technological category; but it is the triumphant dismemberment of the vanquished deity in the conflict and the making of the world from this divine substance which is the central theme. The background to this is twofold. firstly it is a metaphor drawn from the experience of warfare, and its crucial role in the establishment of territory (which is a kind of 'world-creation'). Secondly it draws on the transformative role of sacrifice, which is the ritual means by which one order of reality is transformed into another. We may adapt O'Flaherty 1975, 13: 'the [ancient Near Eastern] universe is a closed system... so that nothing is ever "created" *ex nihilo*; rather, things are constantly rearranged, each put in its proper place, and by doing this... ordered life emerges out of lifeless chaos.' The sacrifice is the medium for this. The dragon-enemy of the creator-god is the transformed enemy, who is sacrificed to the gods. This motif (the 'smiting motif') appears on the pylons of most Egyptian temples, as an offering made by the king to the resident gods.

The Babylonian version of this tradition is the earliest to treat the theme *explicitly* as a cosmogony. However, it is already a late version of the tradition, and all the other derivative versions are given below at §§3(1-16), among which §§3(1-4, 13) are older than the present version.

1   And to Tiamat, whom he had ensnared, he turned back.
The Lord trampled the lower part of Tiamat,
    and with his unsparing mace smashed her skull,
severed the arteries of her blood,
5   and made the North Wind carry it to off as good news...
The Lord rested, and inspected her corpse.
He divided the monstrous shape and created marvels (from it).
He sliced her in half like a fish for drying:
    half of her he put up to roof the sky,
10   drew a bolt across and made a guard hold it.
Her waters he arranged so that they could not escape.
He crossed the heavens and sought out a shrine;
He levelled *Apsû*, dwelling of Nudimmud.
The Lord measured the dimensions of *Apsû*
15   and the large temple, which he built in its image,
......was *Esharra*[1]:
in the great shrine *Esharra*, which he had created as the sky,
    he founded cult centres for Anu, Ellil and Ea.
He created stands for the great gods.
As for the stars, he set up constellations corresponding
......to them.
20   He designated the year and marked out its divisions,

apportioned three stars each to the twelve months[2]...
The spittle of Tiamat [   ]
Marduk [   ]
he put into groups and made clouds scud...
25   He opened the Euphrates and Tigris from her eyes[3]...
'I shall make a house[4] to be a luxurious dwelling for myself,
    and shall found his cult centre within it,
    and I shall establish my private quarters,
    and confirm my kingship...
30   I hereby name it Babylon, 'home of the great gods'.
    We shall make it the centre of religion...
(Dalley 1989, 254-9: *Enuma Elish* iv 128-46, v 1-131, excerpts, adapted)

Anu was the sky-god, Enlil (variant Ellil) the storm-god, and Ea (= Sumerian Enki) the god of water and springs. Nudimmud ('Procreator of Man', 'Image-fashioner') was an epithet of Ea.

This text introduces an important theme, which is taken up in chapter 3, the conflict between two deities. Here it evidently leads to the creation of the world. This element is not so prominent in other versions, but surfaces in various biblical examples. See §§2(15, 16), 3(5-6). In these other versions, another element is paramount: the authority the king derives from the divine victory. (On this motif see Wyatt 1998b and references.)

1   *Esharra* (É.ŠAR.RA) (George 1993, §§1034-7), meaning 'House of the Universe', was a title of several ancient Near Eastern temples. Here it has a more general sense of the universe, but it highlights the idea that the entire universe is a divine abode, and conversely, that a temple (É.GAL: 'great house' — dwelling of a god or king) was a microcosm (the universe in miniature). (The Egyptian term *pr wr*, 'great house', also denotes both a temple and a royal palace. The similar term *pr ʿ3*, 'great house', becomes 'Pharaoh'.) Marduk's temple at Babylon, which was, like others, such a microcosm, was called *Esagila* (É.SAĜ.ÍL, George 1993, §967), 'House whose top is high', because, as satirically expressed in the Tower of Babel story (*Genesis* 11:4, §6(30)), which was modelled on it, *Bābēl* being the Hebrew form of Babylon (Akkadian *bab-ili*), its top 'reached to heaven'. Another name for this temple, equally cosmological in its sense, was É.TEMEN.AN.KI (George 1993, §1088), 'house of the foundations of heaven and earth'. See further at §7. This appears to be a heavenly archetype, since the actual construction of the world takes place in the sequel. See n. 3.

2   Note how time is created as a result of Marduk's victory. The text goes on to detail various subdivisions of time.

3   Note how the material world, and thus space, is also created as a result of Marduk's victory. The text goes on to detail various constituent parts of the world. So space and time are specifically aspects of the created order.

4   Perhaps this reversion to the theme dealt with above (see n. 1) is an indication of redactional activity. But now the emphasis is perhaps on Marduk's own temple as the final seal on the creation.

III   Creation and the Status of Human Beings

The status of human beings within a religious tradition is often represented in its mythology. The order of creation may provide clues as to relative rank: thus *Genesis* 1 (§2(17) below) presents the making of Man (male and female, often construed as androgynous) as the final stage, and thus the culmination of the created order. *Genesis* 2 (§2(18), however, makes the same point by making Man (of very ambiguous sexual type, best construed as initially androgynous) first among the creatures in the Garden. This kind of nuanced treatment of issues will be found in all these texts. Readers should not fall into the trap of thinking that older ideas are necessarily more 'primitive'.

The following ancient texts invite comment on the broad estimate of humans, on moral issues such as social diversity, and theological issues such as the concern of the gods towards their creatures.

2(11)   A Sumerian Tradition from Nippur

A number of creation-story motifs occur in this fragment from the third millennium BCE. Human beings are created as servants of the gods (cf. Adam's role in Eden)[1]. Men are made from clay (cf. *Genesis* 2:7, §2(18)), as was Pandora in Hesiod, *Theogony* 561-89, *Works and Days* 60-82 (where this is restricted to Pandora as proto-woman, in notoriously misogynistic accounts). But Pandora appears originally to have been a goddess, and the god Kulla is made from clay in §8(7). While in the Bible clay ('dust') is mixed with divine breath, in the *Enuma Elish* poem it is mixed with divine blood. Blood is also 'the life' in the Bible (*Deuteronomy* 12:23). Cf. also the divine tears from which men are made in §2(8) n. 4.

  1   'O my son,   [Nammu speaks]
       rise from thy bed...
          from thy...
       work what is wise,
  5   fashion servants of the gods,
       may they produce their...'

       O my mother,   [Enki speaks]
       the creature whose name thou hast uttered,
        ...it exists[2],
 10   Bind upon it the --- of the gods;
       mix the heart of the clay that is over the abyss,
     the good and princely fashioners will thicken the clay,
       thou, do thou bring the limbs into existence;
     Ninmah will work above thee,
 15   [   ] the goddesses of birth will stand by thee
       at thy fashioning;

O my mother, decree thou its fate,
   Ninmah will bind upon it the --- of the gods...
   The ... she (sc. Ninmah) made into a woman
     who cannot give birth.
Enki upon seeing the woman who cannot give birth
   decreed her fate,
20   destined her to be stationed in the 'woman house'.
   The ... she made into one who has no male organ,
     Who has no female organ,
Enki, upon seeing him who has no male organ,
   who has no male organ,
25   to stand before the king decreed as his fate...
Of him whom thy hand has fashioned,
   I have decreed the fate,
   Have given him bread to eat.
Do thou decree the fate of him
30   whom my hand has fashioned,
   do thou give him bread to eat...

                           (Kramer 1961, 70-1)

Enki was the god of the waters (= Ea in §2(10)).

Nammu was the Primaeval Sea (met with as Tiamat in Akkadian texts above, §§2(9-10)), here mother of Enki.

Ninmah was the earth-goddess (from whose substance, clay, people are made); an epithet of Ninhursag, wife of Enki.

Six different human types are made. The state of the tablet allows only the final two, the *enitum* priestess (who must remain childless) and the eunuch, to be identified.

Another translation of part of this appears in *CS* i 516-8. A considerably longer version was published by Jacobsen 1987, 153-66.

1   Heidel 1942, 121-2, contrasted the servile status of men in Mesopotamian myth with his lordship of creation in the Bible. Is this an adequate assessment of *either* tradition? Note that the highest end of man in both traditions was to serve God or the gods. This is also the point of the next passage §2(12) and in §2(14), and is an important biblical idea in §2(17), for Adam will till (√*bd*) the garden, the 'servant of Yahweh' (= the king) is *'ebed yhwh* (√*bd*), and cult, worship, the service at the altar is called *'obdâ* (√*bd*). Interestingly, the Egyptian for 'His Majesty' (the king) is *ḥm.f*, which may be construed as 'his (the god's) servant'. See Gardiner 1957, 581. Frankfort 1948, 45 (cf. von Beckerath 1984, 39), gives a different and perhaps preferable explanation, *ḥm* meaning 'body', so that *ḥm.f* means 'his body', indicating that the king is Horus incarnate: cf. J. P. Allen in *CS* i 5, 'The Incarnation of this god' (citing von Beckerath, n. 9), 'His Incarnation'.

2   This idea, of creating with the utterance of a word, occurs above in Memphis
       §2(7), and in *Genesis* 1, §2(15); it is also present in *Genesis* 2:19-20, where Adam
       names the animals, thus cooperating in their production. This illustrates the
       point that men have always been aware that in a sense they live in a 'linguistic
       universe', where reality is what we construct in words.

2(12) A further Sumerian Tradition from Nippur

Not dissimilar to the previous passage, and also from the third millennium BCE, this
text considers that the life of the gods is deficient until human beings are created to
serve them adequately. Note the various creation motifs: birth, fashioning, cultivation.

1   After on the mountain of heaven and earth,
         An had caused the Anunnaki to be born,
     because the name[1] Ashnan had not been born,
         had not been fashioned,
5   because Uttu had not been fashioned,
         because to Uttu no temenos had been set up,
     there was no ewe,
         no lamb was dropped,
     there was no goat,
10   no kid was dropped,
     the ewe did not give birth to its two lambs,
         the goat did not give birth to its three kids.
     Because the name[1] of Ashnan, the wise, and Lahar,
         the Anunnaki, the great gods, did not know,
15   the grain of thirty days did not exist,
         the grain of forty days did not exist,
     the small grains, the grain of the mountain,
         the grain of the pure living creatures did not exist,
     because Uttu had not been born,
20   because the crown (of vegetation[?]) had not been raised,
     because the lord ... had not been born,
         because Sumugan, the god of the plain, had not come forth,
     like mankind when first created,
     they (the Anunnaki) knew not the eating of bread,
25   knew not the dressing of garments,
     ate plants with their mouth like sheep,
         drank water from the ditch.
     In those days, in the creation chamber of the gods,
         in their house Dulkug[2], Lahar and Ashnan were fashioned;
30   the produce of Lahar and Ashnan,
     the Anunnaki of the Dulkug ate, but remained unsated;
         in their pure sheepfolds milk..., and good things,
         the Anunnaki of the Dulkug drank, but remained unsated;

for the sake of the good things in their pure sheepfolds,

35   man was given breath.

(Kramer 1961, 72-3)

An (Akkadian Anu) was the Sumerian sky-god. See Jacobsen 1976, 95-8.

The Anunnaki were a class of gods of the earth and underworld (the Igigi being those of heaven).

Ashnan (Sumerian Ezinu) was the goddess of grain.

Lahar was the cattle-god.

Uttu was a plant-goddess, daughter of the god of the waters Enki (Akkadian Ea).

1   Note the emphasis on the 'name'. The reality has no full existence until named. Cf. §§2(7) n., 2(11) n. 2, and for a rite based on the written form, §11(26). Here it is the gods who do not yet 'know'. In the subsequent part of the text it becomes clear that they are dependent on human involvement to live a full life.

2   Thus Kramer. Sumerian Du_6-kug, 'the Holy Mound', was the home of the Annunaki. Cf. the *Ben*-stone in Egyptian thought and other omphalos concepts (§§5(1-3), 6(4, 5)).

2(13) The Theogony of Dunnu

An early second millennium BCE composition from Dunnu, in the kingdom of Isin, in which cultural realities are the prime movers in the process of creation. The story is in the form of a theogony, describing the birth of deities, and their cheerful progress through a series of family murders. It bears comparison with the Hittite myths of Kumarbi, the beginnings of *Enuma Elish*, and Hesiod's *Theogony*: see Lambert and Walcot 1965. See Dalley (*ad loc.*) and *CS* i 402-4 for further notes.

1   At the very beginning[?] [Plough married Earth][1]
      And they [decided to establish[?]] a family[?] and dominion.
    'We shall break up the virgin soil of the land into clods!'
      In the clods of their virgin soil[?], they created Sea[2].
5   The furrows, of their own accord, begot the cattle god[3].
      Together they built Dunnu forever[?] as his refuge[?] [4].
    Plough made unrestricted dominion[5] for himself in Dunnu.
    Then Earth raised her face to the cattle god his son
      and said to him, 'Come and let me love you!'
10   The cattle god married Earth his mother,
      and killed Plough his father[6],
      and laid him to rest in Dunnu, which he loved.
    Then the cattle god took over his father's dominion.
      He married Sea, his older sister.
15   The flocks god, son of the cattle god, came
      and killed the cattle god,

and in Dunnu laid him to rest in the tomb of his father.
He married Sea his mother.
   Then Sea slew Earth her mother.
20 On the sixteenth day of Kislimu, he took over dominion
      and rule.
The son of the flocks god married River his own sister,
   and killed (his) father the flocks god and Sea his mother,
   and laid them to rest in the tomb undisturbed[?].
On the first day of Tebet, he seized dominion and rule
      for himself.
25 The herdsman god son of the flocks god married his sister
      Pasture-and-Poplar,
   and made Earth's verdure abundant,
supported sheepfold and pen
      to feed[?] forefathers and settlements[?],
   and [   ] for the gods' requirements.
30 He killed [   ][?] and River his mother
   and made them dwell in the tomb.
On the [   ] day of Shabat, he took over dominion and rule
      for himself.
Haharnum son of the herdsman god married his sister
      Belet-seri
   and killed the herdsman god and Pasture-and-Poplar
      his mother,
35   and made them dwell in the tomb.
On the sixteenth day of Addar, he took over rule
      (and) dominion.
Then Hayyashum son of Haharnum married [   ]
      his own sister.
At the New Year[8] he took over his father's dominion,
      but did not kill him, and seized him alive.
40 He ordered his city to imprison his father ... and...

                    (Text breaks off)

             (Dalley 1989, 279-80: *Theogony of Dunnu*, adapted)

1   Ploughing is often used as a sexual metaphor (e.g. in the Ugaritic text KTU
     1.24.22-3, Wyatt 1998a, 338; note also the elliptical allusion in *Judges* 14:18). On
     'plough-logic' see Berger 1973, 19. It is almost as though the creation were
     dated from the beginning of the Neolithic and the invention of agriculture.
     There may be a hint of scorn for hunter-gatherers.

2   It goes entirely against the grain of other cosmogonies to have the sea a
     product of *earlier* realities. But it is perhaps a matter of economic priorities.

3   Even among early agriculturalists the management of cattle would remain important. But perhaps here it has a secondary role.

4   Apparently the shrine of the cattle god in Dunnu was founded by the gods. Divine choice (usually through ritual techniques, the observation of oracles and omens) was usually recognized in the foundation of cities.

5   Does 'unrestricted dominion' allude to the conception of cosmic rule exemplified in §§3(20-6)?

6   In marrying his mother, the cattle god acts precisely as normal in a matrilineal descent system, whereby property passed down the female line, and males controlled it thorough marriage to the appropriate female. This seems to have been the case in Egypt, was perhaps so at Ugarit (see §11(27)), and also in Israel (Wyatt 1985b). This was the basis of the Oedipus myth (cf. §3(16) introduction), coming from a Cadmid (Phoenician) genealogical line, though when translated to Greek mores, such a marriage became a monstrosity. The present narrative is particularly close to the Greek version, in that the father was killed. It is independent in that mothers are also killed, and sons marry sisters as well as mothers (an Egyptian feature). In a cattle deity killing an agricultural deity, is there also something of the cultural antipathy we find in Cain and Abel (*Genesis* 4)?

7   Presumably the flocks god.

8   The dates, 16th Kislimu (l. 20), first of Tebet (l. 24), the [ ]th of Shabat (l. 32), the 16th Addar (l. 36) and New Year's Day (l. 38), are presumably all of cultic significance, perhaps a calendar of the main city festivals. The months listed are the last four of the year, with the New Year in Nisan (see §2(39)).

2(14) Marduk (Ea) creates Mankind

This passage from the *Enuma Elish* follows a fragmentary section, in which it appears that the gods complain at the work imposed on them, a familiar theme in Mesopotamian tradition (cf. §§2(11) n. 1, 2(12)). Note the caution in the introduction to §8(7) on attempting to harmonize conceptions of this kind.

1   When Marduk heard the speech of the gods,
   he made up his mind to perform miracles.
He spoke his utterance to Ea,
   and communicated to him the plan that was considering.

5   'Let me put blood¹ together, and make bones too.
   Let me set up primaeval man: "Man" shall be his name.
   Let me create a primaeval man.
The work of the gods shall be imposed² (on him),
   and so they (the gods) shall be at leisure…'

10   'It was Kingu who started the war,
   he who incited Tiamat and gathered an army!'
They bound him and held him in front of Ea,

imposed the penalty on him and cut off his blood.
He created mankind from his blood',
15   imposed the toil of the gods (on man)
and released the gods from it.

(Dalley 1989, 260-1, adapted: *Enuma Elish* vi 1-36, excerpts)

1   Man is thus made of *divine* blood. The Babylonian historian Berossus adds
that it was mixed with clay. Cf. §2(17), where it is divine breath mixed with
earth ('dust' — chosen to anticipate the idea of man being merely dust —
Genesis 3:19). See §2(11) introduction.

2   See §2(11) n. 1. The divine element in man (n. 1) precludes the assessment that
man's creation is merely as a chattel.

IV   Creation in Israelite and Judahite Thought

2(15) The 'Priestly Account'

To be dated at some time between the sixth and fourth centuries BCE. This is perhaps
the most familiar account of human creation to modern readers in the West. There is
a constant tendency to read modern theological perceptions into it, which should be
resisted. The narrative is to be assessed in its own context, and against the background
of other ancient Near Eastern stories. This passage is usually treated as prose. For v. 2
as verse see Wyatt 1993, 543-54, and §3(6) below. Here I present the whole narrative as
verse.

1   In the beginning of God's creating¹ of the heavens
and the underworld²,
the underworld was chaotic and empty,
and darkness was over the face of the deep,
and the spirit of God was hovering
over the face of the waters.
5   And God said:
'Let there be light!'
And there was light...
And God said:
'Let there be a firmament in the midst of the waters
10   and let it divide the waters from the waters...'
And God said:
'Let the waters be gathered under the heavens into one place,
and let the dry land appear!'
and it was so...

(*Genesis* 1:1-9)

1   Hebrew *bārâ*: the basic idea is of cutting in two (echoing the conflict myth, for
which see texts in §3). The verb occurs exclusively with Yahweh/God as the

subject. Creation here consists essentially of a series of binary divisions: the primordial soup (1:2) is the raw material of the heavens and the earth; primordial no-light is divided into darkness and light; water and dry land are divided. There is the merest echo of the old conflict tradition, but the common assessment that this indicates the 'demythologization' of the narrative is excessive. See Wyatt 2001a.

2   As transpires in the sequel, *hā 'āreṣ* here must denote the underworld, because the 'earth' (land as a habitable place) is created only in ll. 13-4. Cf. §§2(20-1).

2(16) An Exilic Version of the Creation, from a Lament

This passage is part of a lament over the destruction of Jerusalem. The psalmist appeals to the great work of creation (to which cf. §3) as a demonstration of Yahweh's ability to intervene, now in the time of despair. This is perhaps a less confident expression of the motif than *Isaiah* 51:9-10 (§4(1)).

> 1 Yet, O God, my king from of old,
>> performing saving deeds in the midst of the earth,
> by your power you divided Sea,
>> you smashed the heads[1] of Dragon over the waters!
> 5 You shattered the heads of Leviathan,
>> [giving him as food for the beasts of the wild.]
> [You cleft spring and torrent;][2]
>> you dried up permanent River.
> Day and night are yours:
> 10   you established moon and sun.
> You fixed the boundaries of the underworld;
>> (as for) summer and winter: you made them.

(Psalm 74:12-17)

1   'Heads...' The dragon has seven heads in the Mesopotamian and West Semitic (§4(2b)) traditions. Cf. the seven-headed dragon in *Revelation* 12 (§3(11)). Typhoeus in Hesiod's *Theogony* (§3(14)) n. 2) has a hundred heads!

2   These two lines are intrusive, a later redactional insertion transforming a creation story into an eschatological feast.

Lines 3, 4, 5, 8 give four names for the primaeval dragon: 'Sea, Dragon, Leviathan, River'. 'Sea... River' are paired names for the Ugaritic dragon, called *Litanu*, which later becomes the *Leviathan* of the biblical tradition, and *Ladon* in Greek tradition. Cf. also the Rivers Litani in Lebanon and Ladon in Greece. Cf. the three names in §4(1).

The apparent absence of a cosmogony from Ugarit has been much debated. See Wyatt 1985b for discussion of Day 1985. See also Fisher 1965. Day is entirely right in saying that there is no overt account of creation at Ugarit. But not only does the Baal myth (KTU 1.1-2, §3(4)) tell the same story as *Genesis* 1 (§2(15)), *Psalm* 74 (§2(16)) and other passages which are clearly cosmogonic, but it is followed by KTU 1.3-4, the account of the construction of Baal's temple. This too is in many respects a metaphor for creation, since a temple is a microcosm. Cf. §8(7). The Babylonian account of the myth, which incorporates the construction of Marduk's temple (§§2(9, 10)), is also cosmogonic.

V   The Creation of Man in Israelite and Judahite Thought

The two passages following give parallel accounts of the creation of human beings in biblical thought. While strikingly different in style and narrative detail, both emphasize the primacy of man (and the second has generally been interpreted as the primacy of man over woman, though perhaps without justification). In the first narrative, man (man and woman) is made last, after all other living creatures; in the second, man (evidently androgynous) is made first, and then after the animals have been made, woman is made by the separation from him of his female aspect.

2(17)   The 'Priestly Account'

This is the culmination of the narrative begun in §2(15). In the intervening part (vv. 10-23, not included here) all the life-forms are made 'according to their species' (*mîn*, a term that is used, significantly, in the dietary laws of *Leviticus* 11). Thus creation is as much a classificatory as a formative process. This represents the distinctions throughout experience (cf. light and darkness, day and night, dry land and sea above) which symbolize important aspects of human life (e.g. good and evil), further symbolized by the 'male and female' division below. The principle of Jewish law is 'What God has put asunder, let no man join together'. 'Confusing categories' in disobedience to the divine will amounts to reversion to chaos. See Douglas 1970, 67.

> 1   Then God said
>   'Let us make man in our image,
>   according to our likeness
>   and let them have dominion over[1] the fish of the sea
> 5   and the birds of heaven,
>   and the cattle and all the earth
>   and everything creeping over the earth.'
>   And God created man in his image;
>   in the image of God[2] he created him;
> 10   male and female he created them.

(Genesis 1:24-7)

1   Note the royal aspect: the primal man is essentially a type of the king. Cf. Callender 2000. This is in effect a royal covenant with the Primal Man. Compare the altogether harsher world of the covenant language at the end of the flood story, *Genesis* 9:1-7.

2   This famous metaphor represents almost the apotheosis of man, here an ideal, original and androgynous form. This is no accident, because it is the natural template for the following account (§2(18)), where the original man is androgynous, till the woman (female aspect) is separated out. The emphasis on the image also points to the likely origin of this metaphor, widely used in

ancient Near Eastern tradition. This would be the making of images of the gods, out of clay, and literally made in the image of man (and woman).

2(18) The 'Yahwist's Account' of Creation

Scholars differ widely on the dating of this narrative, between the tenth and the second centuries BCE. The significant theme is the presentation of the 'Adam' figure (= the Man of the previous passage) as royal. The garden here is in the centre of the world, and corresponds to the shrine motif in §6(7, 14), passages which are the sequel to the present one.

1   On the day when Yahweh-God[1] made earth and heaven,
        before any plant of the steppe was on the earth,
        or any herb of the steppe had sprouted;
     for Yahweh-God had not yet caused it to rain upon the earth,
5   and there was no man[2] to till the soil[3],
     a mist was rising up from the underworld[4]
        and watered the whole surface of the ground.
     Then Yahweh-God fashioned[5] man[2] from dust
        from the ground[3],
        and he breathed into his nostrils the breath of life[6],
10   and the man[2] became a living being.

(Genesis 2:4-7)

1   'Yahweh-God'. The Hebrew *yhwh ˁlōhîm* may mean 'Lord of the gods'.

2   Hebrew *'ādām*. The term has royal ideological associations. As made here, the Man is androgynous. He will later become male as the female part of him (the rib) is removed. Thus the Adam here corresponds to the figure embracing *both* genders in *Genesis* 1:27 — §2(17).

3   Hebrew *ˁᵃdāmâ*. The country, *śādê*, 'steppe', requires cultivation to be transformed into productive soil.

4   Hebrew *'ereṣ*. The term has some ambiguity, meaning the earth, and the cosmic dimension lying beneath. Cf. §2(15) n. 2.

5   Hebrew *yāṣar*: lit. 'moulded', or 'crafted'. The term means making things such as a pot. So Yahweh-God is a potter. This idea appears in the Mesopotamian examples above, and also in Egyptian tradition, where the Ram-god of Elephantine (Aswan), Khnum, makes the king and his Ka on a potter's wheel. This supports the interpretation of Adam as a type of the king.

6   An important ritual in the construction of divine images, which transformed them from mere lumps of clay, wood, stone or metal into living deities, was the 'opening of the mouth'. We have details of the *mis pi* ('opening of the mouth') ritual from Mesopotamia and *wnn.r* ritual from Egypt (where it was also applied to the dead). See Dick 1999 for both (with further references). This is perhaps to be seen as the key to the present image-construction by Yahweh himself. He first makes the image, and then performs the vivifying rite (breathing into it) which animates it.

VI   Conceptions of the Universe

2(19) Multiple Levels in the Universe in Mesopotamia

Lambert, in Blacker and Loewe 1975, 58, cites two cosmologies. One precedes the composition of *Enuma Elish* (*ca* eleventh century BCE), the other, cited here, postdates it.

> 1   The upper heavens (i) are of *luludanitu*-stone, of Anu.
>   He settled the three hundred Igigi therein.
>   The middle heavens (ii) are of *saggilmut*-stone, of the Igigi.
>   Bel sat therein on the lofty dais in the chamber of
>   lapis lazuli.
> 5   He lit a lamp of *elmesu*-stone.
>   The lower heavens (iii) are of jasper, of the stars.
>   He drew the constellations of the gods thereon.
>   On the base of the upper earth (iv) he made frail mankind
>   lie down.
>   On the base of the middle earth (v) he settled his father Ea...
> 10   On the base of the lower earth (vi) he shut in
>   the six hundred Anunnaki.

(Blacker and Loewe 1975, 58: KAR 307 obv. 30-8)

The earlier text had simply listed the upper [heavens] of Anu, the middle [heavens] of the Igigi and the lower heavens (of jasper) of the stars. The second has confused things by bringing in dimensions of the earth below, and recognizing the lordship of Bel (Marduk).

There appear to be six separate dimensions here, three heavens above and three earths below (respectively the habitable earth, the *Apsû*, and the Underworld. More commonly, Mesopotamian thought is familiar with seven dimensions. Cf. §2(23), where the seven boundaries appear to separate eight dimensions (the seven levels of the underworld and the world above). For further discussion see Horowitz 1999, 3-6.

2(20) The Threefold Structure of the Israelite Universe i)

The system here reflects the initial division of opposites described in *Genesis* 1 (§2(15), and as a further refinement interposes a third, which perhaps owes something to each of the other dimensions, thus having both celestial (spiritual) and infernal (physical) characteristics, just like the man of *Genesis* 2:7 (§2(18)). Cosmology normally owes something to human conceptions of the self. It would be wrong to suppose that either necessarily derives from the other: rather do they develop in tandem, having a symbiotic relationship. It is probably fair to say that this is true of all human cultures.

> The voice of your thunder was in the dome of heaven,
>   lightnings lit up the world',
>   the underworld shuddered and shook.

> On Sea was your pathway,
>> and your train was on Mighty Waters.

(*Psalm* 77:18-9)

1   The series of binary divisions of *Genesis* 1 — §2(15) — are now separated by the inclusion of a third principle, the 'world' or 'habitable earth', Hebrew *tēbēl*. Similarly in §2(21). This will be removed in §4(8). The 'world' is essentially fragile and transitory, a secondary structure derived from the primary binary division. The dualistic principle, the simplest way of conceptualizing the world, and the initiation of all reasoning, is fundamental and irreducible.

2(21)   The Threefold Structure of the Israelite Universe ii)

> To you belong the heavens and to you the underworld.
>> The world and all that fills it[1] you established.
> Saphon and Sea[2] you divided,
>> Tabor and Hermon delight in your name.

(*Psalm* 89:11-2)

1   Note that the 'infill' ('the world and all that fills it') is set secondarily within the primary 'binary opposition' (§2(20) n. 1). This emphasizes its temporality. This is not intended to denigrate it, but indicates its fragility and ephemerality, and perhaps hints at its own creativity and versatility. It seems that a stark realism lies at the back: try as we may, the entire edifice will eventually come crashing down.

2   The Hebrew reads *ṣāpôn wᵉyāmîn*, 'north and south'. The Greek presupposed *ṣāpôn wᵉyāmîm*, a preferable reading, which is a hendiadys for the dragon, the sacred mountain being constructed from his corpse. See Wyatt 1995a.

2(22)   Barriers in the Underworld in Egypt

Similar to the seven levels both above and below in Mesopotamian thought (§§2(19, 23), Egyptian thought is familiar with a seven-levelled infernal region (though not specifically with a corresponding celestial one). This is most graphically represented in the *Book of the Dead*, a corpus of spells comprising some 192 chapters, of which a selection of about a third appears in any one papyrus. See T. G. Allen 1974, Faulkner 1985 for complete text. The *Book of the Dead* continues a written tradition beginning with the *Pyramid Texts* in the 5th and 6th dynasties (*ca* 2340-2180 BCE) and the *Coffin Texts* from the Middle Kingdom (*ca* 2030-1786 BCE). In the present text, the deceased has to pass through seven barriers (called 'gates', ꜥ*ryt*, and to be differentiated from a later notion of various 'pylons', *sbḫt*, also appearing in the text). At each gate sit various guardians, whose names the deceased must know in order to pass safely through. The first and seventh only are cited here. On knowledge cf. §9(8). For other ritual texts of the present type see §§11(42-5).

The First Gate:

> He-whose-face-is-inverted-the-many-shaped
>> is the name of the keeper;
> Eavesdropper
>> is the name of him who guards it;
> The-loud-voiced
>> is the name of him who makes report in it...

(similar names through to...)

The Seventh Gate:

> He-who-cuts-them-down
>> is the name of the keeper;
> The-Loud-voiced
>> is the name of him who guards it;
> He-who-defends-from-those-who-would-work-harm
>> is the name of him who reports in it.

(Faulkner 1985, 133: BD 144)

2(23) The Realm of Death in Mesopotamian Thought: the Descent of Ishtar

The seven barriers encountered here are similar in conception to those in §2(22) above. In this case the motif, met with elsewhere, of the removal of garments at each barrier appears for the first time. On the far side of the seventh barrier, Ishtar is naked. These infernal boundaries mirror those of the celestial region (§2(19)), though the number system between these two examples does not tally precisely.

> 1   To the Land of No Return, the realm of Ereshkigal, Ishtar,
>> the daughter of Sin, set her mind.
>> Yea, the daughter of Sin set her mind to the Dark House,
>>> the abode of Irkalla[1],
> to the house which none leave who have entered it,
>> to the road from which there is no way back,
> 5   to the house wherein the entrants are bereft of light,
>> where dust is their fare and clay their food,
> where they see no light, residing in darkness,
>> where they are clothed like birds, with wings for garments,
>> and where over door and bolt is spread dust...[2]
> 10 When Ereshkigal heard this, her face turned pale...
> 'Should I drink water with the Anunnaki?
>> Should I eat clay for bread, drink muddied water for beer?
> Should I bemoan the men who left their wives behind?
>> Should I bemoan the maidens who were wrenched from
>> the laps of their lovers?

15 Should I bemoan the tender little one who was sent off
  before his time?'
 'Go, gatekeeper, open the gate for her.
  Treat her in accordance with the ancient rules.'
 Forth went the gatekeeper to open the door for her...
 When the first door he had made her enter,
20 he stripped and took away the great crown on her head...
 When the second door he had made her enter,
  he stripped and took away the pendants on her ears...
 When the third gate he had made her enter,
  he stripped and took away the chains round her neck...
25 When the fourth gate he had made her enter,
  he stripped and took away the ornaments on her breast...
 When the fifth gate he had made her enter,
  he stripped and took away the girdle of birthstones on
   her hips...
 When the sixth gate he had made her enter,
30 he stripped and took away the clasps round her hands
  and feet...
 When the seventh gate he had made her enter,
  he stripped and took away the breechcloth round
   her body...

           (*ANET* 107-8: *the Descent of Ishtar*)

Ereshkigal, wife of Nergal (god of war and the underworld) and daughter of Sin (the moon-god), was the queen of the underworld.

Ishtar (Sumerian Inanna) was the deified planet Venus, goddess of love and war.

1 *Irkalla* ('Great City') was a name of the underworld and by extension, of Ereshkigal ('Mistress of the Great Earth'), the goddess who ruled it.

2 Lines 3-9 also occur in *Gilgamesh* vii (*ANET* 87) and in the myth of *Nergal and Ereshkigal* (*ANET* 509), showing this to be a traditional conception of the underworld. Thus it is no surprise to find it in the Bible: §4(24). Lines 1-9 are cited below as §4(17).

This story in Akkadian is paralleled by a Sumerian version. To this sevenfold structure of the outer reaches of the world (above or below) cf. the image of a sevenfold centre preserved in temple conceptualization and construction, below §6(3). The idea probably comes from the 'fact' of seven planets (Sun, Moon, Mercury, Venus, Mars, Jupiter, Saturn: §2(42)), each of which, as a divine power, gives its attributes in the developed cosmology to the construction of human personality. (Thus we are 'mercurial', 'venereal', 'martial', 'jovial', or 'saturnine'.) This way of thinking was still in fashion in the Middle Ages. Only the rise of modern cosmology really put an end to it, and it survives in some astrological speculations.

The conception of a spherical universe, the earth bounded by the planetary spheres, was widespread in the late antique period (Hellenistic and Roman). Some examples are the following.

Biblical passages: *Deuteronomy* 10:17 ('heaven of heavens'); *1 Kings* 8:27 (plural); *Psalm* 148:4 (plural); *2 Corinthians* 12:2 (at least three); *Ephesians* 6:12 (plural); *Hebrews* 4:14, 7:26 (plural).

Judaeo-Christian non-canonical material: *3 Baruch* (five heavens are listed); *Testament of Levi* 2:7-3:8 (seven); *2 Enoch* 20:1, 28:1 (seven), 22:1 (ten); *3 Enoch* 19:7, 34 (seven, surrounding the *Merkabah* of God); *Ascension of Isaiah* (seven); *Chagigah* 12 (seven).

Mithraism, in which the initiate ascended a ladder piercing the cosmos, each stage representing one of the levels of initiation, and corresponding to the planetary spheres.

Poimandres (part of the *Corpus Hermeticum*), where the Anthropos, born of the spiritual Nous, descended through the cosmic spheres (the 'Harmony') in chs. 12-4, assuming planetary characteristics as he did so, finally becoming ensnared in the material world. Salvation was achieved, through gnosis, by ascending through the spheres again in chs. 24-6.

In the cosmology of Basileides, 365 concentric spheres bounding the material world corresponded to the 365 days of the year (Irenaeus, §58.1 in J. Stevenson 1965, 81).

There is a curious tension between the concept of being somehow imprisoned in life in the late systems, with a consequent freedom by ascent to the outside of the universe, and the older view, apparent in the present passage, that somehow one travels from the real world of the living to a half-world of the dead. There has been a reversal in the symbolism (the historical context of which is discussed in §13). That the older view really does come first is seen by its consistency with the idea of ultimate reality being at the heart of the universe, in the sanctuary of the temple (§6, *passim*). This belongs to the older view of religion as mechanism for the living of the full life here and now. This was later transformed into various emphases, according to local theological system, on the preparatory (or even false) nature of this life, fulfilled or transformed into reality in the next. To complete the paradox, some *Pyramid Texts* explicitly identified the king with various stars, particularly the circumpolar stars to the north, which never set, and Orion to the south.

VII   The Cartographic Imagination

A number of maps drawn on clay have survived from ancient Mesopotamia. Some are quite realistic, giving plans of cities or localities. This is the oldest surviving attempt at a representation of the whole world. It is shown in a highly stylized form, as a disc of land bisected by the Euphrates, surrounded by the sea, with remote areas beyond the sea. It seems strange only to the modern viewer not familiar with the mediaeval Islamic and European tradition, which perpetuates precisely the same symbolic form. See *2.6 n. 1 for references to some examples. In mediaeval examples, Jerusalem or Mecca are located at the centre of the world. In the present case, the actual centre is the hole made by the compass-point, but the nearest significant feature is the rectangle just above the centre, identified in the text as Babylon.

2(24) The Babylonian Map of the World

a) TEXT ON THE OBVERSE:

[   ] the rui[ned] cities [the vas]t [Sea] which Marduk sees. The bridge in[side her²] and the ruine[d] gods which he set[tled] inside the Sea [   ] are present; the viper, great sea-serpent inside. The Anzu-bird, and scorpi[on man, moun]tain goat, gazelle, zebu, [p]anther, bull-m[an, l]ion, wolf, red deer, ibex, ostrich, cat, chameleon, [   ] beasts which Marduk created on top of the res[t]less Sea, [U]tnapishtim, Sargon, and Nur-[D]agan the King of Buršaḥa[nda, w]ings like a bird, which no one can com[prehend].

1	Mountain	6	xxxx	11	City	16	[O]cean	21	[Reg]ion
2	City	7	Swamp	12	Habban	17	Oce[an]	22	Region³
3	Urartu	8	Susa	13	Babylon	18	Great Wall¹	23	—
4	Assyria	9	Channel	14	Ocean	19	Region²	24	—
5	Der	10	Bit Yakin	15	[Ocean]	20	[Regio]n	25	—

(numbers in list corresponding to the numbers on the map):

1   Text continues: 'six leagues in between where the sun is not seen'.

2   Text continues: 'six leagues in between'.

3   Text continues: 'eight leagues in between'.

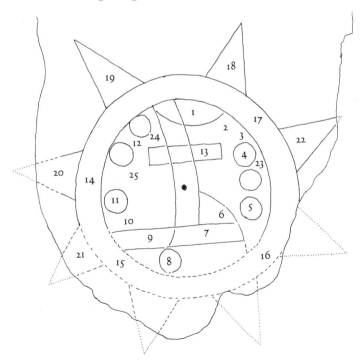

The Babylonian Map of the World (BM 92687)

b)   TEXT ON THE REVERSE:

[wo]nde[rs²   ] great s[ea²   ]

[The first region², when one ent]ers it you tra[vel…] leagues…

to the second region] where you travel seven lea[gues…]… below…

[to the thir]d region, where you travel seven leagu[es   ]. A winged [bi]rd cannot safely comp[lete its journey.]

[To the fo]urth region, where you travel seven lea[gues… [   ] are thick as a *parsiktum*-measure/vessel, twenty fingers [   ]

[To the fif]th region, where you travel seven leagues [is] its height/flood; 840 cubits is its […] its frond/rain; as much as 120 cubits is [its   ]. Its blood he does not see [which we c]limb², where you t[ravel   you/]I will travel seven le[agues   ]. The departure which² is in [   ] its [   ] he crossed [   ]

[To the sixth] region, where you travel [seven leagues   on²] top, I…

[   ] [To the seven]th region, where you travel [seven leagues…   ] where cattle equipped with horns [   ] they run fast and reach [   ] To the [ei]ghth region, where you travel seven leagu[es…   the p]lace where… dawns its entrance². [   ] of the Four Quadrants of the entire […   ] which no one can compre[hend   ]. [   ] copied from its old exemplar and colla[ted   ] the son of Iṣṣuru [the descend]ant of Ea-bēl-il[ī].

(Horowitz 1998, 20-5, excerpts: BM 92687, adapted)

The list of eight regions supports the view that there were originally eight triangles round the ocean, though they are not equidistant, so that certainty is impossible. While described only as 'regions', the shapes certainly suggest cosmic mountains (often appearing as four, in two pairs to East and West such as in Egypt), or alternatively, or as well, the cardinal points and the intermediate points.

2(25) Further Aspects of Egyptian Cosmology i):
The Idea of the Celestial Nile

The economic and strategic life of Egypt was dominated by the Nile, which bisected the country from south to north. South of Memphis the habitable land consisted of little more than the narrow flood-plain of the river. Sailing up and down the river, or crossing it, readily became figures for freedom of movement in general (and hence widely used in mortuary texts, designed to free mortals from the constraints of the tomb). Just as life in Egypt was managed by the use of the Nile, so it was seen as a symbol of the workings of the cosmos as a whole, and was believed to have celestial and infernal counterparts, along or across which respectively travelled the gods and the dead. We are nowhere told precisely how the entire cosmos was envisaged, but since the *ben*-stone, from which all dry land derived, emerged from the centre of Nu, the primordial ocean, and was in turn bisected by the Nile, it seems that a similar mental picture was held as we saw in the Babylonian world-map above. This image may have been reconciled with another similar one, of a sky held aloft by four pillars (to which cf. the eight mountain regions outside the ring of the ocean in the Babylonian map.

The 'great hymn to the Aten', from which these lines are taken, was inscribed on the walls of the tomb of Ay (Tutankhamun's father-in-law and successor as king) at Amarna (the capital city Akhetaten of Akhenaten) *ca* 1350 BCE. It is an extraordinary composition, envisaging the sun-god's universal nature and control of the whole world. It has often been compared with *Psalm* 104, but allegations of a literary connection are, in my estimation, rather exaggerated. In the passage cited, the Aten (the divine sun-disc) is credited with the making of the celestial Nile specifically for the benefit of foreign peoples.

> All distant foreign countries, thou makest their life also,
>> for thou hast set a Nile in heaven,
> that it may descend for them
>> and make waves upon the mountains, like the great green sea,
> to water their fields in their towns.

(*ANET* 370: from *The Hymn to the Aten*)

2(26) Further Aspects of Egyptian Cosmology ii): The Four Pillars of Heaven

In this *Coffin Text*, the deceased claimed identity with Horus the sky-god, to whom the limits of the world were nothing in his divine flight from the underworld to the heavens. The point of the identification is that the king is Horus, and ordinary people, through the democratization of the mortuary system, adopted the royal claims. The motif of the horizon (see §2(8) n. 1) is present here, even when implicit. In §§2(27, 28) it becomes explicit.

> I am Horus, I have come here from the limits of the sky
> and the nether world,
> I have passed by the Ka-chapel of Hathor,
>> on which are fixed the four supports of the sky...

(Faulkner 1977 ii 12: *CT* 378)

2(27) Further Aspects of Egyptian Cosmology iii): Ra's Crossing of the Celestial Nile

This statement of the means whereby Ra, the sun-god, crossed the celestial Nile on his daily journey across the heavens, was an affirmation of the king's destiny, since he was assimilated to Ra by the power of the spell. A variant of this theme, common in iconography, was of Ra sailing in the celestial boat over the body of Nut, the watery sky-goddess, who stood on fingers and toes, overarching the sky. Harakhte ('the horizonal one') was the form of Ra as he traversed the horizons at east and west, in his transition from celestial to infernal god and *vice versa*.

> The reed-floats of the sky are set down for Ra by the day-bark
>> that Ra may cross on them to Harakhte at the horizon.

The reed-floats of the sky are set down for Harakhte by
the night-bark
that Harakhte may cross on them to Ra at the horizon...

(Faulkner 1969, 161: *PT* 473)

2(28) Further Aspects of Egyptian Cosmology iv):
The Osirian Destiny of the King

Two broad views of the king's destiny are expressed in terms of what happened to him
on his death. In one formula, which appears to refer to the actual day on which the
king died, we read that the king's body merged with the sun-disc as it fell into the west.
In the other formulation, which probably relates to the funerary rites performed on the
king's body, he was conveyed across the river. This passage, from the Harris Papyrus,
describes the funeral of Seth-Nakht of the 20th dynasty, predecessor of Rameses III.
It provides the practical experience from which the theological force of §2(27) could be
applied to the king.

Seth-Nakht was the Pharaoh of the exodus according to de Moor 1997. This formula
is similar, but not identical to the previous one. Now, identified as Osiris, the king
goes to his tomb ('horizon') as a god goes to his shrine ('horizon'). Cf. §7(10) for a
solar emphasis.

He went to rest in his horizon, like the gods; there was done for him that
which was done for Osiris; he was rowed in his king's barge upon the
river, and rested in his eternal house west of Thebes.

(*ARE* iv 200, §400: from P. Harris)

2(29) Further Aspects of Egyptian Cosmology v):
The Idea of the Infernal and Celestial Nile

Here the celestial Nile, destined for foreign peoples (cf. §2(25) above), is contrasted
with the infernal Nile, whose task is to nourish Egypt. While its origin way to the
south of Nubia and Ethiopia was well-known to the Egyptians, there was also a mythic
tradition that it emerged from the underworld at Philae (sc. at the first cataract, Egypt's
southern frontier). This is a further extract from the great Hymn to the Aten.

1 Thou (Aten) makest a Nile in the Underworld,
      thou bringest it forth
    as thou desirest to maintain the people of Egypt
      according as thou madest them for thyself...
5 The Nile in heaven, it is for the foreign peoples
      and for the beasts of every desert that go upon their feet;
      while the true Nile comes from the Underworld for Egypt.

(*ANET* 370: from *The Hymn to the Aten*)

2(30) Greek Images of the Surrounding Sea i):
Homer and Hesiod

Greek allusions to the world-surrounding ocean are evidently from the same conceptual background as the Mesopotamian material, with an admixture of Egyptian thought. The derivation of the technical terms from Akkadian or Sumerian (below) is further evidence of a close cultural relationship with the first region. It was primarily through Greek thought, adopted by the Latin West, and melded with the cognate biblical cosmology, that this thinking also heavily influenced early European thought.

ἀψορροος ᾽Ωκεανος: back-flowing[1] Ocean[2]

(Iliad 18:399, *Odyssey* 20:65, *Theogony* 776)*

1   The Greek term ἀψορροος is explained by Greek writers and Lexicons as meaning 'backward-flowing'. This could mean just 'flowing round in a circle', but this would lose the 'backward' element. The Greek word appears only in this cosmological context. A better explanation would be to derive it from Akkadian *Apsû* (Sumerian AB.ZU), which is also the source of Greek ἀβυσσος, 'abyss'.

2   The Greek ᾽Ωκεανος has been given a number of etymological explanations. The most plausible among the following is perhaps West's view. Astour (see Noegel 1998, 413, n. 11), derived it from Sumerian A.KI.AN.A(K), 'the water of heaven and earth', though he later rejected this view (personal communication). M. L. West 1971, 50, noted the Aramaic terms *'ōgānā*, 'basin' (cf. also Akkadian *akūnu*, Ugaritic *agn*, Hebrew *'aggān*, all loaned from Egyptian *ikn*: Muchiki 1999, 63) and *'ōgen*, 'rim', as 'the least implausible etymology'. Cf. the temple basins (§§6(31, 32) which replicated the ocean, and the 'four rims' which surround the earth (§§3(22) n. 1, 3(23)). Neiman 1967, 377, related it to Hebrew *gîhôn* (LXX γηαν), which he linked with *gāhôn*, the 'belly' of the snake in *Genesis* 3:14. Noegel also mentioned Egyptian *wg3*, meaning 'a type of water or flood', and cited Bernal 1991, 83-5. Bernal in turn linked Og, Ogygos and Ogygia with the Semitic √ᵏ*wg*, 'to draw a circle'. Cf. Wyatt 2001c.

2(31) Greek Images of the Surrounding Sea ii): Hesiod

At the ends of the earth...   along the shore of deep and tumultuous Ocean...

(Works and Days 168-71)*

2(32) Greek Images of the Surrounding Sea iii):
the Homeric Hymns

By the streams of Ocean, at the ends of the earth...

(Hymn to Aphrodite 227)*

Over the river of Ocean and the ends of Earth...

(The Cypria 8)*

2(33) Greek Images of the Surrounding Sea iv): Herodotus

It (the Nile) flows from the Ocean, which flows round the entire world.

(Histories ii 21*)*

I do not know of the river of Ocean, and I think that Homer or some other poet invented the name and introduced it into his poetry.

(Histories ii 23*)*

As for the Ocean, they (the Greeks) say that it flows from the sunrise round the entire world, but they cannot prove it…

(Histories iv 8*)*

(Inept cartographers, who) draw the world as circular as if done with compasses, encircled by the river of Ocean, and Asia and Europe of the same size.

(Histories iv 36*)*

This reads almost like a satirical comment on the Babylonian world map noted above (§2(24)).

2(34) Greek Images of the Surrounding Sea v): Pindar

And they reached the open seas of Ocean and the Red Sea…

(Pythian Odes iv 251*)*

2(35) The Cosmic Ocean in Biblical Tradition:
Passages mentioning *Yam Sûf*

On the Hebrew expression *yam sûf* see Montgomery 1938, Snaith 1965; Batto 1983, Wyatt, 1990a, 71-2; id. 1996b, 84-9; id. 2001c. The etymology based on Hebrew *sûf*, 'come to an end', is preferable to the common explanation based on Egyptian *twfy*, 'reed' (thus 'Sea of Reeds', still espoused by *HALOT* ii 747). Cf. the Jewish divine title *'En Sôf*, 'the One without End'. The 'Red Sea' interpretation comes from the Greek Bible (ἐρυθρα θαλασσα). The following instances are good examples of the evidently cosmological, rather than merely geographical, sense of the term.

> The chariotry of Pharaoh and his army he cast into the sea,
> and the choicest of his charioteers were submerged in the Sea of Extinction.

(Exodus 15:4*)*

> The Sea of Extinction he smote[1],
> and he brought them out of the depths[2].

(Psalm 106:9*)*

1   Or: 'he dried up'. Text modified (Wyatt 1996b, 85-6).

2   While on the usual interpretation this refers naturally enough to the depths of the sea, its power is greatly increased in recognition of the Sea of Extinction as threshold of the underworld. Yahweh brings Israel up from Egypt as the land

of the dead. This constrasts nicely with the second colon of *Exodus* 15:4, where the reverse image is used of the wicked Egyptians. Cf. §§5(6) ll. 6-7, 8(9) l. 33 and 8(11) n. 3.

2(36) Marduk and the Kingship of the Gods i)

The exercise of kingship (sc. control of territory) as a consequence of the appropriation by warrior-kings of the cosmic victory won by the gods *in illo tempore* is widely attested in the ancient Near East. It is particularly well-developed in Babylonian and Assyrian, Hittite, Ugaritic and biblical thought. For the textual evidence see Wyatt 1998b, and below, §3. The following two passages describe the rise of Marduk to kingship among the gods, which in turn legitimized the rule of the kings of Babylon.

> 1   If I am indeed to be your champion,
>   if I am to defeat Tiamat and save your lives,
>   convene the council, name a special fate,
>   sit joyfully seated together in the *Ubšu-ukkinakku*[1],
> 5   my own utterance shall fix fate instead of you!
>   Whatever I create shall never be altered!
>   the decree of my lips shall never be revoked,
>   never changed[2].

> (Dalley 1989, 243-4: *Enuma Elish* ii 123-9, adapted)

1   The 'Court of Assembly' (Sumerian UB.ŠU.UKKIN.NA), where the gods meet in council. See also §§7(13, 15 [text §9(2)]). The same idea is found in Ugarit (the *ğr mʿd*, where the *pḫr mʿd* — 'the convocation of the council' — meets: this is apparently the place where Baal fights Yam, §3(4)); and in Israel (the *har mōʿēd*, §5(8)). The visions of Isaiah (§7(18)) and Micaiah (§11(11)) confirm that the assembly is also the divine throne-room. Egyptian thought may be similar in conception to these examples, though it is less clear-cut (§7(12)).

2   To this idea cf. *Isaiah* 55:11:
>   ... the word which goes out from my mouth
>   does not return to me empty,
>   unless it has done what I desire
>   and has accomplished what I sent it out to do.

This 'apotheosis of the word' is what underlies the solemnity of name-giving, of oaths, legal decisions and royal decrees in the ancient world. Something of it survives in the modern world. Marduk's utterance is a *tour de force*: placed in his mouth by the poet, a Babylonian priest, it gives Marduk the irrevocable authority to be the chief god of the pantheon.

2(37) Marduk and the Kingship of the Gods ii)

> 1   They founded a princely shrine for him[1],
>   and he took up residence as ruler before his fathers[2],
>   (who proclaimed)...
>   O Marduk, you are honoured among the great gods

5   Your destiny is unequalled, your word (has the power of) Anu!
     From this day onward your command shall not be changed.
     yours is the power to exalt and abase...
     O Marduk, you are our champion!
     We hereby give you sovereignty over all of the whole
         universe.'

(Dalley 1989, 249-50, adapted: *Enuma Elish* iv 1-14 excerpts)

1   This would be Esagila, Marduk's shrine at Babylon (see §2(10) n. 1). The
     statement that the gods as a group founded the shrine was a mark of its special
     prestige. Cf. §8(7).

2   The idea that Marduk should rule over gods older than himself is deliberately
     phrased to highlight the paradox. This sort of statement is a means whereby all
     older traditions are subsumed under the authority of the new. But of course
     the 'new' is itself dated from the time of the creation of the world.

In this passage the other gods of the pantheon concede Marduk's demand in §2(36).
Anu had previously been the recognized head of the pantheon (see l. 5): now this
authority passes to the younger god. The conception of 'older' gods who give way to
younger ones is common to many cosmogonic contexts: they are the 'Urgötter', the
primordial gods. Thus in Egypt we have the Ogdoad of Hermopolis (§2(3) n. 1), and
deities such as Geb and Nut, Shu and Tefnut from the Heliopolitan Ennead; in Greece
there are the Titans, and in India the Asuras (who become demons), in Scandinavia the
Vanir, and so on.

VIII   Miscellaneous Elements

2(38) Calendars i): The Egyptian Calendar

The human ability to distinguish the different structures of time, the independent
phases of the moon and the solar year must go back many thousands of years.
Pantheons in India and Syria can have 33 members, suggesting a basis in the lunar
month (30 + 3), which was evidently the basis of calendrical computations. With the
rise of urban life, and the needs of regular cult and administration, attempts began to
be made to coordinate the lunar (354 days) and solar ($365^1/_4$ days) years, and above all
to aim for exactitude in the latter (since all early calendars failed to recognize the
quarter day), usually by 'intercalations' of days or months to bring errant calendars
back in line with the real world. See *ERE* iii 61-141, Richards 1998. Some calendars
began with the Spring equinox, others with the Autumn equinox, some with both, and
the Egyptian one with the beginning of the annual inundation of the Nile at the end of
July. There were thousands of variations, and wars and schisms took place over
calendrical niceties. There is evidence of a 364-day calendar in use at Qumran
(Wintermute 1985, 39; Vanderkam 1998, 71; cf. §4(9) below), and the sectaries' view of
second temple Judaism in Jerusalem was that they had defied the divine command in
the construction of their calendar.

The appearance of Sirius (Egyptian *spdw*, Sopd, 'the Harbinger') in the southern sky in late July was linked in predynastic times with the imminent pouring into the Nile valley at Aswan of the flood-waters from the sources of the Nile in Uganda and Ethiopia. This marked the end of the old year and beginning of the new. Over a period of four months the Nile rose and covered the entire flood-plain of the Nile valley. In early times this would have swamped villages and destroyed many structures. Cooperative behaviour in anticipating the flood, and harnessing it to good advantage, was probably an important catalyst in the formation of powerful, central control, which culminated in the unification of Egypt at the end of the fourth millennium. During the next season, dikes constructed to retain as much flood water as possible were gradually tapped to release the water under controlled conditions to irrigate crops. During the dry season, a gradual dessication settled on the land, though water could still be pumped up for irrigation.

SEASON	GREEK NAME OF MONTH	DEITY IN CONTROL (= EGYPTIAN NAME?)	TIME
3ht Akhet (Inundation)	*Thouth*	Tekhi (Thoth?)	Jul-Aug
	Phaophi	Ptah, Menket, Apet	Aug-Sep
	Athyr	Hathor	Sep-Oct
	Khoiak	Sekhmet, Kaherka	Oct-Nov
prt Pert (Coming forth)	*Tybi*	Min, Shefbeti	Nov-Dec
	Mekhi	Rekh-Wer	Dec-Jan
	Phamenoth	Rekh-Netches	Jan-Feb
	Pharmouthi	Rennunet	Feb-Mar
šmw Shemu (Summer)	*Pakhon*	Khonsu	Mar-Apr
	Payni	Horus-Khenti-Khatit	Apr-May
	Epiph	Apet	May-Jun
	Mesore	Horus Iakhuti	Jun-Jul

12 months, each of 30 days, giving 365-day year, adding 5 epagomenal days before reform in 239 BCE; 5 or 6 after

2(39) Calendars ii): Some other Near Eastern Calendars

PERIOD	SUMERIAN	AKKADIAN[1]
Mar-Apr	*Barzagga*	*Nisanu*
Apr-May	*Gusisa*	*Ayaru*
May-Jun	*Sigga*	*Simanu, Sivanu*
Jun-Jul	*Šunumun*	*Du'uzu*
Jul-Aug	*Nenegar*	*Abu*
Aug-Sep	*Kinninni*	*Ululu*
Sep-Oct	*Du*	*Tašritu*
Oct-Nov	*Apindua*	*Araḫsamu*
Nov-Dec	*Gangan*	*Kislimu*
Dec-Jan	*Ziz*	*Tebetu*
Jan-Feb	*Abbar*	*Šabatu*
Feb-Mar	*Šegurku*	*Adaru*

[1]   Eighteen month-names are known from Emar on the Euphrates (Fleming 2000, 200-1, fig. 19). The above lists represent a standardized form, from which there were undoubtedly many departures.

PERIOD	UGARIT	ISRAEL I[1]	ISRAEL II
Mar-Apr	*ḥallatu*	*Abib*	*Nisan*
Apr-May	*gunu*		*Iyyar*
May-Jun	*iṯibu*	*Asiph*	*Siwan*
Jun-Jul	?[2]		*Tammuz*
Jul-Aug	?[2]		*Ab*
Aug-Sep	*ittbnm*[3]		*Elul*
Sep-Oct	*riš yn*		*Tishri*
Oct-Nov	*niqali*		*Marhešwan*
Nov-Dec	*magmaru*		*Kislev*
Dec-Jan	*pagrūma*		*Tebet*
Jan-Feb	*ibʿalatu*		*Šebat*
Feb-Mar	*ḥiyaru*		*Adar*

[1]   A few references to the old Israelite calendar appear in pre-exilic passages.

[2]   The missing Ugaritian ones are perhaps *kislīmu* and *addaru*, but their order is unknown. Note the failure of similar month names to denote the same months in Akkadian, Ugaritic and Hebrew. The Ugaritian calendar is slightly modified in Pardee 2001, 19 n. 21.

[3]   Vocalization unknown.

2(40) Calendars iii): The Gezer Calendar

Sep-Oct	Two months *'sp*	Olive Harvest, Ingathering
Nov-Dec	Two months *zrᶜ*	Planting
Jan-Feb	Two months *lqsh*	Late planting
Mar	(One) month *ᶜṣdt psht*	Flax harvest
Apr	(One) month *qṣr sᶜrm*	Barley harvest
May	(One) month *qṣr wkl*	Harvest and feasting
Jun-Jul	Two months *zmr*	Vine tending and vintage
Aug	(One) month *qṣ*	Summer fruit

This calendar, found at Tell Gezer in Israel, appears to run from September to August (the autumnal equinox therefore probably being the New Year) and is perhaps a school exercise. The precise month equivalents are conjectural.

2(41) Deities of the World Structure

ZONE	EGYPT	SUMER	BABYLONIA
Celestial Waters	Nut	AB.ZU	Apsû
Heaven		An	Anu, Marduk
Air	Shu	Enlil	Igigi, Enlil
Earth	Geb	Enki	Ea
Under-world	Osiris		Anunnaki, Nergal
Infernal Waters	Nu, Nun	AB.ZU	Ti'amat

ZONE	UGARIT	ISRAEL	GREECE
Celestial Waters	*thmt*	*tᵉhôm*	Ocean
Heaven	Baal	Yahweh	Zeus
Air			
Earth			Poseidon
Under-world	Mot, *arṣ*	*Šᵉ'ôl, 'ereṣ, Māwet*	Hades
Infernal Waters	*thmt*	*tᵉhôm*	Ocean

These words are divine names, or can be, even though also appearing as common nouns. Note that Israel has only Yahweh. But while the other gods were in many respects personifications of their sphere of influence, or even the substance, Yahweh was not identifiable with any of these phenomena. He may have been a moon-god in his prehistory, but this is not certain (see §2(42) n. 3). There is evidence of parallels to the surrounding cultures: thus Asherah (Yahweh's consort, the southern counterpart of Ugaritic Athirat) may have been solar.

2(42) The Number Seven i): Sun, Moon and the Planets

It is well-known that there were seven 'stars' in the sky in ancient cosmology: that is, the following celestial bodies were taken to be divine rulers. Surprisingly, they cannot all be identified with certainty, and the precise history of their development is unknown. The following identifications are known.

PLANET	SUMERIAN[1]	AKKADIAN[1]	UGARITIC	ISRAELITE
SUN	UTU	Shamash	Shapsh, Athirat, Rahmay	Shemesh, Asherah
MOON	Nanna	Sin	Yarih, El	El = Yahweh[3]
MERCURY	GU$_4$-UTU[2]	Nabu		
VENUS	Inanna	Ishtar	Ashtar, Ashtart	Ashtarot
MARS	Nergal	Nergal	Reshef	Reshef
JUPITER		Marduk		
SATURN		Kayamanu		

PLANET	HURRIAN	EGYPTIAN	GREEK
SUN	Shimegi	Khepri, Ra, Atum, Horus, Amun	Apollo
MOON	Nusk	Thoth, Khonsu	Semele
		(Seth)	Hermes
VENUS			Aphrodite, Astarte
MARS		(Reshef)	Ares
JUPITER		(Horus)	Zeus
SATURN		Horus the Bull (Geb)	

1   The planets were called *bibbu*, 'wild sheep', while the fixed stars compared with domesticated cattle and sheep: Horowitz 1998, 153.

2   GU$_4$-UTU, 'the Bull of the Sun'.

3   El and Yahweh both appear to have been emancipated from their lunar background by the Late Bronze. Hints survive in the language of theophany in the Hebrew Bible (e.g. *Exodus* 24:10, §7(23), *Deuteronomy* 33:2, *Judges* 5:4 = *Psalm* 68:8, EV 7, *Psalm* 19:2-7, EV 1-6: see Wyatt 1995b). The toponym Sinai (*sînāy*) is best explained as 'belonging to Sin', where Sin was the Babylonian moon-god. Nabonidus, the last king of Babylon before the Persian conquest, promoted the cult of Sin in western Arabia (Lewy 1945-6).

There is reason to think that it was not originally in a spatial, but in a temporal context, that the number seven initially became important. A month could be conveniently divided into four equal parts. The Sabbath is generally supposed to have originated in Israel. However, it seems to be present, in the form of sets of seven days, probably quarter-days of a lunation, in Ugarit before 1200 BCE.

2(43) The Number Seven ii): in Time and Space

Once its temporal use was established, it could be attributed to the divine powers controlling time, viz., the seven 'planetary' deities above, and thus readily transferred to spatial contexts. We shall see below that both the world at large, and the temple as microcosmic replica of the world could have a sevenfold structure.

Some examples of seven as a symbolic number in this volume:

§3(5): *Psalm* 29: the seven voices of Yahweh;

§4(2b): seven heads of Litan (= Leviathan), corresponding to other ancient Near Eastern dragons;

§4(4-6, 8): seven days and nights;

§4(6): seven levels in Utnapishtim's ark;

§4(8): seven pairs of 'clean' animals;

§4(9): seven floodgates of heaven and the deep: *Jubilees* 5;

§4(18): seven portions of food;

§6(3): seven (concentric?) zones in El's palace;

§6(9): seven branches to Menorah (candelabrum) and seven lamps;

§6(13): seven lamps;

§7(13) n. 1: Enmeduranki seventh king of Sippar;

§7(19): Enoch seventh generation from Adam;

§7(21): seven stars;

§9(2): seven days without the south wind;

§9(2) n. 2: seven *Apkallus*;

§10(2): seven rams of one sacrificial category;

§10(5): figurines seven finger-breadths high used in rites;

§11(28): seven years drought as result of Danel's curse;

§12(7): 'seven thousand' perhaps means the entire population.

From its originally spatial, and thence temporal function as a metaphor, it seems that seven came to represent further metaphorical levels of reality, such as holiness, perfection or universalism. The continuing extension of forms, which were already metaphors, in the further conceptual exploration of human possibilities is common enough in all language, as any perusal of an etymological dictionary will show. But it is a particular feature of religious thinking, which constructs increasingly complex models for the validation of growing complexities in social structure and historical, or even personal experience. Once voiced, even mere possibilities can rapidly become central facts, a fact being merely some construction which a critical mass of people in a culture regard as beyond dispute.

Chapter 3

SPACE, TIME AND WATER I:
WATER AND THE BEGINNING OF THE WORLD

Some of the texts already given mention the idea of 'cosmic water', whether conceptualized as an ocean — §§2(9, 10, 15, 20, 21, 24 [Map]), or as a river — §§2(25-9), or as both — §§2(30-4). The two ideas are often merged, or represented as alternative perceptions of the same reality.

There are a number of ways in which water plays an important role in cosmology. We may isolate three:

i)   its role in origins, in which it is often personified as a great serpent or dragon, and cut in two;

ii)   its semi-permanent status as boundary to the habitable world, which may be viewed in two- or three-dimensional aspects;

iii)   its appearance in narratives of world destruction (notably flood stories).

We shall examine the first two aspects of the theme here; the third will come in the next chapter (§4).

Suggested Reading:

Batto 1993; Day 1985; Eliade 1958, 188-215; Fawcett 1970, 110-1; Heidel 1942; Wensinck 1918; Wyatt 1996b, chapters 2, 3; id. 1998b; id. 2001c.

3.1   Introduction

3.1.1   We are concerned in the present chapter with a widespread myth of the origins of the universe, found throughout Europe and Western Asia. We have numerous examples, from Mesopotamia, Syria, Israel, Egypt, Anatolia, Iran, India and Europe (Greece and even Ireland). The Israelite tradition survives in a number of Christian traditions (§§3(9-12). This is a further application of the type of creation ('cosmogony') myth that uses violence as a metaphor (§§2(9-10 above). While this is one way of classifying the motif (alongside sex, technology and speech, as we have seen), another is to see it as using the medium of water (as distinct from breath in speech, clay in technology, or semen in sexual generation).

3.1.2   Water is a universal symbol of the origin and source of all things: its psychological foundation. Perhaps it is evidence of pre-natal memories; certainly from the experience of parents watching birth; memories of floods; the crucial nature of water supply for survival, the ritual use of water in purifications, libations and so forth. It carries ideas of birth, death and rebirth, as well as the sustenance of life.

3.1.3   As seen from §§2(30-35), the idea of a world bounded by water is a powerful one. Even when not explicitly stated in myth or references like these, it is generally the picture of the universe as a whole, and this is true of Egypt and Mesopotamia as well. The heavens above and the underworld below are likewise believed to be contained by an ocean (Sumerian AB.ZU and derivatives: see §2(30) nn. 1 and 2).

3.2   Egypt

Egypt has no explicit creation myth of this kind, though it does have a flood story (§4(3)), and the creation and flood traditions are probably related. But we have noticed the motif of the *ben*-stone, arising out of the primordial flood (§§2(2) n. 1, 2(5) and 5(1-3) below). The reason for the absence may lie in the regularity of a relatively manageable flood in the Nile Valley, which replenished the soil each year (so that recreation was implicit). Floods in the Tigris-Euphrates flood-plains are generally extremely destructive, and the *Chaoskampf* (conflict) theme emphasizes the similarly portentous event of creation, creation and destruction (flood) balancing each other. There may even be historical reasons behind the diverse approaches (§§3(16) n., 4(14) n.).

3.3   Mesopotamia

3.3.1   The oldest example of the myth, of which two fragments survive (§§3(1, 2)) dates from about 2400 BCE, with the Amorite storm-god Tishpak as hero. In chronological order, the Mesopotamian (Akkadian) versions are then from Mari (§3(3) from *ca* 1760 BCE, and from Babylon (§§2(9-10)) from *ca* 1100 BCE. The last of these, featuring Marduk, is the only one explicitly to link the killing of a dragon, sea monster or watery goddess with the creation of the world.

3.3.2   However, the persistence of symbols in mythic narratives and allusions leads us to propose that creation, even if only indirectly, is the key to understanding the story. And 'creation' can take a number of forms in myth, since all myths have an archetypal nature, and describe (and 'validate' or 'authenticate') the true beginning of human life and culture.

3.3.3   The Mari version (§3(3)) is very informative. It provides the clue as to how the entire tradition should be understood. The storm-god Adad sends an oracle through a priest. He hands King Zimri-Lim some sacred weapons. He states that these are the weapons which he (Adad) used to conquer Tiamat. The implication, borne out by numerous allusions to the motif in political and historical texts (see Wyatt 1998b), is that real warfare is seen as a struggle against the powers of chaos. The same kind of rhetoric is used in modern political propaganda.

3.4   The West Semitic World: Ugarit and Israel

3.4.1   The biblical versions of this tradition (§§3(6-8)) are probably familiar through numerous allusions and several narrations.   These versions, which in turn inspire later Jewish and Christian variations (§§3(9-12)), are themselves heavily influenced by §3(4), the Ugaritic (commonly referred to as the 'Canaanite') version.

3.4.2   The Ugaritic account, with Baal as the hero, has been most intensively studied, and was long held to be an elaborate allegory of the passage of the seasons.   This view has now been discredited, and the implications of the Mari text (§3(3)) recognized to have a greater explanatory force (Wyatt 1998b).   The poem has harnessed the tradition to the requirements of royal ideology.

3.4.3   Four examples are given (§§3(5-8)), out of some fifty biblical accounts or allusions.   *Psalm* 29 (§3(5)) is one of the oldest compositions in the Hebrew Bible.   The expression 'the voice of Yahweh (*qôl yhwh*)' occurs seven times (cf. §2(43)), and is agreed to be an echo of the formula 'seven thunders' used of Baal in Ugaritic poetry, as are various other allusions in the poem.   It celebrates (like the Ugaritic version) the conquest of the sea-god and the enthronement of the victorious figure. 'Over the heavenly Ocean' (l. 20) may be translated as 'on...', the corpse of the dead sea-god becoming Yahweh's throne.   Cf. §§6(16-25)) where the cosmic tent, a symbol of the temple as a microcosm, is the corpse of the sea-god.   *Genesis* 1 (v. 2 given at §3(6); cf. §2(15)) appears at first glance to have no conflict element.   This is because the power of the sea to resist the divine power is futile.   But the elements are hinted at here, and in the 'creating' of v. 1 (*bārā'* = 'divide').   A short excursus gives four Christian examples of the continuing life of the tradition (§§3(9-12)).

3.5   Other Versions

3.5.1   The Hittite version (§3(13)) appears to have been adapted to another purpose, the social conflict between matrilineal and patrilineal societies. The storm-god (Tarḫund) wins his victory at the price of killing his son. However, a diversion of the myth from its original cosmogonic intent is not complete, for it is the application of a cosmogonic (and therefore archetypal) motif to a new social institution.   The biblical versions are comparable.

3.5.2   The Greek versions deal respectively with creation ((§3(14), the *Theogony*) and the royal claim to the throne through victory over a sea-monster (Perseus and Andromeda, §§3(15, 16)).   These are closely related.

The story of Perseus (as a Semitic name, Perseus means 'Slicer') is in fact a Greek telling of the Baal-Yam Canaanite myth, from which the seemingly quite different *Theogony* also derives, together with its Mesopotamian input.

3.6   The Diffusion of the Myth

3.6.1   This is essentially theoretical. The problem is that the myth is found throughout Eurasia. The earliest Indian examples (*Ṛg Veda*) are uncannily close to the Ugaritic. How can this be? A diffusionary explanation is inescapable. I argued some while ago (Wyatt 1988b) that the presence of Sanskrit speakers in the Near East could explain this (i.e., a proto-Indian version came west). The subsequent discovery of the Mari evidence (supported by that from Eshnunna) disproves it, because it is too early. But a new theory about the flood tradition opens up a better possibility.

3.6.2   This is to see some merit, despite reservations, in the argument of Ryan and Pitman (see §§3(16) n. and 4(14) n.). What I would add to their argument is the likelihood that the Black Sea inundation caused the dispersal, in Neolithic times, of many peoples found subsequently in a ring around (Hatti, Mesopotamia, Iran, India, Syria, Israel, Egypt) who not only have flood stories, but except for Egypt also have a conflict myth (*Chaoskampf*). As can be seen from their treatment here (chapters 3 and 4), there is a case for seeing these as essentially two versions of the same basic myth, one dealing with world-creation and the other with world-destruction by a reversal of the process. This comes out most explicitly in the biblical account of the creation and the flood (*Genesis* 1, 6-8, §§2(15), 4(8)), where the second is deliberately represented as the undoing of the first.

3.7   Ocean Imagery

3.7.1   The vocabulary of the cosmic waters is dealt with briefly in the notes to §§2(30-4) ('Ocean' and 'Abyss'), 2(35) (Hebrew *Yam Sûf*). The wide borrowing of Sumerian terminology shows Sumer's considerable cultural influence in the region. Egypt's cosmology was rather too localized to have the same influence. The ocean was a 'reversionary symbol', always pointing the way home, leading the mind, consciously or unconsciously back to its birth.

3.7.2   The persistent interest in the Ocean as 'cosmological fact' did not simply exist in a vacuum: it was an important motif in political thought. Early societies, just like modern ones, felt a profound need to be in control of their environment. (Indeed, in the contemporary crisis in environmental terms, concerning human responsibility for the world as an ecosystem, we can look back with justice to this ancient imperative as sowing the seeds of ecological destruction.) The most pervasive expression of this need for territorial mastery was found in the idiom of 'ruling from sea to sea'. A number of passages are cited (§§3(17-26)) which illustrate the nature of such thought, and its link with the cosmogonic theme of the conflict myth.

I   Myths of the Primaeval Battle

We noted that violence as a means of creating the world is the theme of the Babylonian *Enuma Elish* story (§§2(9-10)). This is by no means the oldest version of an important myth attested throughout Eurasia. The oldest version thus far known comes from Amorite culture in Eastern Babylonia (the city of Eshnunna), but it originates, on present evidence, from West Semitic culture (cf. later Amurru, southern neighbour of Ugarit on the Syrian coast). There are also fragments indicating that there were Sumerian versions, which may be independent of the Amorite tradition.

3(1)   Amorite Version From Eshnunna i)

The earliest extant versions are originally Amorite (West Semitic) traditions, as are the examples below from Ugarit and Israel. I have not given here the Babylonian account — see §§2(9-10) — which is also Amorite in origin (cf. Eshnunna below) but has been more influenced by Sumerian traditions. The Babylonian account is the only *overtly* cosmogonic one apart from some of the biblical texts — §§2(15, 18). Such an interpretation probably lurks in the background of those whose primary purpose is now the installation of the king as heir to the cosmic victory. (On this see Wyatt 1998b, and below, §3(3).)

Eshnunna (Tell Asmar) lay some 80 km northeast of Baghdad. The tradition here, dating from *ca* 2350 BCE, is derived from Amorite culture, the Amorites (people from the northwest, in Syria) having brought it with them in their long-drawn out settlement in Mesopotamia.

> 'Steward of Tiamat, fierce warrior, arise!
>   Tishpak, steward of Tiamat, fierce one, arise!
> God, king of...'

(Westenholz 1974-7, 102: MAD i 192)

3(2)   Amorite Version From Eshnunna ii)

> 1 'Who will go and [slay] the raging dragon,
>   [and] deliver the wide land [   ]
>   and exercise kingship [   ]?'
>   'Go, Tishpak, sl[ay] the raging dragon,
> 5   and deliver the wide land [   ],
>   and exercise kingship [   ].'

(Lewis 1996, 31-2: CT 13.33-4, 17-22)

The background to these fragments can only be reconstructed with some difficulty. It appears that Eshnunna was threatened by a dragon (*labbu, mušḫuššu*) 80 km long. (Did this represent a long flooded river-valley?) Tishpak, the storm-god of the city, was prevailed upon to defeat it, his reward being the rule of the city (sc. as the city-god, here called its 'king'). This royal ideological dimension to the myth is in fact crucial to its overall understanding, as becomes particularly clear in §3(3).

3(3)   Amorite Version From Mari

The city of Mari (modern Tell el Hariri), destroyed by Hammurabi of Babylon *ca* 1760 BCE, lies on the Euphrates just north of the Syro-Iraqi frontier. A huge archive was found in the extensive royal palace and administrative buildings. The present text (A 1968, published in Durand 1993) dates from *ca* 1780 BCE, and describes the delivery of an oracle to King Zimri-Lim, the last monarch. He had regained his throne, to which he was heir, after an Assyrian seizure of power by Shamshi-Adad of Assyria some years previously (Kuhrt 1995, i 98). This is here attributed to the agency of his patron deity, Adad the storm-god.

Thus speaks Adad:...

I have brought you back to the throne of your father, and have given you the arms with which I fought against Tiamat[1]. I have anointed you with the oil of my victory, and no one has withstood you.

(Wyatt 1998b, 842: *ARMT* A 1968)

[1]   It seems that ritual weapons were handed to the king at his enthronement. He would use these (so ran the theory) in his own wars, thus replicating the primaeval battle. Thus was war virtually apotheosized, and conceptualized as a reenactment of divine battles. For numerous examples of this rhetoric see Wyatt 1998b, 842-7.

Mari was also heir to Amorite (West Semitic) culture. This text, combining oracular, ritual and ideological elements, has proved to be the key to understanding the whole tradition of the conflict myth. It is the first text to provide a context for the myth. Its message, delivered here by an oracle from Adad (who appears in his Western guise as Baal in the following text, and is also known as Haddu at Ugarit, and in Israel and Damascus as Hadad), refers back to the god's cosmic victory in the primordial myth as guaranteeing royal victories (with the same 'divine weapons', though of course in reality these would be housed in a temple) to the king. The ritual of handing over the weapons belongs to an enthronement. The sequel, an oracle, is cited at §11(4).

3(4)   Ugaritic Version: Baal Fights Yam

This version from *ca* 1200 BCE has been developed into a long poem of six tablets, of which about half is extant. The present text is the climax to the first part, which deals with the triumph of Baal among the competing gods. The second part treats his acquisition of a palace (the same term *hkl* means 'palace' and 'temple': §2(10) n. 1), while the third has a combat with Mot (Death) similar in literary form to the present episode. A further tablet may have been the conclusion, with Baal marrying Anat. The marriage motif is present in other versions (see §3(12) introduction).

1　Kothar[1] fashioned two maces,
　　and pronounced their names:
　　'You, your name is "Expeller".
　　Expeller, expel Yam[2], → Sea
5　　expel Yam from his throne,
　　Nahar[3] from the siege of his dominion!
　　You must leap from the hand of Baal[4],
　　like a falcon from his fingers.
　　Strike the shoulders of Prince Yam,
10　the chest of Ruler Nahar!' → River
　　The mace leapt from the hand of Baal,
　　like a falcon from his fingers.
　　It struck the shoulders of Prince Yam,
　　the chest of Ruler Nahar.
15　But Yam was strong:
　　he did not flinch.
　　His joints did not tremble;
　　his face was not discomposed
　　Koshar brought down two maces,
20　and he pronounced their names:
　　'You, your name is All-Driver.
　　All-Driver, drive Yam away,
　　drive Yam from his throne,
　　Nahar from the siege of his dominion!
25　You must leap from the hand of Baal,
　　like a falcon from his fingers.
　　Strike the skull of Prince Yam,
　　the brow of Ruler Nahar!
　　Let Yam collapse in a heap,
30　and let him fall to the ground.'
　　Then the mace leapt form the hand of Baal
　　like a falcon from his fingers.
　　It struck the skull of Prince Yam,
　　the brow of Ruler Nahar.
35　Yam collapsed in a heap;
　　he fell to the ground.
　　His joints trembled,
　　and his face was discomposed.
　　Baal gathered up
40　and drank Prince Yam to the dregs;
　　he exterminated Ruler Nahar.
　　By name Ashtart chided him:

'Dry him up, O Valiant Baal!
Dry him up, O Charioteer of the Clouds!
45 For our captive is Prince Yam,
for our captive is Ruler Nahar!'
Then Baal went out...
Valiant Baal dried him up...
'Yam is indeed dead!
50   Baal will rule...!'

(Wyatt 1998a, 65-9, KTU 1.2 iv 11-32)

1   Kothar (*ktr*, 'skilful') was the Ugaritian artificer god, probably derived from Ptah of Memphis (also called *qsr*, borrowed from the Semitic). He was ambidextrous, a quality now recognized of his Greek counterpart Hephaestus (§6(20) introduction).

2   Yam (*ym*, 'sea') was the Ugaritian sea-god.

3   Nahar (*nhr*, 'river') was an epithet of Yam, the two names commonly appearing in parallel, as in this passage. Note the riverine quality of the Ocean in Greek idiom, §§2(30-4), and cf. the Hebrew usage in §§3(7, 24-6).

4   Baal was the title given in Ugarit to Haddu the West Semitic storm-god (= Adad of §3(3)). The title 'Baal' was given him by virtue of him being the patron deity of the city. It is by no means certain that the same title in the Bible always refers to the same deity.

Mythic narratives are frequently brief to the point of obscurity. This lovingly drawn-out narrative, working its leisurely way to the climax, is part of an exhaustive reworking of the tradition by Ilimilku, perhaps on the occasion of a royal wedding (see Wyatt 2001b). Its implicit applicability to royal ideology, and hence its suitability for such an occasion, is established on the basis of §3(3). The old 'seasonal' or 'fertility cult' interpretations are irrelevant.

3(5)   Israelite Version: Yahweh Fights Leviathan

There are numerous versions of the tradition in the Hebrew Bible, and many further allusions to it. See particularly Day 1985 for detailed discussion. *Psalm* 29 is an archaic composition, from the early first millennium BCE, and some scholars have even supposed it to be a translation or adaptation of an old 'Canaanite' hymn. While there is no need to draw this conclusion, its proximity to Ugaritic poetry, even using some of the same phraseology, is striking. The 'voice of Yahweh' (*qôl yhwh*), mentioned seven times in the text (see §2(43)), appears to echo the 'seven lighning-flashes, eight bundles of thunder' of Ugaritian Baal (Wyatt 1998a, 388, KTU 1.101.3-4). It continues the theme of the enthronement of the victorious god (ll. 20-1).

1 Give to Yahweh, sons of El,
give to Yahweh honour and strength,
give to Yahweh the honour of his name:
worship Yahweh in the courts of the Holy Ones.

5 The voice of Yahweh over the waters,
   Yahweh over multitudinous waters!
The voice of Yahweh in strength,
   the voice of Yahweh in splendour;
10 the voice of Yahweh breaks cedars,
   and Yahweh shatters the cedars of Lebanon;
and he makes Lebanon skip like a calf,
   and Sirion like the son of a bull.
The voice of Yahweh strikes with flames of fire;
15 the voice of Yahweh makes the desert tremble,
   Yahweh makes the holy desert tremble.
The voice of Yahweh shakes the oak trees
   and strips bare the forests;
   and in his temple everything shouts: 'Glory!'
20 Yahweh has taken his throne over the heavenly ocean[1],
   and Yahweh is enthroned king forever.
Yahweh gives strength to his people;
   Yahweh blesses his people with well-being.

(Psalm 29)

1   In the Ugaritic tradition, Yam is firstly enthroned 'over Baal', who is bound and lies beneath the throne (cf. the symbolic representation of captured and bound enemies on Egyptian royal footstools). Subsequently, Baal takes his throne (the same throne) on top of Mount Saphon, which is itself probably to be construed as the corpse of Yam. Thus the relative positions of the gods are reversed. Yahweh's enthronement 'over', or perhaps 'on' the heavenly ocean (*lammabbûl*) is similar in conception. The preposition here is curious, and may have altered an original 'upon' (*'al*), a spatial term, into 'until', a temporal term, indicating Yahweh's rule until some future cataclysm at the end of time, or world cycle.

3(6)   An Echo of the Battle Motif
from the Genesis Creation Story

See §2(15) n. 1 for the significance of the Hebrew term *bārâ*, 'create'. The conflict element being now sublimated, we move directly from the scene-setting phrase of v. 1 to the initiation of creation itself in the present verse. The divine spirit hovers, half triumphantly, half caringly, over the raw materials it is about to organize into the differentiated world. Is it perhaps an avian metaphor, as found in §§2(3-5)? The process of organization which follows is to be compared with that in the Babylonian account of *Enuma Elish*, §2(10). Both are a series of divisions of unitary principles into binary ones.

> Now the earth was chaotic and empty,
>   and darkness was over the face of Deep,
>   and the spirit of God was brooding over the face
>   of the waters.

(*Genesis* 1:2)

This is the conflict element from §2(15). Note that the sense of tension has been entirely removed. The erstwhile dragon-foe (cf. Babylonian Tiamat) is now apparently the inert *T*hôm* ('Deep'). But note the implicitly divine aspect of this in the present passage. Grammatically, having no article, the term still has the echo of a name. Note how the prosody requires the equation darkness = spirit of God. (See Wyatt 1993.)

3(7) An Allusion to the Myth in an Oracle of Isaiah

The text below betrays its editorial history. See Wyatt 1998a, 68 n. 150 for discussion. This is an interesting example of the appropriate mythological allusion for a political oracle, probably composed in the Persian period (Kaiser 1974, 99). The ancient poets had treated the exodus in *Exodus* 15, and even the end of the exile (*Isaiah* 40, 51:9-11) in terms of the conflict myth. Now Egypt's political impotence can be parodied by further allusion to it.

> And drunk are the waters (of) {from} Sea,
>   and River is {dehydrated and} dried up.

(*Isaiah* 19:5)

The reduction of the divine enemy which we saw in §3(6) cannot be said to have happened here. This is a clear allusion to the motif of the drying up of the vanquished sea-god in §3(4). Again, the lack of definite articles invites us to recognize both Sea and River as names (and the same ones as in §3(4)). Ambiguities in texts like this warn the reader against the rather simplistic view that the Bible is uniformly monotheistic. Poets are not constrained by matters of doctrinal purity, and in any case, doctrine is frequently read into earlier texts by later interpreters.

3(8) Daniel and the Dragon

This late story, from the second or first century BCE, attached to the book of *Daniel* (see further §6(10)), is a parody of the mythic tradition. Daniel has shown King Cyrus that Bel (= Marduk) is not really a god: his priests take away his food so that it looks as though the image has eaten it. Cyrus kills the priests and their families: Daniel destroys the image of Bel. The satire is also perhaps evidence of the use of an image of Tiamat in the Babylonian cult.

Now there was a great dragon in Babylon, and the Babylonians also worshipped it. Then King (Astyages) said to Daniel: 'You cannot tell me that this is not a living god? So worship it!' Daniel replied: 'I worship the Lord my god; for he is the living god. but if you give me permission, O king, I shall kill the dragon using neither sword nor club.' 'I give you permission', said the king. Then Daniel took some pitch, some fat and some hair and boiled them up together, rolled the mixture into balls and put them into the dragon's mouth; the dragon swallowed them and burst. Daniel said: 'Now look at the sort of things you worship'.

(*Daniel* 14:23-28 Greek text Θ)

This splendid satire is based on the writer's and readers' intimate familiarity with the conflict myth tradition. One of its undercurrents, given the royal ideological significance of the original myth (see §§3(1-3) notes), is undoubtedly the spurious nature of the Persian king's rule, in addition to its specifically theological attack on Persian religion. The story tells of Babylon, which had become a cipher for falsity in religion and government.

Excursus (§§3(9-12): Christian Versions

The following four narratives do not strictly fit into an ancient Near Eastern anthology: but they do represent retellings of the same basic myth, and are included for completeness.

3(9) Christian Version i): Jesus Stills the Storm

As the following four examples show, the motif survives into Christian tradition. Heil 1981, Madden 1997 and Aus 1998, 51-133 have noted the connection between the first two examples and the older tradition. *Matthew*, *Luke* and *John* have variants. The main narrative has been split into its two logical halves: the first account (§3(9)) describes the battle, in which the mere word of command of the deity now stills his foe; the second (§3(10)) describes his triumphant trampling of the corpse of his slain enemy, to which cf. *Job* 9:8 (§6(17)) and parallels.

The narrative of Jesus stilling the storm may already be a partial hybrid, since it echoes the motif of the flood tradition too, and may be compared with §4(10), which is more clearly linked to the tradition of Noah (§§4(8, 9)).

And he said to them on that day, as evening came, 'Let us cross over to the other side'. And leaving the crowd behind they took him just as he was in the boat; and there were other boats with him. Then a great raging storm blew up, and the waves broke into the boat so that it was almost swamped. Now he was in the stern, his head on the cushion, asleep. Then they woke him and said to him, 'Teacher, do you not care? We are sinking!' And he woke up and rebuked[1] the wind and said to the sea, 'Quiet! Be calm!' And the wind dropped, and it became very calm. Then he said to them, 'Why are you so frightened? How is it that you have no faith?' They were filled with awe and said to one another, 'Who can this be? Even the wind and the sea obey him!'[2]

(*Mark* 4:35-41)

1   The Hebrew tradition speaks of the victorious god 'rebuking' ($\sqrt{g'r}$) the sea: see McCurley 1983, 46-52. This seems to be an echo of it.

2   The point of the disciples' questions is that while they only haltingly catch a glimpse of the nature of Jesus, the reader knows only too well: here is the primaeval contest fought anew: the conquering god overwhelms the forces of chaos. Attempts to rationalize the narrative in psychological terms (e.g. Jesus calms the disciples' fears with his voice, so that they experience an inner peace) completely miss the mythological power of the story.

3(10) Christian Version ii): Jesus Walks on the Sea

On the surface an entirely independent tradition form §3(9), this is on the contrary closely related. The battle is now won, and in this later narrative in the gospel, the victor tramples the corpse of his enemy.

Straightway he told his disciples to embark on the boat, and to set off across to the other side, to Bethsaida, while he sent the crowd away... And when it had become late, the boat was in the middle of the sea, and he was alone on the land. He could see that they were making heavy weather of it, for the wind was against them. And about the fourth watch of the night he came towards them, walking on the sea. He was intending to pass them by, but when they saw him walking on the sea they thought it was a ghost and cried out, for they had all seen him and were terrified. But he spoke to them immediately, and said: 'Courage! It is I[1]! Do not be afraid.' Then he got into the boat with them, and the wind dropped[2]. They were utterly and completely dumbfounded...

> (*Mark* 6:45, 47-51)

1   Jesus says ἐγώ εἰμι, 'I am', which cannot fail to remind the percipient reader of Yahweh's expression in the Septuagint at *Exodus* 3:13: ἐγώ εἰμι ὁ Ὢν, 'I am the One who is', for the Hebrew *'ehyê "šer 'ehyê*, 'I am as I am' (or similar). The Hebrew is already mysterious enough. The Greek gives it a formal ontological character. Thus in the present narrative the victor of the battles of creation and the exodus is now the victor against Satan's kingdom. There is therefore a typological dimension to the narrative: that is, the New Testament is couched in such language as to show for those with eyes to see that a narrative or prophecy in the Old Testament is now fulfilled, or recapitulated. An informal typology informs *all* retelling of myth.

2   This seems to be an almost unconscious allusion to the earlier story. The state of the wind is immaterial here.

In these two examples, the force of the narrative is the demonstration that Jesus is divine. There is a further quasi-typological relationship between these two passages and the following one.

3(11) Christian Version iii): Michael Fights the Dragon

The time-reference of this vision is unclear. Contemporary Jewish tradition thought in terms of a primaeval war in heaven, in which Satan and his angels were cast down to the earth or underworld (*1 Enoch* 86, where the star of v. 1 is to be identified with the star of *Luke* 1:18 and 'Lucifer' in *Isaiah* 14:12). This tradition was evidently linked in *1*

Enoch 6-7 with the curious story in *Genesis* 6:1-4, which served in part as an introduction to the flood story (§§4(8, 9)), by indicating how corrupt the world had become. It thus showed how the world had come to be fallen (paralleling the developing understanding of *Genesis* 2-3 (§9(4)), and also explained the continuing presence of fallen angels who continued to impede the divine purpose. Is this the subject of John's vision here? On the other hand, it is closely linked to the image of the woman and her child, which might be a primordial type of the incarnation, but more probably relates to this as an event which had already happened. The following could therefore alternatively be listed under §4, since it may deal with a cosmic battle at the end of time. Note the precise wording of *Revelation* 1:1. But as Gunkel recognized in his famous epigram *Urzeit wird Endzeit* ('the original time will become the final time'), the two really coalesce in the 'eternal present' (*illud tempus*) of the religious imagination. Cf. §9(6).

And war broke out in heaven, with Michael and his angels attacking the dragon[1]. And the dragon fought back with his angels, but they did not prevail, and no place was left for them in heaven. And the great dragon, the primaeval serpent, known as the Devil or Satan[2], who had deceived all the world, was hurled down to the earth and his angels were hurled down with him...

(*Revelation* 12:7-9)

[1] This dragon appears in threefold guise in *Revelation*. The complexity of the dragon symbolism is well treated by Barker 2000, 212-25.

[2] The dragon is to be traced back to Leviathan in Israel and Litan in Ugarit (§4(2)), and to Tiamat in Mesopotamia (§§2(9, 10, 14, 36), 3(1-3)). It already appeared as *labbu* (literally 'lion') in Akkadian texts (see discussion at Wyatt 1998a, 116 n. 11, and 2001c), and had both oceanic and terrestrial forms. The serpent in *Gilgamesh* xi 313 is called *labbu irṣiti*, 'lion of the earth (or, underworld)'. Mot says in §4(18) that his appetite is that of **lbim thm* (text *lbim thw*), that is, in Akkadian **labbu ti'amat*, 'lion of the deep'. See Wyatt 1998a, 116 n. 11. Its identification with Satan belongs to the interpretation of the serpent of *Genesis* 3 (§9(4)) as a form of Satan. The Hebrew term *śāṭān* means 'opponent' in a forensic sense. 'The Satan' of *Job* 2 is the prosecutor in the divine court, whose task is to check out people's deeds and motives. The Greek term διαβολος is simply a translation of this. But the definite article disappeared from the Hebrew, so that Satan became the *name* of the opponent, who then developed into an enemy of the deity (he had originally been divine, being a 'son of God', *Job* 2:1), and traditions grew up of how his enmity began. A further tradition, in *The Life of Adam and Eve* 12, told how Satan had refused to worship Adam in the Garden of Eden, and was thus deposed. This version was taken up into Islamic thought in the *Qur'ān*, Suras 2, 7, 15 and 18. The primordial figure of the dragon becomes an eschatological character during this overall historical development, and its origins may be traced back, tentatively, at least to Ugarit. See Wyatt 1998a, 115 n. 4.

3(12) Christian Version iv): George and the Dragon

It may seem indulgent to cite a mediaeval text in a collection of ancient Near Eastern literature. But the present text is an example of the remarkable continuity that may sometimes be encountered between the ancient and more recent worlds. The story of George and the Dragon has a complex prehistory. One underlying element is the myth of Perseus and Andromeda (§§3(15, 16)), which takes place, surprisingly for a *Greek* myth, at Joppa. ('Andromeda's rock' can still be seen as a shoal in the mouth of the harbour at Jaffa.) Note the range covered here, from Cappadocia to Libya! A mysterious figure, called Khidr, also appears in Islamic folklore, who seems to be traceable back to George (*Jirjis* in Arabic) and ultimately to Baal of Mount Saphon, victor over the sea-god in §3(4). We are a long way from the original plot in this telling of the story. But one constant remains, though it is not always visible. The fragmentary myth of *Astarte and the Tribute of the Sea* (*ANET* 17-8, *CS* i 35-6) suggests that a sub-plot of the conflict myth is the marriage of the victor, as part of his assumption of royal power. Thus Baal may marry Anat as part of the Ugaritic version (Wyatt 2001b), there are hints at the connection of the two in *Psalm* 8 (Wyatt 1994, 412), the woman in *Revelation* 12 is giving birth, and it is part of the Perseus tradition (§§3(15, 16)). Thus here it is a king's daughter whom George rescues. We should expect him to marry her, but this theme has been sidelined by the need to preach the gospel, and no doubt by the mediaeval prizing of virginity above marriage. But note the painting in the Tate Gallery, London, by D. G. Rossetti, of the wedding of St George to the Princess Sabre.

George was a native of Cappadocia... Once he came to the province of Libya, and to the city of Silena. In this town there was a lake, where dwelt a dragon, who had many times put to flight the people who came armed against him. He would come to the city walls and killed all whom he found with his breath. The result was that the citizens were obliged to offer him two sheep every day to pacify him... But in time the number of sheep was so reduced... that they gave him one sheep and one human being each day. The name of a child, youth or maiden was drawn in a lottery... No one was exempt... And one day the lot had fallen upon the only daughter of the king...

So she walked down to the lake. Blessed George, passing that way, saw her in tears, he asked her the cause of her woe...

(She tells him to get away while he can...)

While they were speaking, the dragon reared his head up out of the lake. Then, trembling, the maiden cried: 'Away, lord, away, and hurry!' But George mounted his horse, arming himself with the sign of the cross, and bravely attacked the dragon... and wounded the monster, throwing him to the ground. And he said to the damsel:

'Cast your girdle about the dragon's neck! And fear nothing, lovely girl!' Thus she did, and the dragon... followed her like a well-behaved little dog.

Now when they had led him to the city, and the people saw him, they began to flee to the mountains and the valleys...

Blessed George signed to them, and said to them: 'Have no fear, for our Lord has sent me to deliver you from the crimes of this dragon! Just believe in God, and be baptized, and I shall slay the dragon.' Then the king and all his people were baptized... and St George, drawing his sword, slew the dragon...

> (after Dunne-Lardeau 1997, 425-7, §56:
> Jacques de Voragine *La Légende Dorée*)

3(13)   Hittite Version: the Storm-god and Illuyankas

There are two rather different versions of this tradition. Hoffner 1990, 11-4, gives both. The translation of A. Goetze given here is of the second version.

The Dragon Illuyankas vanquished the Storm-god and took his heart and his eyes from him. The Storm-god sought to revenge himself upon him. He took the daughter of the poor man for his wife and he begot a son. When he grew up, he took the daughter of the Dragon Illuyankas in marriage. The Storm-god instructed his son: 'When you go to the house of your wife, ask them for my heart and my eyes!' When he went there, he asked them for the heart and they gave that to him. Later he asked for the eyes and they gave him those too. He brought them to the Storm-god, his father. Thus the Storm-god got back his heart and his eyes. When his frame had been restored to its old state, he left to the sea for battle. When he engaged the Dragon Illuyankas in battle, he came close to vanquishing him. But the son of the Storm-god, who was with Illuyankas, shouted up to heaven to his father: 'Count me as with him! Spare me not!' So the Storm-god killed the Dragon Illuyankas and his son too. In this way the Storm-god got even with Illuyankas.

> (*ANET* 126: *Illuyankas*)

This version has been turned into a treatment of problems of social structure, matrilineal *versus* patrilineal loyalties, so that the spatial aspect (which is originally a matter of winning territory) is now a metaphor for priorities in family loyalties (closer to this or that family). The storm-god, Tarḫund, wins his victory at the cost of losing his son, whose loyalty is now towards the family of his wife. He has not so much gained a daughter as lost a son! The same dilemma was explored in Egyptian thought. See §8(2).

3(14)   Greek Version i) Zeus destroys Typhoeus (Typhon)

Greece owes a considerable debt to the Near East in terms of its cultural, literary and religious heritage, both in second millennium trade and cultural interchange (Ugarit was first discovered after the find of a 'Mycenaean' tomb near Tell Ras Shamra in 1928), and for centuries after with Ionian Greek settlements on the coast of Anatolia.

This has been increasingly recognized in the last forty years (Walcot 1966; Astour 1967; M. L. West 1971; id. 1997; Lambrou-Philippson 1990; Penglase 1994; D. R. West 1995).

Hesiod wrote in the eighth century BCE, after a considerable period of absorption and naturalization of the old oriental myths. But the basic pedigree of the myth of Zeus and Typhon is clear enough. It is a further version of the conflict myth, and judging by Typhoeus' name (n. 1), it is derived primarily from the West Semitic version. The twist in the plot is that Typhoeus was created out of jealousy by Hera, when Zeus showed himself perfectly capable of reproduction without her, having androgynous qualities, like other ancient creator gods, such as Amun, Atum, Ra, Ptah, El and Yahweh, Ulomos (= ʿÔlām, Eusebius *Praeparatio Evangelica* i 10 1), Zurvan (M. L. West 1971, 30) and Prajāpati. As M. L. West noted, many of these figures represented the deity of time, if not deified time.

1   But when Zeus had driven the Titans from heaven,
    huge Earth bare her youngest child Typhoeus[1]
of the love of Tartarus,
    by the aid of golden Aphrodite.
5   Strength was with his hands in all that he did
    and the feet of the strong god were untiring.
From his shoulders grew an hundred heads[2] of a snake,
    a fearful dragon, with dark, flickering tongues,
and from under the brows of his eyes in his hundred
    heads flashed fire,
10   and fire burned from his heads as he glared.
And there were voices in all his dreadful heads
    which uttered every kind of sound unspeakable;
for at one time they made sounds such that the gods understood,
    but at another, the noise of a bull bellowing aloud in
    proud ungovernable fury;
15   and at another, the sound of a lion, relentless of heart;
    and at another, sounds like whelps, wonderful to hear;
    and again, at another, he would hiss, so that the
    high mountains reechoed.
And truly a thing past help would have happened on that day,
    and he would have come to reign over mortals and immortals,
20   had not the father of men and gods been quick to perceive it.
But he thundered hard and mightily:
    and the earth around resounded terribly and the wild heaven
    above,
    and the sea and Ocean's streams and the nether parts of
    the earth[3].
Great Olympus reeled beneath the divine feet of the king as
    he rose
25   and earth groaned thereat.

Through the thunder and the lightning,
>and through the fire from the monster,
>and the scorching winds and blazing thunderbolt.
The whole earth seethed, and sky and sea:
30   and the long waves raged along the beaches round and about,
at the rush of the deathless gods:
>and there arose an endless shaking.
Hades trembled where he rules over the dead below,
>and the Titans under Tartarus who live with Kronos,
35   because of the unending clamour and the fearful strife.
So when Zeus had raised up his might and seized his arms,
>thunder and lightning and lurid thunderbolt,
he leapt from Olympus and struck him,
>and burned all the marvellous heads of the monster about him.
40   But when Zeus had conquered him and lashed him with strokes,
Typhoeus was hurled down, a maimed wreck,
so that the huge earth groaned...
>And in the bitterness of his anger Zeus cast him into wide
>   Tartarus.

(Evelyn-White 1914, 139-43, adapted: Hesiod, *Theogony*, 820-68)

1   Later versions call him Typhon (a Typhon appears already in *Theogony* 305). Plutarch used this name in his Greek account of the myth of Osiris to denote Seth. (On this see §§8(1-4) and discussion.) The Greek forms Typhon (Τυφων) and Typhoeus (Τυφωευς) derive from Ugaritic ṣapunu (Hebrew ṣāpôn), which is the name of the sacred mountain in Ugarit and Israel (Wyatt 1995a). This suggests that Typhoeus denotes a figure based on Yam, the sea-god, and that as in Indian versions of the myth, the sacred mountain is constructed out of the corpse of the primordial dragon. See further at §5(5).

2   A considerable enhancement of the seven heads of the earlier tradition!

3   Cf. §§2(30-4).

There is a tripartite division of the cosmos in Greek thought, between Zeus (sky), Poseidon (Sea) and Pluto-Hades (earth, underworld). This corresponds to a relationship that is not formally stated in the West Semitic cosmology, between Baal (sky, weather), Yam (sea) and Mot (earth, underworld). In practice Zeus and Baal respectively each controls the land too (Baal is called *zbl bʿl arṣ*, 'The Prince, Master of the Earth'). This is further circumstantial evidence of the link between the traditions.

3(15) Greek Version ii)
Strabo's Account of Perseus and Andromeda

Note the *Levantine* (§3(15) or even *African* (§3(16)) location of this *Greek* myth, indicative of its derivation from Oriental tradition. See §3(12) introduction. The name Perseus as a Semitic form would mean 'Slicer' (cf. Gordon 1969, 288, related to

Akkadian *parāsu*), while Andromeda is perhaps to be derived from West Semitic
*Anatu Ramitu, 'Anat raised up'.

Then one comes to Iope (= Joppa), where the seaboard from Egypt,
though at first stretching towards the east, makes a significant bend
towards the north. Here it was, according to certain writers of myths, that
Andromeda was exposed to the sea-monster; for the place is situated at a
rather high elevation...

(Jones 1930, vii 275: Strabo, *Geography*, 16.28)

3(16) Greek Version iii)
Apollodorus' Account of Perseus and Andromeda

Danaë daughter of Acrisius was destined to bear a son who would kill his father (cf.
the Oedipus myth, which is a 'dry' version of this 'wet' myth, and which, like this, may
owe something to West Semitic royal ideology). So she was locked up in a tower.
Here Zeus, in order to seduce her, descended upon her as a shower of gold. She gave
birth to Perseus. She and her child were put in a box and sent out to sea, washing up
on the shore of Seriphos, where Dictys ('fisherman') found it on the beach, and
brought Danaë and Perseus to his brother, King Polydectes. The latter wished to
marry Danaë, and Perseus, now grown up, was sent to fetch a gorgon's head as a
means of getting rid of him… With help from Athena and Hermes, Perseus killed
Medusa, one of the gorgons, and the only mortal one, by looking at her reflection in
his shield as he slew her, for looking directly at her would turn him to stone. On his
way back to Seriphos, with Medusa's head, he came upon Andromeda chained to a
rock (see §3(12) introduction), and showed Medusa's head to the threatening sea-
monster, which was turned to stone. On returning home, Perseus also showed the
head to Polydectes…

Having received from Hermes an adamantine sickle, he flew to the ocean
and caught the Gorgons asleep. They were Stheno, Euryale and Medusa.
Now Medusa alone was mortal; for that reason Perseus was sent to fetch
her head. But the Gorgons had heads twined about with the scales of
dragons… and golden wings by which they flew; and they turned to stone
such as beheld them. So Perseus stood over them as they slept, and while
Athena guided his hand and he looked with averted gaze on a brazen
shield, in which he beheld the image of the Gorgon, he beheaded her…
Perseus put the head of Medusa in the wallet and went back again...

Being come to Ethiopia, of which Cepheus was king, he found the king's
daughter Andromeda set out to be the prey of a sea-monster. For
Cassiepea[1], the wife of Cepheus, vied with the Nereids in beauty and
boasted to be better than them all; hence the Nereids were angry, and
Poseidon, sharing their wrath, sent a flood and a monster to invade the
land. But Ammon[2] having predicted deliverance from the calamity if
Cassiepea's daughter Andromeda were exposed as prey to the monster,
Cepheus was compelled by the Ethiopians to do it, and he bound his
daughter to a rock. When Perseus beheld her, he loved her and promised

Cepheus that he would kill the monster, if he would give him the rescued damsel to wife. These terms having been sworn to, Perseus withstood and slew the monster and released Andromeda...

(Frazer 1921 i, 157-61: Apollodorus *The Library*, 2.4.2-3)

1   A variant spelling of Cassiopeia.

2   This is Amun, the Egyptian god, appropriate for the Ethiopian setting of this account.

The motif of the creation of the world out of the cadaver of a primordial chaos-monster is found, as we see here, in a wide-ranging group of cultures. The *same* cultures also preserve stories of the flood, as we shall see in the next chapter (§4). The theory proposed by Ryan and Pitman 1998, of the cultural consequences of a sixth millennium Black Sea inundation (discussed below, §4(14)) makes it possible that the dragon-killing and the flood narratives, which represent respectively the beginning and the end of the world, are to be seen as both dependent upon the same folk memory.

II   Some Passages Describing the Idea of the World-encircling Ocean

For these, see §§2(30-5) above.

It is evident that the image of a world-encircling ocean is a symbolic representation of a dynamic condition: the two, land and sea, are in constant opposition, and controlled by the efficacy of temple rituals, which manage time and space for the maintenance of civilized life. Thus the ocean is repelled and overcome in the primordial myth, which is reiterated in the rituals of kingship, and in such contexts as the Babylonian Akitu festival, at which the whole of the *Enuma Elish* was recited. An analogous ritual was performed daily in Egypt, in which the victory of Ra (or Seth as his agent) over Apepi, a subterranean monster, was celebrated and enabled by the destruction of a papyrus drawing of the monster, and the utterance of appropriate curses (§8(5)).

The ocean even enters into temple architecture, requiring to be tapped at crucial times, for it is life-giving water, and by representation in architectural form its taming and control is celebrated. See §§6(31-3).

The potential for the return of the ocean, and the overwhelming of the earth, is described in the myths which deal with the flood motif, §4.

III   The Ends of the Earth

This section is not concerned with the end of the earth or world, in a temporal sense. That is the concern of §4. We are here concerned with the ends of the earth in a spatial sense, which, as will become clear, relates to the origin of the world and its continued management, largely in political terms. The Hebrew term *'epes* (cognate with Ugaritic *aps*), meaning 'end', or 'extremity', as in *'apsê 'ereṣ*, 'the ends of the earth', has been linked etymologically with Akkadian *apsû*, Sumerian AB.ZU, by Pope 1955, 72 and Reymond 1958, 170-1. *HALOT* cites these references as possible explanations for *'epes*. Let us examine the usage to see whether it provides any firm evidence in support. §§3(17, 18) give interesting examples of each usage. Note also the nuanced use of the Egyptian concept of the horizon (§§7(1-11)).

3(17)   The Limit to Earthly Kingship in Ugaritic Thought

This is an excerpt from §7(16) below.   The narrative is of course about the enthronement of a god, not a man.   But it can be argued that it represents the ideology of human kingship (which was in reality a kind of 'divine kingship', since kings were regarded as divine in certain contexts (enthronement, activity in the cult, cosmic ruler — see immediately below — and so forth).   This is true, in varying degrees, throughout the ancient Near East.   (See Wyatt 1999 for West Semitic evidence.)   The present text is an antecedent of a whole family of traditions of legitimate (§§7(17-21)) and illegitimate (§§5(8-10)) ascents.   The former category are the means by which kings, prophets and sages acquired wisdom; the latter where arrogant monarchs characterized by hubris were brought down.

> Athtar the Brilliant went up into the uttermost parts of Saphon;
>> he sat on the throne of Valiant Baal.
> [But] his feet did not reach the footstool,
>> his head did not come to its top[1].

> (Wyatt 1998a, 132: KTU 1.6 i 56-61)

1   Ugaritic *apsh*. The oceanic sense we might expect from a cognate of Akkadian *apsû* (§2(30) n. 1, 7(21) n. 3) is not obviously present.   But the term means, as its Hebrew counterpart indicates, the remotest part of the cosmos, which is where the cosmic ocean is encountered.   We are therefore to understand this divine throne as an *axis mundi*, reaching vertically through the whole universe.   The image of *Isaiah* 66:1 (from about 800 years later) provides a clear means to its understanding, where Yahweh (= El of the Ugaritic text) declares:

> *haššāmayim kis'î*   The heavens are my throne
> *wᵉhā' āreṣ hᵃdōm raglāy*   and the *'ereṣ* (underworld)
>   is my footstool.

The supra-firmamental waters are 'mystically present', as it were, in the very form *haššāmayim*, since the word contains the element *māyim*, 'waters'.   Thus the upper limit to which Athtar's head does not reach, is in distinction from Baal's head, the aqueous location of which is described in a hymn to Baal, KTU 1.101.5-8:

> His head is magnificent,
>> His brow is dew-drenched.
>> his feet are eloquent in (his) wrath.
> [His] horn is [exal]ted;
>> his head is in the snows in heaven,
>> [with] the god there is abounding water.

3(18)   The Term *'epes* in Hebrew

The Hebrew term is similarly used to Ugaritic *aps* in §3(17).   This is a particularly instructive example.   Two translations are offered.   The first is conventional, simply reading the Masoretic Text as found in printed Hebrew Bibles.

> All the nations are as nothing[1] before him;
> as far as he is concerned they are (as) utter waste[2].

(Isaiah 41:17)

1   'As nothing': Hebrew k^e*ayin*.

2   'Utter waste': Hebrew *mê*'*epes wātôhû*. The initial *mê* is better explained not as the Hebrew preposition *m*', 'from', but as *mê* (construct plural of *māyim*) with genitive: 'the waters of the end/*apsû*'. While '*epes* and *tôhû*, 'waste', have standard meanings in Hebrew, the latter term undoubtedly carries for the poet echoes of *t*'*hôm*, 'abyss', which in turn invites the recognition of the cosmological overtones of '*epes*. We may even conjecture that '*ayin*, 'nothing', n. 1, has been selected because it evokes '*ayin*, 'spring, well'. It is perhaps going too far to say that these are here the primary meanings, but the poet surely evokes nonentity less in abstract, conceptual terms as in spatial terms: reality is that which is contained within the bounds of the universe, and all is bounded by water. If we wished to be perhaps a little over-bold, we might offer the following as grasping at the meaning implied:

> All the nations are as well-water before him;
> as far as he is concerned they are the upper and lower seas.

The sense, on this reading, would imply that the nations, so precious to those who belong to them, are merely the raw material of creation from a divine perspective. They can be remade at any time. It would amount to a hydrological equivalent to the sentiment that 'all flesh is grass!' (*Isaiah* 40:6).

3(19) The Scope of the King's Rule: Sargon's Conquest as far as the 'Upper Sea'

Kings frequently claimed in public inscriptions or liturgical texts to rule the entire world. This is easily dismissed as propagandistic language, an elevated style common to royal proclamations, often defined as *Hofstil* ('courtly style'). But to take it as essentially vacuous, a mere form of words, is to misconstrue the psychological and religious impulses giving rise to it. We have seen how important is the conception of the spoken or written word and its substantival nature (§§2(11) n. 2, 2(36) n. 2, 2(37)). There are two aspects to such language. Firstly, kings saw themselves as echoing by command of, and as sons of, the national deity, and as recapitulating, in their victories, the divine victory. §3(3) from Mari was the classic example of this, echoed in any number of similar texts, of which we have a selection above. Secondly, the theme of control, and ideally total control (the modern conception of 'empowerment' is similar), motivated many actions. So any kingship gave the incumbent a total control over his subjects, and in an ideal world, complete command of all surrounding territory. In practice, of course, diplomacy and trade gave a fair substitute, but once the taste for battle, and its heroic image, had been experienced, it operated under its own logical rules (Berger 1973, 19). This was therefore *necessary* rhetoric, and played its part in the conception, and consequently the realization, of the vision. It may plausibly be argued that all culture is rhetoric, of which the cogency persists in the believing community.

This excerpt is from a statue inscription (later copied onto clay tablets) recording the earliest known military adventure, of Sargon, king of Agade (2334-2279 BCE). For background see Kuhrt 1995, 44-57.

Sargon... conquered É-NIN-MAR.KI and tore down its walls.   He conquered its territory as well as Lagash (down) to the sea; he washed his weapons in the sea...

Sargon, king of the Land: Enlil did not give him a rival, (but) he gave him indeed the Upper Sea and the Lower (Sea) From the Lower Sea to the Upper Sea citizens of Akkad (now) hold governorships.

(CS ii 243, adapted)

There are three elements of note here. The first is Sargon's ritual act in washing his weapons in the sea. As I have argued (Wyatt 1998b, 844-5, following Durand 1993, 57) this is a widespread formulation of complete victory, to the practical limits of the world, the sea being the cosmic ocean. This does not require that Sargon believe this to be the end of the world. He acted *as though* it were (the rhetoric, the form of words, made it so). This was a ritual act. He also traded with ships from Meluḫḫa (sc. the Indus Valley culture), showing a knowledge of a much broader real geography.

Secondly and thirdly, there are the two parts of the sea named. The 'Lower Sea' was without doubt the upper reaches of the Persian Gulf. The 'Upper Sea' could conceivably be the Black Sea, but is rather to be identified as the Mediterranean Sea, in view of other locations mentioned in Naram-Sin's repetition of the expedition (§3(20)).

3(20) Naram-Sin's Conquest as far as the 'Upper Sea'

This appears to be broadly a repetition of Sargon's campaign (or at any rate of Sargon's account of his campaign, for Naram-Sin appears to have wished to emulate his predecessor).

From of old, from the creation of men, no one among the kings had overthrown Armanum and Ebla: with the help of the weapon of Nergal[1], Naram-Sin, the Mighty, opened the only path there and he (Nergal) gave him Armanum and Ebla. He also granted him the Amanus, the Cedar Forest and the Upper Sea...

(CS ii 244-5, adapted)

1   The king's weapon is identified with that of Nergal, implying the ritual of weapon-giving illustrated in §3(3).

The places named help locate the expedition. Arman is not precisely located (Bottéro 1971, 325-6: perhaps on the Balikh?), while Ebla is Tell Mardikh south of Aleppo, the Cedar Mountain may be Lebanon, but is more likely the Amanus, also identified by name, all suggesting that a north-*westerly* location is required.

3(21) The Campaign of Yahdun-Lim of Mari

King in late nineteenth-century BCE Mari, Yahdun-Lim sought to expand westwards. This is an account of a campaign as far as the Mediterranean.

... Yahdun-Lim, son of Yaggid-Lim, powerful king, wild bull of kings, by means of his strength and overpowering might went to the shore of the sea, and made a great offering (befitting) his kingship to the sea[1]. His troops bathed themselves in the sea[2].

(*CS* ii 260, adapted)

1   Or 'to Sea', sc. the sea-god.

2   This appears to be an extension of the ritual of washing weapons, as in §3(19).

3(22) Ruling from Sea to Sea: Hammurabi of Babylon

Hammurabi, king of Babylon from 1792 to 1750 BCE, whose law-code, inscribed on a stela, is now in the Louvre, was son of Sin-muballit. This excerpt comes from the prologue to the code, iv 70, v 1-20.

The mighty heir of Sin-muballit, with royal ancestors for generations; the mighty king, the sun of Babylon who shines all over the lands of Sumer and Akkad; the king who has made the four parts of the world[1] listen; the one beloved of Ishtar.   And so when Marduk urged me to direct the people of the land to adopt correct behaviour, I made the land speak with justice and truth...

(Richardson 2000, 41)

1   The expression 'the four parts (of the world)' (or 'four quarters...', 'four rims...' or 'the universe', according to translator), is the formula *kibrāt arba'im*, variant *kibrāt erbettim*. The term *kibru* (singular of *kibrāt(u)*) means a bank of a river, or the shore of the sea. So the four represent the cardinal points, and the sense is of the furthest limits of the world, bounded by the ocean (*Apsû*).

Another inscription of Hammurabi (*CS* ii 257), recording the digging of a canal, begins 'Hammurabi, mighty king, king of Babylon, king who makes the four quarters be at peace, who achieves the victory of the god Marduk...'   The last two phrases mean much the same thing: his conquest (attributed to Marduk) involved the pacification of outlying peoples.

3(23) Esarhaddon of Assyria as Universal Ruler

Esarhaddon ruled Assyria from 680 to 669 BCE.   In about 671 he conquered Lower Egypt, thus extending the imperial boundary much further than hitherto; his successor Ashurbanipal added Thebes.   The ancient formula has not changed.   Note the historical appeal to the ancient kingdoms of Sumer and Akkad, long-since swallowed up, the 'regency' of Babylon, as though in recognition of *its* ancient precedence, and the appeal to ethics and divine choice. Cf. also §11(8).

Esarhaddon, great king, legitimate king, king of the world, king of Assyria, regent of Babylon, king of Sumer and Akkad, king of the four rims (of the earth), true shepherd, favorite of the great gods...

(ANET 289: from Esarhaddon Prism B)

3(24) The Aspiration to Cosmic Rule in the Psalms

We have seen something of the Israelite conception of the cosmic sea above (§2(35)). The *yam sûf* could denote this, or at times simply the Mediterranean Sea, or the Red Sea. A number of passages which may be simple geographical allusions may however have deliberate cosmological echoes. This is particularly the case with §3(24); with §3(26) the issue is less clear-cut. The pettiest king could echo the imperial grandiloquence, for the absolutist claim to power is the same. For extent of rule in a spatial sense, we really have to read absolutism in a local context. The kingdom of Judah did not even reach the sea when Philistine power was strong!

> May he reign from sea to sea,
> and from the river[1] to the ends[2] of the earth!

(Psalm 72:8)

1   The term 'river' here is often identified as the Euphrates. See further at §3(25). But its sense here must be determined by context. 'Sea to sea', rather than referring to the Mediterranean and the Dead Seas, which at times were the geographical limits of Judah, alludes to the cosmic sea surrounding the world, and therefore the boundaries, in opposite directions, of an ideal kingdom. The second colon, as commonly in Semitic poetry, merely rephrases and extends this sense. The 'river' is another designation of the cosmic sea, while 'the ends of the earth' refer to its uttermost limits, sc. at the sea's edge.

2   Hebrew *'apsê*. See §3(18).

This psalm has the superscription *lišlōmô*, 'concerning (or 'to') Solomon'. This has probably no strict historical reference, however, unless in retrospect, rather expressing an editorial idealization of Solomon's wealth and power. Verse 5 (Greek) also gives the reign temporal limitlessness. But the psalm may have originated in the royal cult, though from which era, preexilic or Hasmonean, cannot be determined with certainty.

3(25) The Israelite Aspiration:
the Divine Promise at the King's Enthronement

The following psalm appears to be more specifically linked to a royal coronation (cf. *Psalm* 2), but still evades precise location. Its allusion to the king's Davidic antecedents is to be expected, whatever its age.

> So I shall set upon the sea his (left) hand[1]
> and on the rivers[2] his right hand!

(Psalm 89:26)

1   The hands are frequently mentioned as a pair; when the term 'hand' (*yad*) is unqualified, but parallels 'the right hand' (*yāmîn*), it is to be understood as the left hand. In fact, both hands are understood to be used together. The

distinction is rhetorical. The laying on of hands, no doubt with a ritual background, not only confers authority, but also denotes the superiority of the person doing it. Thus it signifies the king's cosmic authority.

2   The text reads *n^ehārôt* (plural). But 'sea' in the first colon is singular (both are plural in Greek). They should be harmonized, and 'River' be read as singular. It and 'Sea' (or 'Yam') are probably the divine names, as in Ugaritic (having no article). But at any rate they have cosmological reference.

3(26) Historiographical Allusions in the Bible

These passages at first glance belong in historiographical contexts, and therefore to demand assessment as historical statements. A closer look however reveals their poetic, and possibly liturgical nature. For more on history see §§12 and Epilogue.

a)   Yahweh Covenants with Abram

This passage still has powerful political and ideological echoes in contemporary Israel and Palestine. Generally attributed to the 'Yahwistic' source in the Pentateuch, it used to be dated to as early as the tenth century BCE (any earlier date, such as during a 'patriarchal age', being generally discounted by scholars). Van Seters 1975, however makes a strong case for an exilic (sixth-fifth century BCE) dating for traditions about Abra(ha)m.

> To your descendants I give this land,
>
> from the river of Egypt[1] to the great river[2].

(Genesis 15:18)

1   The 'river of Egypt' may be the Wadi el Arish, which roughly marks the Afro-Asiatic boundary. But since Egypt is sometimes conceptualized as lying 'beyond' the sea (the *yam sûf* (§2(35)), it is possible that the cosmological overtone should be recognized here.

2   In the following two passages 'the great river' is glossed as the River Euphrates. With no such gloss here, it is likely that the cosmological sense is paramount. That is, 'the great river' means the ocean.

b)   Divine Instructions in Deuteronomy

Every place where the sole of your feet tread will be yours, from the desert and the Lebanon, from the river, the River Euphrates, to the western sea shall be your frontiers.

(Deuteronomy 11:24)

c)   Moses' Words to Joshua on the Eve of the Conquest of Palestine

From the desert and the Lebanon, and to the great river, the River Euphrates, and all the land of the Hittites, and to the great sea where the sun sets shall be your frontiers.

(Joshua 1:4)

These two passages evidently have a close literary relationship. They appear to develop something of the thought of *Deuteronomy* 1:7, and c) is evidently a much reworked version of b). Already here, the phrase 'the River Euphrates', which glosses 'the river' (note how it becomes 'the *great* river' in c), as in a)), is the only real geographical location ('Lebanon' qualifies under the language examined in §1 (col. 3) as a geographical term for 'north'). Otherwise 'river… sea' may act as poetic designations of the cosmic ocean, as above in §§3(24) and a) above.

Chapter 4

SPACE, TIME AND WATER II:
WATER AND THE END OF THE WORLD

Just as water precedes the existence of the habitable world, as well as surrounding it, so it often appears in mythology to outlast it. In a sense, these stories are recapitulations of the primordial narrative (§4 I), or reversals of it (§4 II). This is particularly clear in §4(8).

Suggested Reading:

Dalley 1989; Davila 1995; George 1999; Heidel 1949; Holloway 1991, id. 1998; Hendel 1995; Lambert and Millard 1969; Ryan and Pitman 1999; Wyatt 2001c.

4.1 Introduction

4.1.1 The subject matter of this chapter is in a strict correspondence with that of chapter 3, but now with a futuristic reference. This need not be entirely eschatological, since flood stories, our theme, are generally set in the past, just like creation. Thematically however, they must have a future reference in principle, in that they deal with the end of the world, even if this has already happened, to be succeeded by a subsequent re-creation (as is clearly so in the *Genesis* account). As will be explored later (§13, Epilogue I), this conception belongs in the context of beliefs in 'world cycles', which find expression in later (first millennium BCE) literature.

4.1.2 The link between past and future is evident before we even turn to flood stories, as can be seen in texts §§4(1, 2a, 2b). Here we see the specifics of the dragon-killing, long a national myth of Israel's origin, cited as the basis for the conviction that Yahweh will again help his people, now exiles in Babylon. A new exodus is about to take place! The link is explicit in §4(1). In §4(2b) we have simply a futuristic account, echoing the old myth. §4(2a) is cited as a matter of interest, since this late thirteenth century Ugaritic text evidently lies behind the much younger (sixth-fifth century BCE) biblical text.

4.2 Egypt

§4(3) is an isolated example of a flood tradition from Egypt. Note its clear reference to a return to the primordial ('pre-creation') state, when Nu, the primordial flood, covers everything. This may of course be construed as referring to no more than the regular *annual* inundation. But it seems as though something more emphatic than this underlies the text, because the speaker, the dead person, sees himself alone surviving, as Nu.

4.3   Mesopotamia

4.3.1   This region is rich in flood traditions, and it appears as though the other Near Eastern versions (Israel and Greece) are dependent upon it. The region is prone to substantial flood destruction. However, given that the tradition is even more widespread than the ancient Near East, but is also found in the Indo-Iranian tradition, the surmise of §4(14) n., that the Black Sea flood of the 6th millennium BCE is the ultimate source of the tradition has something to be said for it. But this only strengthens the case for *one* flood being behind all the versions.

4.3.2   The earliest version is probably Sumerian. The hero is Ziusudra (perhaps the Sumerian form of Utnapishtim: §4.3.3), a king (his kingdom is not identified, but is probably Shuruppak). The text is fragmentary, and no motive is given for the flood.

4.3.3   Two Akkadian versions survive. In the first, §4(5), a free-standing composition, Atrahasis ('the supremely wise', this may be an epithet originally applied to Ziusudra), a king of Shuruppak, is the hero. The reason for the flood is twofold: overpopulation and the noise people are making, which prevents the gods sleeping.

4.3.4   In the other version, *Gilgamesh* tablet xi, §4(6), Atrahasis, king of Shuruppak, is still the hero, also called Utnapishtim (' He saw Life'?). Gilgamesh has seen his friend Enkidu die, and goes off (tablet x) to find immortality. Utnapishtim tells him the story. Again there is no apparent motive, though in the context (Gilgamesh seeking immortality) it may be just to emphasize human mortality.

4.3.5   In Eusebius (§4(7)) we have fragments of a late version told by Berossus (Xisuthros is a Greek form of Ziusudra).

4.4   The West Semitic World: Ugarit and Israel

4.4.1   Ugarit has not yet yielded a native version of the tradition. However, fragments of both *Atrahasis* and *Gilgamesh* have been found, indicating local familiarity with the tradition. A *Gilgamesh* fragment has also been found at Megiddo in Israel. So it seems that the Levant was acquainted with the tradition long before the biblical account was written.

4.4.2   The biblical narrative (§4(8)), evidently owes much to the Mesopotamian stories, but has its own distinctive elements. Noah ('Consolation') is the hero. The motive is clear: Yahweh is out of patience with human sin. It seems that two stories have been conflated. In one version there is a pair of each species, and it rains for forty days and nights; in the other sluices above and below open to allow the cosmic ocean back into the sphere, and there are seven pairs of clean animals, one pair of unclean ones. See biblical commentaries (especially Skinner 1910 and Westermann 1984) for discussion. §§4(9, 10) are derivatives.

4.5   Greek Versions (also recorded in Latin)

Human pride and disobedience are to be punished in these versions. Deucalion is the hero (in one Latin version he is called Cerambus).

4.6   The Religious Significance of Flood Stories

4.6.1 The real importance of these tales is not so much whether they are historically true, or how much imagination has been used, as the moral aspect which they reveal. Why did the gods send a flood? And why did one man, or a man and his family, receive a warning and thus survive? And does the boat have any symbolic significance?

4.6.2 We should not necessarily make too much of the different motives recorded, in the sense assumed by some biblical commentators, that only the Noah story is really 'moral'. Overpopulation, noise, and general wickedness are all much of a muchness in moral terms. They all show human beings out of control, and evidently not obeying divine commands. The narrators are all succinct to the point of obscurity, but probably have a range of sins in mind.

4.6.3 There is not much mileage to be made in contrasting the monotheistic (Jewish) and polytheistic (all the others) backgrounds in terms of moral superiority (e.g. Heidel 1949, 225-7). This is firstly to read far too much meaning into the biblical account, and secondly to fail to do justice to other versions. Even in *Genesis* Yahweh appears to have limitations: he is sorry (*Genesis* 6:6) for having made people. It is better to examine the particular symbolism. This is most readily studied in the comparison of the Mesopotamian and biblical accounts.

4.6.4 In each case the hero is a model of the pious man. He is also an Adam figure, because at each flood the world begins anew. This is why he is presented as a king (and a priest: Davila 1995), because kings are 'Adam' figures, archetypes, and 'sons of God'. They are in fact divine. In both contexts the king is the 'servant' or 'gardener' of God or the gods (Wyatt, 1988a, 1990b). Morality is measured primarily in terms of cultic propriety. Holiness is both integrity (wholeness) and the observance of category distinctions. (See §2 (17) introduction.) The breakdown of divinely ordained boundaries leads to chaos, and the flood represents a reversion to chaos. Divine grace ensures that a righteous remnant survives.

4.6.5 Holloway (1991) has drawn attention to an important feature in both *Gilgamesh* and *Genesis*: in each case the ark is designed in such a way as to replicate a temple. We shall see later (§6) that temples are models of the human body and of the world (echoes of §1). In the present case, the ark-temple serves as a refuge from the chaos which otherwise irrupts into human lives. To 'dwell in the temple of the Lord' is a universal ancient aspiration. Temples, like the ark, are 'founded on the *apsû*'.

4.6.6 The flood leads to a new creation. This is indicated most graphically in the *Genesis* narrative. God's words to the First Man (*hā'ādām*) in 1:28-30 are to be compared with those to Noah in 9:1-17. The former is implicitly a covenant; the latter explicitly so. This is to be read against the tradition of the covenant in *Exodus*, and both are derived from the experience of exile in the 6th century.

4.7   Death

The ultimate reference of flood traditions (witness Gilgamesh's motivation: to avoid dying) is the human consciousness of mortality. §§4(15-27) illustrate general attitudes; some of the passages are chosen because they use end of the world or flood imagery. The underworld lay hard against the cosmic abyss (the waters below the earth), and so Jonah's words (§4(27)) are entirely typical of the ancient world view.

I   Reenactment of the Primordial Conflict,
now Projected into the Future

At §3(11) we cited Gunkel's famous epigram *Urzeit wird Endzeit*, which encapsulates a fundamental quality of much mythical thought and expression: the stories that are told about *illud tempus*, the Primordial Time, appear to have the capacity to transform the present, and also to shape the future. This is a fundamental quality of human cognition, for we use our past experience to lead us what to expect, and to anticipate the future. This was the main temporal significance of the ideas discussed in §1.

4(1)   Recapitulation in Biblical Prophetic Thought

In view of the mythic capacity to recapitulate and represent through anamnesis, we should not be surprised to encounter the following passage in *Isaiah*. Chapters 40-55 are often distinguished from 1-39 ('Proto-Isaiah', or 'Isaiah of Jerusalem', an eighth century figure) and 56-66 ('Trito-Isaiah'), an early post-exilic poet, as 'Deutero-Isaiah', an anonymous figure of the exilic period. The history of the text is very complex, and this neat distinction oversimplifies the literary problem. However, the present passage, evoking the exodus ('as in days of yore'), serves as a paradigm for what Yahweh is about to do, for it continues with exhortations to the hearers (living in exile in Babylon) to anticipate a repetition of the event. For similar passages in the same body of poetry, see *Isaiah* 43:1-5, 16-21 (v. 18: 'Do not remember the former things, nor consider those things which are past!' is a graphic expression of the power of anamnesis, which appears to make memory superfluous!).

1 Awake, awake!
  clothe yourself in power, arm of Yahweh; *military image* [handwritten]
  awake, as in days of yore,
    of generations long past!
5 Was it not you who smote Rahab, → *corpse* [handwritten]
    transfixing Dragon?
  Was it not you who dried up Sea,
    the waters of the great abyss,
  who made the valleys of Sea a path
10   for the passage of the redeemed?

(*Isaiah* 51:9-10)

In §2(16) four names were given to the sea-god ('Sea', 'Dragon', 'Leviathan', 'River'). Here two of them, 'Dragon' and 'Sea', are accompanied by a further one, Rahab (Hebrew *rāhāb*, 'storm'). Rahab may also be a cipher for Egypt, as in *Psalms* 87:4 and 89:11 (English 10), and Spronk 1995, col. 1292 (= 1999, 684) suggests that it may be cognate with *labbu* (§3(11) n. 2).

4(2) An Ugaritic Figure and its Biblical Transformation

a) Mot's words to Baal

Mot challenges Baal, telling him that although he had fought Yam and his allies (these appear to be names of Yam), he will find himself, Mot, an altogether more formidable foe. Baal appears to capitulate with surprising speed.

Though you smote Litan the wriggling serpent,
    finished off the writhing serpent,
    Encircler-with-seven-heads…

(Wyatt 1998a, 115[1]: KTU 1.5 i 1-3)

1 See Wyatt 1998a, 115 n. 4 for discussion of the relationship of these two passages §§4(2a, 2b). This is a classic example of the close relationship of the Ugaritic and Israelite poetic traditions.

b) A Biblical Adaptation of the Ugaritic Motif

The following passage from Deutero-Isaiah (see §4(1) introduction) is evidently cognate with the above, from Ugarit. Now it is given a futuristic reference.

On that day Yahweh will punish
  with his relentless sword, great and sharp,
Leviathan the fleeing serpent,
  yea, Leviathan the writhing serpent,
  and he will slay the Dragon which is in the sea.

(*Isaiah* 27:1)

Deutero-Isaiah is looking forward to an imminent day of redemption, of liberation from exile. Passages such as these are often described as 'eschatological'. This classification is not always appropriate, since eschatological thought, though attested in Persian (Zoroastrian), Jewish and Christian thought, is not an obvious feature of other ancient Near Eastern religious thought. Eschatology basically concerns the end of the world, and the end of history. It may even be defined as an attitude of despair towards history, since it usually arises when religions address times of crisis, and offer alternatives to a historical resolution of the problem. Classic examples of such conditions in Israel were the Maccabean period, mid-second century BCE, when the anti-Jewish policies of Antiochus IV Epiphanes were put into effect, and the latter part of the first and early second centuries CE, when Roman policy towards the Jews led to two destructions of Jerusalem in 70 and 135 CE. (General beliefs about the *post-mortem* destiny of humans, while often treated under the rubric of eschatology, are a separate issue.) The passages above are rather to be described as futuristic, looking to a redemption of Israel (in exile at the time of writing) in the imminent *historical* future. They were, however, to inspire much eschatological speculation later on, in Hellenistic and Roman times. See Epilogue.

II   Some Examples of Flood Stories

4(3)   An Egyptian Account: Atum addresses the Deceased

The *Book of the Dead* belongs substantially to New Kingdom times (from *ca* 1550 BCE), though its roots are older (§§2(8) notes and 2(22) notes). The present passage has all the qualities of a flood story, but appears not to be directly cognate with the Asiatic traditions. Its time-reference is obscure. Is it an allusion to the regular annual inundation, or to some more dramatic and cataclysmic event? There was a belief in the eventual swallowing up of the whole universe in Nu. Cf. Hornung 1996, 151-69. But this is due to general cosmic entropy, not the wickedness of human beings. Atum, the ancient sun-god of Heliopolis, emerged as an androgynous figure from the primordial ocean (Nu) (see §2(1)), and here predicts a return to the first condition.

1   You shall be for millions on millions of years,
       a lifetime of millions of years.
   I will dispatch the Elders
       and destroy all that I have made;
5   the earth shall return to the Abyss,
       to the surging flood,
       as in its original state.
   But I will remain with Osiris,
       I will transform myself into something else,
10   namely a serpent,
       without men knowing or the gods seeing.

(Faulkner 1985, 175: *BD* 175)

The words are spoken to the deceased, identified as Osiris, by Atum. He appears to be saying that in spite of the coming dissolution, he (Atum) will remain, and will guarantee the continued existence of Osiris (sc. the deceased) as well. The deceased therefore appears to become an eschatological flood-hero.

4(4)   Mesopotamian Accounts i): Ziusudra

Common to all the following cognate versions of the narrative is the curious feature of divine ambivalence.   The gods wish to destroy human beings, but not entirely. Somehow, a survivor must be left to continue the species (singular survivor, because all the emphasis is on him as righteous or wise: his wife is a mere adjunct to later procreation)'.   What this means, of course, since all theological speculation is a *human* activity, is a deep ambivalence in human beings.   Do they deserve to live, or to die? Are they somehow responsible for the condition of the world they inhabit?   Are they making the best use of a second chance?

The earliest accounts of the flood appear to be Sumerian, according to Kramer 1961, 97.   But it is perhaps safer to use the inclusive term 'Sumero-Akkadian' here, or 'Sumero-Babylonian', as used by Lambert and Millard 1969, 1.   The real source, in local terms, is unlikely to be resolved, and much Sumerian literature was common material recorded in what had come to be regarded as the 'classical' language.   See further discussion at §4(14).   This fragmentary version from Nippur tells of a pious king from Sumer who is saved by Enki, who also warns Atrahasis and (somewhat indirectly!) Utnapishtim.   It is possible that the latter two forms are simply epithets of the one hero Ziusudra.   The name of the hero is preserved in the classical forms Xisuthros (Greek) and Sisithrus (Latin).

1   Burkert 1992, 24, points out that both *Atrahasis* (DT 42 [W] 8) and *Gilgamesh* (xi 85 = §4(6) l. 40) include some craftsmen for later reconstruction!

1   All the windstorms, exceedingly powerful, attacked as one,
        the deluge raged over the surface of the earth.
    After the deluge had raged in the land
        for seven days and seven nights,
5   and the huge boat had been tossed about on the great waters,
        Utu came forth, who sheds light on heaven and earth.
    Ziusudra opened a window of the huge boat,
        Ziusudra, the king, before Utu prostrated himself,
    the king kills an ox, slaughters a sheep...
10   Ziusudra, the king, before An and Enlil prostrated himself;
    life like a god they gave him,
        breath eternal like a god they bring down for him'.
    In those days, Ziusudra, the king,
        the preserver of the name of ---- and man,
15   in the mountain of crossing, the mountain of Dilmun²,
        the place where the sun rises, they caused to dwell

(Kramer 1961, 97-8)

1   The granting of eternal life to the survivor of the flood is a common feature in the Mesopotamian versions, which is not preserved in their derivatives.   But one conception of 'eternal life' in early Jewish thought was that a man 'lived on in his sons'.   So Noah may have become immortal too, in a roundabout way.

This fragment does not tell whether Ziusudra fathered later generations of humans.

2   Dilmun, the Sumerian 'paradise', is usually identified with modern Bahrain. Cf. §5(4).

4(5)   Mesopotamian Accounts ii): Atrahasis

This is the classic form of the Mesopotamian tradition. The main material, found in Ashurbanipal's library at Nineveh, can be dated (Lambert and Millard 1969, 5) to a great-great-grandson of Hammurabi, Ammi-ṣaduqa, *ca* 1650 BCE, but of course represents the culmination of centuries of growth, if not more.

1   Enki made his voice heard,
         and spoke to his servant...
     'Make sure you attend to the message I shall tell you!...
     Dismantle the house, build a boat,
5   reject possessions, and save living things.
     The boat that you build...
         roof it over like the *Apsû*
         so that the sun cannot see inside it!
     Make upper decks and lower decks.
10   The tackle must be very strong,
         the bitumen strong, to give strength.
     I shall make rain fall on you here...'
     The elders [   ]
         the carpenter [brought his axe,]
15   the reed worker [brought his stone,]
         [a child brought] bitumen.
         The poor [fetched what was needed]...
     The face of the weather changed.
         Adad bellowed from the clouds.
20   The winds were raging even as he went up
         and cut through the rope (and) released the boat...
     No one could see anyone else,
         they could not be recognized in the catastrophe.
     The flood roared like a bull,
25   like a wild ass screaming the winds [howled],
         the darkness was total, there was no sun...
     What was Anu's intention as decision-maker?
         It was his command that the gods his sons obeyed,
     he who did not deliberate, but sent the flood,
30   he who gathered the people to catastrophe...
     For seven days and seven nights
         the torrent, storm and flood came on...

He put down [   ]
  provided food [   ]
35 The gods smelt the fragrance,
  gathered like flies over the offering[1].

(Dalley 1989, 29-33: Atrahasis III i 15-v 35 excerpts)

1   This is a standard expression in Akkadian, signifying the acceptability of sacrifice. Cf. §4(6) below, and *Genesis* 8:21 (§4(8)), *Leviticus* 1:9 (§10(4) and n. 6).

4(6) Mesopotamian Accounts iii): Utnapishtim

The *Epic of Gilgamesh* is one of the great rediscoveries of literature through the agency of archaeology. It was extremely popular, surviving, often in fragmentary form, over a wide range of sites in Mesopotamia, with fragments discovered at Ugarit and Megiddo. It was the culmination of a long growth in folklore concerning a historical figure, king of Uruk in the third millennium BCE. A number of supplementary stories also circulated concerning him. In Sumerian texts his name appeared in the form 'Bilgamesh'.

The present episode comes towards the end of the narrative. Gilgamesh, two thirds divine and one third human, was a heroic king, with all the blemishes of heroism. The gods determined to tame him, and Enkidu, a wild man, was created, who would outdo him in spirit and thus overcome his arrogance. However, Enkidu was himself tamed by a woman sent to seduce him, after which the wild animals fled from him. After an initial contest, he and Gilgamesh became fast friends, and set out for heroic adventures. They insulted Ishtar, who demanded that one of them died. Enkidu expired, and Gilgamesh, for the first time aware that he too was mortal, went off to seek the key to immortality, from Utnapishtim, the survivor of the flood. §9(1) is the sequel, describing the futility of his search. But first, Utnapishtim tells him the story of the flood.

1 Utnapishtim spoke to him, to Gilgamesh,
  'Let me reveal to you a closely-guarded matter, Gilgamesh,
  and let me tell you the secret of the gods.
  Shuruppak is a city that you yourself know,
5   situated on the bank of the Euphrates.
  That city was already old when the gods within it
  decided that the great gods should make a flood.'

  There was Anu their father,
  Warrior Ellil their counsellor,
10 Ninurta was their chamberlain,
  Ennugi their canal-controller.
  Far-sighted Ea swore the oath of secrecy with them,
  so he repeated their speech to a reed hut:
  'Reed hut, reed hut, brick wall, brick wall,
15 listen, reed hut,

and pay attention, brick wall'[1]:
Man of Shuruppak, son of Ubara-Tutu,
  dismantle your house, build a boat.
Leave possessions, search out living things.
20   Reject chattels and save lives!
Put aboard the seed of all living things, into the boat.
  The boat that you are to build
shall have her dimensions in proportion,
  her width and length shall be in harmony.
25 Roof her like the *Apsû*'...

On the fifth day I laid down her form.
One acre was her circumference,
  ten poles each the height of her walls,
  her top edge was likewise ten poles all round.
30 I laid down her structure, drew it out,
  gave her six decks,
  divided her into seven...
I loaded her with everything there was,
  loaded her with all the silver,
35   loaded her with all the gold,
loaded her with all the seed of living things, all of them.
I put on board the boat all my kith and kin.
  Put on board cattle from open country,
wild beasts from open country,
40   all kinds of craftsmen.

Shamash had fixed the hour:
'In the morning cakes,
  in the evening a rain of wheat[2]
I shall shower down:
45   enter into the boat and shut your door!'
That hour arrived...
  I went aboard the boat and closed the door.
To seal the boat I handed over the (floating) palace with
    her cargo
  to Puzur-Amurri the boatman.

50 When the first light of dawn appeared,
  a black cloud came up from the base of the sky.
Adad kept rumbling inside it...
The calm before the Storm-god came over the sky,

everything light turned to darkness...
55 Even the gods were afraid of the flood-weapon.
    They withdrew; they went up to the heaven of Anu.
    The gods cowered, like dogs crouched by an outside wall...

For six days and [seven?] nights the wind blew,
    flood and tempest overwhelmed the land;
60 when the seventh day arrived the tempest, flood and onslaught
    which had struggled like a woman in labour, blew themselves out?.
The sea became calm,
    the *imhullu*-wind grew quiet,
    the flood held back.
65 I looked at the weather; silence reigned,
    for all mankind had turned to clay...
The boat had come to rest on Mount Nimush,
    the mountain Nimush held the boat fast
    and did not let it budge...

70 When the seventh day arrived,
    I put out and released a dove.
The dove went; it came back,
    for no perching place was visible to it, and it turned round.
I put out and released a swallow.
75   The swallow went; it came back,
for no perching place was visible to it, and it turned round.
I put out and released a raven.
    The raven went, and saw the waters receding.
It ate, preened?, lifted its tail and did not turn round.

80 Then I put everything? out to the four winds,
      and I made a sacrifice,
    set out a *surqinnu*-offering upon the mountain peak...
The gods smelt the fragrance,
    the gods smelt the pleasant fragrance,
85   the gods like flies gathered over the sacrifice...
As soon as Ellil arrived he saw the boat.
    Ellil was furious, filled with anger at the Igigi gods:
'What sort of life survived?
    No man should have lived through the destruction!'

             (Dalley 1989, 109-15: *Gilgamesh* xi 8-175 excerpts)

1   The urge to tell someone is overwhelming! Thus the secret is out, and unstoppable. Cf. the secret of Midas' 'ass's ears'.

2   'Cakes' (*kukku*)... 'wheat' (*kibtu*): referring to darkness (*kukkû*) and hailstones, a common Akkadian metaphor (*kibittu* = 'heaviness').

The discussion between Holloway and Hendel (Holloway 1991, 1998; Hendel 1995) on the shape of the ark, is of interest. Holloway argued that Utnapishtim's ark, and Noah's in imitation, was modelled on the shape of an ideal ziggurat, thus forming a 'nave', an image surviving in church architecture and Christian iconography.

4(7) Mesopotamian Accounts iv): Xisuthros (Sisithrus)

Fragments of the Babylonian tradition are found in Berossus, a historiographer writing on the island of Cos *ca* 300 BCE. His version is referred to by Josephus in his account of the flood (*Antiquities* 1.3.9) and quoted scrappily in Eusebius, who also cites Abydenus, an Assyrian historian.

This deluge and the ark are mentioned by all who have written histories of the Barbarians, among whom is Berossus the Chaldean. For in narrating the circumstances of the flood, he describes it thus:

'It is said that there is still a portion of the vessel in Armenia near the mountain of the Cordyaei, and that persons scrape off and carry away some of the pitch. And the people use what they carry away chiefly for charms to avert misfortunes.' This is also mentioned by Hieronymus the Egyptian, who wrote *The archaeology of Phoenicia*, and by Mnaseas, and several others. Nicolaus of Damascus gives an account of them in his 96th book, speaking thus: 'There is above Minyas a great mountain in Armenia called Baris, to which, as the story goes, many fled for refuge at the time of the deluge and were saved; and a certain man borne on an ark landed on the top of the mountain, and the remains of the timbers were preserved for a long time.' So writes Josephus.

But after mentioning the Median and Assyrian records from the work of Abydenus, I will set before you his statements concerning this same story, as follows:

'After him reigned among others Xisuthros, to whom Kronos foretold that there would be a great rain on the fifteenth of Desius, and commanded him to hide everything connected with literature at Heliopolis in the country of the Sippari. And when Xisuthros had accomplished this, he straightway sailed up towards Armenia, and immediately what God had predicted overtook him. But on the third day, when the rain had abated, he proceeded to let loose some of the birds, to try whether they saw land anywhere that had emerged from the water. But as they were met by a vast unbroken ocean, and were at a loss where to find a haven, they came safe back to Xisuthros, and others after them did the same. But when he was successful with the third set, for they came back with their feet full of mud, the gods removed him from men's sight; but in Armenia the ship supplied the people of the country with wooden amulets as antidotes to poison.'

(Gifford 1908 iii 445-6: Eusebius, *Praeparatio Evangelica* ix 11-2)

4(8) Jewish Accounts i) The Genesis Account of Noah's Flood

This version is the primary source of all subsequent Jewish versions, though itself evidently indebted to the earlier Mesopotamian versions. Even the story of Jesus stilling the storm (§3(9)), taking place in a boat, may draw on this symbolism. In this sense it amalgamates the two traditions, the rebuke pointing to the conflict myth tradition, the boat to the present theme. The Genesis flood story is generally recognized as composite, melding an account of a forty day and night rainstorm, and one of an irruption from outside the cosmos (the opening up of windows and sluices) of the cosmic ocean.

Now Yahweh saw how great was the evil of mankind on the earth... And Yahweh was sorry that he had made mankind on the earth. Then Yahweh said, 'I shall wipe out mankind (*'ādām*), whom I have made, from the surface of the ground (*'ᵃdāmâ*), man and beast, creeping things and birds, for I am sorry that I ever made them!' But Noah had found favour in Yahweh's sight...

Then God[1] said to Noah... 'Make yourself an ark (*tēbâ*) with ribs of cypress... And this is how you will make it: the ark must be 300 cubits long, 50 cubits wide, and 30 cubits high. You must make a roof for the ark... and you shall put a door in the side of the ark, (and) put in lower, middle and upper decks. For I am going to bring a flood upon the earth, to destroy all flesh with the breath of life in it under heaven: everything on earth shall perish...'

'Go with all your family aboard the ark, for I have found you (alone) righteous in this generation. From all pure animals you are to take seven (pairs?), male and female, and from the animals which are not pure you are to take two, a male and a female... For in seven days' time I shall make it rain for forty days and forty nights I shall destroy every creature I have made...In the 600th year of Noah's life, on the 17th day of the second month , on that very day, all the springs of the great deep burst forth, and the windows of heaven were opened[3]. Then it rained on the earth for forty days and forty nights...

Now the flood was forty days on the earth. And the waters rose up, and lifted the ark, and it rose above the earth. And the waters rose up increasingly above the earth, and the ark floated upon the surface of the waters. And the waters rose up even more over the earth and all the highest mountains under heaven were covered... And he (Yahweh) destroyed every creature on the surface of the ground, from men to cattle, and every creeping thing, and all the birds of heaven; he destroyed them, and only Noah and those with him in the ark remained...

Now at the end of forty days Noah opened the hatch he had made in the ark, and released a raven, which flew back and forth (and returned?[4]) till the waters dried up from the earth. Then he released the dove to see whether the waters had receded from the ground. But the dove could find no perch and returned to him in the ark, for the water was over the entire surface of the earth... So he waited seven days more, and released the dove again from the ark. And the dove returned to him in the evening with a fresh olive-leaf in its beak, and Noah knew that the waters were receding from the earth. Then he waited seven more days and released the dove, and it did not return to him again... Then Noah built an altar to Yahweh... and he burnt holocausts upon the altar. And Yahweh smelt the soothing odour[5], and said to himself, 'I shall never again curse the ground on account of man...'

(*Genesis* 6-8, excerpts)

1   Note that the narrative varies in its reference to the deity, now Yahweh, now God ('*elōhîm*). This has often been seen as evidence for a conflation of the two versions of the story (the so-called P and J sources) mentioned in the introduction. The story is certainly composite, since it records different times for the flood, different meteorological processes, and so on.

2   The same term is used for the 'basket of bulrushes' in which the infant Moses is placed. The symbolism is inescapable.

3   The cosmological theme is particularly clear here: the story is an anti-cosmogony, a reversal of the process of creation. Formerly (§§2(15), 3(6)), the primaeval waters had been separated by the interpolation of the 'world' (*tēbēl*, the habitable world, §§2(20-1)). Now this process is reversed, as the barriers are pierced with windows and sluices opening. This image is far stronger than the weaker idea of forty days of rain: an older (rain) account has been melded with a younger (anti-cosmogonic) one, as a powerful metaphor for the destruction of the Jewish state ('their whole world'!) by Babylon in 597, 587-6 and 582 BCE. Cf. also §4(18). Consequently, Noah's subsequent emergence from the ark represents a new creation.

4   Did the raven return? The text reads *wāšôb*, the infinitive absolute of *šûb*, 'to return': but see English translations, which follow the Greek, omitting the verb.

5   A technical term from the cult, of 'acceptable' sacrifices. Cf. the Mesopotamian descriptions §4(5, 6) and 10(2).

The birds featuring in the ancient Near Eastern versions:

Ziusudra	—	—		—	
Atraḥasis	—	—		—	
Utnapishtim	Dove	Swallow		—	Raven
Noah	Raven	Dove	Dove (Olive Branch)	Dove

Ravens often appear as divine messengers in ancient Near Eastern tradition.

4(9) Jewish Accounts ii): From the Book of Jubilees

The Book of Jubilees, written in the second century BCE, gives an account of the primaeval and early 'history' of Israel (as told in the Pentateuch), with a number of additions from the pseudepigraphical materials. Time is measured in 'weeks' (a 'week' is seven years) and jubilees (seven 'weeks' = forty-nine years), based on a 364-day calendar, as apparently at Qumran, where cosmology was perhaps influenced by *Jubilees*.

And the Lord said that he would destroy everything which was upon the earth, both men and cattle, and beasts, and fowls of the air, and that which moveth on the earth. And he commanded Noah to make him an ark, that he might save himself from the waters of the flood. And Noah made the ark in all respects as he commanded him, in the 27th jubilee of years, in the fifth week in the fifth year (on the new moon of the first month). And he entered in the sixth year thereof, in the second month, on the new moon of the second month, till the 16th; and he entered, and all that we·brought to him into the ark...

1   And the Lord opened seven flood-gates of heaven[1],
     and the mouths of the fountains of the great deep,
        seven mouths in number.
   And the flood-gates began to pour down water from the heaven
5   40 days and 40 nights,
   and the fountains of the deep also sent up waters,
        until the whole world was full of water[2].
   And the waters increased upon the earth:
        fifteen cubits did the waters rise above all the high mountains,
10   and the ark was lifted up above the earth,
        and it moved upon the face of the waters.

And the water prevailed upon the face of the earth five months — 150 days. And the ark went and rested on the top of Lûbâr, one of the mountains of Ararat... All the mouths of the abysses of the earth were opened, and the water began to descend into the deep below... And on the new moon of the third month he went forth from the ark, and built an altar on that mountain.

And he made atonement for the earth, and took a kid and made atonement by its blood for all the guilt of the earth; for everything that had been on it had been destroyed, save those that were in the ark with Noah.

(Charles 1913, 20-1; *Jubilees* 5:20-6:2)

1   It is not clear whether we are to imagine the single firmament with seven apertures, or whether there is one aperture for each of seven increasingly remote heavens. On the latter conception cf. §§2(19, 23). The idea of more than three heavens (up to nine) is found in several late Jewish texts. See Charlesworth 1985, 959-60 for references.

1   Note the conception of the world as a hollow space that can be filled with water. Strictly, the *tēbēl* (the 'habitable earth'), appears to have been a disc, but here it includes the space above, presumably as far as the firmament.

4(10) Jewish Accounts iii): The Patriarchs at Sea

The Testaments of the Twelve Patriarchs are a series of writings, originating in the second century BCE, with a number of early Christian additions, and purporting to be death-bed confessions by the sons of Jacob, and anticipating the tribe's future in the eschatological era.

This seems to a hybrid story, like §3(9); it combines the motifs of the boat (Noah's flood) with a storm which is calmed (an echo of the conflict myth). It is evidently a parable of some period in history, possibly the exile and return, or perhaps a later era. The linking of Levi and Judah echoes the doctrine of two messiahs, current in the Hellenistic era and in Qumran (§§6(13), 11(14)).

I saw our father Jacob standing at the sea of Jamnia and we, his sons, with him. And behold, a ship came sailing by without sailors and pilot, and the ship was inscribed 'Jacob'. And our father said to us: 'Let us climb into our ship!' As we entered, there came a violent storm, and a tempest of strong wind. And our father, who was holding the helm, was taken from us. And overtaken by the storm we were driven over the sea. And the ship was filled with water, beaten here and there by the waves, so that it was shattered. And Joseph fled upon a little boat. And we also were divided upon ten planks. And Levi and Judah were together. We were all scattered then to the ends of the earth. But Levi, girt about with sackcloth, prayed for us all to the Lord. And as the storm ceased, the ship came upon the land as in peace. And behold, our father came, and we all rejoiced with one accord.

(Charles 1913, 338; *Testament of Naphtali* 6:1-10)

4(11) Greek Accounts i):
Apollodorus' Account of Deucalion and Pyrrha

Apollodorus flourished in Athens in the second century BCE, and wrote a compendium of Greek mythology. Prometheus angered Zeus by bringing fire to men. When men became corrupt, Zeus sent a flood. Deucalion, king of Phthia in Thessaly, son of Prometheus, was warned by his father.

When Zeus would destroy the men of the Bronze Age, Deucalion by the advice of Prometheus constructed a chest, and having stored it with provisions he embarked in it with Pyrrha. But Zeus by pouring heavy rain from heaven flooded the greater part of Greece, so that all men were destroyed, except a few who fled to the high mountains in the neighbourhood. It was then that the mountains in Thessaly parted, and that all the world outside the Isthmus and Peloponnesus was overwhelmed. But Deucalion, floating in the chest over the sea for nine days and as many nights, drifted to Parnassus, and there, when the rain ceased, he landed and sacrificed to Zeus, the god of Escape (Zeus Phuxios). And Zeus sent Hermes to him and allowed him to choose what he would, and he chose to get men. And at the bidding of Zeus he took up stones and threw them over his head, and the stones which Deucalion threw became men, and the stones which Pyrrha threw became women. Hence people were called metaphorically 'people' (λαος) from 'a stone' (λαας).

(Frazer 1921 i, 53-5: Apollodorus, The Library, 1.7.2)

4(12) Greek Accounts ii):
Lucian's Account of Deucalion and Pyrrha

Lucian came from Samosata in Syria, living in the second century CE. *De Dea Syria*, from which this comes, is an account of the cult of Atargatis of Hierapolis, modern Membij. It appears to be a retelling of Apollodorus' account, but Lucian has the event take place in Asia, with the receding waters disappearing into a hole in the ground at Hierapolis, over which Deucalion built the temple of Hera (Atargatis). For all Lucian's assurance that this is how the Greeks tell the story, it is of course Semitic in origin.

The men of the original creation... were rebellious, and wilful, and performed unholy deeds, disregarding the sanctity of oaths and hospitality, and behaving cruelly to suppliants; and it was for these misdeeds that the great destruction fell upon them. Straightway the earth discharged a vast volume of water, and the rivers of heaven came down in streams and the sea mounted high. Thus everything became water and all men perished; Deucalion alone was saved for another generation, on the score of his wisdom and piety. The manner of his salvation was as follows: he placed his children and his wives in an ark of vast size, and he himself also entered in. Now, when he had embarked, there came to him wild boars and horses, and generations of lions and serpents, and all the other beasts which roam the earth, all in couples. He welcomed them all. Nor did they harm him; and friendship remained amongst them as Zeus himself ordained. These, one and all, floated in the ark as long as the flood remained. This is the legend of Deucalion as told by the Greeks.

(Strong and Garstang, 1913, 50-1: Lucian *De Dea Syria* 12-3 adapted)

The narrative continues at §6(31).

4(13) Latin Account in Ovid i) Deucalion and Pyrrha

Ovid was born in 43 BCE, and travelled widely in the Mediterranean world. His composition the *Metamorphoses* is a long poem about mythological transformations.

1   'Wherever old Ocean roars around the earth,
       I must destroy the race of men...'
    He laid aside the bolts which cyclopean hands had forged.
    He preferred a different punishment,
5   to destroy the human race beneath the waves
        and to send down rain from every quarter of the sky.
    Straightway he shuts the North Wind up in the cave of Aeolus,
        and all blasts soever that put the clouds to flight;
        but he lets the South Wind loose.
10 Forth flies the South Wind with dripping wings,
        his awful face shrouded in pitchy darkness.
    His beard is heavy with rain;
        water flows in streams down his hoary locks;
        dark clouds rest upon his brow;
15   while his wings and garments drip with dew...
    The wrath of Jove is not content with the waters from
            his own sky;
        his sea-god brother aids him with auxiliary waves...
    Neptune himself smites the earth with his trident...
    Most living things are drowned outright.
20 Those who have escaped the water,
        slow starvation at last overcomes through lack of food.
    Mount Parnassus lifts its two peaks' skywards,
        high and steep, piercing the clouds.
    When here Deucalion and his wife, borne in a little skiff,
        had come to land...
25   they first worshipped the Corycian nymphs and the mountain
            deities,
        and the goddess, fate-revealing Themis, who in those days kept
            the oracles.
    There was no better man than he,

none more scrupulous of right,
nor than she was any woman more reverent of the gods...
30   When now Jove saw...
that only one man was left...
and but one woman too,
both innocent and both worshippers of God,
he rent the clouds asunder...
35   Then too the anger of the sea subsides...
The world was indeed restored.
But when Deucalion saw that it was an empty world,
and that deeps silence filled the desolated lands,
he burst into tears...
40   The goddess was moved and gave this oracle:
Depart hence,
and with veiled heads and loosened robes
throw behind you the bones of your great mother!'...
And the stones —
45   who would believe it unless ancient tradition vouched for it? —
began at once to lose their hardness...
to grow soft slowly,
and softened to take on form...
Hence come the hardness of our race and our endurance of toil;
50   we give proof from what origin we are sprung.

(Miller 1956 i, 15, 21-31:
Ovid *Metamorphoses* 1.186-7, 259-415, excerpts, adapted)

I   On the twin peaks of Mount Parnassus cf. §5(5).

4(14) Latin Account in Ovid ii): Cerambus

Another brief allusion by Ovid, in which a further survivor of the flood is disclosed.
Cerambus was also mentioned by Pausanias.

Old Cerambus...
by the aid of the nymphs borne up into the air on wings,
at the time when the heavy earth had sunk beneath the overwhelming
sea,
escaped Deucalion's flood undrowned.

(Miller 1956 i, 367: Ovid *Metamorphoses* 7.353-6)

The apparent absence of a flood-story from Ugarit is deceptive. A small fragment (RS
22.421) of a version of *Atrahasis* was found in 1959. A fragment of *Gilgamesh*, which if
complete would have given another account, was found in 1994, in addition to a
fragment at Megiddo (*4.4.1). There are also fragments from Hattusa, the Hittite
capital, from Assyrian sites, and from Emar on the central Euphrates. It appears, then,
that the flood tradition was known throughout the Fertile Crescent.

There has been much debate over the years about the matter of the historicity of the 'Flood'. As a plausible historical event (even if often repeated) it is obviously more credible than a creation story. Naturally enough, there have been many enquiries into its possible origin(s) as a narrative. This has been given a fascinating twist by a recent publication, Ryan and Pitman 1999, which examines evidence for a catastrophic flooding of the Black Sea depression *ca* 5600 BCE, as a result of the rise of sea levels following the end of the last Ice Age (*ca* 10000 BCE). This would have resulted in a dispersal of Neolithic communities settled around the earlier freshwater lake, and explains subsequent distinctive cultural changes in south-eastern Europe, the Crimea, the Balkans and Anatolia, with further implications for Egypt, Mesopotamia and the Levant. The earliest Flood story in literature (*Atrahasis*) is from *ca* 1700 BCE, but is copied from older texts. These in turn undoubtedly derive from earlier oral tradition. As noted above (§3(16)), there are substantial reasons for suspecting the flood and dragon-killing traditions to be essentially two versions of the same tradition: one treats it cosmogonically, the other eschatologically, and floods lead to new creations. Whether an ultimate link with the 'Black Sea event' can be sustained for either is another matter, however. See Mallowan 1964 for an attempt to locate the flood in the early third millennium BCE. Initial reactions from scholars specializing in Ancient Near Eastern studies are at least very cautious, when not simply negative.

Though they have a number of mythic features, it is tempting to treat the traditions, for all their extravagances, as deriving from an early historical core. But we must remember that even today history can be heavily ideological and even mythical in character, and the hope we can establish 'historical facts' (already so difficult to establish in modern historiography!) in ancient materials is likely to prove elusive. In the present instance, the problem is further beset with the intrinsically symbolic nature of the material.

III Conceptions of and Attitudes to Mortality

A few passages are cited here to give an indication of general conceptions of death and the afterlife in ancient Near eastern thought. While there was a considerably variety of ideas (particularly in Egypt) there was a general pessimism. Death means the undoing of a person's world (cf. the flood stories above), and a return to the precosmic conditions of the primaeval sea is a frequent metaphor.

Such passages belong here, because conceptions of the afterlife obviously related to both temporal and spatial aspects of experience. In so far as 'life' continued (that is, that something survived the death-experience) it was believed to live on, often in attenuated form, in a parallel-time world which could intersect with real time, in a narrative such as *1 Samuel* 28, where Saul invoked the ghost of Samuel (§11(16)). This other world, often conceptualized nowadays in terms of heaven, was generally entirely chthonian, that is, underworldly, in conception.

4(15) Realism in Egypt: Pessimism in the Face of Death

Morenz cites a number of passages like this, which indicate that for all the ritual power and the elaborate mythic constructions, ordinary Egyptians had a healthy fear of death.

Thou who wast rich in people, thou art in the land that likes solitude. He who loved to spread his legs in walking is bound, enwrapped and obstructed. He who liked to dress himself in rich fabrics sleeps in yesterday's cast-off garment.

(Morenz 1973, 187)

4(16) The Mesopotamian View of Death: Utnapishtim's Words to Gilgamesh

Gilgamesh has already been warned off his adventure by the goddess Siduri, who exhorted him to take comfort in family life. Now he has reached Utnapishtim beyond the sea, and he too now warns him of the fragile nature of human life.

1 Do we build a house for ever?
   Do we seal contracts for ever?
   Do brothers divide shares for ever?
   Does hatred persist for ever in the land?
5 Does the river for ever raise up and bring on floods?
   The dragonfly leaves its shell
   that its face might but glance at the face of the sun.
   Since the days of yore there has been no permanence;
   the resting and the dead, how alike they are!
10 Do they not compose a picture of death,
   the commoner and the noble, once they are near to their fate?

(*ANET* 92-3: *Gilgamesh* x col. vi 26-36 = x 309-18)

As well as the watery image of l. 5, note the *context* of the episode: Gilgamesh has crossed the *Apsû* to meet Utnapishtim, hero of the flood. That is, he is *outside* the normal boundary of the cosmos. On the important theme of crossing cosmic boundaries, see §7.

4(17) The Mesopotamian Conception of the Underworld

1 To the Land of No Return, the realm of Ereshkigal, Ishtar,
      the daughter of Sin, set her mind.
      Yea, the daughter of Sin set her mind to the Dark House,
      the abode of Irkalla,
   to the house which none leave who have entered it,
      to the road from which there is no way back,
5 to the house wherein the entrants are bereft of light,
      where dust is their fare and clay their food,
   where they see no light, residing in darkness,
      where they are clothed like birds, with wings for garments,
      and where over door and bolt is spread dust...

(*ANET* 107: *The Descent of Ishtar*)

Cited from §2(23) lines 1-9.

4(18) Dying in Ugarit i):
Death as a Divine Power — the Appetite of Mot

Baal has sent messengers to Mot, the god of death. This is part of the truculent response they bring back from him.

> 1 My appetite is the appetite of the monster of the deep[1],
>   the desire of the shark in the sea.
>   As wild bulls yearn for pools,
>   or the hind longs for the spring,
> 5   so I find them indeed,
>   my throat consumes clay,
>   I devour it by the handful,
>   if my seven portions are on the plate,
>   and Nahar[2] has filled my cup...

(Wyatt 1998a, 116-9, adapted; KTU 1.5 i 14-22)

1 Literally 'lion of the deep', reading conjecturally *lbim thm*. See §3(11) n. 2, and cf. Wyatt 1998a, 116 n. 11 for this as an alternative translation. The idea of Death as the primordial monster is another example of the way in which the world's destruction is represented by the mirror image of its creation. Cf. §§4(8) n. 3, 5(7) n. 1.

2 'River': a name of Yam the sea-god.

4(19) Dying in Ugarit ii): a Description of Mot's Gaping Jaws

Mot is not simply 'the god of death'. He is death personified. Ultimately, he devours the entire universe, this description appears to say, giving visual effect to his threat of §4(18).

> [A lip to the ea]rth,
>   a lip to the heavens,
>   and a tongue to the stars.

(Wyatt 1998a, 120; KTU 1.5 ii 2-3)

This is a description of the gaping, all-devouring mouth of Mot, god of death. Cf. the description of Kṛṣṇa's open mouth, devouring the world, in *Bhagavad Gītā* 11.

4(20) Dying in Ugarit iii):
Aqhat's Response to Anat's Offer of Everlasting Life

Aqhat, offered everlasting life by Anat in exchange for his bow, rebuffs her offer with this statement of realism in the face of death. See further at §9(3).

> 1 Man, (at his) end, what will he receive?
>   What will he receive, a man (as his destiny?
>   Silver? will be poured on his head,
>   gold?[1] on top of his skull,

5 [and] the death of all I shall die,
    and I shall surely die.

(Wyatt 1998a, 274; KTU 1.17 vi 35-8)

1   'Silver... gold...'. See Wyatt 1998a, 274 n. 115 for discussion of the textual
     difficulty. Pardee 2000, 63, is unhappy with my approach. The proper
     appreciation of the relationship between archaeology and philology is often
     rather fraught.

Excerpt from §9(3). Aqhat's apparent allusion to death masks may refer to those
discovered in Mycenaean tombs, and replicated in the faces on anthropoid coffins in
Egyptian and Philistine funerary practice. The tombs at Ugarit, corbelled stone
structures underneath the floors of houses and palaces, are of Mycenaean type.

4(21) Dying in Ugarit iv):
The End of the World, and Entrance to the Underworld

Baal is feared dead. Invited to go to meet Mot, he had abjectly obeyed the summons.

[We travelled to the en]ds of the [e]ar[th, to the edge of the abyss];
we came to 'Pleasure', the land of pasture,
'Delight', the steppe by the shore of death.

(Wyatt 1998a, 126; KTU 1.5 vi 3-7)

1   Ugaritic *qṣm arṣ* (restored from KTU 1.16 iii 3) is similar, though without the
     allusion to the ocean, in conception to the *aps* (Hebrew *'epes*) discussed at
     §3(18).

Here, the divine messengers report to Anat, describing how they go as far as the
cosmic boundary in the search for the dead Baal. Note the spatial metaphor for death.
In the next example, §4(22), Pharaoh and his army are destroyed because they try
improperly to cross the *yam sûf*, the cosmic boundary. Cf. §§4(8) n. 3, 4(16) n., and §7,
for the idea of crossing boundaries.

4(22) The End of the World in Israelite Thought i):
Hymn to Yahweh

This is a hymn ostensibly sung by Miriam, celebrating the Exodus (the 'Song of the
Sea'). The *yam sûf* marks the end of the world and the death of Pharaoh and his army.
It marks the end of the world, but new life for the Israelites. The sea is a medium of
transformation, from one dimension to another, be it life to death, or death to life. It
thus becomes a cipher of resurrection to new life in baptism.

The chariots of Pharaoh and his army he cast into the sea:
    and the choicest of his warriors were overwhelmed
        in the Sea of Extinction.
The deeps covered them:
    they went down into the depths like a stone.

(*Exodus* 15:4-5)

4(23) The End of the World in Israelite Thought ii):
The Two Deeps

The present psalm is cast in the form of a lament by the devotee on his way to the tabernacle (v. 4), perhaps on the Feast of Tabernacles? He mulls over his doubts, and meditates on the two deeps, which well up to overwhelm him. On the other hand the mutual colloquy of the two deeps appears to bring a message of renewal and hope. On the conception of two deeps see §6(2), Ugarit, and §6(33), Israel, where they speak. This appears to be the junction of the bodies of water sometimes distinguished as *apsû* and *ti'amat* in Akkadian texts.

> Deep is calling to deep; at the roar of your cataracts,
> All your breakers and your billows wash over me.

(Psalm 42:8)

Cf. citation of this passage at §6(33) n. 1.

4(24) The Underworld in Israelite Thought i):
The Conception of the Underworld in Job

The book of *Job* was probably composed in the fifth or fourth century BCE, though it is undoubtedly founded on older tradition. For its possible prehistory see de Moor 1994. It is an attempt at a comprehensive theodicy, pitting the righteous Job against the wiles of an energetic adversary (*haśśāṭān*, forerunner of Satan: see §3(11) n. 2). The eschatological meaning commonly read into *Job* 19:25-6 ('And I know that my redeemer is alive…') is certainly not original to the sense of the text. The present passage and the following, §4(25), more accurately reflect Job's real beliefs. His anger is precisely because he believes that he must be vindicated in the present life.

> 1 Are not the days of my life coming to an end?
> Withdraw from me, leave me a little joy,
>   before I go to the place of no return,
> the land of darkness and deep shadow,
> 5   a land of gloom like the dead of night,
>
> deep shadow with no distinctions[1]
> and it is like the dead of night.

(Job 10:20-2)

1   That is, it is too dark for distinctions to be made. The final verse is somewhat ponderous, and maybe a number of glosses have been incorporated into the text.

To this passage cf. §2(23) 1-9 = §4(17) for the similar Mesopotamian idiom.

4(25) The Underworld in Israelite Thought ii): Job's Discomfort

This continues the sentiment of §4(24), and gives it even more horrible detail. Sheol has nothing positive to offer the dead.

> 1 All I anticipate is Sheol[1] for my home,
>   and making my bed in the dark.

I tell the grave: You are my father,

and call the worm my mother and my sister[2].

5 Where then is my hope?

Who can see any happiness for me?

Will they go down with me into Sheol,

or sink with me into the dust?

(Job 17:13-6)

1   The underworld.

2   'Father... mother... sister...' Poetic rigour requires that either 'and my sister' be omitted, or 'and my brother' be inserted after 'my father'.

4(26) Death as Ultimate Separation from Yahweh

This passage gives the theological basis for the despair (or at any rate profound resignation) that can be discerned in some texts illustrating Israelite religion, implicit in §§4(24, 25).

Come back, Yahweh, rescue my life[1],

Save me for the sake of your steadfastness.

For no one in death remembers you:

who sings to you in Sheol?[2]

(Psalm 6:5-6, EV 4-5)

1   Hebrew *napšî*. The term *nepeš* can have a variety of nuances. Its primary sense is probably 'thorax', seat of breath, and by extension breath as a sign of life. It can mean little more than 'me'. Note that it is parallel to the 'me' of the following colon.

2   A graphic expression of separation from Yahweh, and therefore of the futility of a frail survival. In this archaic world-view, death is not total annihilation: the dead descend into the underworld (Sheol), and have a shadowy, unhappy existence, or are deemed to be asleep. It also implies that Yahweh has no jurisdiction in the underworld. This represents an early Israelite view, in which Yahweh's authority is limited to the territory of Israel. The underworld is not in his domain. This is probably however not a formal limitation on Yahweh, but a matter of delegated responsibility. Cf. Ugaritic thought, in which there appears to be a division of the universe between Yam (ocean), Mot (underworld) and Baal, the world of living things, while El, their father, remains in overall control. Contrast *Psalm* 139:8, where the conception of Yahweh as cosmic lord is emphasized, and the divine presence is in the furthest reaches of the heavens and the underworld. The earlier view precedes the rise of monotheism, while the later one presupposes it (the delegees have been paid off, though soon replaced by infinite hierarchies of angelic bureaucrats). *Deuteronomy* 32:8-9 represents an intermediate stage, where El (= Yahweh) is already supreme deity (as El had always been, head of the pantheon), and delegates the control of other nations (and thus of their territories), to various other gods (who later become angels).

4(27) Jonah's Hymn in the Belly of the Fish

The story of *Jonah* was probably composed in the Persian period, to counter narrow introspection and exclusivism on the part of Israel's theological leaders. The poem cited is almost certainly an independent composition drafted in to express Jonah's distress in the belly of the great fish (*dag gādôl*: it is *not* said to be a whale, though we may ask, purely rhetorically, whether the author has in mind the same monster as threatened Andromeda). It gives an eloquent account of the conception of the underworld in watery terms (for Yam and Mot virtually coalesce in the underworld, which is the location of the subterranean ocean, Yam, and the domain of death, Mot. For a good coverage of the imagery used to describe the underworld see Tromp 1969.

> 1 I called in my distress to Yahweh[1],
>   to Yahweh, and he heard me.
>   From the belly of Sheol I cried for help:
>   you heard my voice.
> 5 You cast me into the depths,
>   into the heart of Sea,
>   and River encircled me.
>   All your breakers and your waves passed over me.
>   ...
>   Waters washed round me up to my throat;
> 10   Deep encircled me.
>   Extinction was wound round my head
>   at the roots of the mountains.
>   I went down into the underworld,
>   its coils were about me for ever.

(Jonah 2:3-7)

1   Hebrew *lî*. I have taken this to represent *lyhwh*. The Greek supports this.

For discussion of this passage see Wyatt 1996b, 102-5. Note the water imagery in §§4(16, 22-3) and here. The *yam sûf* image (§2(35)) is explicit in the allusion to 'extinction' in l. 11 (v. 6). The term *sûf* is translated differently in different versions (e.g. JB 'seaweed').

Chapter 5

THE MOUNTAIN AT THE CENTRE OF THE WORLD

The cosmic centre is reality, and is commonly represented by a mountain, either a local landmark, or even an artificial construction such as a temple platform. It is seen as the source of all benefits, and as a point of intersection of all dimensions of the world. It is the point of access to heaven, and the place at which benefits may be drawn up from the underworld.

Suggested Reading:

Clifford 1972; Keel 1978, 113-20; Stadelmann 1970; Wensinck 1916; Wyatt 1995a; id. 1996b, 27-52.

5.1 Introduction

5.1.1 If the end of the world is bounded by the ever-flowing and fluid Ocean, whose liquidity (always 'becoming') symbolizes its lack of 'being', its ontological opposite is the hard place, the cosmic mountain, at the centre of the world. So powerful is this a symbol of durability, strength and security, that it is hardly surprising that Yahweh is frequently called 'my rock' (or: 'my mountain').

5.1.2 The classic image of creation in Egypt (§§5(1-3)) was the *ben*-stone (the first dry land) emerging from the abyss (Nu). All temples, whose floors rose gently from the threshold to the sanctuary as the high point, claimed to be the location of the *ben*-stone. Thus temples were intimately linked with creation theology. This principle also lay behind other temple traditions, and all temples were theoretically built on the cosmic mountain. The *ben*-stone belonged to the symbolic complex primaeval mound (*bn*), pyramid (*bnw*), pyramidion (*bnw*), phoenix (*bnw*) and sunrise (*wbn*).

5.1.3 Tower-temples ('ziggurats') in Mesopotamia probably arose naturally, like all tells (ruin-mounds), out of the debris of previous construction. But already by the end of the third millennium BCE it is evident that they were believed to constitute holy mountains. The paradise described in §5(4) is a temporal rather than a spatial image (Dilmun = Bahrain). But as an island surrounded by the sea (*apsû*) it was a type of all world-centres (and therefore of all shrines).

5.1.4 The West Semitic world was dominated by the mental construction of Mount Saphon (§5(5)). This was a 'mountain in the mind', a high point of refuge, which could be variously identified wherever people went. In Ugarit it lay on the northern horizon; in Jerusalem it lay immediately north of the old city, the temple mount (Zion identified with Saphon: §5(12)).

Other sacred places in the Lebanon, Greece, Anatolia and Armenia, appear to have been so identified, and even a sand dune on the border of Egypt was so named, after a local promontory temple (see Semple 1927[1]).

5.2   **The Mountain**

5.2.1   Mount Saphon in Syria has two main peaks (*Kasion* and *Anti-Kasion* in Greek, *Casios* and *Anti-Casios* in Latin). This feature is not only recorded in iconography (and corresponding mythology) but it links it thematically to other mountains (§5(5) n.). Nice examples from the Levant are Gerizim and Ebal at ancient Shechem, and Lebanon and Anti-Lebanon (= Hermon) in the Lebanon.

5.2.2   An important feature of sacred mountains is their implicit, and sometimes explicit, identification as an Omphalos (Greek ὀμφαλος = 'navel'). See §§6(4, 5) for references. Another omphalos in Palestine besides Jerusalem and Gerizim is Mount Tabor, whose name is not to be distinguished from *ṭabbûr*, 'navel'. The omphalos may be the mountain itself, or a specific stone on it, and is commonly associated with a sanctuary, of which remains can be seen on Mount Gerizim.

5.2.3   The idea of the omphalos brings us full circle, to the theme of §1, where we saw our human subjectivity as the source of all perception. The centre of the mountain, which is the centre of the world, is also *our* centre.

---

[1]   While this article does not deal in detail with the Levantine coast, it mentions Baal Saphon (map, p. 354, marked '5') on the northern coast of the Sinai, Tyre, Sidon and (marked but not named) Byblos. The principle of the 'templed promontory', at which local gods were invoked to ensure safe passage by sea, would also cover most settlements up the Levantine coast — Baal Zephon, Tell Haror, Tell Mevtrach, Joppa, Nahariyah, Tell Dor, Carmel, Acre, Zarepath, Beirut, Sarba, Batruna, Tripoli, Orthosia, Antarados (Tartus), Arad (Arwad island), Baniyas, Ras Ibn Hani and Ugarit, and Ras el Bassit (Posidium)... This is a prime example of the use of religion to manage space and make it accessible to human use. On the edge of the ocean, the threshold of oblivion, these shrines brought all the power of the cosmic centre to control chaos. They would also have constituted landmarks visible to sailors at sea. The two temple towers of Ugarit were probably markers for safe navigation through coastal shoals into the haven of Minet El Beida (ancient Maḥadu, 'Port-Town'). On their vertical aspect, see §7 II introduction, n. 2. See also Brody 1998, 39-61.

5.3   Mythology

5.3.1   We might expect an important sacred mountain to feature in mythology. We find that this is the case with Mount Saphon, and the apparent absence of such traditions with other mountains may be that this tradition dominates all others. On the distinctly biblical mythology see below.

5.3.2   Mount Saphon almost plays the part of an actor in the great Baal cycle of myths from Ugarit (Wyatt 1998a, 34-146). It sits, lowering and immobile at the heart of the action; El, chief god, sits enthroned there; the throne is passed from god to god till Baal wins it. It is also the throne of kings (§5(11): cf. §§7(24-26 below).

5.3.3   An important motif implicit in the name Saphon (Ugaritic *ṣapunu* perhaps plays on the idea 'stretched out': Wyatt 1995a, though its formal etymology suggests it is the place where the god 'looks out') is an echo of the conflict myth dealt with above (§§2(9, 10), 3(1-16)). It is the idiom of creation in §5(7). This is tied up with temple symbolism (§§6(16-25)), when the sanctuary is represented as a tent. The biblical tradition echoes an older theme, also found in Greece, Mesopotamia and India, that the fabric of the tent, which is, of course, a microcosm, is made from the skin of the vanquished sea-dragon.

5.3.4   Allusions to the motif in the Bible deal now with victory, now with creation. It also points to the theophany (appearance in glory, in the cult) of the deity, as in §6(24). The psalmist in §6(25) appeals to this tradition as a guarantee that Yahweh will come amongst his people.

5.3.5   We shall see below (§7) the importance of location in the symbolism of contact between gods and men. We anticipate this in §§5(8-10), three passages from an important royal myth, concerning the enthronement of the king. But in these texts, from *Isaiah* 14 and *Ezekiel* 28, the royal figure is a symbol of disobedience: he has overstepped the mark, and appears to want to challenge God himself (El, Yahweh). He will be cast down into the underworld. This is the prototype of myths concerning the fall of Satan. The theme is nuanced, for the king does in fact, in the cult, climb the mountain, as we shall see.

5.3.6   A distinctive element in biblical mythology is the concern of the tradition to make all the different mountain traditions into a coherent series: all are really one and the same (§§5(13-15)). Thus the mountain in the Garden of Eden (in *Ezekiel* 28, not *Genesis* 2-3) is the location of an altar on which Adam sacrificed. Cain and Abel also sacrificed there, as did

Noah (§5(13)). One tradition (§5(13) n.) even identified this mythical altar explicitly with that in Jerusalem. Abraham's offering of Isaac (§5(14) and nn.) in a place called Moriah is in turn explicitly linked with the temple mount in Jerusalem by the Chronicler (§5(15)) when he locates Solomon's temple there, thus identifying Zion and Moriah.

5.3.7   Much of this speculation is found in post-biblical books (the 'Pseudepigrapha'). It has been fashionable to dismiss this as flimsy nonsense detracting from the sublimity of the original biblical text. This view cannot be sustained. The (Hebrew) Bible was a living organism right down to the early years of Christianity, and much of the pseudepigraphical materials were evidently already of considerable antiquity, in many regards preserving first temple (pre-exilic) ideas, which are absent from the *text* of the post-exilic Bible, but obviously not from its thought world.

I   Structures — the Making of Sacred Space

5(1)   The *Ben* Stone in Egypt i): Thebes

This idea represents a typical Egyptian word-play: 'arise' of the sun = *wbn*; the '*ben*-bird' is the Phoenix, the purple heron[1] (*bnw*), a symbol of the rising sun; the '*ben*-stone' is the primaeval mound (also *bnw*) on which the heron alights, represented by the pyramidion (*bnw*) at the top of an obelisk; '*ben*-house' is the temple containing the *ben*-stone in its sanctuary. The image also lies behind §2(2). The main temples in Egypt all identified the sanctuary with the *ben*-stone, and progress down the axis of many temples is a gentle rise to the shrine, where the god took up residence in his divine image, on the highest floor-level in the building.

Thebes (modern Luxor and Karnak, ancient Wast — *w3st*, 'Power', or *iwnw rswt*, 'Heliopolis of the South', *iwnw šm'w*, 'Heliopolis of Upper Egypt') rose to national importance with the rise of the Middle Kingdom, when the Theban kings of dynasties 11 and 12 reunited Egypt under central control. Political legitimacy required theological legitimacy, and the present passage presents Thebes as the archetypal city, dating from creation.

1   The purple heron, *Ardea Purpurea*, is probably intended by the Greek term φοινιξ, which means 'purple'. Cf. §11(45).

1   Thebes is normal beyond every other city.
    The water and land were in her from the first times.
        Then sand came to delimit the fields
    and to create her ground on the hillock;
5   thus earth came into being.

Then men came into being in her,
  to found every city with her real name,
for their name is called 'city'[1]
  only under the oversight of Thebes, the Eye of Ra.

(ANET 8: P. Leiden I 350)

[1]   The Egyptian word *niwt*, 'city' was used as a name for Thebes (cf. 'the city' for London today).

5(2)   The *Ben* Stone in Egypt ii): Heliopolis

Heliopolis, northeast of Cairo, was the seat of the ancient sun-god Atum, an androgynous figure who created the other gods and mankind (see §2(1)). The sun was represented from Old Kingdom times in three forms, as Khepri (*ḫpri*, 'the one who becomes, takes shape' and *ḫprr*, 'scarab') the rising sun, Ra (*rʿ*, 'day, sun') the sun at its zenith and Atum (*tm*, 'completion') the setting sun. Here the sun-god appears as the first and third combined as a merism, thus representing all three forms.

O Atum-Kheprer, you became high on the height,
  you rose up as the *benben*-stone in the Mansion
    of the Phoenix (*bnw*) in Heliopolis,
you spat out Shu,
  you expectorated Tefnut...

(Faulkner 1969, 246: PT 600 adapted)

5(3)   The *Ben* Stone in Egypt iii): Hermopolis

Hermopolis, ancient *ḥmnw*, modern Eshmunein — both Egyptian and Arabic words mean 'Eight-(Town)', referring to Thoth's Ogdoad (see §2(3) n. 1) — was the seat of Thoth, the god of the moon, time and wisdom. This passage from *the Book of the Dead* is part of a long catechism of the theology of Ra. Here Thoth, the creator god of Hermopolis, is identified with him.

I was Atum when I was in the abyss (*nw*);
  I was Ra in his glorious appearings when he began to rule
    what he had made.
What does it mean? It means Ra when he began to rule what he had made,
when he began to appear as king, before the supports of Shu[1] had come into being, when he was upon the hill which is in Hermopolis...

(Faulkner, 1985, 44: from BD 17)

[1]   Shu was the air god. He appeared in iconography as a kneeling figure with raised arms (reminiscent of the Ka), separating Nut the sky goddess from Geb the earth god.

5(4)   Paradise in Sumerian thought — Dilmun

We encountered Dilmun at §4(4), as the place beyond the sea where Ziusudra lived after surviving the flood. It is implicitly the place where Gilgamesh visits Utnapishtim in §4(6), and is identified with modern Bahrain. This is a place where all the common ills of everyday life, with disease, thirst, evil omens and predation, are absent.

1   The Land Dilmun is pure,
      the land Dilmun is clean;
    the land Dilmun is clean,
      the land Dilmun is most bright...
5   In Dilmun the raven utters no cries,
      the *ittidu*-bird utters not the cry of the *ittidu*-bird,
    the lion kills not,
      the wolf snatches not the lamb[1],
      unknown is the kid-devouring wild dog...
10 the sick-eyed says not 'I am sick-eyed',
      the sick-headed says not 'I am sick-headed',
      its old woman says not 'I am an old woman'...
    From the 'mouth whence issues the water of the earth'
      bring thee sweet water from the earth...
15 Let him make thy city drink from it the waters of abundance..
      Let thy well of bitter water become a well of sweet water,
    let thy furrowed farms and fields bear thee grain...

(*ANET* 38: from *Enki and Ninhursag*)

1   Cf. the paradisal image of *Isaiah* 11:6-9, 65:25 (§9(5)).

5(5) Ugaritic Conceptions of the Cosmic Mountain i): Saphon as the Divine Dwelling

Mount Saphon (Jebel el Aqra on the Syro-Turkish frontier) plays an important part in the cosmology not only of Ugaritian, but also Hittite, Greek, Phoenician, Israelite and even Egyptian religious thought. See at §3(14) n. 1. The present two passages should be compared with §§6(2, 3), where further discussion is offered. Each line here unfolds a new dimension of the sacred mountain, dealt with in notes 1-5.

1   Come, and I shall reveal it in the midst of my divine mountain[1],
      Saphon,
    in the sanctuary,[2]
  on the mountain of my inheritance,[3]
    in Paradise,[4]
5   in the hill of victory.[5]

(Wyatt 1998a, 78: KTU 1.3 iii 28-31)

1   As the centre of the world, where deity ultimately resides (because the centre is 'real', §1), the mountain is where oracles and revelation are sought.

2   The sanctuary at Ugarit in the temple of Baal was probably identified with the divine seat on Mount Saphon, as the *ben*-stone was reified in the sanctuary of Egyptian temples.

3   The Baal myths (KTU 1.1-6) deal with a succession of gods who occupy the throne of El. Baal's occupation signifies the 'real' world of historical Ugarit, where Baal was the patron deity, and this relationship of deity and people (and its territory) is expressed in terms of an inheritance. This is the apotheosis of land-tenure. The image is found in Egypt, with great emphasis on Egypt as the inheritance of Horus (§8(3)), occurs of Mot's domain in §5(6) below, and is carried on in Israel, where Zion is Yahweh's, that is, Israel's inheritance. See particularly *Exodus* 15:17 (inheritance as the outcome of divine conflict, as in Ugaritian tradition); *Psalm* 79:1 (lament for loss of temple, 'your inheritance' parallel to 'your temple', which is on Mount Zion); and more generally *Deuteronomy* 32:9 and numerous other passages, where the land in general, epitomized by the mountain, is Israel's inheritance.

4   Ugaritic *n'm* means 'gracious', 'select', 'delightful'. Here it is used as a noun, the name of a place. This mythical location corresponds to the royal garden in the palace grounds, comparable to the 'king's garden' in Jerusalem. See §6(7) and Wyatt 1990b.

5   The mountain is the place of triumph after the victory, but the relationship is more intimate. The substance of the mountain is to be understood as the corpse of Yam (cf. the imagery of the stretching out of the cosmic tent, §§6(16-25)), as the substance of Tiamat is made into the world (§2(10). This may lend an intriguing nuance to the image of Yahweh as 'rock' in *Psalm* 18:3 (EV 2) etc.

Mount Saphon has two peaks, and these appear as an important motif in iconography (see Dijkstra 1991). Two peaks (Gerizim and Ebal) flank the ancient city of Shechem in Israel. Parnassus has two peaks in §4(13). The Lebanon is split by the Beqaa valley separating Lebanon from Anti-Lebanon. Hurowitz 1999 discusses various connections. On the pairing of mountains, cf. the pairing of the tree in Eden, §6(7). The Egyptian term *akhet* (*3ḫt*, 'horizon') is represented by a hieroglyph representing the sun rising over a twin-peaked mountain: ☼. See Wilkinson 1992, 134-5 and §§7(1-11). The following text probably refers to this motif.

5(6) Ugaritic Conceptions of the Cosmic Mountain ii): The Entrance to the Underworld under the Mountain

Baal, now in possession of his palace (temple), sends his messengers to challenge Mot, who considers himself supreme. The content of his message is unfortunately missing, but we have a graphic account of the nature of the underworld. It is a subterranean realm, where Mot rules, a concave kingdom almost parodying the convex kingdom (the mountain) above. This is also the archetypal tomb, for all the dead inhabit Mot's kingdom.

1   So set your face towards the rock of *trǵzz*,[1]
        towards the rock of *trmg*,[1]
        towards the twin peaks of the Ruler of the Underworld.
     Raise the mountain on your hands,
5   the hill on top of your hands,
     and go down into the house of the couch of the earth,

be numbered among those who go down into the earth.
Then set your faces indeed towards his (Mot's) city 'Muddy',
  a pit is the seat of his enthronement,
10   a crevice the land of his inheritance.

(Wyatt 1998a, 112-3: KTU 1.4 viii 1-14)

1   These two terms are Hurrian forms, and remain opaque. The second, *trmg*,
       may contain a naturalized form of the Hurrian divine name Shimegi (the sun-
       god). The two names here probably represent twin peaks of the same
       mountain (Mount Saphon), as in the note to §5(5). The narrative seems to
       equate these with the twin peaks of Saphon. The Greek name of the mountain
       was Κασιον, which is to be interpreted as a transcription into Greek of the
       Ugaritic word *kasiu* (= Hebrew *kissē'*, *kēs*), 'throne'. This is confirmed by the
       fact that the Greeks also called it 'Mount Throne' (Θρονος), and that it was
       called *ks*, 'throne' in Ugaritic in KTU 1.1 iii 12. These mountains form a
       horizon, almost in the Egyptian conception (§§7(1-11)), as the point of
       transition between two dimensions of reality.

5(7)   Israelite Passages on the Mountain i): Creation in Job

This is the image of pitching of the cosmic tent (made of the skin of Yam), as a figure
for creation. See further at §§6(16-25).

He stretches Saphon over chaos (*tôhû*)[1]
  and hangs the underworld over nothingness.

(*Job* 26:7)

1   Cf. Hebrew *tᵉhôm* ('Deep'). Perhaps this should be read here? At the least
       there is a deliberate echo. Cf. §4(18) n. 1.

5(8)   Israelite Passages on the Mountain ii):
The Usurpation of the Divine Throne by the King of Babylon

Caution often leads scholars to treat this and the following passages in isolation. But
they all deal with the same theme, and represent different emphases on it, so that a
synthetic appraisal is not only possible, but required. This is confirmed by many other
passages. Thus the result is a world that is made from the skin and corpse of the sea-
god; at its centre is a mountain, the omphalos, which serves as the divine throne, and
by extension as the royal throne. This is the locus of the sacred garden ('Paradise'),
where the king communes with the gods. It is the place from which he can be
expelled ('cast down') by divine decree. This symbolic geography can be superimposed
on real geography, to fit various localities.

The arrogant claim in this passage is based on a legitimate ascent of the king, whereby
he enters heaven to receive divine authority and wisdom, before coming down to earth
to rule (as does Athtar in §§3(17), 7(16)), where the cultic origin of this tradition is
evident. The whole point of this passage from *Isaiah* is that the king is identified with
Hēlēl ben šaḥar, 'Bright One, son of Dawn' in v. 13, who is Venus as the morning star.
Athtar (Venus) is the apotheosis of kingship. See also §§7(17-21).

I[1] shall ascend to heaven:
  above the stars of El I shall exalt my throne,
and I shall sit on the Mount of Assembly,
  in the recesses of Saphon[2].

(*Isaiah* 14:13)

1   The figure parodied is variously supposed to be an Assyrian, a Babylonian or
         even a Persian king.

2   The Hebrew *yark^{e}tê ṣāpôn* translates the Ugaritic expression *ṣrrt ṣpn*.

5(9)   Israelite Passages on the Mountain iii):
The King of Tyre Speaks

I am El[1]:
I dwell[2] in the dwelling-place of the gods,
  in the heart of the sea[3]...

(*Ezekiel* 28:2)

1   The enthroned king is legitimately 'son of El' (*bn il* = 'a god') in West Semitic
         royal ideology, but to claim identity with El goes beyond acceptable limits.

2   Or: 'am enthroned' (Hebrew *yāšabtî*).

3   Or: 'seas'. This no doubt refers to Tyre as an island fortress. It was only
         joined to the mainland by Alexander the Great, who built a causeway across
         during his siege of the city in 332 BCE. But there is also a cosmological level of
         understanding, which may indeed have been part of the Tyrian worldview, but
         is here used by Ezekiel as his own worldview (that of Israel).

5(10) Israelite Passages on the Mountain iv):
The King of Tyre is Taunted by Ezekiel

This passage combines the imagery of the cosmic mountain and the Garden of Eden,
by giving them the same location. This is undoubtedly to be identified with Mount
Zion, the temple mount, in Jerusalem. For discussion see Wyatt 1990b. While the
identification is explicit only here in the Bible, it is probably to be understood as
implicit in *Genesis* 2-3.

In Eden, the garden of God[1] were you...
  I set you on the holy mountain:
a god you were -
  you walked upon stones of fire.

(*Ezekiel* 28:12, 14)

1   Or: 'the gods'.

5(11) Israelite Passages on the Mountain v):
Yahweh's Declaration at the King's Enthronement

Psalm 2 was part of the enthronement liturgy of the king in Jerusalem. This passage, in which Yahweh says that he has enthroned the king, is comparable to the continuity of divine occupancy of El's throne in the Ugaritian tradition. The throne that is implicitly referred to here is Yahweh's own. Cf. *1 Chronicles* 28:5, 29:23 (= §7(26)).

> But I (Yahweh) have installed my king
>   upon Zion my holy mountain.

(Psalm 2:6)

5(12) Israelite Passages on the Mountain vi):
A Hymn Concerning Mount Zion

Zion's priority over Memphis and Saphon, sacred centres of Egypt and Syria respectively, and even its incorporation of their claims, is here asserted.

> 1 Great is Yahweh and much to be praised,
>   in the city of our god is his holy mountain!
> As beautiful as Memphis,
>   the exaltation of the whole world,
> 5 Mount Zion,
>   in the recesses of Saphon
>   is the city of the Great King!

(Psalm 48:1-2)

For discussion of this passage see Wyatt 1996b, 31-3.

II   The Mountain as Unifying Principle in Tradition

5(13) Noah-Moriah

No explicit link is made in the Hebrew Bible between Noah and Mount Moriah. But rabbinic tradition identified his place of sacrifice (*Genesis* 8:20), which the narrative locates in Armenia (Ararat is Urartu), as the temple mount. It was identified with Adam's altar (the Bible has no tradition of Adam offering sacrifice), which was also used by Cain and Abel.

Then Noah built an altar before the Lord — it is the altar which Adam built at the time he was banished from the garden of Eden and on which he offered an offering, and upon which Cain and Abel offered their offerings. But when the waters of the flood came down it was destroyed. Noah rebuilt it...

(Maher 1992, 43-4: *Targum Jonathan* at *Genesis* 8:20)

This is an Aramaic translation of the Hebrew text of the Bible. The 'Targumists' (translators) often introduced an element of commentary and interpretation into their versions. Maher 1992, 44 n. 16, cites *Genesis Rabba* 34:9: Noah offered a sacrifice 'on the great altar in Jerusalem, where Adam sacrificed'.

5(14) Abraham-Moriah

This is the so-called Aqedah (*ᶜᵃqēdâ*, 'binding'), the 'binding of Isaac' in preparation for his sacrifice. This story became a soteriological parallel to the Christian story of the passion.

Now after these events God appeared to Abraham and said to him, 'Abraham!' He answered, 'Here I am!' Then he said 'Take your only son, whom you love, Isaac, and go to the Land of Moriah[1], and offer him up as a holocaust on one[2] of the mountains, as I shall instruct you'.

(Genesis 22:2)

1.   lit. 'The Land of Moriah' (MT *mōriyyâ*; var. Vulgate *terram visionis* (**mōri'â*): √ *r'h*, which would require interpretation as 'visible', 'being seen'; see *5.3.3 on the etymology of Saphon). This may be part of the plot of the story, which gives Abraham a vision of the 'promised land', not as a historical event in remote antiquity, but as a cipher for return from exile, a theme which runs throughout the Pentateuch, an exilic composition. This interpretation is supported by v. 14, where Abraham names the (hitherto unnamed) place *yhwh yir'ê*, not 'Yahweh provides', but 'Yahweh is seen' (the verb should probably be read *yērā'ê*, Niphal: *BHS* app.). The MT *mōriyyâ* supports the Samaritan identification of the place with Mount Gerizim (Moreh), their sacred mountain.

2.   'One of the mountains', or the highest (*ᵃᶜḥād* = 'the most prominent') mountain'. This is Mount Zion, the temple mount.

5(15) Temple-Moriah

Then Solomon began to build Yahweh's temple in Jerusalem on Mount Moriah, where he had appeared[1] to his father David, who had acquired 'the place of David'[2] at the threshing floor of Ornan the Jebusite[3].

(2 Chronicles 3:1)

1.   The Chronicler uses the same √ *r'h* as a midrash on the name Moriah. Cf. §5(14) n. 1.

2.   On the technical sense of *māqôm*, 'place', see §7(22) n. 1.

3.   'Ornan', appearing as 'Araunah' (*'rwnh*, but read *'wrnh*, with Qere) in 2 *Samuel* 24, was the previous king of Jerusalem, to be identifed with 'Uriah the Hittite', whom David had murdered. See Wyatt 1985b.

5(16) Moriah = Zion = Eden

This equation is the implication of §§5(7-12) viewed synoptically. Cf. §5(10) n. It is in turn to be linked with Mount Saphon of the Ugaritian tradition, which in turn is identified as *har mōᶜēd*, the 'Mountain of Assembly', where the gods gather in the divine council, common to all ancient Near Eastern tradition.

Chapter 6

The Temple at the Centre of the World

The observations made of the mountain at the beginning of §5 all apply to the temple. As a human construction, it represents the epitome of all cultural and cultic activity. Its sacred nature is often represented in terms of its divine, rather than human, construction. At the least, the gods or a god chose it, as a point of self-disclosure to his or her worshippers.

Suggested Reading:

Cook 1974; Fox 1988, 1-47; George 1993; Haran 1985; Hayman 1986; Hurowitz 1992; Kapelrud 1963; Keel 1978, 113-20; Parpola 1993; Patai 1948; Shafer 1998; Wensinck 1916; Widengren 1950; Wyatt 1990b, 1996b, 130-71.

6.1 Introduction

6.1.1 It should be clear by now that we are building up a composite picture, with a universe made not just out of 'natural things out there', but of things constructed in the mind by human experience, cerebration and imagination. The world we see and experience is inescapably a world we have created, 'a human world'. Religion is the means by which this world is conceptualized, reified and maintained.

6.1.2 We may recapitulate the two accounts we have already given of the centre, the individual human body (§1) and the cosmic mountain (§5), which we have seen to be constructed from the corpse of the sea-dragon. Thus all the cosmology (with its processes in §§2-4) locks together in a satisfying, if at first glance rather confusing, whole. Note that we include paradise imagery in the discussion, for as *Ezekiel* 28 indicates, the garden ('paradise': Hebrew *pardēs* is borrowed from Persian *pairi-daēẓa*, a royal garden) lies on the sacred mountain. The biblical Garden of Eden is to be identified with 'the king's garden' in Jerusalem (Wyatt 1990b).

6.1.3 Temples in the ancient world had gardens. For they were primarily the houses where the gods dwelt; and just as any person of importance lives in a spacious dwelling with a large household of staff, and gardens for pleasurable strolls, so the gods were provided with leisure space. Even the Bible is familiar with this world of thought, for Yahweh 'strolls in the garden in the cool of the day' (*Genesis* 3:8). The garden had trees, and a familiar cultic theme was the tree of life, frequently represented in iconography on reliefs and paintings.

6.1.4   However, our main theme in this chapter is the centrality of the temple, for it is, as we have seen, to be identified with the omphalos, the cosmic mountain, and finally, human subjectivity. The centre is reality.

6.2   Egypt

The passages at §§2(3), 5(1-3) reflect the tradition that Egyptian temples were built on the first land to emerge from the primordial abyss, the *ben*-stone, on which the primaeval sun-god, the Phoenix (*bnw*), alighted. Some Egyptian temples are well-preserved, and their main features are clear. The seven-fold cosmic symbolism (§§2(19-23) of the structure at Edfu is clear, as you walk from the temenos entrance up the main axis to the shrine-room.   §6(1), from the dedication inscription of Seti I's mortuary temple at Abydos, takes the symbolism of centrality for granted rather than describing it, but sees the axis of divine father and son as reaching out to the underworld and the heavens. Abydos, as 'region of eternity', has the aura of a world-centre.

6.3   The Temple at the Centre: West Semitic Imagery

6.3.1   El dwells in a shrine which is a) a tent-shrine and b) seven-fold in structure (§§6(2-3)). We have also noted the omphalos imagery of §6(4-5). All sanctuaries are *implicitly* 'navels of the earth', for these are architectural representations of human subjectivity.

6.3.2   Sacred trees appear in the iconography of many traditions, and no doubt real trees featured in the cult. Thus in the royal cultus at Luxor the leaves of the Persea Tree were inscribed with the names of the Pharaoh, and in the *Book of the Dead* (§6(6)) a tree-goddess nourished the dead. Assyrian reliefs depict the king performing a ritual act around a tree, which may be the pollination of the flowers. Parpola 1993 has traced the tree's symbolism down to the early mediaeval construction of the Jewish kabbalistic tree of life. There is otherwise little direct evidence of the ritual use of trees outside Israel.

6.3.3   In Israel, we are familiar with the *two* trees, of knowledge and of life, in the Garden of Eden (§6(7), a world centre (§6(14)), and the garden of the royal temple cult. They belong to royal ideology. The tree (probably of life) was identified with the goddess Asherah (recently recognized as consort of Yahweh), who was mother of the king. A stylized tree probably signified her presence in the sanctuary. It was later regarded as offensive, and destroyed (§6(8)). The tree (probably in this case of knowledge) also represented kings, and developed into a messianic symbol (§§6(10-13)). Knowledge, in the form of royal wisdom, was an important attribute of kings. The tree survived in Jewish iconography in the form of the Menorah, symbolizing creation, the Light of the World, and the King.

6.3.4 We see how the tent, prototype of the temple, is made from the skin or the corpse of the primaeval dragon (Tiamat and analogues: §§5(7), 6(16-25)). There is evidence that early tent shrines were in use before brick and stone ones were constructed (cf. the biblical symbol of the tabernacle, prototype of the temple), and this lived on in iconography. A tent sanctuary was discovered at Timna in southern Israel.

6.4 The Temple Joining Heaven and Earth

While this is the practical effect of temple cult, putting people in touch with their gods, it is expressed in more deliberately cosmological terms. The point of the junction is communication between the two, allowing the benefits of cult to reach the gods (they were seen as being fed by their servants, like great lords), and for their power to be transmitted downwards as blessing (a materialistic concept, as in *Deuteronomy* 28:1-8). Names of temples (§6(29)) reflected their role, and the parody of the Babel story (§6(30)) accurately captures their function in stabilizing, unifying and empowering society (all good political aspirations!).

6.5 The King as Temple Builder

6.5.1 We have seen how the gods first of all managed their own affairs, and men were made as substitutes, to serve them (§2(12, 18)). Thus the gods originally made their own houses (sc. temples), §8(7). Afterwards, the (human) servants did so. 'The servant of god X' is a common expression for a king. Adam is put into the Garden of Eden to till the soil. He is Yahweh's 'servant' or 'gardener' (*ᶜebed yhwh*). The Egyptian king is *ḥm.f*, which may mean 'his (the god's) servant'[1]. So temple building is an important part of a king's public duties. Numerous inscriptions attest the fact (e.g. §§6(26-7, and cf. 28)). This is in turn an outworking of the king's representative role as the chief inhabitant of the gods' world. It is a signal mark of royal piety.

6.5.2 The king as a warrior repeats in his battles the primordial battle fought by the god who killed the dragon (Wyatt 1998b, §3(3) n.). Since the

---

[1]   But see §2(11) n. 1.

myth had cosmogonic overtones, even when these are not explicit, it follows that this element too is transferred to the king. The representation of the king as temple-builder makes a theological statement about the king (see §7 for further discussion), which, since he represents the whole community, is a general affirmation of life and the establishment of culture.

6.6   The Temple constructed over the Ocean, with Access to It

6.6.1 We have noted that the Gihon (the name of the spring below Jerusalem) was also a cosmic river (§6(14)) and the surrounding world ocean (§§2(30) n., 2(31-5)). This water needed to be tapped to bring life to the community. So water-symbolism, and indeed water works, were an important part of temple construction and practice. Temples had a replica of the Ocean. Some in Egypt are still visible, and even full (as at Karnak). The one at Hierapolis is mentioned (§6(31)), and we see that the subsiding flood was drained off through it or an associated rock (omphalos), and that it gave access to it for ritual purposes.

6.6.2 While no explanation is given, the 'bronze sea' in the Jerusalem temple may have served such a purpose (§6(32)), and a similar chasm gave access to the underworld (see §6(33), where its ritual purpose is clear). If the *'eben štiyyâ* ('stone of foundation') under the Dome of the Rock is indeed the temple site, this would provide access to the ocean through its crevices. See §§4(23), 6(33) n. 1 for *Psalm* 42:8.

Such physical constructions confirm the interpretation we have offered for narratives like *Genesis* 2 (§2(18)), which describes a cultic centre.

6.7   The Temple as Microcosm

This should by now be clear: the temple symbolizes almost every aspect of 'reality', that is human experience and validation through religious activity of that experience. Houses are extensions of ourselves, and we have seen how we are also microcosms. We make them reflect our personalities by décor and pictures, arrangement and use. The temple, in all the ancient languages a 'great house' (see §2(10) n. 1: the same words also denote the palaces of kings) was the chief public building, generally far better endowed than domestic dwellings. It represented the communal identity of the population and the epitome of all social action. By sharing ritual meals (sacrifices) with the gods, contact was effected and maintained with these supernatural extensions of the nation, who with theological developments had become autonomous, and could judge and destroy, as well as succour and sustain, the community.

I   Egypt

6(1)   The Dedication of a Temple at Abydos

The following passage is an excerpt from the remarkable dedication inscription on the walls of the mortuary temple of Seti I at Abydos, in which his son and successor Rameses II addresses him. See *ARE* iii 102-17, §§251-81 for entire inscription and introduction. A feature of a mortuary temple was that the deceased king, now worshipped as a god, was able to communicate with both the underworld and the heavens, being identified with various of their inhabitants. Abydos was a site associated since the rise of united Egypt with Osiris.

Then spake the King of upper and Lower Egypt, Rameses I, given life, sending up that which he had done for his father, the Osiris, King Menmare (Seti I), triumphant; saying: 'Awake thou, (lift) thy face to heaven, that thou mayest see Ra, O my father, Merneptah (Seti I), who art a god[1]. Behold, I am making thy name to live, I have protected thee, I give attention to thy temple, thy offerings are established. Thou restest in the Nether World, like Osiris[2], while I shine as Ra[3] for the people, being upon the great throne of Atum, like Horus, son of Isis, who protected his father. How happy for thee, who begattest me... since thou comest as one living again. I have fashioned thee, I have built the house thou lovest[4], wherein is thy statue in the cemetery of Abydos, region of eternity[5]. I have founded offerings [for] thy s[tatues], the daily offerings come to thee. I am he that doeth all that is lacking to thee; I do it for thee, every desire of thy heart, the excellent thing in thy name... I have come myself... in order to see thy temple beside Wennefer[6], sovereign of eternity. I have finished the work in it, I have laid out the ground[7], I ... that which thou desirest, making thy every house wherein I have established thy name forever.

(*ARE* iii 113, §272, adapted)

1   The Egyptian king was a god in his lifetime, but there appears to be a greater emphasis on his transcendent nature after death. Only now was cult specifically offered *to* him.

2   Not a comparison so much as an identification. Osiris was restored to life, but a subterranean life in the underworld.

3   The king was commonly Horus, and son of Ra. Such a bold and explicit identification with Ra was unusual.

4   Sc. the mortuary temple. This was quite distinct from the king's tomb, which was prepared in the Valley of the Kings at Thebes (VK 17). In addition, there

was a Theban mortuary temple at Qurna on the west bank. In the Old Kingdom, in the first dynasty, kings appear to have had two tombs, at Saqqara, the necropolis of Memphis, and Abydos. The first three kings of the 19th dynasty, Rameses I, Seti I and Rameses II all had temples at Abydos, as though reviving ancient custom. That of Seti I, subject of the present text, had incorporated, to its great prestige, the Osireion, the traditional tomb of Osiris himself.

5   This expression could merely refer to the cemetery, but probably qualifies Abydos.

6   Osiris restored. See §9(7) n. 1.

7   That is, Rameses II claims to have founded Seti's temple. Reliefs on temple walls frequently represent the king ploughing furrows marking out the lines of a new temple.

See also texts §§2(5) and 5(1-3) above. These indicate how the same conceptions underlay different temple-construction theories. There is no question of any one of these falsifying other such claims. Indeed, during the historical period of Egyptian unification, in which high officials might be priests in a number of temples, we should think rather of a generally synthetic process, in which comparisons were made not out of a sense of rivalry, but because each local claim reinforced other claims (and such claims often had a political underpinning). We should not underestimate the possibility of the concept of a 'sacred landscape' extending throughout all Egypt, linking different sanctuaries. This is partly evidenced in the great festivals, when divine images would make long journeys to honour other deities at their festivals. A good example of this was the annual visit of Hathor of Denderah (that is, the image of the goddess) to Edfu.

II   The West Semitic Conception: El Dwelling at the Centre of the World

Mount Saphon (Jebel el Aqra on the Syro-Turkish frontier) is nowhere explicitly said to be an 'omphalos' in Ugaritic tradition. We have already noticed its importance, however, in §§5(5, 6), and the likelihood that it was so regarded is supported by the iconography of a bronze coin of Trajan from Seleucia Pieria (near Antioch), on the north side of the mountain. The obverse has the head of Trajan. The reverse depicts an omphalos-baetylos in a temple, with an eagle flying above. The formula ZEUC KACIOC ('Zeus Casios') appears below. See Lipiński 1992, 61 fig. 40.

6(2)   Kothar Travels for an Audience with El

This is formulaic language, used on a number of occasions when a deity visits El. He dwells at the centre of the world, which is here indicated by a number of features.

1   Then he set his face indeed towards El

at the source of the rivers[1],
amidst the springs of the two deeps.
He rolled back the tent of El

5   and entered the pavilion of the King, father of the Bright One[2].

At the feet of El he bowed down and fell on his face,
he paid him homage and honoured him.

(Wyatt 1998a, 52: KTU 1.2 iii 4-6)

1   Their number is disputed, many translators understanding there to be two (parallel to the two deeps, since 'rivers' and 'deeps' are in parallel). But I think it likely that the image of centrality expressed in the biblical image of *four* rivers (§6(14)) is probably to be understood. Certainty is impossible. Cf.Wyatt 2001c.

2   Ugaritic *šnm*. I construe this as 'the Bright One', and a designation of Shapsh, the sun-goddess, in her role as the rising sun. On the sun-goddess (geminated as Athirat and Rahmay) as daughter(s) of El, an androgynous parent, see KTU 1.23.32-3 (Wyatt 1998a, 330 and n. 33.)

The text is partially reconstructed from parallel accounts. Note the tent imagery used here, which recurs at §§6(15-25). On two deeps cf. §§4(23), 6(33).

6(3)   El Replies to Anat

Anat has travelled to visit El (according to the formula of §6(2)). On hearing her approach, and knowing her volatile temper, El is careful to remain out of sight. We are to understand this as various layers of fabric constituting the cosmic tent.

El replied from within the seven chambers,
through the eight façades of the closed rooms.

(Wyatt 1998a, 86: KTU 1.3 v 25-7)

On the significance of seven, here a spatial figure, cf. §§2(42-3). On the tent metaphor see §§6(15-25) below, and notes.

III   The Omphalos Motif in Israel and Judah

A problem in dealing with the Omphalos motif in Israel concerns its antiquity. Did it go back to Bronze Age beliefs (thus Terrien 1970; G. R. H. Wright 1970)? Or is it the outcome of much later thinking, perhaps influenced by Delphi in Greece (thus Alexander 1997)? Cf. also Thomas 1951. The issue is determined by the relative age accorded to the texts below, on the surface too early for Delphic influence, but conceivably modified or reinterpreted in the light of later ideas.

6(4)   Gaal sees the Troops of Abimelech Approaching

According to the narrative of *Judges* 9:22-41, Abimelech, king of Shechem, had taken up position on the flanks of Mount Gerizim, just south of the city. He attacked the city at dawn, to destroy a rebellion led by Gaal son of Ebed. The 'Navel of the Earth' is here evidently a name given to Mount Gerizim, at Shechem, indicating its local status.

He said: 'Look! There are people coming down from the Navel of the Earth.'

(*Judges* 9:37)

6(5)   An Allusion by Ezekiel

This is part of Ezekiel's oracle against Gog and Magog, remote peoples who, he predicts, will invade Israel. Here the Navel of the Earth is to be identified with Mount Zion at Jerusalem.

... the people... dwelling on the Navel of the Earth.

(*Ezekiel* 38:12)

IV   Tree Imagery

The 'Tree of Life' is a persistent motif in ancient Near Eastern iconography. While it carries a number of symbolic associations with different nuances in different cultures, its underlying symbolism is fairly constant, and overflows from ancient usage into Christian, Jewish (Kabbalistic) and Islamic tradition. Trees stand out particularly starkly in the Near East, where in the intense sunlight the soil is usually a dusty beige, and vegetation (apart from modern farmed crops) tends to a dusty grey. Trees stand out sharply with their abundant vegetation, thus promising life and nourishment. They also outlast a human lifespan, thus contrasting with the ephemeral 'grass' of other vegetation. They are thus popular symbols of the everlasting life of the gods. This comes out particularly in the story of the 'Fall' (§6(7)).

Two main themes occur widely: the tree is both an *axis mundi* (cf. the mountain in the same role, §3(17) n. 1), that is, the central pillar of the universe, supporting the sky, and separating it from the earth below, so that it maintains the cosmos in its created state (that is, as intended by the gods at creation); and an allomorph (alternative form) of the (androgynous) Primal Man. Thus goddesses are associated or identified with the tree (§6(5)), as are kings (§§6(9-12)).

6(6)   The Tree in Egypt: a Spell from *the Book of the Dead*

This spell accompanies a scene with a goddess appearing in the branches of the tree (she is identified variously in the iconography as Isis, Hathor or Nut) and pouring out life-giving water to refresh the dead. The iconographic form also occurs independently, as a common element in tomb-decoration.

The spell for breathing the air and having power over the water in the realms of the dead. O you sycamore of the sky[1], may there be given to me the air which is in it, for I am he who sought out that throne in the middle of Wenu[2] and I have guarded this Egg of the Great Cackler[3] If it grows, I will grow; if it lives, I will live; if it breathes the air, I will breathe the air.

(Faulkner 1985, 68: *BD* 59)

1   Egyptian *nwt*, meaning either 'sky' or Nut', the goddess of the sky.

2   Hermopolis.

3   A primaeval gander (sometimes identified with Amun, and perhaps hermaphrodite), which laid the first egg, representing the creation of the world.

6(7)   The Tree in the Hebrew Bible i): the Garden of Eden

Perhaps the most important myth in western culture, this narrative has had an incalculable effect on society (making 'original sin' the foundation of western self-assessment, and particularly in its deleterious effects on the status of women); on the environment (after the dangerous exhortations of *Genesis* 1:28-9 and 9:1-7 it almost appears to give fallen man an *excuse* for depredation); and even on horticulture (the formal garden, developed from the eighteenth century CE, and the fore-runner of today's enthusiasm for private gardens large and small, was an attempt to recreate Paradise).   It is the very paradigm of western consciousness of the world centre, represents idealized world-*space*, and has been classically projected into the future as a *post-mortem* home for the redeemed.

And Yahweh-God planted a garden in the beginning[1] and he placed there the Man ('*ādām*)[2] whom he had fashioned. Then Yahweh-God caused to grow from the ground every tree that is pleasant to the sight and good for eating, and the Tree of Life in the middle of the garden, and the Tree of the Knowledge of Good and Evil.[3] And a river was coming out of Eden to water the garden, and from there it divided and became four rivers...[4]

And Yahweh-God took the Man and put him in the garden of Eden[5] to till it and care for it. And Yahweh-God commanded the Man, 'From every tree in the garden you may indeed eat. But from the Tree of the Knowledge of Good and Evil you shall not eat. For on the day that you eat it you will certainly die...'

(*Genesis* 2:8-17)

1   Hebrew *miqqedem*. Not 'in the east', as most translations, the term being temporal here, not spatial. See Wyatt 1981. This is the temporal extension of the term noted in §1(1).

2   This first man ('Primal Man'), androgynous till the female dimension is separated out as woman, is a figure for the king. This androgynous character derives from the king's relationship to the chief deity, who as creator is also androgynous. Cf. §§2(17, 18).

3   The second tree here *reads* like an afterthought. The narrator has probably geminated one tree in the elaboration of the story. In Christian iconography one tree serves both purposes. But the duality fits the late Jewish idea of two messiahs, since the tree is also a royal symbol (§§6(11-13)).

4   For the intervening verses see §6(14).

5   The image of the man placed in the garden is a perfect microcosm. Though the garden is to be identified with a particular place (the royal burial ground in Jerusalem, called 'the King's Garden'), it is at the same time a figure for his position in the world.

See also §9(4) for the sequel.

6(8)   The Tree in the Hebrew Bible ii): the Asherah

The book of *Deuteronomy*, whose core probably originated among a dissident Yahwist community in the northern kingdom of Israel in the late tenth century BCE or a little later, following Jeroboam's religious secession (see Wyatt 1992), demanded a return to a single shrine, which 'Yahweh [would] choose to give his name a home'. This was Jerusalem[1], to which they had continued to go for festivals until prevented by Jeroboam (*1 Kings* 12:27). The enlarged book contained legislation for a centralized cult (*Deuteronomy* 12), and consequently the writers of *1* and *2 Kings* condemned all cultic activity outside Jerualem (which involved writing off the entire northern kingdom), as well as most popular manifestations within.

1   The place was later identified by the Samaritans as Shechem.

Then he (Josiah) removed the Asherah from the temple of Yahweh right out of Jerusalem to the Wadi Kidron, and he burnt it in the Wadi Kidron. He reduced it to ashes and had its ashes thrown on the common burial ground. He pulled down the houses of the sacred male prostitutes (*qᵉdēšîm*)[1] which were in the temple of Yahweh, where the women wove clothes for (the) Asherah.

(2 Kings 23:6-7)

1   This is the usual translation of the term. It could however be read as 'Holy Ones' (sc. the other gods dwelling in the temple). Perhaps the term catches both senses, that is, the divine images are represented satirically as mere prostitutes (here male). The image of marriage is often used of Israel (cf. *Hosea* 1-2) of the practice of true religion, while adultery and prostitution are consistent metaphors for syncretism, polytheism and apostasy. If 'Holy Ones' is read, the preceding 'houses' (Hebrew *bottê*, plural, but singular in Greek text) should be translated as 'shrines'.

The goddess Asherah, who is increasingly recognized as having been the consort of Yahweh in the Solomonic temple, and the mythical mother of the king, appears to have had a stylized tree as one of her iconic forms (she was primarily the sun-goddess and the apotheosis of the Queen mother). Cf. Wiggins 1993, Wyatt 1995c. The tree of life in the Garden of Eden undoubtedly represents an important cultic tree in the royal sanctuary in Jerusalem. The narrative from *2 Kings* shows that it was not always in favour. To the motif of the tree-goddess cf. §6(6). The late recognition of Asherah's importance may be explained by a number of factors, not least a reluctance among Biblical Studies scholars to engage with other disciplines (e.g. Ugaritic Studies), or even to accept as of importance the iconographic tradition that has been unearthed for Palestine by archaeologists. The work of Keel and Uehlinger is important here, and students of the subject should consult such works as Keel 1978, id. 1998; Keel and Uehlinger 1998. There is the danger of seeing Israelite culture as entirely literary in nature (and even canonical!), which is implausible.

6(9)   The Tree in the Hebrew Bible iii): the Menorah

This passage is from the Priestly source, which in *Exodus* 25-31 gives instructions for the construction of the Tabernacle, a type of the Jerusalem temple. This is often taken to be a historical tent-shrine dating from before the settlement in Palestine (i.e. *ca* 1200 BCE). It is preferable to interpret it as a much later (fifth or fourth century BCE) text, echoing ancient cultic language about tents (see §6(15), an example from Ugarit), and see it as an adumbration of the post-exilic ('second') temple. The Menorah was already an ancient motif, appearing on the thirteenth century BCE Lachish ewer, and an earlier relief from Susa dating from *ca* 3000 BCE.

You shall make a lamp-stand of pure gold; the lamp-stand is to be made of wrought metal, base and stem. Its cups — knots and buds — must be of one piece with it. Six branches are to extend from its sides, three branches of the lamp-stand from one side, three branches of the lamp-stand from the other. The first branch is to carry three almond-shaped cups; the second branch too... Then you shall make lamps for it, seven of them, and set them so that they throw their light towards its front...

(*Exodus* 25:31-40)

Cf. Also *Exodus* 37:17-24. Note that the Menorah (*mᵉnōrâ*, 'lamp'), the seven-branched candelabrum, was a stylized almond tree. Cf. §6(12) below. In synagogue mosaics in Palestine two Menorot flank the scroll shrine. This was a representation of the temple (= Garden of Eden) with the two Trees, of Life and of Knowledge, as in Genesis 2-3 (§6(7)). The trees are also messianic symbols: §§6(11-13), 9(5). The Menorah is probably what Moses is understood to have seen as the burning bush in *Exodus* 3. See Wyatt 1979, and cf. the painting of the Burning Bush by Ernst Fuchs (of which a copy can be seen in Halevi 1979, 48-9).

6(10)   The Tree in the Hebrew Bible iv):
Nebuchadnezzar's Dream

The book of *Daniel* (see also §3(8)) was composed for the most part in the second century BCE, and addressed the crises of Jewish identity in the face of the aggressive policies of Antiochus IV Epiphanes. It used narratives set in Neo-Babylonian and Persian times, when Judah had previously been a pawn in imperial politics, as parables of the present day and its problems. The present excerpt comes from an account of a dream by Nebuchadrezzar, king of Babylon, which his wise men were unable to interpret. Daniel rose to the occasion, and was able to interpret it. On the interpretation of dreams in Jewish thought see Husser 1994, 1999.

'I saw a tree in the middle of the world. And it was extremely tall. The tree grew taller and stronger, until its top reached the sky, and it was visible from the very ends of the earth. Its foliage was beautiful, its fruit plentiful, and there was food for all on it. For wild animals it provided shade, and in its branches rested the birds, and from it every living creature fed...'

'That tree... is yourself, O king...!'

(*Daniel* 4:7-9, 17, 19)

Note that the tree is here a royal symbol. It is no accident that the Tree of Life is associated or identified with Asherah, the divine mother of the king. This implies that the Tree of Knowledge represents the king. (Cf. also the two Menorot in §6(9) n. and two olive-trees in §6(13).)   An essential element in royal ideology is the secret knowledge to which the king becomes privy during the royal ascent at his enthronement. The importance of the tree in symbolic geography is particularly clear in this passage: this is a huge structure holding up the sky, as the *axis mundi* (the 'world axis'): cf. also §3(17) n. 1. The king is represented as himself the *axis mundi*.

Although the figure is probably based primarily on biblical conceptions, it also corresponds remarkably closely to Assyrian ones, undoubtedly held in common with Babylonian ideology. An important iconographic motif in Assyria shows the king tending the tree of life. The royal palace at Nineveh had panels with reliefs of the cult of the tree surrounding the throne room. The king was thus represented precisely as Adam, who walked in the garden. Cf. Parpola 1993. See also Widengren 1951 for a general treatment of the royal associations of the tree.

6(11) The Tree in the Hebrew Bible v):
The Tree as Symbol of the Messiah

Set in a narrative of the wilderness wandering of Moses and the tribes of Israel before the settlement, the book of *Numbers*, substantially from the fifth-fourth century BCE, is largely a collection of laws, the narratives giving them a quasi-historical context. The present narrative is a crux in the history of the transmission of ideology in the post-exilic period: now the ancient powers of the king are transferred to Aaron, the high priest.

Then Yahweh spoke to Moses saying, 'Speak to the Israelites, and take from each of them a branch (*maṭṭê*)[1], one for each tribe[2], from the leaders of each tribe... Write (the name of each) on his branch[3]; and write the name 'Aaron' on the branch of Levi... Then put them in the Tent of Meeting before the testimony[4]... Now the man whose branch sprouts shall be the one whom I have chosen...'

On the following day Moses came to the Tent... and there, Aaron's branch had already flowered, for the House of Levi[5]. The buds had opened, the flowers had blossomed, and the almonds had ripened.

(from *Numbers* 17:1-8, Hebrew 16-23)

1   The word *maṭṭê* also means 'tribe' (the arboreal metaphor is familiar to us in the language of 'family trees', 'stock', 'scion' etc.). The same image occurs in the next passage. It also means a sceptre, and the narrative plays on this ambiguity.

2   Literally 'from each house of a father'. We should understand these to be tribal representatives, i.e. twelve in number.

3   While not an exact copy, this perhaps reflects the writing of the names of the king of Egypt on the leaves of the sacred Persea tree (*išd*) at the time of his coronation. The royal dimension is certainly present.

4   'In the Tent of Meeting before the testimony': *bᵉʾōhel mōʿēd lipnê hāʿēdût*. In v. 7, (Hebrew 22) we read *lipnê yhwh bᵉʾōhel hāʿēdût*, 'before Yahweh in the tent of the Testimony'. A number of concepts have been interwoven here *ʾōhel mōʿēd* recalls not only the ancient idea of deities living in tents (cf. §6(15)), but also of the divine council, where decisions were taken. The phrase *lipnê* means, literally, 'before the face of ', originally denoting presence before a divine image, though once images were discontinued in Judaism the formula still represented the symbolic presence of Yahweh. General discussion in Haran 1985. The *hāʿēdût* possibly referred to an item of royal regalia, later transferred to the priesthood. See Widengren 1950, 25, for the interesting proposal that the 'testimony' was the tablets of law, handed to the king at his coronation. He cited *2 Kings* 11:12. He further linked it with the 'tablet of destinies' (or 'tablets of destiny') given to the king in Mesopotamia (§7(13)), and linked them in turn with the *Urim* and *Tummim* (*'ûrîm wᵉ tummîm*). See §11(15) for an example of their use in oracular procedures. The bringing down of two tablets of the law from Mount Sinai by Moses (*Exodus* 24:12, 32:15-9, 34:27-30) may have constituted the biblical myth of their origin.

5   Levi was a tribe without a territory. A suitable symbol for the new 'priestly monarchy', a king without a kingdom.

6(12)   The Tree in the Hebrew Bible vi): A Royal Vision of Zechariah

Zechariah lived in the late sixth century BCE, at the time of the construction of the second temple. Under apparently benevolent Persian rule (so far as religious policies were concerned) Judah was allowed considerable freedom. Zerubbabel, a descendent of the royal line from Jehoiakin, was widely expected to restore the monarchy. Zechariah even had a vision of Zerubbabel's coronation (*Zechariah* 6:9-14). However, Zerubbabel mysteriously disappeared from the scene, and with the increasing theocratization of nascent Judaism, the High Priest, Joshua, was substituted in the text for Zerubbabel. See further at §6(13).

Then he (Yahweh) showed me Joshua the High Priest standing before the angel of Yahweh'... 'Is not this man a burning log snatched from the fire?'...

'Now listen, Joshua, High Priest... For I now mean to bring out my servant Branch²...'

(from Zechariah 3:1-10)

1   See §6(11) n. 4. Note that an angel was now required to mediate between deity and priest.

2   Hebrew *ṣemaḥ*, 'branch (of tree)'. This is an allusion to the arboreal conception of the king. Since Joshua is being addressed in the last part, it must

refer to somebody else, sc. Zerubbabel, even though it had been Joshua at the beginning who was identified as the 'burning log'. The editorial process has obviously been incomplete, preserving elements of both stages in redaction.

6(13)   The Tree in the Hebrew Bible vii):
A Second Royal Vision of Zechariah

It was perhaps the shift from a royal to a priestly aspiration (which we see half frozen in the process in §6(12)) that the doctrine of two messiahs had its origin. Zechariah sees the Menorah. Cf. §11(14).

The angel who was speaking to me continued… asking me, 'What can you see?' I replied: 'I see a solid gold lamp-stand with a bowl on top; seven lamps are on the lamp-stand, and seven spouts for the lamps on it. And two olive trees are beside it, one to the right of it and one to the left.'…

'What are these two olive trees?'…

'These are the two anointed ones[1] who stand before the lord of the whole world.'

(*Zechariah* 4:1-14)

1   Hebrew *bᵉnê hayyishār*, 'sons of the oil'. This is an expression of the doctrine of two messiahs. See §§4(10), 11(14).

V   The image of the River

6(14) The Rivers of Paradise in Genesis

This passage skilfully combines the idea of one cosmic river (presumably to be identified with the cosmic ocean) with four rivers flowing out from the centre to the ocean. The two main rivers of Mesopotamia (Tigris and Euphrates) feature, together with Pishon, which appears to be identified with the Arabian Sea. On the Gihon see below. On the number four cf. §6(2) n. 1.

A river came out of Eden to irrigate the garden, and from here it divided into four sources (*rāšîm*). The name of the first is Pishon: this encircles the whole land of Havilah, where gold is found. And the gold of this land is pure. Bdellium and carnelian are also found there. And the name of the second is Gihon: this encircles the whole land of Cush. And the name of the third river is Tigris: this flows this side of Assyria. And the fourth river is the Euphrates.

(*Genesis* 2:10-4)

Note the symmetrical structure of the Garden, a microcosm: four rivers represent the four cardinal points, and thus between them irrigate the whole 'garden', that is, the whole earth. The Gihon is particularly interesting. In addition to being a river of Eden it is a name of the cosmic ocean. Here, flowing round Cush (that is, Ethiopia, or Abyssinia, 'the Land of the Abyss') it is the main stream which *becomes* the Cosmic Ocean, but flows from the centre of the Garden. Cf. §§2(24, 30-5).

But Gihon is also the name of the underground stream which flows beneath Jerusalem, and by means of underground tunnels, such as the one commonly attributed to Hezekiah, provides the city's main water supply. Thus is Jerusalem declared to be the centre of the world, a theme we have already noted (§6(5)).

VI The Cosmic Tent

There are numerous allusions to the cosmic tent in the Hebrew Bible (§§6(16-25)). Apart from these, the entire tradition of the 'Wilderness Tabernacle' of the Pentateuch is a complex metaphor for life in exile rather than a historical record for an institution in the time of Moses. It also occurs in Ugaritic tradition (§§6(2, 15)). While not present in literary form, it appears in much older architectural forms in both Egyptian and Mesopotamian religious thought, and also in the Kenite site of Timna near Eilat. The earliest shrines were made of reeds and animal hides, and the earliest stone and brick constructions preserved the basic forms. Thus columns made of tied reeds became the stone columns with their tell tale foliate form in Egypt. For another important example of this motif see §6(2) above.

6(15) An Ugaritian Example

> The gods blessed him (Keret) and went away,
> > the gods went away to their dwellings
> > the family of El to their tents.

(Wyatt 1998a, 212: KTU 1.15 iii 17-9)

6(16) Israelite Examples i): a Joban Account

The Israelite forms are distinctive in using a mythological metaphor in conjunction with the architectural tent-construction image. See Habel 1972. The cosmic tent is made from the hide of the slain sea-monster. This corresponds to the construction of the world out of the cadaver of Tiamat in Mesopotamian tradition (§§2(9-10)). Since the motif is also found in Indian tradition (Indra against Vṛtra), it quite possibly goes back to the putative Neolithic dispersal of the original mythic tradition. See notes to §§3(16) and 4(14) above. The Babylonian example (§2(10)), using architectural terms, is in principle a younger version than this, more metamorphosed: the Hebrew tent tradition (evidently deriving from the Ugaritic antecedent), is more archaic in conception, despite its later chronological date.

> (El) stretching out (the) heavens by himself,
> > and striding on the back of Sea.[1]

(*Job* 9:8)

---

1   To the final colon cf. *the Story of Sinuhe* B140-1 (Parkinson 1997, 33):
        I felled him with his own axe,
        and gave my war cry on his back.
    El's procedure also appears to be a dance of triumph on the corpse of his enemy, just as was Marduk's (§2(9) l. 18). See also §9(6) n. 6.

The divine name El (or the generic term *'eloâ*, 'God') is used throughout the poetic sections of the *Book of Job*, until Yahweh enters the drama as a character and gives Job his answer in chapter 38. The relationship between El and Yahweh is much disputed, and need not detain us here, beyond noting my view that Yahweh originates as a local form of El. See §4(26) n. 2 for my estimate of the evidence of *Deuteronomy* 32:8. They are roughly, but perhaps not formally equated in *Job*, and the evidence of this text points to an archaic tradition of El as the adversary of Yam. See Wyatt 1987b.

6(17) Israelite Examples ii): from Deutero-Isaiah

§§6(17-22) all come from so-called Deutero-Isaiah (see §4(1) introduction), the anonymous exilic poet to whom *Isaiah* 40-55 are generally attributed. Living, it seems, during the exilic period (sixth century BCE), he used the conflict myth tradition (see §4(1) and cf. §4(2b)) as a means of applying the ancient traditions to the immediate future, as a message of hope to his hearers and readers. Many of his poems are statements of self-glorification by Yahweh, now unequalled, indeed the only god (*Isaiah* 45:7). His people have more than paid for their sins (*Isaiah* 40:2), and can look forward to a new creation, guaranteed in these affirmations of Yahweh's (re-)construction of the world and his shrine as its epitome. For the tent metaphor belongs as specifically to the sanctuary as it does to the world in general, and renewed victory in the conflict leads on to its reerection. Each reference is turned to a particular application, as noted.

The reference here is primarily to Yahweh's temple, which will be reconstructed. Given the powerful symbolism of the destruction of the temple in Jerusalem by Nebuchadrezzar II in 586 BCE, and its devasting effects on public morale, this is an equally powerful message of hope for national regeneration. At the same time, an implicit extension of this figure is a promise of new homes for the exiles.

> who stretches out like a veil the heavens,
>   and spreads them like a tent to dwell in.

(Isaiah 40:22)

6(18) Israelite Examples iii): from Deutero-Isaiah

Here the final line extends the meaning to economic regeneration. It is no use hoping to return to a ravaged land.

> Thus says El-Yahweh,
> creating the heavens
>   and stretching out the firmament,
>   the earth and its produce.

(Isaiah 42:5)

6(19) Israelite Examples iv): from Deutero-Isaiah

Two features are present in this allusion to the motif, firstly the unicity of Yahweh (this is on the verge of monotheism, but how far it succeeded at the time is much debated), and secondly the alternative figure of Yahweh the metal-worker (cf. Yahweh the potter in *Genesis* 2: §2(18) n. 5).

> I am Yahweh who made everything,
> > stretching out the heavens by myself,
> > beating out the earth on my own.

> (*Isaiah* 44:24)

6(20) Israelite Examples v): from Deutero-Isaiah

This time Yahweh's skill is emphasized in the apparent allusion to his ambidextrous nature (cf. Kothar in Ugarit: Wyatt 1998a, 43 n. 23), and is followed by a military allusion. Note too that Hephaestus was known by the name Ἀμφιγυεις, which LS 90b translated as 'with both feet crooked', Evelyn-White 1914, 121 as 'Limping (god)', but which M. L. West 1988, 20, rendered 'Ambidexter'. Yahweh controls the entire host of heaven (implicitly a polytheistic figure, though the gods are probably in the process of being redefined as angels).

> As for me, my two hands stretched out the heavens,
> > and all their hosts I commanded.

> (*Isaiah* 45:12)

6(21) Israelite Examples vi): from Deutero-Isaiah

Yahweh's ambidextrous nature is perhaps implicit in this commoner idiom, with its reference to each hand. Though in parallelism the 'hand' and 'right hand' may simply be the same (the poetic usage commonly has *yād* parallel to *yāmîn*), it is probable that the first allusion here is to the '(left) hand'. Note too the idea of the fixing of the earth: that is, stopping any turmoil and motion, and bringing order.

> It was my hand that fixed the earth,
> > and my right hand that spread out the heavens.

> (*Isaiah* 48:13)

6(22) Israelite Examples vii): from Deutero-Isaiah

A rhetorical question, but perhaps one that made sense to a people cowed by deportation and exile. The essential function of memory is discussed at **1.3.2, 1.8, 8.1.

> And have you forgotten Yahweh your maker,
> > stretching out the heavens
> > > and fixing the earth?

> (*Isaiah* 51:13)

6(23) Israelite Examples viii): Psalm 104

There is a wisdom element here, with an interest in the construction details of the universe. Cf. the catalogue of *Job* 38:4-39:30, which develops into a general catalogue of nature.

> (Yahweh) stretching out (the) heavens like a tent-curtain,
> > fixing on the waters the beams of your store-chambers.

> (*Psalm* 104:2-3)

6(24) Israelite Examples ix): a Theophany Account

The description of a theophany here represents it as the triumphant self-disclosure of the victor of the divine conflict.

> He stretched out the heavens and came down,
>   and a dark cloud was beneath his feet.
> And he rode upon a cherub and flew,
>   and flew on outstretched wings.
> He made darkness his hiding-place round about him,
>   his shelter the darkness of the waters.
>   {clouds of darkness}

(Psalm 18:10-2)

Cf. *2 Samuel* 22:10-12, which is the same, except that v. 12, cited below, reads differently. The text above is preferable, without the final line, marked {}.

> And he made darkness around himself a shelter,
>   a mass of waters (into²) clouds of darkness.   *(2 Samuel* 22:12)

6(25) Israelite Examples x): a Prayer for a Theophany

While §6(24) describes a theophany as it happens (probably to be interpreted as a poetic account of the passage of the divine image or symbol in the temple), this passage is a prayer for such a self-disclosure to occur. As well as beginning with an allusion to the tent-pitching, heaven-stretching motif which recalls the divine victory, it goes on to invoke a further victory against the forces of chaos, exhibited in two forms, the threats of the irruption of the cosmic sea, and of invasions by foreign powers.

> 1 Yahweh, stretch out your heavens and come down!
>   strike the mountains so that they smoke!
>   Flash your lightning-bolts and scatter them,
>   Discharge your shafts and confuse them!
> 5 Stretch out your hand from on high:
>   remove me and snatch me away
>   from (the) mighty waters,
>   from the power of foreigners!

(Psalm 144:5-7)

VII   Temples, their Location between and Junction of Heaven and Earth

6(26) The Temple's Foundations in the Earth i): Egyptian Tradition

Coronation Inscription of Tuthmosis III at Karnak. The passages treating the foundations of Egyptian temples on the *ben*-stone (§§5(1-2)) have correspondences elsewhere. Reliefs on temple walls frequently represent the king, measuring out the plan or, plough in hand, 'cutting the first sod' of a new temple foundation. This may cover original construction, or, as below, repair and renovation work too, regarded as a new foundation. This was almost a mythical view of temple-construction: each remodelling or repair happened, as it were, *in illo tempore*, thus claiming a foundation going back to the beginning of the world.

Construction at Karnak continued from the Middle Kingdom down to Roman times, successive kings regarding it as the primary site at which to represent their piety and triumph in permanent embellishments to the sacred site. This inscription describes the works of Tuthmosis III (1504-1450 BCE).

[He built the temple of Amun⁷] anew, together with a 'Divine Abode', a monument of fine white sandstone. The king himself performed with his two hands the stretching of the cord and the extension of the line, putting (it) upon the ground, and furnishing on this monument the exaction of work, according to the command of [Amun⁷] enduring work of their hands.

(*ARE* ii 64 (§152; cf. §157))

6(27) The Temple's Foundations in the Earth ii): Assyrian Tradition

The following inscription, from the reign of Shalmaneser I of Assyria (1274-1245 BCE) is typical of a large number of dedicatory inscriptions, usually found buried in the foundations of temples. As is clear, the crucial element in any temple construction or reconstruction was that it was founded on the bedrock, below any signs of human habitation. The theory behind this was presumably that it obviated any risk of pollution, and more effectively linked the earth below with the heavens above.

When Ehursagkurkurra¹, the temple of my lord Aššur, which Ushpia, priest of Aššur, my ancestor, had built aforetime, fell into ruins, then my ancestor Erishu, priest of Aššur, restored it. One hundred and fifty-nine years passed after the reign of Erishu and that temple again fell into ruins. Then Shamshi-Adad, priest of Aššur, restored it. Five hundred and eighty years elapsed, and that temple which Shamshi-Adad, priest of Aššur, had restored, became old and weak, fire broke out in it, its sacred edifice, every sanctuary, the shrines, the vestments, yea, all the property of the temple of Aššur my lord, burned with fire.

At that time I tore down the temple in its totality, I cleared away the earth from it, went down to its foundations, built its foundation walls with mighty stones, like the structure of the mountains. An illustrious temple, a lofty dwelling-place, a noble shrine, a magnificent abode, whose front was higher than (that) of the earlier (shrine), cunningly constructed, manifesting glory, befitting the dignity of his exalted divinity, worthy of his sovereignty, I restored with great care...

When the lord Aššur enters that temple and makes his joyful abode in its noble shrine, may he look upon the splendid work(s) (which I performed upon) that temple, may he rejoice, may he hear my prayers, listen to my supplications…[2]

(Luckenbill 1926, i 41-2, §§119-21; *KAH*, 1, 13)

1   É.ḪUR.SAĞ.KUR.KUR.RA ('House, Mountain of the Lands') was the name of Aššur's cella in his temple at Aššur (George 1993, §486). Notice the comparison with the mountains in the second paragraph. Cf. also the tent shrine (above §§6(15-25)), which in West Semitic tradition is made from the corpse of the sea-dragon, and identified with Mount Saphon.

2   Note the form of a prayer at the end. The inscription was intended for burial in the temple foundation, for the god's eyes only.

6(28) The Temple's Foundations in the Earth iii): A Late Jewish Tradition

David wished to build the temple on virgin soil (cf. §8(7)). He dug down 1,500 cubits ($^1/_3$ mile!) and, just as he thought he had reached the bedrock, he found a potsherd.

'After all the trouble I have taken, now I find this sherd!' Whereupon God gave a voice to the sherd and it said, 'This is not my original place, but when the earth was split asunder (at the giving of the Torah at Mount Sinai) I descended here. If you do not believe me — behold, *Tehom*, the Deep, lies beneath me.' David picked up the sherd and the waters of the Deep rose to engulf him. David said: 'Whosoever knows a word that will put a stop to this *Tehom*, and does not say it, may he suffocate!' And Ahitophel, who stood there, spoke the word and arrested the Deep.

(Patai 1948, 55: *Midrash Samuel* 26)

6(29) The Temple's Summit in Heaven i): Some Mesopotamian Temple Names

The idea that a temple reaches to heaven, and thus has direct contact with the gods, shows how the temple can be seen as an architectural representation of the mountain, where the gods dwell. We see it graphically in Egypt, for example, where the pylons, the gate-towers of the temple, replicate the mountains of the horizon, between which the sun rises. This is also a representation of the written form for 'horizon', *akhet* (*3ḫt*, written ◠, §5(5) above), which we shall see (§§7(1-11)) serves as a metaphor for the transition from one dimension to another. It is also evident in the construction of Mesopotamian 'temple-towers' ('ziggurats'), both architecturally, and in their names. For examples of these see §6(29).

The temple of Ishtar of Nineveh at Babylon was called both É.ḪUR.SAĞ.AN.KI.A: 'House, Mountain of Heaven and Underworld', and É.GIŠ.ḪUR.AN.KI.A: 'House of the ordinances of Heaven and the Underworld' (George 1993, §§409, 475).

Another temple of Ištar at Kar-Bel-Matati, near Babylon, was called É.AN.KI: 'House of Heaven and Underworld' (George 1993, §68). The same name was given to the sanctuary of Anu at Uruk (George 1993, §69). The whole temple of Anu at Uruk was called É.AN.NA: 'House of Heaven' (George 1993, §75). It was also the name of a shrine of Inanna (= Ishtar) at Lagash (George 1993, §76), and of Inanna at Girshu (George 1993, §77), as well as of other shrines.

6(30) The Temple's Summit in Heaven i):
The Story of the Tower of Babel

We tend to think of the very name of this story as a parody, as perhaps intended by the author, who plays with the terms *Bābēl*, 'Babylon' (in Akkadian *Bāb-ili*, cf. §11(5)) and *bālal*, 'confuse' (cf. English 'babble'). However, we may also call it more neutrally 'the tower of Babylon'. For exiled Jews, the claims of Babylonian theology, which were implicit in ziggurat architecture, were a mere mockery of the very similar claim of their own temple tradition: cf. §7(22). The story probably conflates two original versions of the tale, one concerning a city, and the other a tower. Cf. Skinner 1910, 223. This is not merely a parody of Babylonian theology; it is also a mythical account of how the Jews were exiled to Babylon and elsewhere, with the resulting loss of a common language as they ceased to be a united nation.

Now all the world had one language and one vocabulary. Now as they wandered around in the beginning[1], they found a plain in the land of Shinar[2], and they settled there. And they said to one another, 'Come now, let us make bricks and let us fire them in the kiln'. So they used bricks for stone, and bitumen for mortar[3]. 'Come!' they said: 'Let us build ourselves a city and a tower[4] with its top in the heavens, and let us make ourselves a name lest we be scattered all over the surface of the earth.'

Now Yahweh came down to see the city and the tower which the people had made. Then Yahweh said, 'Look! They are one people and they all have one language; and this is but the beginning of their doings. Now nothing that they plan to do will be impossible for them. Come, let us go down and confuse their language, so that no one can understand his neighbour's language.'

And Yahweh scattered them from there all over the surface of the earth, and they stopped building the city. So he called it Babel (*Bābēl*), because there Yahweh confused (*bālal*) the language of the whole earth, and from there Yahweh scattered them all over the surface of the earth.

(*Genesis* 11:1-9)

1   Hebrew *miqqedem*. Rather than 'in (or from) the east'. Cf. §6(6) n. 1.

2   Shinar is the Hebrew name of Sumer.

3   This note explained to Palestinian hearers and readers (who built with stone and mortar) the curious practice of Mesopotamia, where bricks and bitumen were used.

4   City or tower? The former leads to a scattering, the second to a confusion.

Note how the story changes an intended vertical movement (human planning) up towards the divine abode into a horizontal movement (divine planning) away from the divine abode. Was Babylon here a cipher for corrupt Jerusalem, from which the exiles were indeed scattered? The tale works on a number of levels, thus creating a very rich reservoir of meanings. The same play on different axes is implicit in §§5(8-10) and 9(4).

6(31) The Temple's Contact with the Ocean i):
the Temple Receptacle at Hierapolis

Temples generally had water containers, ranging from the Olympic-size pool at Karnak to stone and metal receptacles. These not only provided water for ritual purposes, but symbolized the cosmic Ocean, which while obviously far removed from a building at the centre of the world, could nevertheless be tapped, signifying its life-giving properties and the power of ritual to harness and control it. Temples thus represent the human capacity to control and manage the environment. See §6(27): the potsherd acts as plug to the Ocean below.

This passage describes the receptacle at Hierapolis (Membij), following Lucian's account of Deucalion and Pyrrha, and the flood. Cf. §4(12)

The men of the holy city tell a marvellous tale, how in this land a great chasm opened up, and received all the water (of the flood). And when this happened, Deucalion had an altar built, and had a temple dedicated to Hera[1] built over the chasm. I saw the chasm, which is beneath the temple, quite a small one. If it was once great and has become small, I know not; but the one I saw is small.

Concerning this story they speak thus. Twice each year[2] water comes from the sea to the temple. It is not only priests who bring it, but all Syria and Arabia. Many people come from beyond the Euphrates to the sea[3], and they all bring water, which is poured out in the temple. It then runs down into the chasm, and while the chasm is small, it certainly swallows an immense quantity of water. And in doing this they say that it was ordained by Deucalion for the sanctuary, in memory of the tribulation[4] and the subsequent blessing.

(Strong and Garstang, 1913, 51-2: Lucian, *De Dea Syria* 13)

1   Hera was the Greek equivalent of Atargatis (usually explained as a syncrasia of ᶜAthtart and ᶜAnat: ᶜ > ', ᶜAttart > 'Atar; ᶜAnat > ga(n)t + -is) .

2   Many Near eastern cultures had two New Year festivals each year, as the year could begin with either the Spring or the Autumn equinox. We see this in Israel where the Passover and Day of Atonement rites diverged from a common source.

3   This phrase confirms the suspicion that the 'sea' is not the Mediterranean, which is some hundred miles from Hierapolis. Besides, the 'sea' used in the

ritual refers to fresh, not salt, water. Lucian is probably referring to a receptacle in the temple.

4 Sc. the flood. Various localities were credited with being the drain-hole of the receding flood: Gezer in Palestine, and the temple of Zeus in Athens.

6(32) The Temple's Contact with the Ocean ii): the Temple Receptacle in Jerusalem

1 Kings 6-7 narrate the construction of the Solomonic temple in Jerusalem, *ca* 930 BCE. §6(28) supposes that Solomon's father David built it, from the predictable desire that the first king in Jerusalem should be regarded as its author. The cosmic sea was amorphous, uncontained and chaotic. The construction of a receptacle for it in the temple, as described here, was part of the cultic process of taming chaos, by containing it, and thus reducing it to order and manageability.

He (Solomon) made the sea of cast metal, ten cubits from rim to rim, circular in shape and five cubits high; a cord thirty cubits long gave the measurement of its girth. Under its rim and completely encircling it were gourds surrounding the sea; over the length of thirty cubits the gourds were in two rows, of one and the same casting with the rest. It rested on twelve oxen, three facing north, three facing west, three facing south, three facing east; on these, their hindquarters all turned inwards, stood the sea. It was a hand's breadth in thickness, and its rim was shaped like the rim of a cup, lily-shaped. It could hold 2,000 measures.

(*1 Kings* 7:23-6)

6(33) Jerusalem: the Entry into the Underworld and the Cosmic Ocean

On the water-libations poured out in the temple, at *Rôš haššānâ* (New Year) and the associated Feast of Tabernacles (*Sukkôt*) see the discussion by Patai 1948, 24-53. He quotes the following passage (p. 41).

Again, Rabbi Eliezer said: 'When on the Feast of Tabernacles the water-libations are carried out, Deep says to Deep[1], "Let thy waters spring forth; I hear the voice of two friends, (namely) the water and the wine poured onto the altar[2]"'.

(Patai 1948, 41: B. *Ta'an* 25b)

1 This is almost certainly an allusion to *Psalm* 42:8 (EV 7):
 Deep is calling to deep; at the roar of your cataracts,
 All your breakers and your billows wash over me. (= §4(23))
 This passage perhaps recalls the Flood Story in its context, as an occasion when all men were overwhelmed, but the righteous (Noah and family) survived. The psalm reads a spiritual meaning into the ritual process of libations poured on the altar, or more likely on the rock which stood in the Holy of Holies, and is now under the Dome of the rock.

2   The altar here is probably to be equated with the rock of n. 1, which is natural
        bedrock, though, Jean-Michel de Tarragon tells me, somewhat eroded by
        Roman quarrying.

Chapter 7

BOUNDARIES AND HOW TO CROSS THEM:
ASPECTS OF THE CULT

Boundaries that require crossing, because they impose unwelcome limitations, such as death, on people, may be seen in terms of space or time, or a combination of them both. The language used in the following texts is spatial. The language of people breaking through boundaries points to a number of issues. Firstly there was the initiation of cult-specialists (kings, priests, prophets and shamans) which gave them prestige and power. There was also the acceptance that people of high degree, such as kings, had a special destiny of assimilation to the divine realm. Then there was the slow filtering down of such beliefs in a supernatural experience to common people, so that the Egyptian king's destiny gradually became the foundation for universal salvation. The process of democratization probably occurred elsewhere as well, but is not so clearly documented. We should consider under what conditions space was a metaphor for other dimensions, such as time, in which the person who transcended a boundary was moving from ordinary time into an extraordinary mode of time. See introductory note to §8 for discussion of the concept of *illud tempus*. One interesting avenue for research is the pharmacological basis for the experiences described, which correspond closely to modern accounts of the effects of LSD or opium. Opium was widely used from Neolithic times in cultic contexts, and the extensive use of incense and anointing oils (see Wyatt 1999, 857 n. 13) presumably contributed to a range of psycho-somatic experiences. The role of music would also have been of paramount importance.

Suggested Reading:

Barker 1987; id. 1991; Collins and Fishbane 1995, 15-58; Douglas 1970; Eliade 1964, 487-94; Fletcher-Lewis 1997; van Gennep 1909; Haran 1985; Himmelfarb 1993; Kvanvig 1988; Rowley 1967, 71-110; de Vaux 1961, 271-344; Widengren 1951; Wyatt 1986, id. 1987; id. 1990c.

7.1   Introduction

7.1.1   Two issues constitute an entrée into our discussion: firstly, we have so far dealt with two seemingly opposed ideas, that of the end of the world (§§3, 4), often represented by the notion of a 'cosmic ocean', and that of the centre of the world (§§5, 6). How do the two relate? Secondly, the crucial element here is the notion of boundaries, of categories, and their distinctions. Why are they made, and what is the significance of their rupture, by accident, or deliberately?

7.1.2   These two ideas are really two sides of the same coin. We have noticed the basic division of reality into 'binary oppositions' (the classic essay is Lévi-Strauss 1968, chapter 11). Thus in facing east, we have the past in front in opposition to the future behind; similarly the left and right hands are opposed (§1). We find such basic divisions throughout the universe, often originating from a single divisive sword-stroke. See §§2(10, 15 and n. 1) and 3 *passim*. §2(15) separates light from darkness; waters above the firmament from those below the earth; land from sea, and all the *distinct* species of life from one another. Their distinction is a symbol of order (cf. the dietary laws in *Leviticus* 11 = *Deuteronomy* 14 and Douglas' treatment, Douglas 1970).

7.1.3   Now there are two fundamental human activities. The first is the management of daily life, and may be symbolized as the maintenance of the created order and divisions. Thus sacred and profane, clean and unclean, living and dead are not to be mixed. This is seen most graphically in the Jewish dietary laws, and in Douglas' analysis. At the same time we have the second: something impels human beings to try to recapture the primordial situation in which there was no differentiation, no alienation, no death, in short, to make things whole, or one, which is what the idea of 'atonement' represents. The cult, paradoxically, serves to bring together that which has been sundered as well as to maintain the distinction of things which otherwise become confused (Wyatt 1987a)[1].

7.1.4   This may sound entirely illogical. Religion often does, though 'counter-intuitive' is a better description. In fact it is the key to the whole: we are alienated as human beings (the animals won't speak to us, to start with… as the tamed Enkidu discovered, §4(6) introduction). We are pulled two ways. The alienation is the very driving force of culture (Berger 1973), and so has to be maintained. Ritual action can do this. But at the same time we long for paradise, for the repaired relationship, for mystic union. In the cult, this is also achieved. In practice, the cult-specialists (among whom was the king) tended to try to keep this latter secret to themselves.

7.2   Boundaries: a Theoretical Example: the Egyptian Horizon

7.2.1   As an example of the kind of symbolism operating, let us consider the Egyptian term *akhet* (*3ḥt*), meaning 'horizon' (§§7(1-11). It has the following distinct applications in the passages cited:

1)   The horizon we see, the boundary of earth and sky (§7(1));
2)   the horizon as location of a natural event interpreted theologically: 'the sun rises' means 'Ra appears' (§7(2));

---

[1]   See also Erikson 1966, 339, cited below, *10.5.2.

3)   the symbolic application of 1) and 2): 'the mysteries of the two horizons' refers to those unseen (and therefore implicitly supernatural) realities lying beyond (§7(3));

4)   the symbolic application of 2): the doors of a temple represent the boundary between earthly and heavenly realities, and therefore acts as a horizon (§7(4)); and for 'like' ('Thy doors are like…') we may read 'as', which identifies doors and heaven: this is where the god appears to his people (§7(8));

5)   this symbolism is applied to the whole temple (§7(5)), for the temple is the place where the god appears; the same is true in (§7(6)), where the Holy of Holies, called 'the Great Seat', is this horizon; it is the earthly replica of a pattern in heaven (§§7(7, 8)) (this idea takes on enormous importance in late Judaism, Christianity and Islam);

6)   'He went to his horizon' means 'he died': language used of a king, who was divine (§§7(9, 10)).

7.2.2   While the vocabulary of the other ancient cultures is nowhere so clearly expressed as this in terms of one coherent metaphor, the same significance is attached to boundaries.

7.3   The Concept of the Heavenly Journey

7.3.1   All the remainder of the texts in §7 narrate real or fictitious events interpreted according to one basic idea: that the subject ascended to, and entered, 'heaven', where he (we have no accounts of women doing this[2], and female rulers such as Hatshepsut of Egypt called themselves 'kings') was divinized. Even the real (sc. historical) events narrate a fiction, because they put a supernatural gloss on an event which also had a naturalistic explanation. We thus have the ritual form (a banal act), and the ritual significance (the transcendent reality achieved).

7.3.2   Let us consider §7(12) as a type. This reflects the crucial need in Egypt to identify the next king among all the numerous princes of the blood. A divine choice must be signalled. No doubt it could be manufactured. Here the image of Amun, in transit through the Karnak temple, 'saw' the young Tuthmosis, and gave a sign that he was chosen

---

[2]   There were of course female cult-functionaries, choristers, priestesses and prophetesses. What is generally lacking is any record of activities or experiences particular to them. Cf. however the interesting reconstruction of the installation of Baal's high priestess at Emar: Fleming 1992.

(this was formalized in the expression *meri-Amun*, 'Beloved of Amun' or 'Begotten of Amun', which kings used in their titulary: Wyatt 1985). There followed an ascent to heaven and the receiving of divine honours, which was not perceived by those around him ('they were remote from the faces of mankind…'). It was thus a purely subjective experience.

7.3.3   §7(13) is a similar Mesopotamian account: Enmeduranki, king of Sippar, also entered into the divine assembly. This was located in 'Ebarra' (but see n. 1). That is, like §7(12), it actually took place in the temple. Among the gods (present in their images), the king was taught the secrets required for the management of the world and society. The story of *Etana* (§7(14)) is an account of the spatial imagery implied in ritual by giving a bird's eye view of the earth from heaven. In this we have a glimpse of the idea of multiple heavens (ll. 35-6) as an indication of the degree of transcendence achieved in such journeys.

7.3.4   We see the use of the imagery in *Adapa* (§7(15) = 9(2)); here the hero is summoned to heaven (a temple, that of Anu, lies behind the image) to account for his sin. We may compare it with Adam and Eve challenged by Yahweh in the garden (= the sanctuary) in *Genesis* 3 (§9(4)).

7.3.5   The story of *Keret* (§7(17)) is at first glance altogether more down to earth. Keret merely climbed up to the top of a temple. But the language of ascent corresponds to what we have seen, and the ritual stages (n. 3) represent the transformation in the ritual of the king from human to divine status. This is a story. But the ritual texts from Ugarit confirm this interpretation, with rituals of 'sacralization' and 'profanation' which transform the king at beginning and end of the cult (Wyatt 1999).

7.3.6   §7(16), from Ugarit, the enthronement of Athtar, is a narrative entirely in mythic mode. But the kings of Ugarit were mystically identified with the god, and this ascent of the sacred mountain and the divine throne (in this story) were the type and model for the throne the king ascended. This can be seen with the similar cosmology in Israel in the curious wording of §7(25). Note ll. 8-10 in §7(16), suggesting the use of aromatherapeutic herbs in the anointing oil.

7.3.7   There are numerous Jewish texts which tell the same story from different aspects (§§7(18-25)). Some describe the ascent (§§7(19-22)), others the ritual activity which generated the ascent in the mind's eye (§§7(18, 23, 25)). The motif occurs as a parody in §5(8). §6(30) also belongs in such a category, and the present chapter provides interesting illustrations of the story's presuppositions. §§7(24, 25) belong to the enthronement rite of Judah, which in turn shaped all the language of messianism, and also of the rituals of European monarchies.

7.4 The Symbolism of the Entry into Heaven

7.4.1 Note the paradox of the language of elevation to denote arrival at the centre (see §7(20) n. 2). The counterpart to this is the language of expulsion in §9(4), which is a parable of the deposition and banishment of the king of Judah in the exile to Babylon. Thus horizontal and vertical images are allomorphs of one another (i.e. they frequently say the same thing, the one being a metaphor for the other).

7.4.2 What are we to make of this strange language? The symbolism operates on a number of levels, literary, theological and sociological. In literary terms the ascent often forms a climax to the narrative. It is based, after all, as theology would assert, on the highest aspirations, realized in the ritual behaviour of the king, who entered heaven, was transformed, and thus effected as representative figure the transformation ('redemption') of society. Such a process, by deliberate transformation, actually preserved both worlds intact (*7.1.4 above), held them in tension, and was the nearest we can get to resolution of the intrinsic problems of life (a ritual counterpart to myth, as analysed by Lévi-Strauss 1968).

7.4.3 Sociologically, the bottom line was the preservation and management of society. Of course this was distinctly to the advantage of the king, rather than his subjects. But such revolutionary thought was alien to the ancients, who saw society strictly in pyramidal terms, and never questioned the justice of the system. This was surely of importance in the rise of complex societies, for it was in the division of labour, and rule of the many by the few, that leisure activities, literacy, philosophy and the slow betterment of society developed. We shall give different assessments of this according to whether we start from a psychological, a theological or an anthropological perspective.

I   The Egyptian Concept of the Horizon

The term *akhet* (*ꜣḫt*), denoting a boundary between two dimensions, is of particular interest in conceptualizing 'boundaries' in religious thought, and serves as a useful introduction of the topic. See *7.2 for the general range of meanings. A 'horizon' is the point of intersection or contiguity of any spatial or qualitative difference (such as from earth to sky, or from profane to sacred), a *limen*, or threshold. In its use in the context of death (§§7(9-10) it is further developed to present a spatial metaphor for a temporal and ontological transition. The following are examples of the different nuances of the term.

7(1)   From the Catechism of Ra

For *BD* 17 see §5(3) introduction. On one level this passage simply describes a natural event. But in Egyptian thought it was also the epiphany of a god.

Ra when he rises in the eastern horizon of the sky...

(Faulkner 1985, 44: from *BD* 17)

7(2)   Hymn to Harakhte from *the Book of the Dead*

The epiphany aspect is particularly evident here. The appearance of the sun-god brings hope to his people.

> How beautiful is your shining forth from the horizon
>> when you illumine the Two Lands[1] with your rays!

(Faulkner 1985, 41: from *BD* 15)

1   On the fundamentally dualistic conception of Egypt see §7(12) n.

7(3)   From the Myth of the Secret Name of Ra

In an attempt to trick Ra into revealing his secret name, Isis created a poisonous snake, which bit him; she then offered to heal him, requiring knowledge of his names to have power over the poison. This is one of his numerous names which Ra recites, before she manages to obtain the secret one. The text was probably used in healing rites for snakebite.

> I am he who made the heaven and the mysteries of
>> the two horizons,
> so that the soul of the gods might be placed therein.

(*ANET* 13: from Turin P. and P. Chester Beatty XI)

7(4)   Inscriptions Concerning the Temple of Ptah

Inscriptions of Rameses II and III concerning the temple of Ptah at Memphis, describing work they had had done.

> 1   Thy doors are like the horizon of heaven,
>> causing strangers to praise thee...
> I restored the House of Ptah[1], thy great seat[2],
>> I caused it to be like the horizon,
> 5   wherein Ra is[3]...
> I made its august throne[4] like the horizon of heaven...

(*ARE* iii 181, §412, inscription at Abu Simbel;

ARE iv 165, §§314, 315, from P. Harris)

1   The temple was called 'The House of the Ka of Ptah' (*ḥwt k3 ptḥ*), and because of its symbolic significance, as the premier shrine of Egypt, was borrowed as a generic term for the city and the country (Ugaritic *ḥkpt*, Greek Αἴγυπτος), modern 'Egypt'.

2   This is a term for the throne of the image, and then for the temple, on the principle of synechdoche. We preserve the usage in such ideas as a ducal seat.

3   Solarization was an almost natural feature of all state religion in Egypt. This was Ptah's temple, but he was implicitly a form of Ra.

4   A further reference to the throne for the divine image in the sanctuary.

7(5) A New Shrine in Hermopolis

P. Harris is a long account of the good deeds of Rameses III of the 20th dynasty (1184-1152 BCE). The largest surviving papyrus from Egypt, it was written to be placed in his tomb. This passage details construction work at Hermopolis.

I did numerous benefactions in Hesret[1] for my father Thoth, dwelling in Hermopolis. I built for him a house anew in his court; it was a mysterious chapel for the All-Lord[2]. I made for him another house as a dwelling-place; it was the horizon of heaven before him. When he appeared, he was contented in heart to rest in them; he rejoiced and was glad to see them. I supplied them with food and provisions, containing the products of every land...

(ARE iv 179, §356, from P. Harris)

1   Hesret was a town in Hermopolis Nome with an important sanctuary of Thoth.

2   'The All-Lord' was Ra.

7(6) Karnak Inscription of Tuthmosis III

This inscription on the wall of the temple of Amun at Karnak tells how Tuthmosis was chosen by Amun to be king (see the account in §7(12)), and goes on to list the king's pious benefactions.

Behold, My Majesty erected for him an august Holy of Holies, the favourite place of Amun, named His-Great-Seat-is-like-the-Horizon-of-Heaven[1]...

(ARE ii 64, §153)

1   This may be compared with the Mesopotamian temple names at §§2(10) n. 1, 6(27) n. 1, 6(29) and 11(5) n. 1. See also §7(7).

7(7) Inscription at Medinat Habu

The Medinet Habu temple on the west bank at Thebes was the mortuary temple of Rameses III (twentieth dynasty). It contains a number of important shrines, including, in the second court, that of Amen-Apet, a self-regenerating form of Amun, represented as ithyphallic, which is probably the subject of the present inscription. The long temple-name is that of the mortuary temple as a whole.

He (Rameses III) made it (the second court of the Medinet Habu temple) as his monument for his father, Amun-Ra, making for him The-House-of-Usermaat-Ra-Meri-Amun-Possessed-of-Eternity-in-the-House-of-Amun, like unto the great palace of the horizon, of fine sandstone.

(*ARE* iv 6, §7)

7(8)   Inscription of the Edfu Shrine of Horus

The Ptolemaic temple of Horus at Edfu is the best preserved of the temples of Egypt. The diorite shrine box is intact, except for its doors, and this is part of the inscription round the architrave. It offers a brief theology of the resident deity, the falcon god. He was also worshipped in the form of the winged disc as Horus of Behdet, a warrior god, and hero of the myths of conflict between Horus and Seth inscribed on the ambulatory walls. The following excerpt is an important document for the understanding of the Egyptian conception of the relationship of a god to his image. Its spatial language is used to express the superimposition of two orders of reality, the transcendent and immaterial, and the immanent and material.

There is one horizon in the sky of Him-of-the-Horizon[1], and there is another on earth with his image. The western horizon in the sky holds Ra, but the Temple of Edfu on earth[2] holds Him-of-Behdet. When the two doors of the Temple are opened[3] the disc rises like[4] Ra shining in the horizon.

As the firmament is afar off with Ra, so is the Temple exalted with his image.[5]

(Blackman and Fairman 1941, 398, adapted)

[1]   Harakhte (*ḥr 3ḥty*) is a title of Ra (Ra Harakhte) at the point of his crossing the boundaries of the horizons, so that it implicitly embraces the rising sun-god (Khepri) and the setting sun-god (Atum). In the following text, it is evident that Harakhte is in turn identified with Horus of Behdet.

[2]   That is, the present shrine, as a boundary between the the transcendent and the immanent dwellings of the god.

[3]   The temple doors would be opened at dawn, to coincide with the rising of the sun, and ritually, to effect that rising.

[4]   Or, 'as'. Not a comparison but an identification.

[5]   The sense is that the transcendent quality of the firmament is transferred to the temple by virtue of the image, which embodies the god's presence on earth.

7(9)   The Death of the King in the Old Kingdom

The *Pyramid Texts* offer a considerable range of destinies for the deceased king (§2(8) n. 1). The present formula, spoken by Ra, not only assimilates the king to the sun-god on the horizon, but identifies him with Harakhte himself (§7(8) n. 1).

> The king my son is my beloved;
> I have given to him the two horizons
> that he may have power in them as Harakhte.

(Faulkner 1969, 1: PT 6)

7(10) The Death of Amenemhet I

Amenemhet I (1963-1934 BCE) was the founder of the twelfth dynasty, and reunited Egypt under Theban control (the Middle Kingdom). *The story of Sinuhe*, of a man exiled to Palestine, was set in the years following his death, during the reign of Sesostris I. This is a standard formula for the death of a king. See §2(28) for the Osirian emphasis in the statement concerning Seth-Nakht.

The god[1] ascended to his horizon[2]; the King of Upper and Lower Egypt Sehetep-ib-Ra[3] was taken up to heaven and united with the sun-disc[4].

(ANET 18: Story of Sinuhe, adapted)

1   The living king was regarded as divine.

2   That is, he died. Notice the idea of ascension (sc. to the sky); the timing of this ascension was linked with the setting of the evening sun. The accession of the successor king was timed to sunrise the following day. Another nuance may be that the king was transfigured in his laying to rest in his tomb ('horizon').

3   This is the fourth royal name (see the titulary in §7(12)), meaning 'The Heart of Ra gives Peace'.

4   The Aten (*itn*), which in the reign of Amenhotpe IV (Akhenaten) in the eighteenth dynasty was at the heart of the 'Amarna revolution'. It is often regarded as an early form of monotheism.

7(11) Boundary Stela Inscription at Akhetaten

This excerpt from one of the southern boundary stelae of Akhenaten's (Amenhotpe IV) new city of Akhet-Aten at el Amarna, dating from *ca* 1350 BCE, uses the term *3ht* with several of its nuances.

On this day, when one[1] was in Akhet-[Aten][2], his Person[3] [appeared] on the great chariot of electrum — just like Aten, when he rises in his horizon and fills the land with the love and [the pleasantness? of] the Aten. He set off on a good road [toward] Akhet-Aten, his place of the primaeval event[4], which he made for himself to set within it daily[5], and which his son Wa-en-Ra[6] made for him — (being) his great monument which he founded for himself; his horizon, [in which his] circuit comes into being, where he is beheld with joy while the land rejoices and all hearts exult when they see him.

(Murnane 1995, 74, adapted)

1   The king.

2   Akhet-Aten (*3ḫt itn*), 'the Horizon of the Sun-Disc', was the name of the new capital. Its primary sense was no doubt in the sense of 'sanctuary' (as in §7(8)). It perhaps played on a tradition that the site was revealed to the king by a sunrise (interpreted as an epiphany) between two high points (representing the hieroglyphic form ⟨𓈌⟩) on the eastern horizon. See §§5(5) n., p. 153.

3   The king again, but this time specifically as an incarnation of the Aten, thus emphasizing his divine nature.

4   While the foundation of Akhet-Aten is well-rooted in eighteenth dynasty history, it is here projected back to primordial times, an absolute requirement of any claim to sanctity.

5   The deity is here credited with the foundation of his own shrine.

6   Wa-en-Ra (*wˤ-n-rˤ*), 'Ra is One', the fourth name of the king. The unassociated identity of the Aten (*itn*, 'sun-disc') should not be overemphasized. The Aten was a manifestation of Ra.

II   Heavenly Journeys

There is a striking similarity of structure in accounts of kings, priests, or wise men, who ascend to heaven. This was a metaphor for the notion of transcendence, which may be regarded as a universal feature of religion from very early times. The idea of entering the presence of a god, which in the real world means walking through the boundary separating the main hall from the shrine room of the deity in a temple (the 'cella' or 'holy of holies'') during the cult, appears to be universal, the horizontal movement being transformed into a vertical movement[2], which emphasizes hierarchical and moral transformations. Shamanism, associated in particular with the Altai peoples of Siberia, has in fact been almost universal in its incidence, and undoubtedly had its roots in Palaeolithic culture. The ancient Near Eastern examples had their roots in the pre-urban cultures of the Neolithic, and betray shamanic elements. Ascents were also associated with dream-experiences, and hallucinations experienced while under the influence of various narcotics. The use of powerful aromatherapeutic substances was very common, ranging from herbs selected for use in base oils in unction (see §7(16)) below) to intoxicants such as alcohol and opium[3] and even cocaine, supposedly found in a number of New Kingdom mummies.

1   'Holy of holies' (in Hebrew *qᵉdôš qᵉdôšîm*) is a superlative, meaning 'the holiest', and alluded to the progressive degrees of purity, sanctity and separation from the profane world as progress was made into the inmost part of a shrine, where the cult-image of the deity was usually placed in a shrine-box. We see this structure particularly clearly in the Temple of Horus at Edfu.

2 In the case of ziggurats, tower-temples (particularly associated with promontory sites (see *5.1.4 n. 1), and aspects of the cult involving roof-shrines in Egypt, the vertical movement was already directly represented.

3 Evidence of the use of opium is found very widely in Neolithic contexts. Many ritual vessels from Europe and the Near East from the earliest ceramic finds are shaped like poppy-heads. Figures of deities wearing a crown of poppy seed-pods have been found in Crete. Poppy-seeds from *ca* 4200 BCE have been found in ritual contexts in Spain. The Ebers papyrus (*ca* 1500 BCE) gives notes on the medicinal use of opium. And so-called 'incense altars' found widely in the Near East may have been used for more interesting substances.

7(12) An Egyptian Account: the Ascent of Tuthmosis III

See §7(6) introduction. The following account describes the divine choice of Tuthmosis by Amun-Ra during the course of him serving in the Karnak temple as a junior priest. The movement of the image, whether deliberate or inadvertent on the part of the priests carrying it, was interpreted as the sign of the divine choice of the heir. We do not have to see here a real mystical experience by a susceptible teen-ager! The language is entirely stereotypical, and this text was undoubtedly composed on the king's behalf at the time of its inscription in the temple. This was spin-doctoring on a monumental scale! The text ends with the king's fivefold titulary, usually given to him at his enthronement. Here Tuthmosis claims that it was revealed to him on the occasion of this theophany.

We may tentatively use this passage as a guide to the interpretation of the enthronement rites of Egypt, with parallels *mutatis mutandis* elsewhere in the ancient Near East.

The god Amun is my father, and I am his son. He commanded that I should be upon his throne, while I was still a nestling. He begot me from the very middle of his heart and chose me for the kingship... There is no lie, there is no equivocation therein — when My Majesty was only a puppy, when I was only a newly-weaned child who was in his temple, before my installation as prophet had taken place...

While I was in the guise and role of the Pillar-of-his-mother priest, like the youth of Horus in Khemmis, and I was standing in the north colonnaded hall, Amun-Ra came forth from the glory of his horizon. He made heaven and earth festive with his beauty, and he began a great marvel, with his rays in the eyes of men like the rising of Harakhte. The people gave him praise when he halted at the... of his temple. Then His Majesty offered him incense upon the flame and presented to him a great oblation of oxen, cattle, and wild beasts of the desert... The procession made the circuit of the colonnaded hall on its two sides, but it was not in the heart of those who were present to his actions, in seeking out My Majesty everywhere.

Then he recognized me, and he halted... I touched the ground; I bowed myself down in his presence. He set me before his majesty, I being posted at the Station of the Lord. Then he worked a great marvel over me...

These things really happened, without equivocation, though they were remote from the faces of mankind and mysterious in the hearts of the gods... There is no one who knows them; there is no one who can judge them...

He opened for me the portals of heaven; he spread open for me the portals of its horizon. I flew up to the sky as a divine falcon, that I might see his mysterious form which is in heaven, that I might adore his majesty... I saw the forms of being of the Horizon God on his mysterious ways in heaven. Ra himself established me, and I was endowed with his crowns which were upon his head, his uraeus-serpent was fixed upon my brow... I was equipped with all his states of glory; I was made satisfied with the understanding of the gods, like Horus when he took account of himself at the house of his father Amun-Ra. I was perfected with the dignities of a god... He established my crowns, and drew up for me titulary himself. He fixed my falcon upon the façade; he made me mighty as a mighty bull; he made me appear in the midst of Thebes, in this my name of...

I   Horus: the Mighty Bull, appearing in Thebes.
           He made me wear the two goddesses; he made my kingship to endure
           like Ra in heaven, in this my name of
II   the Two Goddesses: Enduring in kingship like Ra in heaven.
           He fashioned me as a falcon of gold; he gave me his power and his
           strength; I was august in these his appearances, in this my name of
III   Horus of Gold: Powerful of strength, August of appearances.
           He caused me to appear as King of Upper Egypt and Lower Egypt in
           the Two Lands; he established my forms like Ra, in this my name of
IV   King of Upper Egypt and Lower Egypt: Lord of the Two Lands:
                               Men-kheper-Ra.
           I am his son, who came forth out of him, perfect of birth like Him
           who presides over Hesret; he united all my beings, in this my name of
V   Son of Ra: Tuthmosis-United-of-Being, living forever and ever...

                                        (*ANET* 446-7: Karnak Inscription)

The king was normally given his fivefold titulary at his coronation. Here it was given proleptically during the prince's heavenly ascent. The titulary comprised the following features:

I   The Horus name (*ḥr*):
The oldest name, identifying the king as the falcon sky-god.

II   The 'Two Ladies' name (*nbty*):

This understood the king as son and protégé of the titulary goddesses of Upper and Lower Egypt. Nekhbet, the former, the vulture goddess of El Kab, was also the White Crown of Upper Egypt. Wadjet, the latter, cobra goddess of Buto in the Delta, was also the Red Crown. The goddesses 'came together' in the double crown on the king's head, and also as vulture and cobra uraei on his brow.

III   The 'Golden Horus' name (*ḥr nbw*):

The meaning of this is obscure, but was in Ptolemaic times understood as a statement of Horus' victory over Seth 'the Ombite' (*nbty*). But since gold was a symbol of divinity and transcendence, it may originally have been an emphasis on the king's transcendence.

IV   The 'Sedge and Bee' name (*nsw bit*):

Commonly translated 'the King of upper and Lower Egypt', the name plays on the heraldic emblems of Upper and Lower Egypt respectively (*nsw*, 'sedge', also means 'king of Upper Egypt'; *bit*, 'bee', also means 'king of Lower Egypt).

V   The 'Son of Ra' name (*s3 rꜥ*):

This formula was in use from the fifth dynasty.

It is interesting to note, in view of the dualistic tensions in Egyptian cosmology, that the names see the king as a unitary (I, and V) and dual (II, IV) being. The status of the third name in this system is ambiguous, but I prefer to see it as unitary.

7(13)   A Mespotamian Account i): the Ascent of Enmeduranki

Enmeduranki was an antediluvian king in *the Sumerian king-list* (*ANET* 265-7), who ruled for 6,000 or even 21,000 years. He was also the sixth or the seventh king since 'kingship was lowered from heaven'. As king of Sippar, he had a particular devotion to Shamash, (= Utu, the Sumerian sun-god). As king, he would be the god's high priest. These features may have influenced the tradition of Enoch's ascent(s) to heaven: below (§7(19-21)).

Shamash caused Enmeduranki, the king of Sippar, the beloved of Anu, Enlil and Ea, to enter into Ebarra[1]. Shamash and Adad called him to their assembly... Shamash and Adad placed him on a great golden throne; they taught him to inspect oil on water[2], the secret of Anu, Enlil and Ea. The darling of the gods, they caused his hand to seize the tablet of the gods, the bag with the mystery of heaven and earth[3], the cedar staff [4].

(Widengren 1950:7-8, *The Ascent of Enmeduranki*, adapted)

1   Ebarra: read rather É.BABBAR.(RA), 'The Shining House'. This was the name of the temple of Shamash at Sippar.

2   The arts of divination were practised by the *bārû* priests, who looked back to Enmeduranki as their legendary patron. Here the emphasis is on secrecy, for kings were granted divine wisdom during their enthronement, in which context the 'ascent to heaven' — sc. their entry into the sanctuary — took place. For an example of lecanomancy see §11(35).

3   This was the so-called 'Tablet of Destinies' (also referred to by scholars as 'Tablets of Destiny'). See §6(13) n. 4. It has been seen by some as the

prototype of the *Urîm* and *Tummîm* of Israelite ritual practice (§11(15)). The two 'tablets of the law' brought down from Mount Sinai by Moses, seen by some as cuneiform tablets, or at least as stone stelae with divine instructions written on them, was in the tradition of ancient law-codes set up in public for all (literate people!) to refer to. The stela of Hammurabi of Babylon is a fine example in the Louvre.

4   The sceptre of a king. Its cedar form is interesting, since Baal Hadad, the Canaanite storm- and war-god carried a cedar staff. Here it is the king's sceptre. As an extension of the king's person, it is comparable to the king himself identified as a tree or branch (§§6(9-13)).

7(14) A Mespotamian Account ii): the Journey of Etana

Etana was legendary king of Kish. According to *the Sumerian king-list* (*ANET* 265-7), 'Etana, a shepherd, he who ascended to heaven and who consolidated all countries, became king and ruled for 1,560 (or, 1,500) years'. The story of Etana probably had no directly ideological purpose, but is rather a folktale derivative ('an elaborate legend': Speiser, *ANET* 114). But since it was natural for a story-teller to draw on well-known, and especially heroic, motifs, we may relate the accounts of his celestial journeys as derived from the tradition of the ascent of the king.

1   'Come, my friend, let me carry you up [to the sky,]
[let us meet] with Ishtar, the mistress [of Birth].
Beside Ishtar the Mistress [of Birth let us...]
Put your arms over my sides;
5   put your hands over the quills of my wings.'
He put his arms over its sides;
  put his hands over the quills of its wings.
[The eagle] took him upwards for a mile.
'My friend, look at the country!
10   How does it seem?'
'The affairs of the country buzz? [like flies ?],
  and the wide sea is no bigger than a sheepfold!'
[The eagle took him] up a second mile.
'My friend, look at the country!
15   How does it seem?'
'The country has turned into a garden [   ]
  and the wide sea is no bigger than a bucket!'
It took him up a third mile.
'My friend, look at the country!
20   How does it seem?'
'I am looking for the country,
  but I can't see it!
My eyes cannot even pick out the wide sea!'...

> (This attempt to reach heaven is a failure. Etana is told in
> dreams to persevere. The eagle makes a further attempt...)

The eagle...
25 took him up a mile,
   and spoke to him, to Etana:
'See, my friend, how the country seems!
Inspect the sea,
   look carefully for its features!

...

30 The eagle took him up a second mile...

...

The eagle took him up a third mile
   and spoke to Etana:
'See, my friend, how the garden seems!
   The sea has turned into a gardener's ditch!'
35 When they came up to the heaven of Anu,
   they went through the gate of Anu, Ellil and Ea.
The eagle and Etana bowed down together.
   They went through the gate of Sin, Shamash, Adad and Ishtar.
The eagle and Etana bowed down together.
   [   ]
40 He pushed it open [and went inside].

(Dalley 1989, 197-200: from *Etana*)

Note the visual impression of increasing height: 'the wide sea is no bigger than a sheepfold... no bigger than a bucket... my eyes cannot even pick out the wide sea... a gardener's ditch!' The last comparison is anti-climactic after the third (and originally surely the last) of the first series, and points to redactional work. Ishtar, the first deity mentioned at the beginning, is the last mentioned at the end, thus providing an envelope figure. The imagery of *Etana* suggests that it may be the primary source underlying the so-called ascent of Alexander (in Pseudo-Callisthenes, *The Greek Alexander Romance* ii 41, Stoneman 1991, 123). He has two birds captured at the end of the earth, harnesses an ox-hide to them, and using horse's liver as a bait on the end of two spears (on the carrot and donkey principle), gets them to carry him up into the sky. He meets a heavenly being, who tells him to look down. 'I looked down... and saw... a great snake curled up, and in the middle of the snake a tiny circle like a threshing floor.' His companion then says, 'that is the world. The snake is the sea that surrounds the world.'

7(15) A Mesopotamian Account iii): the Summons of Adapa

See §9(2), *Adapa* ll. 45-122, for the narrative: the scene envisaged is a court-room scene; but the assize takes place in the throne-room of Anu, and the entire episode is modelled on the motif of the royal ascent. Adapa, like Adam, is a royal figure and a 'First Man'. Like Adam, he loses potential immortality by taking bad advice. From a god!

7(16) An Ugaritic Account i): the Enthronement of Athtar

This is an excerpt from the late thirteenth century BCE narrative which dealt with the fortunes of the god Baal at Ugarit, establishing him as king of the gods, under the overall control of El. After Yam's enthronement, Baal had challenged him, killed him, and seized his throne, having a great palace (sc. temple) constructed as a token of his power. But he capitulated to Mot, god of the underworld, and Athtar was selected to rule in his stead. This is the myth of the institution of human kingship (cf. §§5(8-10)).

1   Aloud cried El to the Great Lady-who-tramples-Yam:
       'Listen, O Great Lady-who-tramples-Yam.
     Give the first of your sons;
       I shall make him king.'
5   And the Great Lady-who-tramples-Yam replied:
       'Shall we not make king one who has knowledge and wit?'
     And the Wise, the Perceptive god (El), replied:
     'Let the finest of pigments be ground,
       Let the people of Baal prepare unguents:
10   the people of the Son of Dagan crushed herbs!'¹
     The Great Lady-who-tramples-Yam replied:
     'Indeed, let us make Athtar the Brilliant king:
       Athtar the Brilliant shall rule!'
     Immediately
15   Athtar the Brilliant went up into the uttermost parts of Saphon;
       he sat on the throne of Valiant Baal.
     [But] his feet did not reach the footstool,
       his head did not come to its top.
     Then Athtar the Brilliant said:
20   'I shall not rule in the uttermost parts of Saphon!'
     Athtar the Brilliant came down,
       he came down from the throne of Valiant Baal
       and ruled in the earth, god of it all.
     [they d]rew water? from amphorae,
25   [they drew] water? from vases.

(Wyatt 1998a, 131-3, adapted: KTU 1.6 i 43-67)

1   For this translation of ll. 8-10, modifying that of Wyatt 1998a, see Wyatt 1999, 857 n. 13.

This is the mythic account of a royal ascent from Ugarit. While describing the ascent of a god, it is evident that the point is the ascent of a man (the king) who becomes a god. This describes an initial 'royal ascent' (its mythic paradigm), while §7(17) gives an account of its continued reenactment in the cult. See §3(17) for lines 15-20 and discussion.

7(17) An Ugaritic Account ii):
King Keret and the Language of Ritual

This excerpt from a thirteenth century BCE Ugaritic tale is an episode in the story of King Keret, who, having lost his wife and children, was instructed by El how to find a new wife and beget many children. Here the king performs cult, offering sacrifices and libations in the temple. In the cult, by 'entering heaven', the king repeats his apotheosis on a regular basis.

1 He washed himself and rouged[1] himself,
     he washed his hands to the elbow,
     his fingers to the shoulder.
  He entered into the darkness of the tent shrine:
5 he took a sacrificial lamb in his hand,
     a suckling lamb in them both.
  He took the appointed portion of his offering-bread,
     dreg-free wine as a (drink-)offer[ing];
  he poured out wine from a silver rhyton,
10 honey(ed wine) from a rhyton of gold;
  and he went up to the top of the tower[2],
     he mounted up to the summit of the wall.
  He lifted up his hands to heaven;
     he sacrificed to Bull his father, El.
15 He served Baal with his sacrifice,
     the Son of Dagan with his food.
  Keret came down [from the r]oof...[3]

(Wyatt 1998a, 198-9: KTU 1.14 iii 52-iv 9)

1   Rouging with red ochre was practised in ritual contexts over a vast area from Palaeolithic times, probably symbolizing blood and thus life and vitality.

2   Note the vertical element, and cf. *7 II n. 2 (p. 193).

3   Note the following stages in the ritual in *Keret*:
     i) ritual washing;
     ii) rouging;
     iii) entry into the sanctuary;
     iv) various sacrificial and libational acts;
     v) ascent to the highest part of the temple (in this narrative the tower);
     vi) raising of the hands to heaven, in a gesture affirming the link achieved;
     vii) formal offering as a sacrifice, and feeding of the gods;
     viii) descent from the high place, thus bringing the ritual process to an end.
    The ritual texts from Ugarit confirm the implication of this sequence: that a process of divinization took place as the king entered the shrine (stage vii above), which was 'in heaven', followed by his 'reanthropization' as he emerged afterwards. Cf. §7(16) and Wyatt 1999, 859.

7(18) A Jewish Account i): Isaiah's Inaugural Vision

A number of Jewish accounts are found. The symbolism is essentially what we have encountered above, and derives most directly from royal practice, both in enthronement rites and then the priestly role of the king (§§7(16-7)). The link between the Jewish (< Israelite and Judahite) beliefs and practice is generally accepted. It is also evident that this both echoes and perpetuates older forms, such as those above, but also anticipates later forms, such as the temptation and later the ascension of Jesus, and subsequently the enthronement of Christian monarchs.

The present passage originates from *ca* 740 BCE, at the time of Isaiah's inaugural vision. The experience was evidently close in conception to that of the king, with its shamanic qualities. Note how a historical account corresponds largely to the literary ideals: the traditional form evidently derived from real experience, which in turn met the expectations of the culture. (*Isaiah* 40, the beginning of so-called 'Deutero-Isaiah', is modelled on this account.)

In the year of King Uzziah's death I saw the Lord sitting on a high, elevated throne, and his pudenda (*šul'*[1]) filled the temple. Seraphs were stationed around him, each with six wings: with two they hid his[2] face, with two they hid his[2] genitals, and with two they were flying. And one was calling to another, saying,

> 'Holy, holy, holy[3] is Yahweh of Hosts!
> his glory fills the entire earth!'

Then the foundations of the threshold shook at the sound of their call, and the temple was filled with smoke. And I said,

> 'Woe is me, for I am destroyed!
> because a man unclean of lips am I,
> and in the midst of a people unclean of lips I am dwelling —
> for the king, Yahweh of Hosts, my eyes have seen!'

Then I heard the voice of the Lord saying, 'Whom shall I send, and who will go for us?'

And I said, 'I am here: send me!' Then he said, 'Go, and say to this people...'

(Isaiah 6:1-5, 8-9)

1   See Eslinger 1995. The idea of the nakedness of the deity is at first glance surprising. Isaiah has, as it were, butted in. He should ordinarily have only been allowed to see Yahweh clothed. On the other hand, it is the priest, representing the king, who himself clothes the image of Amun in §10(1), and Isaiah's experience is surely conditioned by the expectations of the royal experience.

2   Yahweh's, not their own.

3   The sense is superlative: 'most holy'.

7(19) A Jewish Account ii): The Ascent of Enoch in Genesis

Enoch, the hero of several accounts, first appears in *Genesis* 5:18-24, where he was significantly the seventh generation after Adam. Curiously, among a list of ante-diluvian patriarchs whose ages were generally enormous, he lived for what can only be explained as a brief, symbolic life-span of 365 years (sc. a solar year before calendars were refined to take Leap Years into account. Cf. §§2(38-40)). His similarity to, and perhaps derivation from, the figure of Enmeduranki (§7(13)) is widely accepted. Many important biblical and Jewish ideas probably originated in Mesopotamia as a result of Jewish settlement there following the Babylonian deportations of 597, 586 and 582. (A Jewish community has been resident there ever since.)

These are the lifespans of the patriarchs from Adam to Noah:
Adam (930), Seth (912), Enosh (905), Kenan (910), Mahalalel (895), Jared (962), Enoch (365), Methuselah (969), Lamech (777), Noah (950: *Genesis* 9:29). It is evident that Lamech's age is also of symbolic significance. See further p. 325.

Enoch walked with God, and was no more, for God took him.

(Genesis 5:24)

This abrupt statement (the first part repeats the beginning of v. 22) is cryptic. Maccoby 1982, took it that Enoch was the victim of a human sacrifice, with God accepting the offering. Most take it as an account of an assumption into heaven, and this is how the subsequent Jewish tradition (see below, §§7(20-1)) obviously understood it.

7(20) A Jewish Account iii): Enoch in Pseudepigraphical Tradition i)

There were three 'Enoch' books in the late Jewish and early Christian world: *1 Enoch* (Ethiopic, second century BCE-first century CE), *2 Enoch* (Slavonic, first century CE), and *3 Enoch* (Hebrew, fifth-sixth century CE). They are quite divergent, and are rather independent cycles than translations.

And behold, I saw the clouds. And they were calling me in a vision; and the fogs were calling me; and the course of the stars and the lightnings were rushing me and causing me to desire; and in the vision, the winds were causing me to fly and rushing me high up into heaven...

And I entered into the house[1], which was hot like fire and cold like ice, and there was nothing inside it; (so) fear covered me and trembling seized me. And as I shook and trembled, I fell upon my face and saw a vision. And behold there was an opening before me (and) a second house[2] which is greater than the former and everything was built with tongues of fire. And in every respect it excelled the other — in glory and great honour — to the extent that it is impossible for me to recount to you concerning its glory and greatness. As for its floor, it was of fire and above it was lightning and the path of the stars; and as for the ceiling, it was flaming fire. And I observed and saw inside it a lofty throne — its appearance was like crystals and its wheels like the shining sun; and (I heard[?]) the voice of the Cherubim; and from beneath the throne were issuing streams of living fire[3]... And the Great Glory was sitting upon it — as for his gown, which was shining more brightly than the sun, it was whiter than any snow. None of the angels was able to come in and see the face of the Excellent and Glorious One... The flaming fire was round about him, and a great fire stood before him. No one could come near unto him from among those that surrounded the tens of millions[4] (that stood) before him. He needed no council, but the most holy ones who are near to him neither go far away at night nor move away from him.

Until then I was prostrate on my face covered and trembling. And the Lord called me with his own mouth and said to me, 'Come near to me, Enoch, and to my holy Word. And he lifted me up and brought me near to the gate, but I (continued) to look down with my face. But he raised me up and said to me with his voice...

(Charlesworth 1983, i 20-1: *1 Enoch* 14:8-15:1)

1   The Hebrew *hēkāl*, from Sumerian É.GAL ('great house' = temple or palace), denotes a temple. Cf. §2(10) n. 1. In Jerusalem, the term was also used specifically for that part of the temple immediately in front of the Holy of Holies. This is certainly the sense here, since this 'house' is obviously merely an anticipation of the 'second house' mentioned below (n. 2).

2   This must be the 'Holy of Holies', where God was believed to reside. His abode was at the very centre of the universe (Hayman 1986). Cf. §6 *passim*. The Jerusalem temple had three main sections to the building: *'ûlām* ('threshold'), *hēkāl* ('house': main chamber of the building), *debîr* or *qᵉdôš qᵉdôšîm* ('cella', 'Holy of Holies'). Its threefold structure thus replicated in miniature the three storeys of the Hebrew universe (heavens, world, underworld). This comes out clearly in Josephus' account (*Antiquities*) of the significance of the temple: the court = the sea, the *hēkāl* = the land and the Holy of holies = heaven (summarized in Patai 1948, 112). Cf. the *seven*-fold structure of Mesopotamian and Egyptian temples, echoed at Ugarit in §6(1).

3   Cf. the rivers flowing out of Eden (§6(13)) and the river(s) flowing out from the Jerusalem in *Ezekiel* 47:1 and *Revelation* 22:1-2.

4   The 'ten thousand times ten thousand' of *Daniel* 7:10 add up to a hundred million! But the figure is a standard numerical progression (thousands :: ten thousands) as occurring in *1 Samuel* 18:7.

7(21) A Jewish Account iv):
Enoch in Pseudepigraphical Tradition ii)

And they lifted me up into one place where there were (the ones) like the flaming fire. And when they (so) desire they appear like men. And they took me into a place of whirlwind in the mountain; the top of its summit was reaching into heaven[1]. And I saw chambers of light and thunder in the ultimate end of the depth toward (the place where) the bow, the arrow, and their quiver and a fiery sword[2] and all the lightnings were. And they lifted me up unto the waters of life[3], into the occidental fire which receives every setting of the sun. And I came to the river of fire which flows like water and empties itself into the great sea in the direction of the west[4]. And I saw all the great rivers and reached to the great darkness and went into the place where all flesh must walk cautiously. And I saw the mountains of the dark storms of the rainy season and from where the waters of all the seas flow. And I saw the mouths of all the rivers of the earth and the mouth of the sea…

And I saw a deep pit with heavenly fire on its pillars; I saw them descending pillars of fire that were immeasurable (in respect to both) altitude and depth. And on top of that pit I saw a place without the heavenly firmament above it or earthly foundation under it or water. There was nothing on it — not even birds — but it was a desolate and terrible place. And I saw there the seven stars (which) were like great, burning mountains. (Then) the angel said (to me), 'This place is the (ultimate) end of heaven and earth; it is the prison house for the stars and the powers of heaven…

(Charlesworth 1983, i 22-3: 1 Enoch 17:1-8, 18:11-4)

1   Cf. the Tower of Babel (§6(30)), discussed at §2(10) n. 1.

2   The divine weapons are stored in heaven. These are those used in royal rituals. See §3(3) and Wyatt 1998b.

3   The Sumerian expression AB.ZU (Akkadian *apsû*), 'waters of knowledge' (see §2(30) n. 1), says it all! Cf. the following analogy:
      waters of knowledge : waters of life :: tree of knowledge : tree of life.
      The two trees are really one tree differentiated in the tradition into two roles (see §6(7) n. 3). Similarly with the waters. These same waters appear in Greek tradition, as we have seen (§§2(30-4)), as the ἀβυσσος. As the boundary of the world of the dead (to which cf. the Hebrew *yam sûf*) this is also known by other names, such as Acheron ('Αχερων: 'Afterwards', §1(6)), Styx (Στυξ: 'Abhorrent') and Lethe (Ληθη: 'Forgetting'). This last name has the opposite sense to AB.ZU. Note the Greek word for 'truth': αληθεια, lit. 'not forgetting'.

4   On a mundane level this is the Mediterranean Sea. In reality it is the *yam sûf* (§2(35)), the cosmic ocean.

These two passages are the first of several in *1 Enoch* in which the sage wanders the heavens, learning wisdom. The background to this is the royal wisdom, learned by a king at his ascent. When a king ascended to heaven, he became divine. The various sages who ascended did not make this grade, but were accompanied by angels who allowed them to relate unharmed to the divine. The narratives of the temptations of

Jesus, and his transfiguration, modelled on the ascent of the king, were intended to represent him as divine. On the theme of royal wisdom, cf. *1 Enoch* 41:1: 'I saw all the secrets of heaven'. Cf. also the language of *Job* 38-41, in which Yahweh challenged Job with questions he could not answer. But a king would learn all these answers.

7(22) A Jewish Account v): Jacob's Stairway to Heaven

Cf. the Tower of Babel story at §6(30). There the idea of a way up to heaven, as represented by a ziggurat, is treated satirically. Here it forms part of Jewish traditional thought. Cf. Wyatt 1990c, Husser 1991.

And he arrived at the place[1], and settled down for the night there, because the sun had set. Then he took one of the stones of the place[1] and set it as a pillow, and lay down in the place. And he had a dream: there was a stairway, planted firmly on the earth, with its top reaching heaven[2]. And there were messengers of God[3] going up and down on it. And there was Yahweh standing over him, and saying, 'I am Yahweh, the god of Abraham your father, and the god of Isaac. The earth on which you are lying I give to you and to your descendants…' …

Then Jacob awoke from his sleep, and said. 'Surely Yahweh is in this place[1], but I did not know!… How fearful is this place[1]! This is nothing other than the house of God, and this is the Gate of heaven[4]!'

(*Genesis* 28:11-3, 16-7)

1   Hebrew *hammāqôm*. Since the place has not been named, it must be somewhere immediately identifiable as '*The* Place'. The end of the story identifies it as Bethel (*Bêt-'ēl*, 'Temple of El'), but this is secondary. It is more likely that Jerusalem and its future temple are the location of Jacob's dream. All the following symbolism supports this. The term *māqôm*, literally '(something) raised up', as in a building, often denotes specifically *sacred* places. Cf. §§5(15), 8(8). It is of course possible that *Bêt-'ēl* is to be taken as a cipher for the Jerusalem temple.

2   This is a paradigm for all temples, which communicated between earth and heaven. Its particular reference, though located in Jerusalem on one level, is surely the stepped temples (ziggurats) of Mesopotamia.

3   'Messengers of God… temple of God', or perhaps 'messengers of the gods… temple of the gods': the Hebrew is plural.

4   'Gate of Heaven' is perhaps an allusion to the popular Akkadian etymology of *Bab-ili*, 'Gate of God (or: the gods)', the Akkadian name of Babylon. It may have been in origin a pre-Semitic name. 'Heaven' can be a periphrasis for 'God', so that the Hebrew here may be deliberately intended to evoke Babylon. Jacob seems to dream in both Babylon and Jerusalem: the story is addressed to exiles, promising them restoration of land and temple. See §11(5) n. 2.

7(23) A Jewish Account vi): **Moses on the Mountain**

Excerpts from the narrative concerning the revelation of the Torah on Mount Sinai (Horeb). The narrative is composite, blending various source-materials, and is much reworked (see n. 3!). The second paragraph here, rather older than the first, has been claimed as one of the oldest parts of the Hebrew Bible. It certainly reflects an ancient world-view. Notice how not just Moses, but other representatives go up to converse and feast with 'the god of Israel', and also *see* him. The rest of the narrative is concerned that only Moses approaches God, or sees him. This is because Moses is mysteriously transformed.

And Moses went up to God, and Yahweh called to him from the mountain, and said,

> 'Thus shall you say to the House of Jacob,
> and declare to the sons of Israel...'

Then Moses came and called to the elders of the people, and set before them all these matters which Yahweh had commanded him...

Then Moses went up with Aaron, Nadab and Abihu[1], and seventy of the elders of Israel. And they saw the god of Israel, and beneath his feet there was as it were a sapphire pavement[2], like the very substance of the sky in purity. But he did not stretch out his hand against the nobles of the Israelites. They looked upon God, and ate and drank...

Then Moses turned and went down from the mountain[3], with the two tablets[4] of the testimony[5]... The tablets were the handiwork of God, and the writing was the writing of God[6]...

Now when Moses came down from Mount Sinai[7], with the two tablets of the testimony in his hand(s) as he came down the mountain, Moses did not know that he had horns on his face[8] after speaking to (Yahweh). And when Aaron and all the Israelites saw that Moses had horns on his face, they were afraid to go near him[9]...

(Exodus 19:3, 7; 24:9-11; 32:15-6; 34:29-30)

1   Nadab and Abihu no doubt reflect a particular group of priests. They come to a sticky end in *Numbers* 16.

2   Is this perhaps a lunar theophany? Celestial and planetary language is often used of theophanies in the Hebrew Bible.

3   This is Moses' first 'definitive' descent from the mountain of two main ones (the second treated in n. 7): he comes down as a king following his royal ascent, with his authority, legal documentation and symbols of power. But as a reading of the whole of *Exodus* 19-34 quickly reveals, he is actually up and down the mountain several times. Thus he goes up in 19:3, down in 19:7 (though the Hebrew just says 'came'); up (implicitly) in 19:8, down in 19:14; up in 19:20, down in 19:25; (20:1-21 appear to follow on logically from 19:19, at

which point Moses is still down the mountain, while 20:22-23:33, the so-called 'Book of the covenant', is also apparently given to Moses at the foot of the mountain). He goes up in 24:9 (above), after being warned that he alone may approach the deity (24:2), and presumably down again (no reference to this), because in 24:13, 15 he goes up again, and remains there for forty days and nights. After pleading with Yahweh for Israel on account of the golden calf, he comes down in 32:15 (above); he goes up in 34:4, and down in 34:29 (above), his second 'main descent'.

4   The Hebrew *luḥôt* suggests clay tablets, with cuneiform writing on, like a number of treaty and legal texts from the ancient world. Hammurabi's law-code was written on a large stone stela, now in the Louvre. Cf. also §7(13) n. 4; these tablets and Moses' ascent of the mountain to converse with God (*Exodus* 19-34) is modelled on the royal ascent. Cf. Wyatt 1986. The idea of laws being of divine composition was routine in ancient Near Eastern thought, and the biblical idea conforms to this.

5   Hebrew *ʿēdût*. Cf. §6(11) n. 4.

6   Cf. also the divine origin of the *Qurʾān*. The divinization of any religious or legal principle in this way is a powerful metaphor of its absolute authority. This is why the sermon on the mount was modelled on Moses' law-giving at Sinai. And just as Moses was deified, as shown by his horns (Wyatt 1999), so was the New Moses.

7   This is Moses' second 'definitive' descent from the mountain (see beginning of n. 3). The obvious question is why, quite apart from all the other complications noted in n. 3, Moses should have come down twice with the tablets. The best solution is to see the entire event as a parable of the history of the monarchy. Kingship was instituted, and was immediately followed by the confrontation over the golden calf. See Wyatt 1992 for the historical context of the golden calf motif: Jeroboam's religious secession from Jerusalem. The punishment of the people (rather vaguely phrased and certainly understated at *Exodus* 32:35) represents the exile, which gives rise to a new, and now transformed delivery of the Torah before the second descent. The divinized Moses serves two functions: he represents the true kingship (the faithful servant with whom Yahweh speaks face to face), and he then represents the transformed and theocratic priestly rule of the post-monarchical period, in which the text reached its final form.

8   This is often translated as 'the skin of his face shone', and understood as a transfiguration. For discussion see Wyatt 1999, 871-3. The Vulgate supports the translation above. The horns signify Moses' transformation into a god. This then fully explains the people's fear of him, and the use of a protective veil in vv. 33-5. (We might ask just what a 'transfiguration' was supposed to entail, if not an apotheosis. Cf. *Matthew* 17:1-8 = *Mark* 9:2-8 = *Luke* 9:28-36.)

9   This fear, before the *mysterium tremendum et fascinans* (Otto's phrase, Otto 1950), is the appropriate response to the presence of a deity.

7(24) A Jewish Account vii):
The Enthronement of the King in Judah

This is an enthronement address to the king by Yahweh, who describes the king's mythic generation as his son (cf. *Psalm* 2:7).

> Yahweh said to my Lord[1]:
> 'Take your seat on the throne at my right hand,
>> till I have made your enemies your footstool…
> in the courts of the Holy Ones,
>> from the Uterine[2] at dawn as dew[3] I begot you.

(Psalm 110:1, 3[3])

[1]   The term here refers to the king, and thus assumes that he is divine. He is to be understood as enthroned in heaven (in fact the temple sanctuary).

[2]   The goddess Rahmay ('Uterine') appears twinned with Athirat (= biblical Asherah) in Ugaritic royal mythology (KTU 1.23).

[3]   The third verse (last two lines) is based on the LXX Greek text. Is 'dew' a metaphor for divine semen? Similar language was used of the conception of Egyptian kings.

7(25) A Jewish Account viii): The Enthronement of Solomon

This describes Solomon's accession to the throne of Judah following the death of David.

> Then Solomon sat on the throne of Yahweh as king in succession to David his father.

(1 Chronicles 29:23)

As in §7(24), the ritual takes place in the temple, but 'mystically' it takes place in heaven. Notice that the king sits not on his own throne, but on that of the deity. This is itself a statement of the divine status of the king. *Psalm* 110 (§7(24)) is quoted in the New Testament (*Matthew* 22:44, *Acts* 2:34-5, *Hebrews* 1:13) as proof of the divinity of Jesus.

Chapter 8

Myth and the Past

As before (see introductory note to §7, p. 183), much of the language used in myth is spatial, but has a metaphorical value. I have listed under §9 those myths which, while apparently dealing with the past, are primarily concerned with the future. This will include myths explaining why humans are mortal, since the real point of such stories is to reconcile people to the fact that they are going to die in the future. Much of the mythic material appearing above, being located in the past, could be listed here.

In this chapter we cite examples of myth with a strong temporal bias, directed to the past. We are concerned here with the past as paradigmatic for the present, that is, as establishing norms which are to be maintained in the present. Many of the narratives given in §§2 and 3 could also be cited here. The 'past' in question is not simply anterior in a strictly temporal sense, as though it were historical. Indeed the contrast between the quality of time in myth and that in history ('real time', to use current computing jargon) is a useful one, though at times it has been abused by scholars (see below). Some scholars (following M. Eliade) use the expressions *illud tempus* and *in illo tempore* ('That Time', 'In That Time'). Others speak of 'eternal time' (over against 'temporal time' or 'temporal flow'; others again of 'the eternal present' or 'the eternal now', which sounds confusing, but is intended to express the way in which the time of a myth may be brought into the present, particularly in ritual. A good example of this is the 'myth' of the Last Supper, followed by its making present and actual ('représentation', 'reactualization') in the rite of the Eucharist. This example emphasizes another point: 'myth' is the *quality* of a narrative; it cannot be taken to mean that it is purely fictitious (though whether it is or not has no bearing on questions of 'truth'). So the contrast between myth and history, often treated as though it is the fundamental distinction, between fiction (even fantasy) and fact, can be easily misused, as it was done by a number of Old Testament scholars in the middle of the 20th century. On this issue see Wyatt 2001a. The power of myth is in a sense just an application of the power of memory.

The myth is a narrative, or allusion, which evokes powerful and important memories of 'what must have been'. Thus history, in which the 'canonical account' is what is important for a nation to remember, however fictitious some of it may have been, actually plays an important mythic role as the foundation, the charter, of a community's sense of identity.

Suggested Reading:

Batto 1993; Donald 1991; Eliade 1954, id. 1964; Fawcett 1970; Gibbs and Stevenson 1975; Kirk 1970; Munz 1973; Patton and Doniger 1996; J. Z. Smith 1987; Wyatt 2001a.

8.1   Introduction

8.1.1   Our most precious capacity is memory. To lose our memory is to lose our whole personality and identity. Collective memory serves to perpetuate the communal or national identity. In the absence of facts, the memory can be constructed out of myth and legend. (Cf. the tracing of

Roman identity back to Aeneas in Virgil's *Aeneid*.) So an important element in myth is often its pseudo-historical reference. What is remembered is 'true', simply because memory says so (§7(21) n. 3). This perspective is as valid today as it was for ancient societies. In this chapter we deal with myth as addressing the past. We observed in §1 that we *see* the past, which is before our face. This vision serves in the construction of the present, and authenticates it.

8.1.2 We have two important kinds of memory. There is my own memory of things past in my life. 'I remember it as though it happened yesterday.' There is another memory, individual yet also collective, in which we celebrate the memory, and bring the remembered event (the myth) into the present. We may do this through ritual. Terms such as *illud tempus* ('That Time'), 'the Eternal Present' are used to denote this kind of time, which can be brought into the present with an implicit abolition of time. It is easy to see why this is so crucial to the maintenance of preliterate societies. Unless important things were deliberately remembered, they were lost, and any benefit lost too. So they were narratized, turned into myths, and ritualized, celebrated and renewed in rites. Here was one of the essential parts of our 'humanization', our turning into cultural animals (Donald 1991 offers a good account of this).

8.2   Egypt

8.2.1 For all the wealth of textual information we have from ancient Egypt, our knowledge of Egyptian mythology remains fragmentary. This is largely because texts (such as the *Pyramid Texts*, which provide ritual processing for the dead king) will usually allude to a myth as a well-known tradition, rather than actually citing it. The myth of Osiris, for instance, is known in written narrative form only in Plutarch (first century CE). Early texts however allude to many episodes in the narrative.

8.2.2 §§8(1-5) are various versions of, or allusions to, the most important myth in Egyptian religion, the conflict between Horus and Seth. This is not the place to give a full account of this (see Oden 1979 for the best analysis to date). What is important is its ubiquity, and its polysemy: that is, it not only pervaded religious life, ritual and ideology, but meant discrete (though ultimately related) things in each context. A number of narratives have coalesced in this myth, Horus and Seth being now brothers, now nephew and uncle. Seth kills Osiris (Horus' father) and also fights Horus, but is beaten. The conflict may represent tensions between north and south and their unification under the king (= Horus), with complex and untidy history simplified into a stark set of oppositions (thus Griffiths 1960). But it also represents cosmological, moral and social tensions inherent in any society (te Velde 1977, Oden 1979).

8.2.3 In a nutshell, the myth narrates the conflict between Horus (representing kingship, cosmos, strong government, moral values, etc.) and Seth (representing rebellion, chaos, fragmentation of Egypt, immorality, etc.). While the myth comes to a sort of resolution, it remains open-ended, since the problems it treats are perennial, part of the human condition.

8.3 Mesopotamia

8.3.1 We have already noted excerpts from the great Babylonian 'hymn of creation', the *Enuma Elish*: §§2(9, 10, 14, 36, 37). This was recited as part of the ritual of the *Akitu* festival, which marked the Babylonian New Year in the month of Nisan. The hymn's main function appears to have been the glorification of Marduk, whose fifty names were recited. The myth however served to justify those titles, explaining why he was lord of Babylon, and in effect appealing to his primordial victory as guarantee of the present and future well-being of the city.

8.3.2 But myth dealt not only with great political or existential issues, but with more immediate matters, such as chronic toothache §8(6)! This charming story is not as trivial as it sounds. Cf. §2(6) ll. 10-11, where Amun is credited with the creation of slugs and gnats, not our favourite creatures, but essential to the economy of nature. There is nothing sentimental about ancient religions. The present myth anticipates §10, since the myth was recited as part of the ritual and healing work of the dentist.

8.4 The West Semitic World: Ugarit and Israel

8.4.1 An important myth common to both cultures, as well as others (see 8.3) was the conflict myth, or *Chaoskampf*. We have noted both Ugaritic (§§3(4)) and Israelite (§§3(5-8)) versions of this and their antecedents (§§3(1-3)). As well as providing an important cosmogonic tradition, we have seen how this tradition provided the paradigm for the king's role as warrior.

8.4.2 Yahweh's role as warrior in the *Chaoskampf* also found a place in another important mythic and ritual complex in ancient Israel, the

Passover and associated forms. This probably had very ancient origins among pastoralists moving from winter to summer pastures, who ritualized the move by the sacrifice of young kids and goats. Rituals of this kind frequently had a legendary tale which explained why the rite was being performed. Though with a complex prehistory, this rite, another of the sacrifice or redemption of the firstborn of flock or family (§8(7b)), and yet another of eating unleavened bread to mark the break with the old year (§8(7a)), were merged together into the rite associated with the legendary escape of the Israelites from Egypt (*Exodus* 1-15).

8.4.3   This material constitutes one of the most complex issues in biblical studies. To anticipate our final chapter (§12), this reads like an account of a real event, and has commonly been taken to be historical. It may well be, and in this case we would argue that the event has given rise to a ritual of commemoration. On the other hand there are scholars who suggest that it is the transformative power of the ritual which has generated the story. Neither position can be proved, and it is best to speak of the Passover 'legend', which allows a basis in history, while recognizing the power of narrative to generate meaning. This is an important point: it is the narrative, not the event, that creates *meaning* (see Thompson 1974, 326-7).

8.4.4   The issue that concerns us here is the *mythic* nature of this material. The question of its historical or fictitious status is immaterial here. I have even rejected (Wyatt 2001a) the usual idea that 'myth' is essentially a literary form, and is in any event to be contrasted with history. On the contrary, the historiography of the ancient world, and especially the Hebrew Bible, where Yahweh is one of the chief characters, is myth because of the religious mindset of the writers. The 'mythic mind' of which I write is simply the human mind in religious mode, open to the insights and experiences religion offers.

8.4.5   Let us return to the point raised in the discussion above. The myths we have examined here illustrate the important point that they are remembered down the generations, and are thus generated in past time, continuing to have a formative and authoritative role precisely because the community looks to its past to enable it to deal with its present. These are the collective memory, the received account of things past, of the group, which coheres in so far as people share common memories, common beliefs and common aspirations. It may seem extraordinary that collective memory should be dressed up in such strange tales. But not much has changed, and credibility only becomes a problem when the tale is asserted to be factual in so far as it is true. This is however a relatively modern problem, though some of the Greeks already recognized it.

8.4.6 The matter of truth constantly crops up in such discussions. The position I adopt is twofold. Firstly, all religions are 'true', because they all make truth-claims. Who am I, a mere student from outside a tradition, to assert that this tradition is true, but that tradition is false? Secondly, it all depends on how you define truth. We have seen (§7(21) n. 3) that 'truth' (ἀλήθεια) in Greek is 'memory'. Thus the truth at issue is what the narrative, the remembered myth, says it is. Whether we would accept that this constitutes 'cognitive truth', that is, that it actually relates to what is out there in the world, is another matter. We cannot resolve it. But we have a nice illustration of the issue in the idea of the ascent to heaven treated in §7:

> objectively, *we* see a ritual performed by a person in a temple;
> subjectively, *his* account of it is in terms of a heavenly journey.

We see nothing of the journey. We have to take it all on trust. Within the believing community, this is simply accepted. Our inability as outsiders to share the experience (beyond recognizing a common narrative element in a number of examples) can be partly overcome through our powers of empathy and imagination. We *can* believe that the earth is flat! 'Frodo lives!' 'The Force be with you!' In accepting the power of these words, or any other similar formula, ancient or modern, we can join the community.[1]

I   Egypt: Myths of Horus and Seth

This first theme, occurring in a number of recensions, is a fine example of the role of myth in the terms just described. However contorted and transformed, it treats the issue of Egyptian unity, and the suppression or resolution of the various regional and ethnic tensions which remained, to erupt at times in the breakdown of the central state. It is thus a symbolic statement of the ethos of the warrior state, born and nurtured in bloodshed and conquest. But it is more...

It may rightly be described as the defining myth of Egyptian culture. It has political, social and cultic overtones. Surviving in various recensions, it is also the subject of numerous allusions in cultic contexts (e.g. §10(1)), where sacrifices might be compared with the conflict, the killing of the victim being the slaying of Seth. The tradition has evidently brought together a number of theological traditions. Horus and Seth could

---

[1]   A useful collection of readings on the 'insider-outsider' problem can be found in McCutcheon 1999.

be brothers (§§8(1, 3)), sons of Ra, or they could be nephew and uncle (§8(2)), when Horus was son of Osiris, and Seth his (Osiris's) brother. In Plutarch's late Greek account of the tradition, the attention is focused on Osiris, as paradigmatic for the destiny of the faithful in the late mystery cult centring on him and Isis.

Horus, the falcon-god of Hierakonpolis, became the royal god *par excellence*, incarnate in each living king. A number of local gods coalesced in him, which explains the apparently contradictory elements in the myth, as he was sometimes Seth's brother (and son of Ra and Hathor), and sometimes his nephew (and son of Osiris and Isis).

Osiris was the dead king, father of Horus, the pair representing the continuity of the royal line.

Seth, variously brother and uncle of Horus, was the god of storms and disruptive principles. See te Velde 1977.

8(1)   Allusions in the Pyramid Texts

These are numerous, showing that the myth was well-established by the end of the fifth dynasty (*post* 2350 BCE). Many of the allusions regard Horus and Seth as brothers. In their struggle, Horus' eyes are stolen and restored, while Seth's testicles are stolen and restored. The important feature is the royal nature of both gods, reflecting dualistic conceptions in the elements of kingship in Egypt. These texts are discussed at length in Griffiths 1960.

> Ho, thou ferryman, bring this to Horus,
> > bring his eye;
> bring this to Seth,
> > bring his testicles.

> (Faulkner 1969, 163: *PT* 475)

Every part of the body takes on a symbolic role, and in texts like this the organs were identified with various cultic implements or sacrificial offerings.

> 1   Horus comes,
> > Thoth appears.
> They raise Osiris from upon his side
> > and make him stand up in front of the two Enneads.
> 5   Remember, Seth,
> > and put in your heart this word which Geb spoke,
> > > this threat which the gods made against you in the Mansion of
> > > the Prince of Heliopolis,
> > because you threw Osiris to the earth,
> > when you said, O Seth,
> 10   'I have never done this to him'...
> > 'It was he who attacked me',

when you said, O Seth,

'It was he who kicked me'…

(Faulkner 1969, 164: *PT* 477, adapted)

The coming of the gods Horus and Thoth to assist Osiris alludes to masked priests who performed rituals of which this is the interpretation. Their rites represented the ever-repeated victory of Horus over Seth, and the vindication of Osiris (with whom the dead king was identified).

8(2)   The Contendings of Horus and Seth

This version, dating from the twelfth century BCE, and preserved in P. Chester Beatty I, has often been assessed as essentially satirical in nature. It is certainly a far cry from an entirely serious approach to theological matters. But this is deceptive. The narrative does address serious issues, as shown by Oden 1979. It appears to treat a perennial question in societies in transition between matrilineal and patrilineal descent (cf. §3(13) n.), such as might have occurred in Egypt with the political fusion of quite different peoples. It thus shows the capacity of a myth to deal with changing circumstances, speaking anew to each generation.

This is the judging of Horus and Seth, they of mysterious forms, mightiest of existing princes and lords… Then spoke Shu, the son of Ra, before Atum, the great prince of Heliopolis: 'Right rules might. Do it by saying — "Give the office to Horus".'

Then said Thoth to the Ennead: 'That is right a million times!'… Onuris said: 'Thoth shall take the royal name-ring to Horus, and the White Crown shall be placed on his head!'

Then the All-Lord was silent for a long moment, for he was angry with the Ennead. Then Seth, the son of Nut, spoke: 'Let him be sent outside with me, and I shall let you see my hand prevailing over his hand in the presence of the Ennead, since one knows no other means of dispossessing him.'

Then Thoth said to him: 'Do we not know what is wrong? Shall one give the office of Osiris to Seth while his (Osiris's) son Horus is there?'

… Then Neith the Great, the divine mother, sent a letter to the Ennead, saying, 'Give the office of Osiris to his son Horus, and do not commit those great misdeeds that are out of place, or I shall get angry and the sky will crash to the ground! And let it be said to the All-Lord, the Bull of Heliopolis: 'Double Seth's possessions. Give him Anat and Astarte, your two daughters, and place Horus on the seat of his father!"'…

Then Seth, great of strength, the son of Nut, said 'I am Seth, greatest of strength among the Ennead. For I slay the enemy of Ra every day', standing in the prow of the Bark-of-millions, and no other god can do it. I should receive the office of Osiris!'

Then they said: 'Seth, the son of Nut, is right.'

Then Onuris and Thoth cried aloud, saying: 'Shall one give the office to the uncle while the bodily son is there?'

Then Mendes (*b3-nb-dd*) the great living god, said: 'Shall one give the office to the youngster while Seth, his elder brother, is there?'

> (Isis intervenes, and Seth goes off to sulk on an island, instructing the ferryman not to allow any woman across — lest Isis trouble him further. She bribes the ferryman and comes to the island. Arriving as an old woman, she appears to Seth as a nubile girl.)

Seth... went to meet her... and called to her: 'I am here with you, handsome girl!'

She said to him... 'I was the wife of a herdsman and I bore him a son. My husband died, and the boy began to tend the cattle of his father. But then a stranger came. He sat down in my stable and spoke thus to my child: 'I shall beat you, I shall take your father's cattle, and I shall throw you out!' So he spoke to him. Now I wish to make you his defender.'

Then Seth said to her: 'Shall one give the cattle to the stranger while the man's son is there?'

Thereupon Isis changed herself into a kite, flew up, and sat on an acacia. She called to Seth and said to him: 'Weep for yourself! Your own mouth has said it. Your own cleverness has judged you.'

> (Horus and Seth become hippopotami, agreeing that the one to stay submerged longest would become king. Isis harpoons Horus [inadvertently]. She harpoons Seth, but lets him go when he protests that he is her brother. In his anger, Horus beheads her. Seth comes upon Horus asleep, and removes his eyes, burying them on a mountain. They grow into lotuses. Hathor restores Horus' eyes with gazelle's milk... Seth invites Horus to a feast at his house. At night he assaults him homosexually...)

Horus placed his hands between his thighs and caught the semen of Seth. Then Horus went to tell his mother Isis: 'Come... and see what Seth did to me.' He opened his hand and let her see the semen of Seth. She cried out aloud, took her knife, cut off his hand and threw it in the water. Then she made a new hand for him. And she took a dab of ointment and put it on the penis of Horus. She made it become stiff, placed it over a pot and he let his semen drop into it.

In the morning Isis went with the semen of Horus to the garden of Seth... and placed the semen of Horus on the lettuce (Seth's favourite food).

Seth came according to his daily custom and ate the lettuces which he usually ate. Thereupon he became pregnant with the semen of Horus.

Seth... and Horus... Went to the court together. They stood before the great Ennead... Then Seth said: 'Let the office of ruler be given to me, for as regards Horus... I have done a man's deed to him!' Then the Ennead cried out loud, and they spat out before Horus.

And Horus laughed at them, saying: 'What Seth has said is false. Let the semen of Seth be called, and let us see from where it will answer. Then let mine be called, and let us see from where it will answer.'

> (Seth's semen answers from the marshes; Horus' appears as a sun-disc
> from Seth's head, whence Thoth snatches it and places it in his own.)

And the Ennead said: 'Horus is right. Seth is wrong...'

Seth took a great oath... saying: 'He shall not be given the office until he has been dismissed with me, and we shall build ships of stone and race each other...' Then Horus built himself a ship of pine, plastered it over with gypsum, and launched it... And Seth looked at the ship of Horus and thought it was of stone. He went to the mountain, cut off a mountain peak, and built himself a ship of stone of 138 cubits. Then they went into their ships in the presence of the Ennead. Thereupon the ship of Seth sank in the water. Seth changed himself into a hippopotamus and wrecked the ship of Horus...

> (A letter is sent to Osiris, who commands in his reply that Seth be
> brought in bound, and accused of disobeying the will of the Ennead.)

Atum said to him: 'Why have you resisted being judged and have taken for youself the office of Horus?'

Seth said to him: 'Not so, my good lord. Let Horus, son of Isis, be summoned, and let him be given the office of his father Osiris!'

(Lichtheim 1979, ii 14-23: *The Contendings of Horus and Seth*, excerpts)

Anat and Astarte (Athtart) were West Semitic war-goddesses, who were married to Seth (himself equated with West Semitic Baal Hadad by the Hyksos rulers of the second intermediate period).

Neith was a war-goddess of the Delta, and also a goddess of the Red Crown of Lower Egypt.

Onuris, whose name was self-explanatory (*Ini ḥri.t*: 'He who restores [the Eye]') was sometimes equated with Thoth.

1   An allusion to the myth underlying §8(5).

Oden's paper is essential reading for an understanding of this text. It boils down to the demands of irreconcilable principles, of property inheritance by power (matrilineal society, in which the widow's brother is heir) and by birth (patrilineal society, in which the son of the deceased inherits). We can imagine this being a serious problem in nascent Egyptian kingship, as also apparently in Hittite experience (§3(13)). The resolution is essentially a literary one, by the outworking of the 'semantic rectangle', in which the problem is explored by means of three contests between Horus and Seth, interspersed with many clever reversals, and the 'solution' to the problem by the judgment of Osiris. The narrative also moves from east to west across the river, as an indication of its progression to the source of all wisdom, the inhabitants of the underworld, epitomized by Osiris himself.

8(3)   The Memphite Version

See §2(7) for further excerpts from this important ideological document, claiming the primacy of Ptah of Memphis. It is characteristic of the catholicity of Egyptian theology that due weight was given to every important aspect, and so it is no surprise to find the important motif of the king as Horus incorporated. (Memphis also had its own version, the king being Nefertem, son of Ptah and Sekhmet. Ptah being a chthonian deity, Nefertem became a type of the king restored after death.)

The Ennead gathered themselves to Geb[1], and he judged Horus and Seth. He prevented them from quarrelling further, and he made Seth the king of Upper Egypt in the land of Upper Egypt[2]... Then Geb made Horus king of Lower Egypt in the land of Lower Egypt... Thus Horus stood in one place, and Seth stood in another place, and they were reconciled about the Two Lands. Words spoken by Geb to Seth: 'Go to the place in which thou wert born — Seth, Upper Egypt'. Words spoken by Geb to Horus: 'Go to the place in which thy father was drowned — Horus, Lower Egypt'. Words spoken by Geb to Horus and Seth: I have judged you — Lower Egypt and Upper Egypt.

But then it became ill in the heart of Geb that the portion of Horus was only equal to the portion of Seth. So Geb gave his entire inheritance to Horus... Thus Horus stood over the entire land. Thus the land was united...

(ANET 4: The Shabako Stone)

1   Geb was the earth god. It is hard to avoid seeing him here as an aspect of Ptah, who had absorbed the ancient earth-god of the region, Ta-tenen (*t3 tnn*, 'the rising earth'). Thus Ptah, the local god, was universalized.

2   This is essentially a way of expressing the duality of Egyptian kingship. It is not a historical memory of the North conquering the South, since it was if anything the other way round, according to the Narmer palette: Horus was the divine king of Hierakonpolis. See Kemp 1989, and §12(1).

8(4) Appropriating the Myth

Part of an inscription from a relief of Seti I at Karnak. The context is the smiting scene, which appears on temple pylons, in which Amun receives the sacrifice of captured enemy kings. Amun speaks.

I give to thee (Seti I) the possessions of Horus and Seth, and their victories. The portions of the two gods are made thy portions.

(*ARE* iii 76, §155)

8(5) The Myth in the Cult: Ra and Apepi

See §10(1), in which items and actions in ritual treatment of the image of Amun in the Karnak temple cult are rationalized as embodiments and reenactments of the myth of Horus and Seth. The motif is widely encountered in mortuary texts, which indicate such symbolism in the ritual processes, and much of the mythic material inscribed on the temple walls at Edfu indicates the interlocking of mythic, ritual and political aspects of the theme.

Another interesting example is perhaps the ritual which takes as its basis the myth of the nocturnal struggle between Ra and Apepi, a subterranean serpent which attacks the bark of Ra during its voyage through the underworld. It is highly significant that the deity who nightly destroys Apepi with a harpoon is Seth himself, though we may have suspicions that Apepi is in fact a form of Seth. At least he appears to be in late times when he is given the Greek name Bebon. Also, though the serpent Apepi (*'ppi*) is written with an *'*, and the Hyksos king's name Apepi¹ with an *i*, they may well be the same word, and are indeed identical in their Greek form 'Apophis'. The idea of a god who kills himself, here for the good of the world, is not strange in a land where gods can 'generate themselves' or 'renew themselves', and even father their own fathers! We may be uncertain as to the precise nuance of this language, but it is typically Egyptian. The ritual application comes at the end, and makes sense of the whole procedure. The text comes from the P. Bremner-Rhind, fourth century BCE, but is written in archaic Egyptian, and is certainly a tradition of considerable age.

1   The relevance of the royal name is that it is theophoric, and the deity to whom it referred was almost certainly Seth, since he was identified by the Hyksos and in New Kingdom times with Baal Hadad, the West Semitic storm-god.

1   'He is one fallen to the flame,
        Apepi with a knife on his head.
     He cannot see,
        and his name is no more¹ in this land.
5   I have commanded that a curse be cast upon him;
        I have consumed his bones;
     I have annihilated his soul in the course of every day;
        I have cut his vertebrae at his neck,
        severed with a knife which hacked up his flesh
10   and pierced into his hide...
     I have taken away his heart from its place, his seat, his tomb.

I have made him non-existent:
his name is not,
  his children are not,
15 he is not and his family is not.
  He is not and his false door is not,
  he is not and his heirs are not.
His egg shall not last,
  nor his seed knit together...
20 His soul, his corpse, his state of glory, his shadow and his magic
    are not.
  His bones are not
  and his skin is not.
He is fallen and overthrown...
See thou, O Ra!
25   Hear thou, O Ra!
Behold, I[2] have driven away thy enemy;
  I have wiped him out with my feet;
  I have spat upon him.
Ra is triumphant over thee...
30 Drive thou away, consume thou, burn up every enemy of
    Pharaoh — lph[3]
  — whether dead or living...
Thus thou shalt be in thy shrine,
thou shalt journey in the evening bark,
  thou shalt rest in the morning bark,
35 thou shalt cross thy two heavens in peace,
  thou shalt be powerful,
thou shalt live,
  thou shalt be healthy,
thou shalt make thy states of glory to endure,
40   thou shalt drive away every enemy by thy command;
  for these have done evil against Pharaoh — lph — with all
    evil words:
  all men, all folk, all people, all humanity...
  the easterners of every desert,
and every enemy of Pharaoh — lph — whether dead or living,
45   whom I have driven away and annihilated.[4]
Thou dissolvest, fallen, Apepi.
Ra is triumphant over thee, O Apepi!'

            (to be repeated four times[5]).

'Pharaoh — lph — is triumphant over his enemies!' (to be repeated four times).

This spell is to be recited over Apepi drawn on a new sheet of papyrus in green colour and put inside a box on which his name is set, he being tied and bound and put on the fire every day, wiped out with thy left foot and spat upon four times in the course of every day.[6] Thus shalt say as thou puttest him on the fire: 'Ra is triumphant over thee, O Apepi!' four times and: 'Horus is triumphant over his enemies!'[7] four times and: 'Pharaoh — lph — is triumphant over his enemies!' four times.

(*ANET* 7: P. Bremner-Rhind, adapted)

1   An affirmation of non-existence, in the form of a curse, which is repeated and elaborated in lines 12-17 and 20-22.

2   The priest is speaking. He is playing the part of Seth, in a rather attenuated way.

3   'Life, prosperity, health!' (*'nh wd3 snb*), a formula of blessing on the name of the king.

4   Note the political application. Apepi, like Seth, represents and is the apotheosis of all enemies of Egypt. Thus the destruction of Apepi is a destruction of them too, as manifestations of his evil nature.

5   The fourfold repetition was for completeness, and perhaps entailed facing each of the cardinal points in turn.

6   The rite was performed four times every day (see n. 5). This implies an underlying anxiety of some magnitude.

7   This confirms the suspicion that this is strictly an analogue of the Horus and Seth conflict.

II   Divine Anger in Egyptian Myth

8(6)   Hathor and the Destruction of Mankind

This myth is narrated on the walls of the tombs of Seti I, Rameses II and Rameses III in Thebes. It has two interesting parallels. The image of the goddess wading in blood evokes the similar language used of Anat in Ugaritic mythology (KTU 1.3 ii 5-30, Wyatt 1998a, 73-5). The idea of all the water turning to blood evokes the first plague in Egypt in *Exodus* 7:14-25.

It happened in the time of the majesty of Ra, the self-created, after he had become king of men and gods together: mankind plotted against him, while his majesty had grown old, his bones being silver, his flesh gold, his hair true lapis lazuli[1]. When his majesty perceived the plotting of mankind against him, his majesty said to his followers, 'Summon to me my Eye, and

Shu, Tefnut, Geb, Nut, and the fathers and mothers who were with me when I was in Nun, and also the god Nun; and he shall bring his courtiers with him. But bring them stealthily, lest mankind see, lest they lose heart. Come with them (the gods) to the Palace, that they may give their counsel. In the end I may return to Nun, to the place where I came into being.'

The gods were brought, the gods were lined up on his two sides, bowing to the ground before his majesty, that he might make his speech before the eldest father, the maker of mankind, the king of people. They said to his majesty, 'Speak to us, that we may hear it.' Then Ra said to Nun, 'O eldest god in whom I came into being, and ancestor gods, look, mankind, which issued from my Eye[2], is plotting against me. Tell me what you would do about it, for I am searching. I would not slay them until I have heard what you might say about it.'

Then spoke the majesty of Nun, 'My son Ra, god greater than his maker, more august than his creators, stay on your throne! Great is fear of you when your Eye[3] is on those who scheme against you.' Said the majesty of Ra, 'Look, they are fleeing to the desert, their hearts fearful that I might speak to them.' They said to his majesty, 'Let your Eye go and smite them for you, those schemers of evil! No Eye is more able to smite them for you. May it go down as Hathor!'

The goddess returned after slaying mankind in the desert, and the majesty of this god said, 'Welcome in peace, Hathor, Eye who did what I came for!' Said the goddess, 'As you live for me, I have overpowered mankind, and it was balm to my heart.' Said the majesty of Ra, 'I shall have power over them as king by diminishing them.'[4] Thus the Powerful One (Sekhmet[5]) came into being.

The beer-mash of the night for her who would wade in their blood as far as Henes. Ra said. 'Summon to me swift, nimble messengers that they may run like a body's shadow!' The messengers were brought immediately, and the majesty of this god said, 'Go to Yebu and bring me red ochre in great quantity!' The red ochre was brought to him, and the majesty of this god ordered the Side-Lock Wearer in On[6] to grind the ochre, while maidservants crushed barley for beer. Then the red ochre was put into the beer-mash, and it became like human blood; and seven thousand jars of beer were made. Then the majesty of the King of Upper and Lower Egypt, Ra came together with the gods to see the beer.

Now when the day dawned on which the goddess would slay mankind in their time of travelling south, the majesty of Ra said, 'It is good; I shall save mankind by it!'[7] And Ra said, 'Carry it to the place where she plans to slay mankind!' The majesty of King Ra rose early before dawn, to have this sleeping draught poured out. Then the fields were flooded[8] three palms high with the liquid by the might of the majesty of this god. When the goddess came in the morning she found them flooded, and her gaze was pleased by it. She drank and it pleased her heart. She returned drunk without having perceived mankind. The majesty of Ra said to the goddess, 'Welcome in peace, O gracious one!' Thus beautiful women came into being in the town of Imu.[9]

(CS i 36-7, adapted)

1   This description of Ra, which recurs in a number of texts, may well be the description of an image of the god, since these substances were widely used in iconography. The lapis lazuli would have come ultimately from Afghanistan, by way of long-distance trade networks.

2   Cf. §2(8) n. 6.

3   The Eye of Ra (and of Atum) is a powerful hypostasis, identified with various royal goddesses (Wadjet, Neith, and as here, Hathor), which acts as his avenging agent on earth, (a powerful image in a culture accepting the reality of the 'evil eye'). Ra himself and Thoth, as sun and moon, are also said to be the Eye(s) of Horus.

4   Does this reflect a policy of state terrorism, to bring recalcitrant parties into line?

5   The lion-headed goddess Sekhmet (*shmt*, 'the Powerful One') is here seen to be an aspect of Hathor as the Eye of Ra. The triad Ptah-Sekhmet-Nefertem was the apotheosis of royalty at Memphis.

6   Lichtheim, *ad loc.*, 37 n. 9, identified the 'side-lock wearer' as the high priest of Ra in Heliopolis. More to the point, in the myth, if this is indeed a ritual enactment of it, he was undoubtedly a *royal* person, and perhaps the crown prince himself, and thus Nefertem (n. 5) or perhaps Horus (Harpocrates, *hr p3 hrd*, 'Horus the child', the posthumous son of Osiris). Both were shown in iconography with the side-lock, as was Khonsu, who represented the king's Ka. Since the text is recorded in royal tombs, we might expect the kings in question to feature in the narrative. On is Heliopolis. On (*iwnw*) means 'Pillar-(Town)', after the great pyramidion in the forecourt of the temple of Ra.

7   The idea of a god changing his mind is not uncommon in ancient texts.

8   Maspero 1894, 23, cited in Roberts 1995, 12, wrote the following interesting account of the inundation of the Nile at Aswan:

> The first contact [of the flood-waters] is disastrous to the banks; their steep sides disintegrated and cracked by the heat no longer offer any resistance to the current and fall with a crash, in lengths of a hundred yards and more. As the successive floods grow stronger and are more heavily charged with mud, the whole mass of water becomes turbid and changes colour.

In eight or ten days it has turned from grayish blue to dark red, occasionally of so intense a colour as to look like newly-shed blood.

If we wished to rationalize the imagery in the narrative above, we could note that it is at any rate consistent with the natural event, though given a theological gloss. Is it perhaps a mythical account of one particularly bad inundation which caused widespread loss of life?

9   A charming, if somewhat trivial, aetiology concludes the tale.

III   Mesopotamian Myth

8(7)   Myth in the Cult: Temple Reconstruction

We should not expect a one-for-one correspondence between myths and rituals. The idea that one always presupposes the other, long taken as axiomatic in Religious Studies, has been discredited. See Fontenrose 1971. Having said that, it would be wrong to draw the opposite conclusion, that the two can have no connection. We do in fact find rites which presuppose a certain mythic element. See for example §§3(1-2), the Tishpak myths from Eshnunna, §3(3) for the Adad oracle from Mari, and §2(9), excerpts from the *Enuma Elish*, describing the Babylonian cosmogony, which evidently relate to the rituals of kingship, with an emphasis on territorial appropriation and political affirmation. §7(14), excerpts from Etana, and §9(2), the story of Adapa, do not relate directly to the cult (in any 'organic' sense), yet presuppose cultic realities.

The present example, dating from third or fourth century BCE Babylon, deals with the rituals of temple repair. It validates the present construction on the basis of it reiterating the primordial construction done by the gods themselves. No construction is regarded as new, in the sense that the paradigm was established long ago in mythic time, and yet during repairs care was taken to go down to bedrock, so that each new construction was pristine, on virgin soil. Cf. §6(28).

The latter part of the text amounts to a further creation narrative. Two temptations should be avoided: to harmonize the different traditions of this kind, to construct one coherent systematic theology (the modern penchant in the face of theological diversity); or to see the diversity of view as incoherence and evidence of a 'primitive' mentality.

When the wall of the temple falls into ruin — for the purpose of demolishing and founding anew the temple in question, the *bārû* priest shall investigate its plans. Then, in an auspicious month, on a favourable day, during the night, they shall light a fire for the gods Ea and Marduk and make a sacrifice…

(the text continues with various other ritual elements, and then cites the following for recitation)

1   When the god Anu created heaven,

(when) the god Nudimmud created the *apsû* [1], his dwelling,

the god Ea pinched off a piece of clay[2] in the *apsû*,
   created Kulla for the restoration of [temples],
5   created the reed marsh and the forest for the work of
       their construction,
created the gods Ninildu, Ninsimug, and Arazu
   to be the completers of their construction work,
   created mountains and oceans for everything...
created the deities Gushkinbanda, Ninagal, Ninzadim,
    and Ninkurra for their work,
10   (created) the abundant products (of mountain and ocean)
     to be offerings...
created the deities Ashnan, Lahar, Siris, Ningizzida, Ninsar...
   for making their revenues abundant...
created the deities Umunmutamku and Umunmutamnag
    to be presenters of offerings,
    created the god Kusig, high-priest of the great gods,
15   to be the one who completestheir rites and ceremonies.
Created the king to be the provider...
    created men to be the makers...

             (*ANET* 341-2: Uruk tablet, adapted)

Arazu was the god of prayer(?).	Ninildu was the god of carpentry.
Ashnan was a grain goddess.	Ninkurra was a goddess of
Gushkinbanda was the god of	stonecutters.
goldsmiths.	Ninsar was a vegetation goddess.
Kulla was the brick god.	Ninsimug was the god of metal-
Kusig was the high priest of the gods.	workers.
Lahar was a cattle god.	Ninzadim was the god of engravers.
Ninagal was another god of metal-	Siris was a wine goddess.
workers.	Umunmutamku was Marduk's cook.
Ningizzida and Ninezen were deities of	Umunmutamnak was Marduk's cup-
vegetation.	bearer.

Note the long list of divine beings, many very minor, with no developed cult of their
own, who represented the apotheosis of various cultural realities. Cf. §2(13), and
Hesiod's *Theogony*. To the opening lines of the poem cf. also the beginning of §8(8).

1   The Akkadian term *apsû* is derived from Sumerian AB.ZU, 'the waters of
     knowing'. It became Greek ἀβυσσος, the name of the cosmic ocean, and
     English 'abyss'. See §2(30), n 1, and §§3, 4, *passim*.

2   Note that the deity Kulla (as the brick-god his fashioning out of clay is
     supremely logical!) was made just as men were made.

IV   Myth and Medicine

8(8)   Mesopotamia: Incantation for Toothache

After great themes like the creation, this is, in contrast, almost light-hearted. But it illustrates an important feature of all the theologies of the ancient Near East (Israel included). Evil (which is ultimately that which is injurious to men) was created by the gods. They were ultimately responsible.

This belongs to a genre of medical texts, in which a myth was narrated which had a symbolic link with the ailment or condition to be treated. Here a short poem narrates the origin of toothache. Recitation of the text was part of the treatment, the last three lines being the dentist's application of the general myth to this particular toothache. The text dates to the Neo-Babylonian period, *ca* 600-540 BCE. In that such myths had a continuing function with regard to anticipated (sc. future) healings of the sick, they could also be classified under §9.

1   After Anu[1] [had created heaven],
     heaven had created [the earth],
     the earth had created the rivers
     the rivers had created the canals,
5   the canals had created the marsh,
     (and) the marsh had created the worm —
the worm went, weeping, before Shamash,
     his tears flowed before Ea:
'What will you give me for my food?
10   What will you give me for my sucking?'
'I shall give you the ripe fig,
     (and) the apricot.'
'Of what use are they to me,
     the ripe fig and the apricot?
15 Lift me up
     and among the teeth and the gums cause me to dwell!
The blood of the tooth I will suck,
     and of the gum I will gnaw its roots!'
'Fix the pin and seize its foot.
20 Because you have said this, O worm,
     may Ea smite you with the might of his hand!'

(*ANET* 100-1: *The Worm and the Toothache*, adapted)

1   Or perhaps more neutrally, 'the sky'. But each natural phenomenon is set
     within a genealogy of ancestors of the worm, who has a noble pedigree! This
     may be a light-hearted treatment of the theme taken more seriously in the great
     ideological texts, such as Hammurabi's law-code (brief excerpt in §3(22)). But
     the copying is probably an automatic adoption of the appropriate style.

The time reference of this narrative is to be contrasted with that of the beginning of the creation story (§§2(9-10)), in which events are described initially *before* the creation. See also §§2(13), 8(7).

8(9)   Ugarit: How to Treat Intoxication

This text describes how El held a feast and became drunk, with a bout of *delirium tremens* as he was helped home by his divine subordinates. The cure for a hangover of this severity is given at the end. The god's cure is the paradigm for the patient's. For notes on text and bibliography see Wyatt 1998, 404-13. Perhaps 25% of the narrative portion of the text is missing.

1   In his house El gave a feast of game,
     the produce of the hunt in the midst of his palace.
  He cried:
  'To the carving, gods!
5   Eat, O gods, and drink!
  Drink wine until satiety,
     foaming wine until intoxication!'
  Yarih arched his back like a dog;
     he gathered up crumbs beneath the tables.
10 (Any) god who recognized him
     threw him meat from the joint.
  But (any god) who did not recognize him
     hit him with a stick beneath the table.
  At the call of Athtart and Anat he approached.
15 Athtart threw him a haunch,
     and Anat a shoulder of meat.
  The porter of El's house shouted:
  'Look!
  Why have you thrown a haunch to the dog,
20   (why) to the cur have you thrown a shoulder?'
  He shouted at El his father.
  El summoned his drinking-companions;
     El took his seat in his feasting house.
  He drank wine to satiety,
25   new wine until intoxication.
  El went off to his house;
     he stumbled off towards his dwelling;
     Thukamun and Shanim supported him.
  A creeping monster approached him,
30   with horns and tail!
  He floundered in his (own) faeces and urine:

El fell down as though dead;
   El was like those who go down into the underworld.
Anat and Athtart went out hunting
35 [   ]
  [   ]
Athtart and Anat [returned   ]
  And they brought back meat [   ]
When they had cured him, he awoke.

(This is) what needs to be put on his forehead: dog-hair and the knot of a vine and its juice. They should be applied together with virgin olive oil.

(Wyatt 1998a, 405-13: KTU 1.114)

Athart (Astarte) and Anat formed a close pair in Ugarit, of goddesses of hunting and war. They fused in first millennium BCE Syria, to become Atargatis (see §§4(12), 6 (31) and n. 1).

Thukamun and Shanim, perhaps of Kassite and ultimately Indo-Aryan origin, seem to have been El's attendants, as also in §10(10).

Yarih was the West Semitic moon-god.

We should suspend judgment on a typical modern view of this text as illustrating a debased religion, as maintained by de Moor 1997, 83: 'the poet of this baffling text wanted to vent his disdain for Ilu and his family...' The only way in which a god could really become drunk was through a surfeit of offerings, an oxymoron. The point of the form of the text is that as El was (implicitly) healed, so will be the sufferer who takes the medicine. It is important to see this text in the context of the *marziḥu* institution in which it was probably regarded as appropriate. The *marziḥu* was a voluntary society, which met for conviviality and devotion, often dedicated to one deity as patron.

V   Israel's Foundation Myth

Many have denied the presence of myth in the Bible. For the reasons for and against such a position see Wyatt 2001a, with references to extensive further discussion. When myth is recognized, it is usually assumed to be confined to such narratives as *Genesis* 1 (creation, §§2(15, 17), 3(6)) and *Genesis* 2-3 (the Garden of Eden, §2(18)), or it is even claimed that *Genesis* 1 has been demythologized. It is also recognized in the various versions of the conflict myth (§3(5) and parallels, on which see Day 1985).

The material cited here has a greater claim to be Israel's 'foundation myth', notwithstanding my remarks on texts §§6(7) and 9(4), where the Eden narrative has had a far broader cultural impact. Cf. van der Toorn 1996, 287-315, who entitles his chapter 'Inventing a national identity: the Exodus as a charter myth'. The first two of the present instances would not even be recognized as mythic by many scholars, who prefer to emphasize their historiographical, if legendary, nature. But they certainly *function* as myth in their liturgical usage.

8(10) **The Passover Celebration**

Exodus 12-13 deals with the legislation for the performance of the rituals of Passover, Unleavened Bread and firstborn Redemption, which later appear to have fused into one complex form. This is part of the material dealing with its recitation, as an explanation of why the rites are performed. An ancient pastoral festival celebrating transhumance (the move from winter to summer pastures), ancient seasonal festival from an agricultural background (breaking the cycle by not incorporating [old] leaven in [new] dough) and a separate desacralization of flocks ritual have been rejigged to commemorate a 'historical' event. Some would argue that the 'historical' event, the exodus from Egypt, was an invention generated by the festivals. Others would say that the event has generated a renewed symbolic content for the ancient rites. Perhaps it is fair to say that the two things, the past of the people and the rite, have developed symbiotically. The issue of the conception of history in the ancient world is treated at §12.

The Passover, linked to the Spring equinox, was originally the twin of the scapegoat rites (§10(11)) performed at the autumn equinox. It was a pastoralists' rite, but *not* a nomads' one. The conception of Israel as having a nomadic ancestry is a modern myth, misconstruing the narratives of *Genesis*.

a)   **Unleavened Bread**

Normally in the making of bread, crumbs from the previous baking (the 'leaven') were mixed with the new dough, giving a symbolic continuity of all subsequent bakings. At the feast of unleavened bread, the cycle was broken, thus isolating new time from old. The feast was therefore a means of breaking the flow of secular time, and allowing for social renewal.

And you will explain it[1] (the eating of Unleavened Bread) to your son on that day, saying 'This is on account of the fact that Yahweh did this to me: he brought me out of the land of Egypt.' And this will be a sign on your hand[2] and a memento between your eyes[3], so that Yahweh's teaching shall be on your lips, for by the power of his hand[4] did Yahweh bring you[5] out of Egypt. So you shall observe this ordinance at its appointed time every year."[6]

(*Exodus* 13:8-10)

1   Or, 'impress its significance'.

2   Probably an allusion to *tephillin* worn wrapped round the arm? Cf. next note. Or originally, 'on your penis'? In which case this would be an allusion to circumcision. The Hebrew *yād* has both senses. It is possible that the latter sense is older, subsequently reinterpreted with the rise of literacy.

3   An allusion to phylacteries, small boxes containing sacred texts, bound on the forehead.

4   Or, 'with mighty hand'. Similarly in §b) and §8(9). The allusion, frequent in *Deuteronomy*, which has influenced the present text, is to the sword hand of Yahweh the warrior, in the conflict tradition (§3).

5   The form is singular. This follows the style of parts of *Deuteronomy* in which Israel is addressed in the singular, as Yahweh's son (cf. *Hosea* 11:1). Note that in §b below, the first person plural is used, reflecting the independent prehistory of the traditions.

6   I have taken the last two sentences (from 'And this will be a sign...') to be part of the father's speech to his son. Alternatively, it is part of Yahweh's overall instructions to the father.

b)   Passover and Redemption of the Firstborn

While §a) signified primarily a break in a temporal flow, the present rite both did this, relating to the temporal aspect of transhumance, and the move from winter to summer pastures, and also represented a spatial transition from one to the other. The combination of §a) and §b) was a felicitous new rite to express Israel's conviction of its peculiar relationship with Yahweh, its territory, and its sense of its past. Two parts are given below; the first deals specifically with 'Passover' (*pesah*), and the second with the (originally distinct) routine sacrifice of firstborn. The preamble to this second element shows it to have been grafted on to the Passover.

This month will be the first of months for you, the first month of your year[1]... On the tenth (day) of this month everyone is to take an animal, one for each family... an unblemished male yearling, from the sheep or the goats[2]... (On) the fourteenth... you shall slaughter it between the two evenings[3]. Then they shall take some of the blood and smear it on the door-posts and the lintels of the houses where it is eaten. And the flesh shall be eaten on that night, roasted on the fire. It is to be eaten with unleavened bread and bitter herbs... This is how you will eat it: your loins girded, your sandals on your feet, and your staffs in your hands. And you shall eat it hurriedly, for this is a Passover[4] for Yahweh...

And when your son asks you in the future, 'What does this mean?' you shall say to him, 'By the power of his hand Yahweh brought us out of Egypt, out of the house of servitude. For when Pharaoh refused to let us go, Yahweh killed all the firstborn in the land of Egypt, of men and livestock. This is why I slaughter for[5] Yahweh the firstborn male, and redeem every firstborn of my sons. And it shall serve as a sign on your hand and as a phylactery between your eyes, for with the power of his hand did Yahweh bring us out of Egypt.'

(*Exodus* 12: 2-12, 13:14-6, excerpts)

1   This inaugurates a new calendar, which gives enormous emphasis to the rite as a foundation of the people's very being. It is an 'ontological marker'.

2   This factor, with no discrimination between the breeds, points to the rite's cognate relationship with the *Yôm Kippur* rites (§10(11), six months distant: both belong to New Year ritualizations).

3   This probably means at the point where the 'two evenings' (sc. the late afternoon and the early night), join, at sunset. But cf. Hyatt 1971, 132.

4   Hebrew *pesaḥ* is of obscure etymology and meaning. Akkadian *pasāḫu* means 'be appeased'; Hebrew *pāsaḥ* may mean 'a limping dance'. See discussion in Hyatt 1971, 133-4.

5   Or, 'sacrifice to…'.

The first part here, killing victims and smearing their blood on dwellings, is quite independent of the firstborn sacrifice. The victims are a year old. This is probably a transhumant rite, while it has been grafted on to a more general rite connected to fertility in flocks. Redemption of the firstborn, that is, a sacrificial offering in lieu of the firstborn, was probably very ancient. Its rationale is the practice of sacrificing the first offspring of flocks and herds (a wasteful practice in economic terms). Logic would point to the same principle with firstborn children, which would be regarded as unacceptable, yet require some way out of the logical impasse. §5(14) provides an aetiology of how the principle of substitution came to be employed, when a substitute victim is provided by Yahweh in lieu of Isaac. But this story probably owed little to primitive pastoralist rites, and far more to later theological belief and ritual practice.

8(11)   Another Israelite 'Credo'

The context of the present passage is the offering of first-fruits (similar in symbolic terms to the firstborn offerings of §8(10b)). It presupposes the centralization of the cult (see v. 2). It reads like a summation of past history. Its significance here is however its mythological role, for it narrates the past, historical, legendary or fictitious, as a paradigm which determines meanings, values, and identity in the present.

Then you shall say before Yahweh[1], 'A wandering Aramaean was my father[2], and he went down[3] to Egypt, and dwelt[4] there, few in number, but there he became a mighty people, powerful and great. And the Egyptians treated us evilly, oppressed us, and imposed harsh slavery upon us. Then we cried out to Yahweh the god of our fathers, and Yahweh heard our voice and saw our oppression, our pain and our torment. And Yahweh brought us out of Egypt by the power of his hand and outstretched arm, and with great terror, and signs and wonders. And he brought us to this place[5] and gave us this land flowing with milk and honey. And now I bring the first-fruits of the soil which you have given me, Yahweh.'

(Deuteronomy 26:5-10)

1   The Hebrew *lipnê yhwh* means 'before the face of Yahweh' (see §6(11) n. 4 and cf. *Exodus* 20:3), and referred originally to cult practised in the presence ('before the face') of the image of the god.

2   The narrative is couched in the form of words spoken by one of the tribal patriarchs, a son of Jacob, and eponym of the nation. More prosaically (and thus missing the whole nuance of '*in illo tempore*', a primordial time now recaptured), 'my ancestor'. Use of the expression 'my father' reinforces a sense of identity across the generations, thus bringing the mythic time and the present together. 'Wandering': or 'about to perish'.

3   One always 'goes down' to Egypt in Hebrew. The journey symbolizes dying, and going into the underworld (Wyatt 1990a). See also §§2(35) n. 2, 5(6) ll. 6-7 and 8(9) l. 33. Thus 'coming up', its counter, is implicitly the language of resurrection, and of national revival. In this passage the expression 'brought out' is used, which perhaps emphasizes a sense of liberation, as from a prison.

4   √*gwr* means to lives as a 'resident alien', without full legal rights.

5   Hebrew *hammāqôm hazzê*. The term has a technical sense (as in *Genesis* 28, §7(22)), and refers to the sanctuary in Jerusalem.

Chapter 9

MYTH AND THE FUTURE

Leaving aside Egypt to begin with, because it had its own distinctive beliefs and ritual forms addressing death (see *9.4), there is a community of thought throughout the Semitic world (also with Sumerian elements), illustrated by the texts for discussion. These are selected to show the paradoxical nature of death and its origin. It is as though the means of eternal life are available, but the representative heroes of the myths are easily fooled by smooth-tongued gods or snakes.

These are of course 'existential tales': they start from the facts of human experience. I have listed them here, as myths relating to the future, because they are in reality concerned with the human fear of dying in the future. They are couched in the form of 'Just-So Stories', explaining this condition of mortality arose in the first instance. They would therefore also be listed quite appropriately under §8.

Suggested Reading:

Brandon 1962; A.Y. Collins 1984; J. J. Collins 1998; Eliade 1954; Fenn 1997; Kvanvig 1988.

9.1 Introduction

9.1.1 We have seen that myth is essentially a function of memory, and is therefore linked to the past, which it interprets as the authoritative past, the received account, which in turn determines where a religious community stands, by asserting whence it came. Very often the myth will have a past reference: that is, it is its location in the past that is crucial, for that is what provides authority for the present.

9.1.2 In *Nineteen Eighty-Four* Winston Smith cites the party slogan:

'Who controls the past controls the future: who controls the present controls the past'

(quoted Wyatt 1996a, 373). This sounds cynical, but is absolutely true in any society, and perhaps all the more so in the traditional societies of our present concern. The content of the myth (§8) was in the hands of the present ruling power, the king and the priesthood. They alone had the power to alter it. Any alteration was done deliberately and manipulatively. It would normally be done not out of concern for the past, but because it gave greater future control. Donald (1991, 258) noted that the first thing a conqueror does is to impose the myth of the victor on the vanquished. The vanquished remain unvanquished so long as they can keep the independent tradition alive. The deported Jews in Babylon are a nice example of this survival of myth in spite of conquest. But the conquest transformed the myth, and redirected it towards the future.

9.1.3   Two different aspects of the future should be distinguished, the immediate historical future, and the end of the world, either individually, in death, or universally, in cosmic dissolution. Not all future reference of myth is eschatological. Thus the future gloss put on the conflict myth in §§4(1, 2a) 6(17-22) is not really eschatological, though it is commonly supposed to be. It deals with Israel's redemption in history, in the near future, when Yahweh wins his battle anew. And the power of the conflict myth, examined in §3, lay as much in its present political application as anything else. Kings of all kinds saw themselves as reenacting the conflict, with the very weapons which the victorious god had used (§3(3)), in their own wars. Such power was attributed to the myth that it could be the guarantee of all future victories. This was really nothing more than the logical outcome of the principles enunciated in §1.

9.1.4   Perhaps the most obvious context in which myth was deflected from its past concern to a future one was in the universal fear of death. This is the subject matter of the passages in §9. What was the point of all the grandiloquent affirmation of divine power now, if things were inevitably going to fall apart at death? At first glance it looks like elaborate make-believe, as though believing the impossible will somehow achieve it.

9.1.5   The following myths and associated materials are all futuristic, not in telling what is to happen (they clearly relate what has already happened), but on the future implications of what happened *in illo tempore*. They deal not with a charter or legitimization for what now is, or is now done, but with what will happen in the future: the fact that human beings all die, because of what once happened. (They are myths not because they are not legends or other forms of narrative, but because they deal with the mythic mindset — Wyatt 2001a).

9.2   Mesopotamia

9.2.1   *Gilgamesh* and *Adapa* are two tales originating in Sumer (Southern Iraq), widely known in the ancient Near East. The former was known in Ugarit; a copy of the latter was found at El Amarna in Egypt.

9.2.2   *Gilgamesh* (§9(1)) shows a certain pathos. The red-blooded hero is unaware of death until his bosom friend Enkidu (who has been sent to tame his outrageous libido!) is killed at the command of the gods. He determines to avoid death. He crosses the *Apsû* to find Utnapishtim, the survivor of the flood (§4(6)). He is warned of the futility of the search, but presses on. After all his trouble, a serpent (§3(11) n. 2) steals the plant which would have given him renewed life. The Mesopotamian view of the afterlife is consequently of a shadowy, drear time in the underworld.

9.2.3   *Adapa* (§9(2)) explains how it happened that human beings became mortal. The sage was out in his boat searching for gifts for the gods. When a squall blew up he cursed the south wind and broke his wing. Summoned to Anu's court (sc. his temple) to account for his actions, he was counselled by Ea, the god of wisdom, whom he worshipped, not to be fooled by Anu's trick questions, but to refuse gifts symbolizing death, and accept those symbolizing life. He obeyed to the letter. Unfortunately, Ea had tricked him… Bad news for humans!

9.3   The West Semitic World: Ugarit and Israel

9.3.1   These stories offer similar aetiologies (explanations of cultural facts).

9.3.2   The Ugaritic tale of *Aqhat* (§9(3)) features a hero of that name, a prince, who is given a magnificent bow. The goddess of hunting and war, Anat, greatly desires it, and attempts to wheedle it out of him. She offers him great riches. He is unmoved. She offers him the everlasting life of a god. He is not only unmoved, but calls her a liar, and talks down to her as a mere woman. Definitely *not* how to talk to Anat! She ends up killing him, and doing very nasty things to his corpse.

9.3.3   Adam and Eve live in a wonderful garden (§9(4)), where they may eat what they like, and do what they like, but must not eat from the tree of knowledge. Needless to say, you cannot tell somebody not to do such a thing: it is an immediate challenge. Not only that, but there is a wise snake in Eden. A talking snake! It quite rightly points out to Eve that God ('Yahweh-God') has hardly been straight with her. She is easily persuaded, and has a bite. She offers Adam a bite. They realize that they are stark naked, and run away to hide. God finds out, and throws them all, Adam, Eve and snake, out of the garden, with a curse.

9.3.4   This story is full of amazing subtleties. Note the end, at which we hear of another tree, the tree of life, to which the fallen couple are now forbidden access. The implication is that they would have been able to eat it. Thus it is knowledge which brings mortality. The two trees tend to be identified in later tradition, and are essentially allomorphs (different forms of the same thing). Further aspects are Adam's original androgyny, just like that of a creator god. Eve's name (Hebrew *Ḥavvâ* = 'life') echoes that of a Sumerian goddess NIN.TI, which means both 'Lady of Life' and 'Lady of the Rib'. The garden is transparently the royal sanctuary from which the king, the chief officiant, is now banished. See Wyatt 1988a.

9.4   Egypt

Apotheosis. §§8(1-4) deal with what we called (8.2.1) the dominant myth of Egypt. The key figure for us here is Osiris, brother of Seth, murdered by him, and avenged by Horus.   Osiris may have been a mythical-legendary king.   We first meet him as a dangerous power in the underworld, gradually tamed, becoming the god with whom the dead king was primarily identified (among many other gods).   By the end of the Old Kingdom (time of the pyramids, *ca* 2500-2200 BCE), the dead king was identified with Osiris, and his son, the living king, with Horus son of Osiris.   A process of 'democratization' allowed this idea to filter down, until everybody could be identified with Osiris after death, provided the moral and ritual requirements were observed.   The *Book of the Dead* accompanied the dead to his or her rest (§§9(7, 8)), providing information on how to become Osiris, or any number of other deities (cf. §§11(43-5).

I   The Loss of Immortality

9(1)   Gilgamesh and the Snake

This is the sequel to Utnapishtim's account of the flood-story to Gilgamish (§4(6)). We are told that Gilgamesh is 'two-thirds god, one third man'. He is thus potentially immortal, as are other early kings, and as would Adam and Eve have been, if they had not eaten from the first tree. Gilgamesh lives a care-free and somewhat Clintonian lifestyle, and the gods produce Enkidu, a wild man who will tame him. The opposite happens! After an initial fight, the two become fast friends, travelling the world and performing heroic deeds. When they insult Ishtar, by throwing the testicles (or 'thigh') of the Bull of Heaven in her face, she demands vengeance, and the gods sentence Enkidu to death. In mourning him, and seeing the maggots at work, Gilgamesh suddenly realizes that he too will eventually die, and goes off to visit Utnapishtim, hero of the flood. Here he learns of the plant of rejuvenation.

1   Gilgamesh and Ur-shanabi embarked on the boat.
    They cast off the *Magillu*-boat and sailed away.
His wife spoke to him, to Ut-napishtim the far-distant,
'Gilgamesh came, weary, striving;
5   what will you give him to take back to his country?'
And Gilgamesh out there raised the pole,
    he brought the boat near the shore.
Ut-napishtim spoke to him, to Gilgamesh,
'Gilgamesh, you came, weary, striving,
10   What can I give you to take back to your country?
Let me reveal a closely guarded matter, Gilgamesh,
    and let me tell you the secret of the gods.
There is a plant whose root is like camel-thorn,

whose thorn, like a rose's, will spike [your hands].
15 If you yourself can win that plant,
   you will find [rejuvenation(?)].'
When Gilgamesh heard this,
   he opened the pipe,
He tied heavy stones to his feet.
20 They dragged him down into the *Apsû*,
   and [he saw the plant].
He took the plant himself: it spiked [his hands].
   He cut the heavy stones from his feet.
The sea threw him up on to its shore.
25 Gilgamesh spoke to him, to Ur-shanabi the boatman,
'Ur-shanabi, this plant is a plant to cure a crisis!
   With it a man may win the breath of life.
I shall take it back to Uruk the sheepfold;
   I shall give it to an elder to eat,
30   and so try out the plant.
Its name (shall be): 'An old man grows into a young man';
   I too shall eat (it) and turn into the young man that I once was.'
At twenty leagues they ate their ration.
   At thirty leagues they stopped for the night.
35 Gilgamesh saw a pool whose water was cool,
   and went down into the water and washed.
A snake smelt the fragrance of the plant.
   It came up silently and carried off the plant.
As it took it away, it shed its scaly skin.
40 Thereupon Gilgamesh sat down and wept.
   His tears flowed over his cheeks.
[He spoke to(?)] Ur-shanabi the boatman,
   'For what purpose(?). Ur-shanabi, have my arms grown weary?
For what purpose(?) was the blood inside me so red(?)?
45   I did not gain an advantage for myself,
I have given the advantage to the 'lion of the ground''.

(Dalley 1989, 118-9: *Gilgamesh* xi 270-313)

1   'Lion of the ground' (*labbu irṣiti*) is a mythological term for the snake (§3(11) n.
   2). Cf. a name of the primaeval sea-dragon (*Mušḥuššu*, Tiʾamat): *labbu* AB.ZU
   — 'Lion of the Abyss'. Lions in ancient Near Eastern thought represent chaos
   and danger, and as gods (e.g. sphinxes and door-bolts in Egypt, or sculpted
   door-pillars in Mycenae or Hattusas) are guardians of sacred places.

9(2)   The Story of Adapa

Like *Genesis* 3 below (§9(4)), this is an aetiology of how mortality entered the world, and thus why men are going to die. As a wise man, we would expect Adapa not to have been fooled by Ea, especially since he was his priest, and the episode arose out of him searching for offerings. The whole poem is given. On the theme of divine mockery see Gilhus 1997, 14-8. For other translations see *ANET* 101-3, Hallo, *CS* i 449 (excerpt). A copy of the text was found at El Amarna in Egypt (fourteenth century BCE) and further fragments in King Ashurbanipal's library at Nineveh (seventh century BCE).

(several lines missing)

1   He (Ea) made broad understanding perfect in him (Adapa[1]),
    to disclose the design of the land.
  To him he gave wisdom,
    but did not give eternal life.
5   At that time, in those years, he was a sage (*apkallu*[2]), son of Eridu.
    Ea created him as a protecting spirit[?] among mankind.
  A sage — nobody rejects his word —
    Clever, extra-wise (*atrahasīs*), he was one of the Anunnaki,
    holy, pure of hands, the *pašīšu*-priest who always tends the rites.
10 He does the baking with the bakers,
    does the baking with the bakers of Eridu;
  he does the food and water of Eridu every day,
    sets up the offerings table with his pure hands.
    Without him no offerings table is cleared away.
15 He takes the boat out and does the fishing for Eridu.
  at that time Adapa, the son of Eridu,
    when he had got the [leader[?]] Ea out of bed,
  used to 'feed' the bolt of Eridu every day.
  At the holy quay *Kar-usakar* he embarked in a sailing boat
20   and without a rudder his boat would drift,
  without a steering-pole he would take his boat out
    [   ] into the broad sea…

(gap of uncertain length)

  [   ]
    South Wind [   ]
25   send him[?] to live in the fishes' home.'
  'South Wind, though you send your brothers against me,
    however many there are,
    I shall still break your wing!'
  No sooner had he uttered these words
30   than South Wind's wing was broken;

for seven days South Wind did not blow towards the land.
Anu called out to his vizier Ilabrat,
　'Why hasn't South Wind blown towards the land for seven days?'
His vizier Ilabrat answered him,
35　'My lord, Adapa the son of Ea has broken South Wind's wing.'
When Anu heard this word,
　he cried '(Heaven) help (him)!'
He rose up from his throne:
　'[Send for him to] be brought here!'
40　Ea, aware of heaven's ways, touched him
　　and [　　　　] made him wear his hair unkempt,
[clothed him in] mourning garb,
　gave him instructions.
'Adapa, you are to go before king Anu.
45　You will go up to heaven,
　　and when you go up to heaven,
when you approach the Gate of Anu,
　　Dumuzi and Gizzida will be standing in the Gate of Anu,
(they) will see you,
50　　(they) will keep asking you questions:
'Young man, on whose behalf do you look like this?
　On whose behalf do you wear mourning garb?'
(You must answer) 'Two gods have vanished from our country,
　and that is why I am behaving like this.'
55　(They will ask) 'Who are the two gods that have vanished
　　　from the country?'
　　(You must answer) 'They are Dumuzi and Gizzida.'
They will look at each other and laugh a lot,
　will speak a word in your favour to Anu,
　will present you to Anu in a good mood.
60　When you stand before Anu
they will hold out for you bread of death,
　so you must not eat.
They will hold out for you water of death,
　so you must not drink.
65　They will hold out a garment for you:
　　so put it on.
They will hold out oil for you:
　　so anoint yourself.
You must not neglect the instructions I have given you:
70　　keep to the words that I have told you.'
The envoy of Anu arrived.

'Send to me Adapa,
  who broke South Wind's wing.'
He made him take the way of heaven
75   and he (Adapa) went up to heaven.
When he came up to heaven,
  when he approached the Gate of Anu,
Dumuzi and Gizzida were standing in the Gate of Anu.
  They saw Adapa and cried '(Heaven) help (him)!
80   Young man, on whose behalf do you look like this?
    Adapa, on whose behalf do you wear mourning garb?'
'Two gods have vanished from the country,
  And that is why I am wearing mourning garb.'
'Who are the two gods who have vanished from the country?'
85   'Dumuzi and Gizzida.'
They looked at each other, and laughed a lot.
When Adapa drew near to the presence of King Anu,
  Anu saw him and shouted,
'Come here, Adapa! Why did you break South Wind's wing?'
90   Adapa answered Anu,
'My lord, I was catching fish in the middle of the sea
  for the house of my lord (Ea).
But he inflated' the sea into a storm'
  and South Wind blew and sank me!
95   I was forced to take up residence in the fishes' home.
  In my fury I cursed South Wind.'
Dumuzi and Gizzida responded from beside him,
  spoke a word in his favour to Anu.
His heart was appeased, he grew quiet.
100   'Why did Ea disclose to wretched mankind the ways of heaven
      and earth,
    give them a heavy heart?
It was he who did it!
  What can we do for him?
Fetch him the bread of (eternal) life and let him eat!'
105   They fetched him the bread of (eternal) life,
    but he would not eat.
They fetched him the water of (eternal) life,
  but he would not drink.
They fetched him a garment,
110   and he put it on himself.
They fetched him oil,
  and he anointed himself.

Anu watched him and and laughed at him.
'Come, Adapa, why didn't you eat?
115   Why didn't you drink?
Didn't you want to be immortal?
   Alas for downtrodden people!'
'(But) Ea my lord told me:
'You mustn't eat!
120   You mustn't drink!'
'Take him and send him back to his earth.'

(gap of unknown length to end of story)

(Dalley 1989, 184-7, adapted)

1   Adapa. The word may be related to the Hebrew '*ādām*, 'man', 'Adam'.

2   *Apkallu*. There were seven such persons, though their identities vary. They
         were the legendary founders of the holy cities of Sumer, and were primordial
         wise men (< Sumerian AB.GAL, 'expert', 'wise'). They eventually withdrew
         beyond the AB.ZU as minor gods. See Reiner 1961.

Dumuzi and Gizzida were the door-keepers of Anu's palace-temple. The former
(Akkadian Tammuz) features in a number of women's cults in the ancient world.

Ea was the Akkadian form of Enki (Sumerian EN.KI 'Lord Earth'), god of the waters
and creator of mankind. He was also god of wisdom and ritual power. Note that he
tricked Adapa. Was he malevolent? Was Adapa just stupid? The listener or reader
immediately guesses what is going to happen! Ilabrat was the vizier of Anu.

9(3)   From the Story of Aqhat

See also §4(20). Aqhat, a son for whom Danel had longed, has been given a wondrous
composite bow by the artificer god Kothar. The goddess of war and hunting, Anat,
offers him 'everlasting life' in exchange for it. Aqhat retorts insolently. On the motif
of the hero insulting a goddess cf. *Gilgamesh* tablet vi col. 5. Two conflicting views of
human destiny are described here. Anat offers a destiny based on the death and
restoration of Baal, which may implicitly be that believed to apply to kings. Aqhat
refers to an older and gloomier conception, which has many parallels in ancient
literature. Cf. §4(16), which contrasts with Gilgamesh's aspirations.

1   [   ]
     In lifting up her eyes Anat saw [the bow].
     [beautiful was the for]m of its string,
        like lightning [its arrows].
5   [   ] deeps,
        lightning [   ].
     She coveted the bow, the work of [Kothar-and-Hasis]
        [of which the hor]ns were like a coiled serpent.
     [Her goblet she dropped] to the ground,
10   her cup she spilled [in the dust].

[She lifted up her voice] and cried:
'Listen, pray, [O hero Aqhat]!
   Ask for silver and I shall give (it) you,
   [for gold and I shall be]stow (it) on you.
15 Just give your bow to [Virgin] Ana[t],
   your arrows to the Beloved of the Powerful One!'
But Aqhat the hero replied:
'The mightiest ash-trees from Lebanon,
   the strongest sinews from wild bulls,
20   the hardest horns from mountain goats,
   <the toughest> tendons from the hocks of a bull,
   the sharpest reeds from the great marsh,
   give to Kothar-and-Hasis:
let *him* construct a bow for Anat,
25   arrows for the Beloved of the Powerful One!'
And Virgin Anat replied:
'Ask for life, O hero Aqhat:
   ask for life and I shall give (it) you,
   immortality and I shall bestow (it) on you:
30 I shall make you number (your) years with Baal:
   with the son of El you shall number months.
'Like Baal he shall live indeed!'
   Alive, he shall be feasted,
he shall be feasted and given to drink.
35   The minstrel shall intone and sing concerning him'.'
[And she] said to him:
'Thus shall I make Aqhat the hero live!'
But Aqhat the hero replied:
'Do not deceive me, O Virgin,
40   for to a hero your deceit is rubbish!
Man, (at his) end, what will he receive?
   What will he receive, a man (as his) destiny?
silver² will be poured on his head,
   gold² on top of his skull²,
45 [and] the death of all I shall die,
   and I shall surely die.
[And anoth]er thing let me say:
bows (are for) warriors!
   Will women hunt now?'

(Wyatt 1998a, 271-6: KTU 1.17 vi 10-40)

1   Baal is a god who dies and is restored. Hymns celebrated his resurrection. 'The Powerful One' (*lim*) of whom Anat is 'the Beloved' is another of his titles. Thus Aqhat will gain a divine immortality, a promise he considers vacuous.

2   To the hint here at a gold death-mask cf. those of the kings of Mycenae in Bronze Age Greece. For discussion of the problems of translating these lines see Wyatt 1998a, 274 n. 115. My translation here is slightly modified. Also cited at §4(20).

While this story does not present itself as a myth having universal reference for its hearers and readers, it follows the conventions of such stories, with the chief character Aqhat, a king's son, a hero who is prepared to speak plainly to a goddess, thus expressing what the common man may half think, but not dare to articulate. We may compare the outspoken Job! A breakthrough in the conception of human destiny is put before the hero, but he is not prepared to risk all (and especially not his precious bow!) for a mere form of words, whose veracity there is no chance of proving.

9(4)   Eve and the Snake (the 'Fall')

This story, which has had a profound effect on Western culture, has been variously dated from the tenth to the second century BCE. Certainty is impossible, though a later date may be supported by the apparent ignorance of the tradition by any other part of the Hebrew Bible. *Isaiah* 14 and *Ezekiel* 28 perhaps contain the antecedents. See also discussion at §3(11) and for the remainder of the narrative, §§6(7, 14).

'And Yahweh-God[1] instructed the Man[2], 'From every tree in the garden you may eat; but from the tree of knowing all things[3] you may not eat. For on the day that you eat from it you will certainly die!'...

Now the snake was wiser than all other living things of the country, which Yahweh-God had made, and he said to the woman, 'Did God really say "you shall not eat from every tree in the garden"?'

Then the woman replied to the snake, 'The fruit of the trees in the garden we may eat, but from the fruit of the tree which is in the middle of the garden God has said, "you may not eat from it, nor touch it, in case you die".'

Then the snake to the woman, 'You will certainly not die!' For God knows that on the day that you eat from it your eyes will be opened, and you will become gods[4], knowing all things[5].'

(The man and his wife eat from the forbidden tree.)

And Yahweh-God said, 'Look! The man has become one of us, knowing all things. So now, in case he puts out his hand and takes also from the tree of life, and eats and lives for ever...' So Yahweh-God expelled him from the garden of Eden, from tilling[6] the ground from which he had been taken. And he drove out the Man, and he set before the garden of

Eden the cherubs[8] and the flame of the whirling sword to guard the way to the Tree of Life.

(*Genesis* 2:16-7, 3:1-5, 22-3)

1   'Yahweh-God' (*yhwh-' ᵉlōhîm*): the second term is plural in form. It may have the sense 'Lord of the gods'. Similarly, where 'God' appears, it may have been originally construed as 'the gods'. Note the plural in 3:22: 'one of us'! Cf. n. 1 to §2(17).

2   Hebrew *hā'ādām*: sc. 'Adam'. This is an ideological term, 'the Primal Man'. Implicit in its use is the Man's role as archetypal king.

3   Lit. 'the tree of the knowledge of good and evil'. 'Good and evil' constitute a merism, sc. 'everything'.

4   'Become gods': the Hebrew (*kēlōhîm*) is usually translated as a comparison, 'like gods'. It is stronger than that. Similarly in 3:22, 'one of us'. Cf. Waltke and O'Connor 1990, 203, who define the usage, the *kaph veritatis*, 'the logical outcome of comparison is correspondence or identity'.

5   Literally, 'knowing good and evil', a merism.

6   Rather than 'to till'. The point of the expulsion is banishment from the Garden = the Temple, which prevents cultivation. Cultivation is a metaphor for cult (itself the epitome of culture). See §2(11) n. 1, and Wyatt 1988a, 117-22.

8   These are the key to the formal status of this garden: cherubs (derived from Akkadian *kāribu*, 'intercessory priest, tutelary spirit', sometimes identified as divine) are related to sphinxes (leonine) in Egypt and the winged sphinxes (leonine or bovine) of Mesopotamia, where they were commonly the guardians of temple gates and other boundaries (see §9(1) n. 1). Cf. also the lion-gates of Mycenae and Hattusas. These sphinx-like figures keep unfit people out of the sanctuary. Re-entry to the garden (rebuilding of the temple, or in Christian terms the resurrection of Christ and return of Adam — Wyatt 1990b) will signify the redemption of humanity.

II   The Restoration of Hope in Israel

9(5)   Aspirations to the Renewal of Paradise

Virtually any 'proof-text' used in the New Testament would illustrate the point made graphically by the present passage, though it is, rather surprisingly in view of its literary power, not cited anywhere. On a possible historical context see n. 2 below, though it is impossible to verify. The passage (hardly a formal oracle, more a poem meditating on the glorious tranquillity of an ideal reign) envisages real benefits from a righteous king: mayhem and slaughter, killing and cruelty, the hallmarks of all monarchy, and normal human depredation, will be entirely absent, for this will be a kingship like that lost by Adam in Eden, when all are herbivore (contrast *Genesis* 1:29-30, the ideal world, with *Genesis* 9:3-4, the real one). Historically unrealistic, no wonder it has such a resonance as a messianic aspiration! There is nothing intrinsically eschatological about this passage, but such a meaning is generally given to it.

1   A shoot goes out from the stock of Jesse
      and a scion[1] springs[2] from his root.
    And a spirit of Yahweh rests on him[3]:
      a spirit of wisdom and understanding,
5   a spirit of counsel and valour,
      a spirit of knowledge and the fear of Yahweh...[4]

    And wolf dwells with lamb,
      and leopard lies down with kid.
      and calf and lion-cub and fatling together[5]
10   and a small boy[6] leads them.
    And cow and bear are companions,
      their young lie down together.
    Lion, like the ox, eats straw,
    and suckling child plays over the hole of snake;
15   while over viper's retreat weaned child stretches out his hand.
    they do no evil
      and do no killing[7]
    anywhere on my holy mountain[8],
    for the earth is filled with knowledge of Yahweh
20   as waters cover the sea[9].

                                    (*Isaiah* 11:1-2, 6-8)

1   Cf.§5(4), §6(11-13) for previous passages using arboreal imagery of the king.

2   'Goes out... springs', or 'will go... will spring...': the temporal significance of
    the verbs is uncertain. Its original sense may have been present (as with *Isaiah*
    7:13-25, the 'Immanuel' prophecy, where the sign of the pregnant queen was
    there for the prophet's contemporaries to see), as a message of imminent
    divine intervention, perhaps even addressed to the same crisis, as the Syro-
    Ephraimite military alliance threatened Judahite independence. But it is likely
    that by virtue of its survival, and the principle of reapplicability commonly
    accepted for prophetic texts, it came to be understood in a futuristic way, so
    that it always lay in the future as a message of hope to people in a fresh
    historical crisis, exilic, Maccabean, Roman, mediaeval...

3   This alludes both to royal rites such as anointing: cf. *1 Samuel* 16:13, where the
    spirit of Yahweh alights on David; and also perhaps to the very making of
    Adam, a primal royal figure, in *Genesis* 2:7 (§2(18)).

4   Six spirits are listed (or six manifestations of the one spirit). The fear of
    Yahweh hardly constitutes a plausible spirit. The Greek and Latin (LXX,
    Vulgate)) both read 'wisdom... understanding...counsel... valour...
    knowledge... piety... fear of God', thus giving a list of seven. We might have
    expected seven in Hebrew on the basis of the pattern illustrated at §2(43).

5   Hebrew reads 'and calf and lion-cub and fatling…'. Many translators adjust to read 'calf and lion-cub feed together'.

6   Hebrew *na'ar* can have the sense of noble status. Perhaps translating freely, 'young prince'?

7   All the verbs (as noted in n. 1 for vv. 1-2) probably had a present reference, though they may have come to be understood futuristically. However, for the whole passage, cf. §11(11) n. 1 for a justification for the present in translation, as the *present* vision in the prophet's mind's eye.

8   Note the paradisal image applied specifically to the mountain where the deity dwells. We would have expected this from the imagery of §§5, 6.

9   A curious expression. 'The sea' has the article, the only one in the whole passage apart from 'the ox', which is a comparison. And how do waters 'cover' the sea, as distinct from constituting it? I suspect an allusion here to a reaffirmation of the *Chaoskampf* victory, so that somehow Yam (the sea-god) is covered over to prevent him rising up and destroying this idyllic existence. It would be ironic if he were covered over with his own substance. Cf. the ultimate aspiration in *Revelation* 21:1b.

9(6)   The Man from the Sea

This vision from the fourth book of Ezra (*4 Ezra* = *2 Esdras*), a first century CE composition, is a striking example of the principle enunciated by Gunkel (§3(11) introduction). The text, which may have been composed in Hebrew, and of which a Greek version is also lost, survives in Latin, Syriac, Ethiopic, Arabic, Georgian and Armenian (Hayman 1998), testifying to its enormous popularity among early Christians, and oblivion among Jews. It is cited here since it provides a singular instance of the eschatological application of the Conflict motif (cf. §§2(9, 10), 3(1-10, 12-16), and, similarly eschatological, §3(11)). We can see particularly clearly the similarity between this narrative and the imagery employed in §§3(9, 10). To write of an 'eschatological application', as always, tends to beg the question, since for all we know the original author saw redemption coming in his own historical time (perhaps as Deutero-Isaiah had done, cf. §§4(1 and 2)), rather than at the end of time. The text of *4 Ezra* as a whole, however, is firmly eschatological (see 4:42-3, 5:41, 7:26-44, 8:63, 12:9 etc.). The vision is followed in 13:25-53 by a rather ponderous interpretation, which need not concern us here.

After seven days I saw a vision in the night. And lo, a great wind arose from the sea so that it stirred up all its waves[1]. And I saw, and behold, that wind brought up from the heart of the sea something like the figure of a man[2]. And I saw and, lo, that man flew with the clouds of heaven[3]. And wherever he turned his face to look and see, everything trembled at the sight of him. And wherever a voice came forth from his mouth[4], all who heard his voice melted as wax melts when it feels the fire. And after this I saw, and lo, an innumerable multitude of people were gathered together from the four winds of heaven to make war against the man who had come up from the sea. And I saw that he carved[5] for himself a high mountain and flew and stood upon it[6]. And I sought to see the region or the place whence the mountain was carved. But I could not[7]. After this I saw, and lo, all those who had gathered to wage war with him were exceedingly afraid, yet they dared to fight. And when he saw the onrush of the approaching multitude, he did not lift up his hand nor take hold of a spear or any weapon of war, but I saw only how he emitted from his mouth something like a stream of fire, and from his lips a flaming breath, and from his tongue he emitted a storm of sparks. And all these were mixed together... and they fell upon the onrushing multitude which was prepared to fight, and burned them all up... And I saw and was amazed. After this I saw that man come down from the mountain and call to himself another multitude that was peaceable. And the shapes of many people drew near to him, some of whom were joyful and some sad; some of them bound and some were bringing others as offerings.

(Hayman 1998, 2-5: *4 Ezra* 13:1-13)

1   The vision appears to be modelled on that of *Daniel* 7: cf. 7:2.

2   In the vision of *Daniel* 7, beasts had emerged from the sea, representing enemy empires (Assyria, Babylon, Persia and Greece: Rome was not yet an element in Maccabean history in the second century BCE). The man (in contrast to the animals) is an embodiment of Israel, but more precisely of Israel's triumphant deity, who now will variously punish and champion his people. The evocation is thus of Yahweh, though as in the Bible, he owes much to the West Semitic imagery of Baal.

3   Cf. Baal's title 'Charioteer of the clouds', found also of Yahweh at *Psalm* 68:4, and echoed in Yahweh's description in *Psalms* 18:6-11, 68:33, 104:3, *Deuteronomy* 33:26 etc.

4   Cf. *Psalm* 29 and its Ugaritic *Vorlage* (§3(5) introduction).

5   This is circumstantial evidence in favour of the view that the mountain is carved out of Yam's corpse, as Tiamat had been carved up. See §§2(10), 2(21) n. 1 and 6(28) n. 1.

6   As victor, see §§2(9), 6(16) and n. 1. Note also the iconography of Baal standing on two mountains (Dijkstra 1991).

7   Presumably because this mountain is the *axis mundi*, and disappears from sight above the clouds.

III   Hope in Egypt

9(7)   Osiris as the Source of Future Felicity

This is a hymn to Osiris from the beginning of the *Book of the Dead*. It has no chapter number. It accompanies a scene of the deceased before a table of offerings, dedicated to Osiris. The *Book of the Dead* was the culmination of a long tradition of ritual texts, prayes and hymns dating at least from Old Kingdom times (though many of their forebears, the *Pyramid Texts*, already betray a long oral prehistory). On these see §§2(8) and n. 1, 2(22) introduction, and 7(11). The context of this hymn is strictly eschatological, since it was addressed to the god by the deceased, and related to his future destiny.

1   Worship of Osiris Wennefer[1],
        the Great God who dwells in the Thinite Nome,[2]
    King of Eternity, who passes millions of years in his lifetime;
5   First-born of Nut, Begotten of Geb,
    Heir, Lord of the *Wereret*-Crown,[3]
        whose White Crown is tall,
        sovereign of gods and men.
    He has taken the crook and the flail and the office[4]
        of his forefathers.
10   'May your heart which is in the desert land be glad,
        for your son Horus is firm on your throne,
    while you have appeared as Lord of Busiris,
        as the Ruler-who-is-in-Abydos.[5]
    The Two Lands flourish in vindication (*m-m3ᶜ-hrw*)[6]
15   because of you in the presence of the Lord of All.'
    All that exists is ushered in to him in his name of
            Face-to-whom-men-are-ushered;
        the Two Lands are marshalled for him as leader in this
            his great name of Seker;[7]
    his might is far-reaching,
        one greatly feared in this his name of Osiris;
20   he passes over the length of eternity in his name Wennefer.
        'Hail to you, King of Kings, Lord of Lords, Ruler of Rulers,
    who took possession of the Two Lands even in the womb of Nut;
        he rules the plains of the Silent Land,
    even he the golden of body, blue of head,
        on whose arms is turquoise.
    O Pillar of Myriads, broad of breast,
        kindly of countenance, who is in the sacred land:
    may you grant power in the sky,
            might on earth
            and vindication in the Realm of the Dead,
    a journeying downstream to Busiris as a living soul
        and a journeying upstream to Abydos as a heron[8];
25   to go in and out without hindrance at all the gates of
            the Netherworld.

> May there be given to me bread from the House of Cool Water
>   and a table of offerings from Heliopolis,
>   my toes being firm-planted in the Field of Rushes.
> May the barley and emmer which are in it belong to the Ka
>   of Osiris N.'

(Faulkner 1985, 27: *BD Hymn to Osiris*)

1   Wennefer (*wn nfr*, Greek Onuphris), 'the One Beautiful of Being', was a title of Osiris after his restoration from the dead. He was not resurrected, since he remained in the underworld, becoming lord of it and the type of the deceased, from which he took the name 'Foremost of the Westerners' (or, 'of the dead') (*ḫnty imntiw*), a title taken from the ancient mortuary god of Abydos, Anjeti.

2   This, a town and its nome next to Abydos, was the seat of the earliest kings of the Old Kingdom.

3   Sc. the White Crown (*wrrt*, 'Great One'). This was combined with the feather fetish of Abydos to form the Atef crown, the conventional headwear of Osiris and dead kings.

4   The crook and flail, emblems of pastoralism and agriculture, became symbols of justice, and the attributes of Osiris.

5   'Busiris (*pr wsir*, 'House of Osiris')... Abydos': these cities, in the Delta and Upper Egypt respectively, were important centres of the cult of Osiris.

6   The formula *m3ʿ ḥrw*, 'innocent' (literally, 'true of voice') was pronounced of Osiris in his conflict with Seth, who murdered him. In *the Book of the Dead*, the deceased's heart (seat of the will, and hence moral responsibility) was weighed against the feather of Maat (*m3ʿt*, 'truth' or 'justice', personified as a goddess). When the two were in equilibrium, the deceased was pronounced innocent, and hence able to live on and travel to the fields of offerings, the Egyptian paradise (below, §9(8)).

7   Seker was god of the necropolis at Memphis, and often identified with Ptah. Here he is identified with Osiris, and the three gods often formed a triad.

8   'Heron': *bnw*, the Phoenix. See *5.2 and introduction to §§5(1-3).

9(8)   The Fields of Offerings

The 'Fields of Offerings (*sḫt-ḥtpw*)' represented the Egyptian conception of Paradise in its root sense of a garden (cf. §§6(7), 9(5)). It lay at the end of the long journey the deceased made through the underworld, as a haven of normality and tranquillity. It had a decidedly aristocratic and idyllic quality, of the 'hunting, shooting and fishing' kind, in which *shabtis* (models of servants, which responded, √*wšb*, to commands: see §11(42)) actually performed any chores, while the deceased was represented in the iconography as doing them himself. The Fields of Offerings appear in vignettes modelled on the landscape of the delta, rivers and canals criss-crossing the region, and the islands, complete with jetties and boats at the ready, were given over to agricultural pursuits.

The striking feature here, as in all Egyptian mortuary belief and practice, is the enormous emphasis placed on the physical survival of the dead. It is however dangerous to consider it in a purely materialistic way, since the deceased was also identified with any number of gods. In the case of kings, as evidenced in the *Pyramid Texts*, the dead were resurrected, reborn, and transformed into stars, the sun and other gods. In other words, a whole gamut of metaphors was used for the transfiguration and survival of the individual.

The 'Fields of Offerings' (Hebrew *sᵉdê tᵉrûmôt*) appear, apparently inadvertently, in 2 *Samuel* 1:21. A scribe appears to have misread a formula, *sᵉrê tᵉhômôt*, 'welling up of the deeps', which occurs in Ugaritic. See §§11(28, 29).

Here begin the spells of the Fields of Offerings and spells of going forth into the day[1], of coming and going in the Realm of the Dead, of being provided for in the Field of Rushes which is within the Fields of Offerings, the abode of the Great Goddess[2], the Mistress of Winds; having strength thereby, having power thereby, ploughing therein, reaping and eating therein, drinking therein, copulating therein[3], and doing everything that used to be done on earth by N...

'I rowed in the Bark in the Lake of Offerings; I took it from the limbs of Shu, and his northern stars, his limbs, were set in due order; I rowed and arrived at its waterways and towns, I fared southward to the god who is in it, because I am he who would rest in his fields. I control the Two Enneads[4] whom he loves, I pacify the Combatants[5] on behalf of those who are in the west[6], I create what is good, I bring peace...'

This is Horus[7]. He is a falcon a thousand cubits long. Life and domination are in his hand, he comes and goes at will in its waterways and towns, he rises and sets in Qenqenet[8], the birthplace of the god... This is Hotep[9] who walks throughout this field of his; he partakes of a meal in the birthplace of the god. If he rests in Qenqenet, he will do everything in it as it is done in the Island of fire; there is no shouting in it, there is nothing evil in it.

'I live in Hotep, my bag and bowl are on me, which I have filled from baskets, being one whom the spirits of the Lord of Plenty guide... I am one who recalls to himself that of which I have been forgetful. I plough and I reap, and I am content in the City of God. I know the names[10] of the districts, towns and waterways which are in the Fields of Offerings and of those who are in them; I am strong in them and I am a spirit in them; I eat in them and I travel about in them. I plough and reap in the field; I rise early in it and I go to rest in it. I am a spirit in it as Hotep...'

(Faulkner 1985, 103-4: *BD* 110 excerpts, adapted)

[1]   The title of the whole *Book of the Dead* was *prt m hrw* ('coming forth by day').

[2]   Ta-weret ('Great Earth', *t3 wrt*), a hippopotamus form of Hathor.

3　　Unlike the Christian conception of the afterlife, as expressed in *Matthew* 22:30.

4　　The dead were identified with Osiris. It is as Osiris that the deceased speaks here. The identity of the two Enneads is not explicit, but probably those of Heliopolis and Memphis are intended.

5　　Sc. Horus and Seth, pacified by Osiris in §8(2).

6　　The dead.

7　　Here the deceased is identified with Horus. As son of Osiris, with whom the deceased is also identified, he is now implicitly identified with the king ('life and dominion are in his hand...').

8　　A lake in the underworld ('flowing').

9　　The embodiment of the sacrifice.

10　　The emphasis on gnosis is that of §2(22).

Chapter 10

RITUAL AND THE PAST

This chapter is concerned with the application to the present, in the continuing life of a community, of ritual patterns established in the past. The 'archetypal event', which established a ritual, might be entirely fictitious in nature, or could have a historical foundation, or be a bit of both, as with the Israelite Passover (§8(10)), which began as a seasonal festival, but was then attached to, and became a celebration of, the legendary exodus from Egypt, and thus participated in the creation of 'history' (sc. historiography). Cf. also §12.

Suggested Reading:

Bell 1992; Bourdillon and Fortes 1980; Boyer 1993; Davies 1971; Douglas 1973; T. F. Driver 1991; Fontenrose 1971; Grimes 1995; Patton and Doniger 1996; Rappaport 1997; id. 1999; Segal 1998.

10.1 Introduction

We have seen the importance of the past, and memory, real or imagined, in the construction and validation of the present. Just as narratives about the past provide paradigms for the present (and the future), so do ritual forms. A ritual is never 'invented'. Of course it may well be, but tradition will always maintain that it goes back to an archetype. A familiar example is the Eucharist, which claims that its authority and ritual pattern are based on the Last Supper. Thus ritual parallels myth in implicitly appealing to a remembered past: it is thus a further example of the reinforcement of the collective memory, which is so important for the community (see **1.8 and 8.1 above). Note however that while we may often speak of myth and ritual together, we should not make the further step, which used to be made, of seeing them as inseparable. See Fontenrose 1971 and Segal 1998. They are different strategies (linguistic and behavioural) for achieving the same end, so naturally run in parallel from time to time.

10.2 Regular Cult

10.2.1 Routinization is the key here. This is the routine, automatic following of an archetype: the feeding of the gods is the pattern for feeding the community. Nothing better illustrates Durkheim's dictum that in worshipping the gods, society worships itself. We have four representative examples. The pattern, which is as old as the Neolithic revolution (anytime from 10000 BCE onwards), and with older elements, is still much the same everywhere, with only detail differences.

10.2.2 Karnak (§10(1)): while the treatment of the image is standard, washing, anointing, mouth-opening, clothing, feeding, this action is significantly assimilated to the Horus and Seth myth (§§8(1-4)). Every detail of the cult reenacts the primordial conflict, and affirms Horus' victory. Thus the myth serves for the interpretation and validation of the ritual activity.

10.2.3 Uruk (§10(2)): the text here is far less informative about underlying symbolism of the special kind noted above, but the function of sacrifice on one level of understanding as the daily meals of the gods is clear. Note the various specialized meat products. These are the gastronomic delights of the king's table, shared with the gods.

10.2.4 Ugarit (§10(3)): from Ugarit we have long lists of the type given, detailing precisely how many victims were offered to each deity. No explanation is given, but we note the offering of other commodities such as wine and oil. Precious metals and costly fabrics appear in some lists, and the king's role was prominent. Holocausts (whole victims burnt as offering) and communion sacrifices, in which worshippers and deity shared a meal, are an explicit feature.

10.2.5 Jerusalem (§10(4)): precise details of the ritual preparation, cooking procedures and serving, are given here. Everything must be precise: this was 'silver service' for the deity! This idea draws attention to the seriousness of all such activity. It was hedged about with precise instructions, so that nothing in the elaborate symbolic structure could go wrong.

10.2.6 Lying behind all this butchery and other systems of offering was the temple's role at the centre of the community's economic life. All trade in effect passed through the temple, offered up as gifts for the deity, and then passed on into the economy. The foodstuffs were all channeled into the market, stored, sold, given as provisions to temple staff and so on. The whole economy, from agricultural production through trade, booty from war, bullion and other precious items (ivory, precious stones, spices) was implicitly sacralized and thus made acceptable by this means. 'Religion' in antiquity was altogether more comprehensive than now: it was not just the 'metaphysics of society', the 'concern for eternity', or the 'numinous'. This really *was* 'a way of life'.

10.3   Festival Cult

10.3.1 Over against the routinization of regular ritual practice, the emphasis here is on recollection, anamnesis and renewal through the abolition of time. *Illud tempus* really does become 'the Eternal Present'.

10.3.2 We have taken as our example the important *Akitu* festival from Mesopotamia (§10(5)). By the first millennium BCE this ancient festival took eleven days, and in it a number of different elements coalesced, a sacred marriage rite, one of seasonal change, as the summer arrived, various royal elements, and a shrine called *akitu* (its original meaning remaining obscure, but latterly associated with the sacred marriage on the top level of a ziggurat). It had become the chief New Year festival in various cities, notably Babylon (with Marduk as chief deity), and the Assyrian capitals (Nineveh and Ashur, with Aššur as chief deity). It combined the renewal of the year, represented by the recitation of the entire *Enuma Elish* epic (§§2(13, 14)), culminating in the Babylonian version with the chanting of the fifty names of Marduk, with rites of the renewal of kingship, involving a mock trial and humiliation of the king. Various elements in this festival (the two small figures and the ram decapitated) are probably expiatory in nature and anticipate the next section (10.4). This festival amounted to a renewal of the entire world, and a reaffirmation of the king's role as Marduk's representative on earth.

10.3.3 There has been a long and fruitless search to discover the New Year Festivals of ancient Israel and Ugarit. While there may well have been something akin to the *Akitu* festival (the Israelite Feast of Tabernacles — 'Booths' — certainly looks an attractive candidate), no proof has been forthcoming, and most scholars have abandoned the search. But contained under the general rubric of festival cult we should include the Israelite Passover (§8(10)), where the rite corresponds to the texts narrating the myth. This is a classic case of anamnesis, alive and well today.

10.4 Sin and Atonement

10.4.1 Human beings are constantly aware of the gap between aspiration and achievement, between moral imperative and moral failure. Everything turns to dust. Our best intentions go awry. This is all part of the nature of alienation. It may be summed up in the sense of 'sin'. It is probably universal. We examine a number of examples of this sense, and of the methods used to resolve it, of 'making atonement', thus of making whole that which was broken.

10.4.2 The sense of sin is due in part to that of creatureliness before the divine. See Otto 1950. This comes out rather well in §§10(6, 7): the very conception of 'deity' throws into contrast the frailties of men, and leads to the plea for forgiveness. These would suit well any Christian liturgy, but was abundantly present in the religious consciouness of the ancient Near East.

10.4.3 Let us consider the great Atonement Ritual from Ugarit (§10(10). This was a comprehensive rite, covering all sections of society. It fell into six parts, treating the sins of men and women in turn. It is noteworthy for the moral basis of the sins: they are failures as perceived by various neighbours, or perhaps alien communities resident in Ugarit. These would have limited recourse to the law, and could easily be oppressed. (Cf. the institution of the *gēr*, 'resident alien' in Israel.) Thus social inequalities and injustices would lead to various tensions, perceived not only as damaging to communal tranquillity, but as an offence against the gods. This hardly appears to constitute the recalling of any mythic past (as in *10.3), but is comparable in implying the return to a prior state of ritual and moral purity.

10.4.4 §§10(8, 9) really belong with §10(11), as belonging to its obscure prehistory, developing the sense of substitutionary atonement (still a lynch pin of evangelical Christianity). The idea that things that go wrong are always somebody's (sc. somebody else's!) fault is deeply embedded in society. Note the search for scapegoats in times of disaster and emergency. Girard 1977 gives a fascinating account of the mechanism, in which vengeance for the perceived wrong is the first reaction, slowly channeled into sacrifice, and later into legal systems which take the burden of vengeance from society, thus depersonalizing and defusing it.

10.4.5 §10(8) is a pair of fragmentary texts apparently providing a goat (a 'scapegoat') as the bearer away of guilt, perhaps from someone's tomb, so that the deceased is now guiltless before the gods. Note the problem of interpretation discussed in n. 1.

10.4.6 §10(9) is an anticipation of chapter 11, with its future reference, since it is an omen text. The text is fragmentary, and consequently obscure. But it may allude to some means of ridding the community of sin during a military crisis.

10.4.7 §10(11) contains excerpts from *Leviticus* 16. The whole chapter deserves study, and can usefully be read in conjunction with *Yoma*, the tractate in the *Mishnah* (Neusner 1988, 265-79). See the important article of Davies 1977. In a nutshell, two goats share the burden of communal sin. One takes it to the altar (the centre), where it is sacrificed; the other takes it out to the desert (the *limen*, the end of the world), where it is destroyed. Israel is left, as it were, in its own 'centre', safe from the destructive power of God at the centre (for you cannot see God and live:

he is too holy), and from the baneful, demonic and destructive forces (chaos) at the end of the world. A balance is restored between the centrifugal and centripetal tendencies. The tensions pulling the community in both directions, and therefore apart, are resolved.

10.5 Sacrifice

10.5.1 Sacrifice covered a number of forms, and addressed a number of ritual concerns, in the ancient world. Among these there was, for instance, the feeding of the gods (probably perceived originally as material beings who needed sustenance, just like people), and the idea of commensality, in which the gods, sharing food with their worshippers, were bound in a relationship with them (the theme of covenant, an important theological motif in the Bible, was a development of this conviction, modelled on treaties between peoples). Such behaviour was in effect the formal way of doing ordinary everyday things, and may have had its origins in the concern for conformity to a local culture's values and norms. There was no better way to represent and sanction such activities than by seeing them as revealed by the gods. A substantial body of theorizing about the origins of religion (sc. the worship of gods) sees it as developing out of an older worship of ancestors. The gods were the ancestors raised to a higher ontological level.

10.5.2 Ritual is often regarded, outside anthropological circles, as something devoid of meaning ('empty ritual'). The opposite is the case. Ritual is a behavioural pattern we share with many animals (which indicates how deeply rooted it is in the human constitution), though with a crucial distinction:

> an indispensable aspect of periodic *religious observances*, where the believer, by appropriate gestures, confesses his dependence and his childlike faith and seeks, by appropriate offerings, to secure a sense of being lifted up to the very bosom of the supernatural which in the visible form of an image may graciously respond, with the faint smile of an inclined face. The result is a sense of *separateness transcended*, and yet also of *distinctiveness confirmed*.

and

> ... while ethologists will tell us that ritualizations in the animal world must, above all, be *unambiguous* as sets of signals, we suspect that in man the *overcoming of ambivalence* as well as of ambiguity is one of the prime functions of ritualization.

(both quotations from Erikson 1966:339)

These observations indicate the deep roots of ritual. It is fair to say that the more deeply embedded a behavioural pattern is, the more essential it must be regarded for the survival of the species, and the bottom line is always human beings as a biological species. So the persistence of ritual behaviour, even in today's secular states, speaks volumes for its importance.   Another important aspect is what may be called 'routinization'.   It is crucial that activities which are essential to the management of society and the cosmos (such as religious ritual, though it would apply to any social or technological procedure) should be done correctly, and the best way in which this can be achieved is by learning the procedure by rote, so that it comes 'automatically'.   Driving a car is a good example from everyday life.   And such established patterns are found in governmental procedure, law, and any number of human activities beyond the purely religious sphere.

10.5.3 Religious ritual presents models of human behaviour as well as its routinization.   The involvement of the gods as recipients of offerings validates the human procedure, symbolizes a number of levels of communal membership, loyalty, hierarchy and so on.   They also embody various human values, so that their worship reinforces these values.

I   Regular Cult

By this term I refer to ritual practices carried on routinely in temples and shrines, either on a daily or weekly basis.   Such practice was usually construed as the regular 'cult' of the gods, which would include such things as waking, washing, clothing, feeding and taking on journeys round the shrine.   It is striking that the dominant elements were material: the gods indwelt their images, so that the image *was* the god for purposes of cult; the images were fed real meat, cereals, and honoured with offerings of cloth and precious metals; the god 'came forth', that is his image was transported on journeys round the temple or even, during major festivals, further afield, to visit other gods in their homes.   It is as though a paradigm was being regularly reenacted, rather like children playing with dolls, who act out adult roles. Similarly elaborate rituals were also directed towards kings (cf. §10(1) below), and it is tempting to link the two, and see in ancestral kings the origins of at least some of the chief deities of the ancient Near East.   As will be clear from the quantities of meat used in large temples, the management of temple herds to supply the altars resulted in considerable economic growth, since food-production on behalf of the gods (most of which finally reached the tables of the community itself) increased with the growth in prestige of the god.

10(1) The Daily Cult of Amun in the Karnak Temple

This passage from the Berlin Papyrus gives an account of the ritual directed to the image of Amun in the Karnak temple each morning.   The image, naked (cf. §7(18) n. 1), was sealed with ropes and clay seals in its shrine-box, and at dawn, the duty-priest(s) for the day began as follows.   The text appears to be a list of the precise liturgical utterances to be spoken by the priest at each stage of the rite, and this obviously required to be known by heart for precise recitation.   This ritual behaviour was in all probability very close in form to the daily rituals surrounding the king, and was also typical of the kind of attention to detail and the reality of the world of make-believe in all ancient religions.

The striking thing about the official temple cults in Egypt was the ubiquity in the symbolism of both words and action of what may be regarded as the dominant myth of Egyptian religion, the conflict between Horus and Seth (on which see §§8(1-5)).

The beginning of the utterances of the sacred rites which are carried out for the house of Amun-Ra, King of the gods, in the course of every day by the major priest who is in his day's service.

I *The Utterance for striking the fire.* Words to be spoken:

> 'Welcome, welcome in peace, O Eye of Horus[1],
>> who art glorious, unharmed and youthful in peace!
> It shines forth like Ra upon the horizon.
> The power of Seth has hidden itself before the Eye of Horus,
>> who took it away and brought it back,
>> so that it is put in its place again for Horus.
> Triumphant is Horus because of his Eye.
>> The Eye of Horus drives away enemies for Amun-Ra,
>> Lord of the Thrones of the Two Lands, wherever they may be.

> An offering which the king[2] gives: I am pure.'

II *The Utterance for breaking the clay.* Words to be spoken:
> The clay is broken;
>> the cool waters are opened;
>>> the veins of Osiris are drawn.[3]

I have certainly not come to drive the god from his throne; I have come to put the god upon his throne. Thus thou abidest upon thy great throne, O Amun-Ra, Lord of the thrones of the Two Lands. I am one whom the gods inducted.

An offering which the king gives. I am pure.'

III *The Utterance for loosening the shrine.* Words to be spoken:

> 'The finger of Seth[4] is drawn out of the Eye of Horus,
>> so that it may become well.'

The leather covering on the back of the god is laid off.

> 'O Amun-Ra, Lord of the thrones of the Two Lands,
>> receive thou thy two feathers and thy White Crown as
>> the Eye of Horus,
> the right feather as a right Eye
> and the left as a left Eye.[5]
> Thou hast thy beauty, O Amun-Ra,
>> Lord of the thrones of the Two Lands:

naked, thou art covered;
  clothed, thou art further clothed.

Now I am verily a priest; it was the king who sent me to see the god.'

(*ANET* 325-6: P. Berlin 3055, adapted)

1   The Eye of Horus was a powerful symbol of divine and royal power. Horus' two eyes were respectively the sun (right eye) and the moon (left eye). This was the right eye, as the sequel indicates ('shines forth like Ra...'). Cf. §8(6) and nn. 3, 5.

2   The king was in theory the only priest. All other priests merely deputized. This rite was punctuated by affirmations of the acting priest's legitimacy as representative of the king.

3   Note how every possible symbolic association is wrung from the proceedings. Here the breaking of the seal was likened to the breaking of a dyke during irrigation of the fields, releasing life-giving water, identified with Osiris's blood and body fluids.

4   The bolt was identified as Seth's finger.

5   Note how the feathers of Amun's headdress (tall pinion feathers of the cosmic gander) were here identified with the eyes (cf. n. 1).

10(2) The Daily Cult of Anu and other Deities in the Uruk Temple

On temple names see §6(29). The present passage is part of a longer composition detailing offerings of the regular daily cult. Unfortunately (as also with §10(3)), such lists presuppose a whole network of symbolic relationships (hierarchies among the gods, particular significance of individual cultic elements, perhaps the mythical background of individual elements, etc.), without explanation. It thus remains exceedingly difficult to construct theologies of the cult (as can be more readily done with the Israelite evidence, for instance, though there too many questions remain unanswered). Cultic form is always far more conservative (and thus archaic in principle) than cultic meaning.

(Below are enumerated) the bulls and rams for the regular offerings (to be made) every day of the year to the deities Anu, Antu, Ishtar, Nana, and the other gods dwelling in the Resh Temple[1], the Irigal Temple[2], and the Esharra Temple[3], (which is) the topmost stage of the temple-tower of the god Anu. From the first day of the month Nisan through the thirtieth day of the month Adar, (they shall be offered) for the main meal of the morning.

For the main meal of the morning, throughout the year: seven first-class, fat, clean rams which have been fed barley for two years; one fat, milk-fed *kalū*-ram, of the regular offering — totalling eight rams in all. (Furthermore,) one large bull, one milk-fed bullock, and ten fat rams which, unlike the others, have not been fed barley. Grand total for the main meal of the morning throughout the year: eighteen rams, of which one is a milk-fed *kalū*-ram of the regular offering, one large bull, (and) one milk-fed bullock. While slaughtering the bull(s) and the ram(s), the slaughterer shall recite the... *Mār Šamaš* [4]

Similarly, while slaughtering the bull(s) and ram(s), the chief slaughterer shall speak (a prayer for?) life to the deities Anu, Antu, the Great Star, and the planet Venus; he shall recite it to no other god.

(*ANET* 344: Uruk ritual list, adapted)

1   *Bīt Reš*, 'Head Temple', name of a temple of Anu within the sacred precinct at Uruk (George 1993, §940).

2   É.IRI₁₂.GAL = É.ÈŠ.GAL, 'House, Big House', temple of Ishtar and Nana within the sacred precinct at Uruk (George 1993, §536 = 270).

3   É.ŠAR.A, 'House of the Universe', name of the ziggurat at Uruk (George 1993, §1036). Cf. §2(10) n. 1.

4   'Son of Shamash': the title of a liturgy addressed to Marduk. The divine name Marduk is probably very ancient (written AMAR.UDA.AK in Sumerian) and interpreted as '(calf or) son of the sun' (Abusch 1995).

This was the first of four meals offered to the gods during the day.

10(3) Sacrifices at Ugarit

The syntax of the ritual texts from Ugarit is uncertain (cf. introduction to §10(2)). A number of texts outline the calendar for various months. The role of the king was prominent. It appears at times that he was treated as one of the gods. The present text deals with the month of *riš yn* (September-October: §2(39)). Note the various substances offered besides meat.

In the month of [First-of-the-Wine, on the day of the new moon, a bunch of grapes] is to be cut [for El as communion-offering.] On the thir[teenth (day) the king is to wash himself thoroughly.] On the four[teenth the first of the tribute,] and two rams to [the Mistress of the Temples; two birds for the cultic [personnel]; and a ram (and) a ja[r to Ilsh; a ram to the gods.] [The king] shall sit, being purified, and [shall clap his hands and shall proclaim] the day. Subsequently he is to en[ter the temple]. A gift [, two ewes], and a [fe]ral pige[on] he shall of[fer to Anat], and an o[x and a ram to] El. And by the win[dow] he shall pour (a libation). A heifer to the two gods, Thu[kamun and Shanim]; to Reshef a ewe as a holocaust. And (as) communion sacrifices: two ewes to his god; an ox and a ram to the gods, a heifer to the gods; to Baal a ram; to Athirat [a ram; to Thuka]mun and [Shanim a ram;] to Anat a ram; to Reshef a ram; [to the pantheon of El and the assembly of Baal] a heifer; to Shalem [a heifer].

[And at midday in the retiring]-room of the god[s] (and) lords]: thirty [full chalices and] cups. And the gift that he is to take to the royal chapel: an offering of [myrrh-oil] (and one) of spiced oil, honey (as) a gift, [and feral pigeons in two baskets]. And into the hole, four[teen] pitchers of wine; a measure of flour on the ste[ps of] the altar; for the sanctuary of the goddess, two bir[ds]. [To Saphon, a ram]; to the Sacred Bride a ram and to [; to Yarih] a heifer; to Nikkal [a heifer; to the Mistress of the Temples two] birds; for the [cultic] personnel [a heifer]; to the go[ds] a ewe; Sha[psh a heifer; Resh]ef a holocaust and commun[ion sacrifice; ditto, two ewes.]

His [go]d a heifer; [the gods a heifer; El a e]we; Thukamun and Sha[nim a ewe; the goddess of] the temple two ewes, at [the spring a holocaust and communion sacrifice;] ditto a heifer; to B[aal of Saphon] a l[am]b; to Saphon a heifer; to [Baal] of U[ga]rit a ram; to the go[d] of the ancestor [to Athirat], and two [b]irds to ... [   ] times, both in [the sanct]uary of the Mistress of the [Great] Templ[es and on the al]tars.

On the fifth (day): (at) [the sanctuary of El, a shekel of sil]ver as *kubadu*-offering and a sacrifice; [   ] to Athirat; two birds [for the cultic personnel]. [Re]turn to the altar of Baal. A hei[fer to Baal]; a ewe to Saphon and a lamb [to Baal of Ugarit.] Twenty-two times [   ] a ram, a jar of oil, (and) a heifer. And [the king, being purified] shall respond with a litany. On the sixth (day) two [jars of oil] on top of it; a heifer. [The king, being purified] shall res[pond] (with a litany). On the se[ve]nth (day) as the sun declines the day is desacralized; at [s]un-s[e]t the king is desacralized. And on the day of the new moon, two rams to [Athtar]t...

(Wyatt 1998a, 348-55[1]: KTU 1.41)

1   See full commentary and bibliography *ad loc*. See also del Olmo Lete 1999; Pardee 2000; id. 2001.

10(4) Cult in Jerusalem

The idea that ritual deals specifically with the past comes out particularly clearly in the detailed instructions of *Leviticus*. This book was probably written about the fifth or fourth century BCE, and reflects the usage of the second temple (post-exilic or Persian period) in early Judaism. But it is presented as a narrative from the primordial time of the 'wilderness wandering', actually a metaphor for exile rather than a pre- or proto-historical memory. Moses was presented as the archetypal great king and lawgiver (see §7(23)), and the rules Yahweh revealed to him remain the paradigm for the Jewish ritual. The Tabernacle and the Tent of Meeting allude to ancient views (found all over the ancient Near East) that the gods originally dwelt in tents (§§6(15-25)). Thus these words come down from the primordial occasion, *ab illo tempore*. Antiquity, real or imagined, always confers authority on a tradition.

When any person among you makes an offering to Yahweh of an animal from the herd or flock, let him bring his offering forward. If his offering is a holocaust from the herd, he is to bring a blemish-free male to the door of the Tent of Meeting. Let him bring it as (something) acceptable before Yahweh[1]. Let him place his hand on the victim's head, and it shall be accepted as atonement for him[2]. Then he shall slaughter the animal before Yahweh, and the sons of Aaron, the priests, will offer the blood. And they will pour the blood over the altar, which is at the door of the Tent of Meeting, (and) around it. Then he will skin the victim and will cut it into pieces. Then the sons of Aaron (the priest[3]) will place a fire on the altar and arrange wood on the fire. Then the sons of Aaron, the priests, are to place the pieces, the head and the fat on the wood, which is on the fire on the altar. Then he[4] shall wash the entrails and the legs in water, and the priest shall burn[5] it all on the altar. This is a holocaust of which the savour will appease Yahweh[6]...

(*Leviticus* 1:3-9)

1 The expression 'before Yahweh' (Hebrew *lipnê yhwh* = 'in the face of ') would have originally meant in the presence of the god's cult-statue. But the technical formula outlasted the use of images in Israel. See §6(11) n. 4.

2 Sin must be atoned for at all stages. Creatureliness is sinful in contrast with the purity of the deity. Cf. Otto 1950.

3 The expressions 'the sons of Aaron, the priests', and here, 'the priest' in the singular, betray the history of the text. It is possible that an original instruction alluding to the priest has been incorporated in the larger work which sees Aaron as the eponymous priest, brother of Moses.

4 'He': the lay worshipper, or the singular priest above (n. 3)?

5 Literally 'make it go up in smoke'.

6 Technical term, meaning that the sacrifice is accepted by the deity. Cf. *Genesis* 8:21, *Atrahasis* iii v 34-5 (§4(5)) and *Gilgamesh* xi 160-2 (§4(6)).

II Festival Cult

Early organization of increasingly complex societies, with sedentarization and the gradual rise of urbanism requiring increasingly complex forms of social organization and management, meant that people needed to know how time was to be structured with reference to the flow of the seasons, which determined planting and harvests, and the management of livestock. In addition, the phases of sun and moon, the appearance of important stars (e.g. Sirius in Egypt), and such irregular but repeated events as eclipses, required ritual treatment, to ward off dangers, or to assist the divine power in the fulfilment of his or her tasks.

10(5) Elements of the *Akitu* Festival

An ancient festival, attested from the earliest times in many centres, and evolving considerably over time, focusing on the Sacred Marriage and later on the New Year. The final version lasted for the first eleven days days of Nisan, the first month of the year. It was named after the '*Akitu*-House', a construction set up outside the city, to which the devotees would proceed by boats on the canals. The king was a central figure in the rites, as can be seen from this excerpt dating from the Seleucid era.

On the second day of the month Nisan, two hours of the night remaining, the *urigallu*-priest shall rise and wash with river water. He shall enter into the presence of the god Bel... He shall recite the following prayer... On the third day of the month Nisan at... o'clock, the *urigallu*-priest shall rise and wash... He shall speak the following prayer...

When it is three hours after sunrise, he shall call a metalworker and give him precious stones and gold from the treasury of the god Marduk to make two images for the ceremonies of the sixth day... The two images which the artisans are to make shall be seven finger-widths high... One image shall hold in its left hand a snake made of cedar, raising its right hand to the god Nabu. The second shall hold in its left hand a scorpion, raising its right hand to the god Nabu. They shall be clothed in red garments... until the sixth day of the month Nisan they shall be placed in the house of the god Madan. Food from the tray of the god Madan shall be presented to them. On the sixth day... the slaughterer shall strike off their heads. Then a fire having been started in the presence of Nabu, they shall be thrown into it...

On the fifth day... a *mašmašu*-priest... shall call a slaughterer to decapitate a ram, the body of which the *mašmašu*-priest shall use in performing the *kuppuru*-ritual for the temple. He shall recite the incantations for exorcizing the temple... He... shall lift the body of the ram and proceed to the river. Facing west, he shall throw the body of the ram into the river... The slaughterer will do the same thing with the ram's head. They shall go out into the open country...[1]

They shall bring water for washing the king's hands and then shall accompany him to the temple Esagila... When the king reaches the presence of the god Bel, the *urigallu*-priest shall leave the sanctuary and take away the sceptre, the circle and the sword of the king... He shall... strike the king's cheek... He shall drag him by the ears and make him bow to the ground...

(The king utters disclaimers of all sins of mismanagement and oppression...)

The scepter, circle and sword shall be restored to the king.

He (the priest) shall strike the king's cheek. If... the tears flow, the god Bel is friendly; if no tears appear, the god Bel is angry: the enemy will rise up and bring about his downfall...

(*ANET* 331-5: *Akitu* Ritual Programme, selections, adapted)

Bel ('Lord') was a title of Marduk.

Madan (*Madānu*) was the divine judge, sometimes identified with Marduk or Enlil.

Nabu was the god of scribes and wisdom.

1   Cf. the rituals of *Yom-Kippur* (*Leviticus* 16) in Israel, §10(11).

III   Guilt, Sacrifice and Atonement

In Israel, the experience of deportation, reevaluation of tradition and cult (known as 'the exile') seems to have transformed sacrificial theory into an obsession with atonement for sin. (See Davies 1977.) It comes as something of a surprise, therefore, to discover antecedents to the Israelite scapegoat rites of the Day of Atonement from Ebla (Tell Mardikh), dating to the late third millennium. The Ugaritic text (KTU 1.12) from the thirteenth century seems to be linked to the same tradition. In the form of a myth (with ritual application at the end) it deals with Baal encountering two 'Devourers' in the desert. These seem to be caprid in form. Here there is a twist: it is evidently Baal who, hunting them (?), is killed, and his death is seen as atoning. (On this text see Wyatt 1998a, 162-8.) Another Ugaritic text, KTU 1.127 (§10(9)) below) has an obscure allusion to a goat. In biblical tradition, compare the fates of Ishmael and Isaac in myth: Isaac is taken to the altar for sacrifice (*Genesis* 22, Mount Moriah = 'proto-Jerusalem', §5(14): cf. *2 Chronicles* 3:1 and §§5(13, 15)) while Ishmael is cast out into the desert (*Genesis* 16, 21). This mythic tradition is echoed in the ritual tradition of *Leviticus* 16, §10(11).

10(6) The Experience of Guilt in Mesopotamia i)

A Babylonian prayer to Marduk confessing universal human sinfulness and a life-long frailty on behalf of the worshipper.

1   Who has not erred, who has not offended?
     The way of God — who knows it?
  Against thee have I, thy servant, committed sins,
     God's limits have I transgressed.
5 What I have done since my childhood, witting or unwitting,
     Forget it!
  Let not your heart be troubled!
     Forgive my sin!
     Pardon my misdeed!

(Ringgren 1973, 116-7)

10(7) The Experience of Guilt in Mesopotamia ii)

A prayer to Ishtar confessing sin and lamenting the goddess' alienation. Note the emphasis on the averted face (cf. §6(11) n. 4): no comforting eye contact possible!

1   To thee, O Goddess, I give heed,
      to thee is my mind directed,
   Thee, yea, thee, I call upon:
      Loose my curse!
5   Loose my guilt, my offence,
      My wrong-doing and my sin;
   Pardon my evil deed,
      Receive my invocation!...
   Let my genuflection be pleasing to you,
10   Hear my prayer;
   Look faithfully upon me;
      receive my invocation!
   How long, mistress, will you be wroth with averted face?
      Turn your head, which you averted!
15   Direct your mind to friendly speech!

(Ringgren 1973, 117)

10(8) Two Texts from Ebla

Texts dating between 2400 and 2300 BCE. Ebla was Tell Mardikh, south of Aleppo in Syria. I include these texts here in view of their similarity to §10(9, 11) in the ritual use of goats. Pardee 2000a, 78, refers to a forthcoming study (2000b) in which he treats the texts as ominological.

i *ARET* XI 1 I 19—II 7	ii *ARET* XI 2 i 7-21
And we purge the mausoleum. Before the entry of Kura and Barama	And we purge the mausoleum.
a goat, a silver bracelet (hanging from) the goat's neck,	A goat, a silver bracelet (hanging from) the goat's neck, before the entry of Kura and Barama
towards the steppe of Alini we let her go.	towards the steppe of Alini we *enclose* (*her*)[1].

(Zatelli 1998, 255)

1   'We *enclose* (*her*)' (second text, last line): according to Zatelli this is an error for
      'let her go' (first text) (mistaking *nuwaššar-ši*, 'we let her go' for **nu'assar-ši* 'we
      enclose her'). These were phonetically very similar, and scribal errors are

frequent in cuneiform. Comparison with the biblical text below (§§10(11)) allows us to wonder whether the second text does not, in contrast to the first, refer to a goat sacrificed (at an altar). On this understanding, there is not one victim (thus Zatelli), but two as *Leviticus* 16 (§10(11)). On the other hand, the *penultimate* line being identical in both texts, perhaps Zatelli is after all to be followed.

10(9) An Inscription on a Model Lung from Ugarit

A lung-inscription from *ca* 1300 BCE. The model is covered in short texts relating to different features on the surface. These are the last three, which appear to be connected.

> [   ] a woman, they shall take a goat [   ].

> If the city is captured, then death (*mt*[1]) will attack the population.

> (In) the temple, a citizen shall take a goat, and (the future) will be seen from afar.

(KTU 1.127.26-31)

1   'Death will attack…': or 'Mot (god of death) will attack…'; or 'the man', sc. the enemy king, 'will attack'. All are possible. It is entirely unclear what is done with the goat. Most scholars link it with the above texts and with *Leviticus* 16 below (§10(11)). Note the apparent oracular element at the end.

10(10) A Liturgy for a Rite of Atonement for the People of Ugarit

An atonement liturgy (KTU 1.40) from *ca* 1300 BCE, originally of five or more probably six similar sections, of which five survive, the first two being in extremely fragmentary condition. The highly repetitive and formulaic nature of the text allows a considerable degree of restoration. The sections are addressed to men and women respectively, in order, perhaps offering three kinds of victim (I-II ox [?], III-IV sheep, V-VI donkey). This great 'Day of Atonement' liturgy seems to be an analogue of the rite of *Leviticus* 16 (§10(11)). Note that goats do not feature as victims, as they do on the liver inscription, and that all of the victims are apparently sacrificed at the altar. Only the fifth and sixth sections are given here. They are *verbatim* apart from appropriate changes of gender.

SECTION V (MEN)	SECTION VI (WOMEN)
1 Now we present a donkey for purification,	
	Now repeat the liturgy for puri[fication],
for purification of the men of Ugarit,	for purification of the wo<me>n of Ugarit,

and [atonement for <the
foreigner within the walls
of>] Ugari<t>,

and atonement for Yaman,
5 and atonement for ʿrmt,
and atonement for [Ugarit],
and atonement for Niqmad.
Whenever your state of grace
be changed,
whether by the accusation of
the Qa[tians],
10 [or by the accusation of
the Dadm]ians,
or by the accusation of
the Hurrians,
or by the accusation of
the Hittites,
or by the accusation of
the Cypriots,
or by the [accusation of
the ġbr,
15 or by the accusation of]
your oppressed ones,
or by the accusation of
your p[oo]r,
or by the accusation of qrzbl;
whenever your state of grace be
changed,
either through your anger,
20   or through your impatience,
or through some evil
you have done;
whenever your state of grace
be changed
concerning the sacrifices
and the offering,
our sacrifice we offer:
25 this is the offering we make,
this is the victim
we immolate.
May it be borne aloft

and atonement for the
foreigner within the walls
of Ugarit,
35 and [atone]ment for his wife.

Whenever your state of grace be
changed,
whether by the accusation of
the Qa[tians,]
[or by the accusation of
the Dadm]ians,
or by the [accusation of
the Hu]rrians,
40 or by the accusation of
the Hittites,
or by the accusation of
the Cypriots,
or by the [accusation of
the ġbr,
or by the accusation of]
your op[pressed] ones,
or by the accusation of
your p[oo]r,
45 or by the accusation of qrzbl;
whenever your state of grace be
changed,
either through [your] anger,
[or through your impat]ience,
or through some evil
you have done;
50 whenever [your state] of grace
be changed
[concerning the sacrifices]
and the offering,
our sacrifice we offer:
this is the offering we [make],
[this is the victim
we] immolate.
55 May it be borne aloft

to the father of the gods,	to the father of the gods,
may it be borne aloft	may it be borne aloft
to the pantheon of the gods,	to the pan[theon of the gods],
<to the assembly of	[to] the assembly of
the gods,>	the gods,
30 to Thukamun and Shanim:	to Thukamun [and Shanim]:
here is the donkey.	here is the donkey.

(Wyatt 1998a, 342-7: KTU 1.40.26-43)

Thukamun and Shanim were the attendants of the high god El ('the father of the gods'), and acted as intermediaries between the worshippers and him. Cf. §8(9). (They appear as Kassite deities in Babylon, probably of Indo-European origin.)

10(11) The Day of Atonement in Israel

See introduction to the Passover rites (§8(8)) for its relationship with the present ritual performed in relation to the autumn equinox. The text probably dates from *ca* 400 BCE, but the tradition is much older. Cf. discussion at §8(10).

Now from the assembly of the Israelites he[1] shall take two goats for a sin offering, and a ram for a holocaust. After this he will present the bull (mentioned in v. 3) as a sacrifice for his own sin and shall offer it as an atonement, on his own behalf and that of his family.

Then he will take the two goats and shall set them in Yahweh's presence[2] at the door of the Tent of Meeting. Then Aaron shall draw lots over the two goats, one lot for Yahweh and one for Azazel[3]. Then Aaron shall present the goat on which the lot for Yahweh has fallen, and offer it as a sin-offering.

But the goat on which the lot for Azazel has fallen will be set, still alive, in Yahweh's presence for atonement to be performed on it, by sending it to Azazel, out into the desert...

(*Leviticus* 16, excerpts)

1   'He' = Aaron, who represents all priests subsequently performing this rite.

2   'In Yahweh's presence': lit. 'before Yahweh's face' (*lipnê yhwh*). This may originally have meant in the presence of an image. See §§6(11) n. 4, 8(9) n. 1.

3   'Azazel' (*ʿazāzēl*) was apparently some desert demon to be propitiated, but may originally have been *ʿazāz ʾēl* (two words): 'the goat/powerful one of El', a hypostasis of the deity.

An important discussion of this text is Davies 1977. He discussed the spatial symbolism at work here, and the principles he enunciated may be usefully applied to other scapegoat rites. The world may be divided into three zones on the horizontal plane, going from the centre (symbolized by the sanctuary) through a middle realm (where ordinary people live), and on to the desert (the end of the world, haunt of monsters). There are relative degrees of sanctity. The first goat, in going to the centre, was sacrificed (destroyed by the greater purity of the centre), while the other was thrown out into the desert (representing its destruction: in the *Mishnah* it was thrown over a cliff). The middle was thus freed of the accumulated guilt, which was carried off in two directions. On the spatial symbolism in operation here see also the observations of Erikson 1966, cited at *10.5.2 (p. 257), and Wyatt 1987a.

Chapter 11

RITUAL AND THE FUTURE

While ancient religions turned to the past to construct paradigms for the present, they also had a concern for the future. A number of techniques were in use in the ancient world to anticipate and warn of future events. These may be conveniently divided into a number of categories, which though very different in appearance, had common goals. The use of oracles turns out to have been quite ubiquitous in court and military circles, where no decisions were made until the right sign was received and the right word uttered. Other mechanical techniques were used: the observation of various ritual procedures, outlined below, and the examination of 'natural signs'. The observation of various natural events developed into a complex art of recognizing cause and effect. We may compare these techniques with today's meteorological, economic and strategic forecasts, which are probably no more accurate than ancient systems. The point was probably not so much the accurate forecast as the predisposition of the expectant mind (of king or general) to act decisively.

The common feature of all that follows is that it is based on past experience. In this respect it is no different from myth, in that it is accumulated wisdom and information of the past that leads the mind to expect certain consequences in the future. Strange though some of the evidence sounds today, it is essentially a process of trial and error, even if shot through with what appear on the surface to be elements of irrationality. Not a lot has changed.

Sections §§I-III below all deal with the capacity of the human voice, and by extension, the divine voice, to influence the future. Once a word, human or divine, has been uttered, it has a life of its own, and cannot be unsaid. This is why divine promises and threats were believed to continue to be relevant long after the original occasion was past (see §11(11)). A rash human utterance might lead the speaker to regret having spoken (see §11(20)).

Section §IV deals with mechanical means of construing the future, by reading the 'signs' written obscurely by the gods, but discernible to the trained cultic expert.

Section §V deals with eschatological matters: the ritual provision for the dead. In a sense it is the consciousness of death which underlines all the previous sections, because it is the ruffian on the stairs who shadows every human action and anxiety.

Suggested Reading:

Blythin 1970; Lindblom 1962; Loewe and Blacker 1981; Malamat 1989; Nissinen 2000; Parpola 1997; Starr 1990; Swerdlow 1999.

11.1 Introduction

11.1.1 We have seen that ritual builds on paradigms rooted in the past. It appears to be concerned with the reinstitution of the past, a past unsullied by time, uncorrupted by sin. This comes out particularly clearly in *10.4.7 (see also §10(11)), with the Israelite atonement rite. Such concerns with past sin and its resolution obviously have a futuristic reference, in cleansing the past so that the future is free of it.

11.1.2 But it can also be directed towards the future in a different sense. What emerges is that the past (or past experience) is still used as the model for future possibilities. After all, if something has already happened (say an owl perching on a cottage roof, and somebody dying in the house that night, or the river bursting its banks), there is a chance that the same thing will happen again, so that a perching owl is taken as a warning. What we see here is a very sophisticated science of prognosis, of prediction (and this is where language plays a crucial role: *11.1.3), using evidence from the past and its correlatives as a guide to future contingencies. We have exactly the same principle in operation today in economic, demographic or meteorological forecasting. And still considerable degrees of error, perhaps!

11.1.3 The common feature of the first three categories below is their dependence on language. Even today language has an enormous power. Evidence in court is given on oath, as is the inauguration of a president, or a holder of high office (the oath itself is obviously of religious origin). 'A gentleman's word is his bond' (or was!). Language functions here in two important ways: in generating in the first instance the awareness of time, and especially the future, since giving an account of an inchoate idea is often the way to give it substance; and also in giving authority to the idea uttered. *Quod scripsi scripsi*, said Pilate.

11.2 Prophecy

11.2.1 It may seem odd to place prophecy in a ritual context. However, it seems clear that its origins lie in ritual practice, such as taking narcotics, enduring sensory deprivation, having visions (all the paraphernalia of the heavenly journey, above, chapter 7). Prophets were essentially ritual specialists of a particular psychological type, prone to the necessary experiences, such as the hearing of voices construed as the words of gods. See Jaynes 1976 for a detailed analysis of this as a form of early religiosity and consciousness.

11.2.2 The earliest attested forms, from the 18th century BCE, come from Mari, a city on the Euphrates, just north of the present Iraqi frontier (§§11(1-4)). We are in no case given the circumstances of the oracle. Were drugs taken? Did the prophet hallucinate spontaneously? Whatever the cause, the ensuing oracle was taken with the utmost seriousness. What is perhaps significant is that each was a response to political unrest, with threats of rebellion or invasion, and was addressed to the king. Because of the authority credited to prophets, it was crucial to be able to verify the message. The 'hair and fringe' ritual was a guarantee of the prophet's integrity. As extensions of his or her person, they could be destroyed, with a consequent magical destruction of the prophet.

11.2.3 Prophecy was also found in Assyria and Babylonia. Again it was related to royal functions, as it were the divine management of kingship. The king, who was a child of the gods, and had in early times been explicitly divine, as he remained in Egypt and Syria, required assurance from his protecting deities as a means of dealing with difficult political contingencies. Thus the context of §11(5), now preserved in a longer theological text, was promises of divine oversight to a newly enthroned king. Note how the king's might was taken as a token of his righteousness. §11(6) apparently involved the use of some mechanical oracular technique, as we shall see below. Notice the way the question was asked. It admitted of a 'yes' or 'no' answer. §11(7) has some interesting theological implications about the conception of deity in Assyria (see n. *ad loc.* and Parpola's discussion). Note the fluid identity of the god, and his (and her) parental care for the king. Still wholly political in force, §11(8) promised divine help in victory.

11.2.4 Egyptian examples followed much the same pattern. Here the fiction of the king's own divinity was consistently maintained, so that the deity in question, in §§11(9, 10) Amun-Ra, was father of the monarch ('fashioner of his or her beauty'). But mechanical means were probably still employed, as suggested by the circumlocutions, and the evident ritual context (oblations in §11(10)).

11.2.5 Prophecy in Israel was in the same tradition as the forms already noted. It probably occurred even more widely than is apparent, because of the paucity of the record. The Israelite evidence is voluminous, however, and still attests the political context. Here too oracles were addressed primarily to the king. The main literary difference was that collections of oracles were reedited over centuries, ending up as quite different forms. A distinctive feature (so far as we know) of Israelite prophecy was the experience of the heavenly journey seen in §11(11) (cf. §§7(12-25)). In §§11(13, 14) we see examples of autosuggestion: an everyday occurrence triggers off an association of ideas, and communicates a distinctive message.

11.2.6 §11(15) illustrates an example of a mechanical means of obtaining divine guidance, analogous to the prophetic word. This was the technique using objects called *Urim* and *Tummim* , in which a questioning admitting only a 'yes' or 'no' answer allowed the use of stones or other implements, used in pairs, to communicate the message. It was believed that the deity spoke through the *Urim* and *Tummim*. This verges on other mechanical forms noted below.

11.2.7 Necromancy, the invocation of the dead, is very widely attested, and still used in oracles invoking ancestors in Asia and Africa today. The story at §11(16) shows it in use in Israel, though the narrator is at pains to show the unacceptability of such a practice. For all his efforts, Saul received a very dusty answer.

11.3   Vows

These belong to a very archaic form of religiosity, in which the subject bargains with a spirit to provide some, often material, necessity, e.g. a wife (§11(17)), good fortune (§11(19)), a cure (§11(20, 21)), a child (§11(22)), victory (§11(23)), a safe return (§11(24)), etc. In some cases the content of the vow is not stated (§11(18)). Basically a bargain was struck with a deity on a *quid pro quo* basis: 'if you give me this, I shall do that'. Thousands of votive gifts have been found in ancient Near Eastern sites, often mute testimonies to the ubiquity of this religious expression.

11.4   Curses

The conception of blessing, in which the words spoken by the deity (often put into its mouth by the subject) gave rise to a practical and often material effect, such as health, wealth and progeny (strongly featuring under the category of vows (*11.3)), was widespread. The counter to this (i.e. 'blessing reversed') was equally widespread, and resolved a number of problematic situations. We all find ourselves in circumstances where we are unable to change things. We are the victims of injustice, and no legal sanctions can work, because the deed was done secretly (§11(30)). Or we are just so anguished that we cry out in anger against whoever may have done this or that. The very ground may be guilty, if our child or friend died on it (§§11(28, 29))! Or more mundanely, we just want peace in the tomb, and curse anyone who disturbs our sleep (§11(25)). This not just an expression of selfishness: rather is it an appeal to natural justice. When we are frustrated at every turn, the spirits will intervene. They will even destroy distant enemies, if we cooperate in writing names and destroying them (§11(26)). §11(27) is designed to ensure a legitimate succession to the throne. Treaties between nations generally had sanctions against unilateral breaches of the treaty in the form of curses (§§11(31-3)).

11.5 Omens and other Signs from Nature

11.5.1 A serious science of observation of ritual or natural occurrences and their consequences developed over millennia in the ancient Near East. It was the sheer scale of the evidence which seemed so overwhelming. A basic principle was *post hoc, ergo propter hoc*: this happened after that; therefore it happened *because of* that. We still think instinctively this way today. A number of different techniques were used.

11.5.2 Omens (§11(34)): a by-product of sacrifice was the 'reading' of the victims' internal organs.

11.5.3 Other techniques (§§11(35-7)): these allowed a natural process controlled by the priest to be 'read' as providing answers to implicit or explicit questions.

11.5.4 Observations of natural occurrences: where there was no human input. §§11(38-40) concern meteorological or astronomical occurrences. Eclipses (§11(40)) were considered especially significant. Note the combination of eclipse and liver-inspection, designed to refine the interpretation of the eclipse.

11.5.5 Black cats crossing your path are still taken as ominous by modern people. In §11(41) we see a number of examples of animal movements and typical interpretations.

11.5.6 This may all seem very strange to the modern mind. Thanks to the influence of science on our thinking, we often think counter-intuitively. The ancients tended not to, thus seeing all kinds of obvious associations which no longer command our attention. But the techniques described in this chapter illustrate the determination of people to control their own destiny (even if they expressed it by thinking of the gods controlling their destinies), to be able to proceed proactively, not just reacting, like a modern government, rather ineffectually to each successive crisis. This was a savage, unforgiving world. Simply as strategies for survival, maximizing opportunities and adapting to changing circumstances, rituals directed to the future were of fundamental significance in the advance of culture.

11.6 Mortuary Rites

Four examples of Egyptian 'virtual rituals' are given (§§11(42-5)), to illustrate the power of the *Coffin Texts* and *Book of the Dead*, through word and icon, to effect even the *post-mortem* condition of the subject.

I   Prophecy

'Prophecy' is often regarded as peculiar to Israelite religion, but in recent years a number of interesting texts have been discovered at Ebla (Tell Mardikh) in central Syria, dating to the late third millennium BCE, at Mari (Tell Hariri) in south east Syria (*ca* 1760 BCE), and in a number of Assyrian libraries. Scholars have recognized them as antecedents of the Israelite phenomenon.

11(1)   Prophecies from Mari i): Oracle to Zimri-Lim of Mari

The following accounts of oracles come from the archives of Mari, from the reign of its last king, Zimri-Lim (cf. §3(3)), who was conquered by Hammurabi of Babylon *ca* 1760 BCE. It is interesting that the bureaucracy took care to give a precise record of what occurred in each case, identifying each person involved (this one through a trance of Shelebum). The hair and garment–fringe of the 'prophet' (it seems that various temple-personnel were susceptible of prophetic hallucinations, just as in Israel) were extensions of the prophet him- or herself, and because any harm done to them would be extended to their owner, were guarantees of veracity, if not accuracy. An important, if theoretical, account of the psychology of the prophet, who heard voices and attributed them to gods and their images, will be found in Jaynes 1976. The prophetic experience appears to have been entirely spontaneous, since the subject went into a trance here and in §11(2). In §11(3) it was a dream which occasioned it. But a particular psychological type is implied, and it is possible that mechanical aids, or at least spiritual disciplines were used to enhance the subject's potential for receptivity.

Speak to my lord: 'Thus Shibtu your maidservant. The palace is safe and sound. In the temple of Annunitum[1], on the third day of the month, Shelebum went into a trance. Thus spoke Annunitum: "O Zimri-Lim, with a revolt they would put you to the test. Guard yourself. At your side put servants, your controllers whom you love. Station them so that they can guard you. Do not go about by yourself. And as for the men who would put you to the test, I shall deliver these men into your hand." Now I have hereby dispatched to my lord the hair and the fringe of the cult-player.'

(*ANET* 630: *ARMT* x 6, adapted)

1   An epithet of Ishtar.

11(2)   Prophecies from Mari ii): Oracle to Zimri-Lim

Oracle delivered through a trance of Akhatum.

Speak to my lord: 'Thus Shibtu your maidservant. In the temple of Annunitum in the city, Akhatum, the servant of Dagan-malik, went into a trance and spoke as follows, saying: "O Zimri-Lim, even though you for your part have spurned me[1], I for my part shall embrace you. I shall deliver your enemies into your hand, and the men of Sharrakiya I shall seize and gather them to the destruction of Belet-Ekallim[2]." On the following day Akhum the priest brought me this report together with the hair and the fringe, and sent them to my lord.'

(*ANET* 630: *ARMT* x 8)

1   Presumably it is Annunitum who speaks, perhaps expressing displeasure at the king's cavalier reception of previous oracles.

2   'The Mistress of the House', the divine patroness of the Marian dynasty, according to Moran (*ANET* 630 n. 82). The 'house' is presumably the royal palace. A 'Mistress of the (great) Temples' appears in KTU 1.41 at Ugarit (§10(3)).

11(3) Prophecies from Mari iii): Oracle to Zimri-Lim

Oracle delivered through a dream of Addaduri.

Speak to my lord: 'Thus Adduduri your maidservant. Since the peace of your father's house I have never had this dream... In my dream I entered the temple of Belet-Ekallim and Belet-Ekallim was not in residence nor were the statues before her present. And I saw this and wept[1]... Again I dreamt[2], and Dada, the priest of Ishtar-pishra, was on duty in the gate of Belet-Ekallim, and an eerie voice was crying this over and over, saying: "Come back, O Dagan! Come back, O Dagan!" This it was crying over and over. Moreover the ecstatic rose in the temple of Annunitum and spoke thus, saying: "O Zimri-Lim, do not go on an expedition. Stay in Mari, and then I alone will take responsibility." My lord must not be negligent in guarding himself. I myself hereby seal my hair and my fringe and send them to my lord.'

(*ANET* 631: ARMT x 50)

1   Even for the statue to be absent (indicating that the goddess was 'not in residence'), would be taken as a dreadful portent. The presence of the statue in the shrine was *prima facie* evidence of the deity's benevolent oversight of the city. Thus the first thing conquering kings frequently did was to remove cult statues. It had a deleterious effect on morale, thus making the conquest easier.

2   A second dream, but the two appear to deal with the same crisis, as intuited by the prophet. In the second dream, Dagan's implicit absence echoes that of the goddess in the first dream. Thus Mari was abandoned by its gods, perhaps as Hammurabi's army approached the walls.

11(4) Prophecies from Mari iv): Oracle to Zimri-Lim

This oracle, delivered through a trance of Nur-Sin, is the sequel to the restoration of Zimri-Lim to the throne which was the occasion of §3(3) above, which is also oracular in form, declaring the words of the god.

'Listen to this single word of mine: "When anyone who has a lawsuit appeals to you concerning it, saying, 'I have been wronged!' stand up and give him justice. Respond to him with equity. This is what I want of you: when you set out on campaign, do not depart without having consulted oracles. When I have been favourable in an oracle, then you may set out on your campaign. If this has not happened, do not go out of the gate!" Thus spoke the respondent. Now I have brought the respondent's hair and the fringe of his garment to my lord.'

(after Durand 1993: *ARMT* A 1968)

There is a pathos to these passages, for Hammurabi of Babylon conquered Mari and destroyed it. Zimri-Lim was the last king.

11(5) Prophecy from Babylon: Royal Oracle of Marduk

This text comes from the library of the Assyrian king Ashurbanipal (668-631/27 BCE) at Ashur, but probably dates from the time of Nebuchadrezzar I of Babylon (1126-1105 BCE). It is composed in the form of a divine autobiography, in which Marduk tells of his future blessings on the city of Isin (Beyerlin 1988, 121 n. i). The *Sitz im Leben* of the present passage is however the enthronement of a king, at which Marduk's own spontaneous oracle would be recited. It is interesting to see that the Assyrians valued sacred materials from the rival kingdom to the south.

1   This ruler will be powerful and will have no rivals.
       He will take care of the city,
          he will gather together those who are scattered.
   At the same time he will make the temple of Egalmach[1]
5   and the other sanctuaries splendid with precious stones...
   The door of heaven will constantly be open...[2]

(Beyerlin 1978, 121: fragment from Ashur, Ashurbanipal's Library)

1   É.GAL.MAH, 'Exalted Palace', was the name of a number of Mesopotamian temples (George 1993, §§318-23). This one (§318) was the temple of Gula, in the form of Ninisinna, at Isin. A temple of the same name (§319) was located in Babylon. This is conceivably a case of a usurped oracle. At any rate its validity would be recognized wherever it could be applied.

2   The name of the city of Babylon was *Bāb-ili*, probably of unknown etymology, but construed in Akkadian as 'the Gate of the God (sc. Marduk)'. Cf. §6(29). Temples were generally regarded as points of access to heaven (§§2(10) n. 1, 6(27) n. 1, 6(29) and 11(5) n. 1; see also §7(7)). Cf. too Jacob's words in *Genesis* 28:17 (§7(22)). Here its symbolism has been borrowed with reference to the Egalmach temple at Isin.

11(6) Prophecies from Assyria i):
Esarhaddon's Request for an Oracle

The Scythians were seeking a diplomatic marriage. Esarhaddon of Assyria (who ruled 680-669 BCE) was wary of their motives. The way to discover these was to consult Shamash (that is, to pose leading questions to his image). These may have been framed in such a way as to require a 'yes or no' answer, thus giving the enquirer the initiative in framing the questions to suit the occasion. Such a procedure was followed in the Israelite '*Urim* and *Tummim*' technique (see §11(15)).

Bartatua, king of the Scythians, who has now sent his message to Esarhaddon, king of Assyria, concerning a royal daughter in marriage — if Esarhaddon, king of [Assyria], gives him a royal daughter in marriage, will Bartatua, king of the Scythians, speak with [Esarhaddon, king of Assyria], in good faith, true and honest words of peace? Will he keep the treaty of [Esarhaddon, king of Assyria]? Will he do [whatever i]s pleasing to Esarhaddon, king of Assyria?

(Starr 1990 §20: also given in Kuhrt 1995 ii 529)

11(7) Prophecies from Assyria ii):
Oracle of the Gods to Esarhaddon

The king was chosen and protected by the gods. Here the pantheon of Ashur speaks with one voice in endorsing the rule of Esarhaddon.

'Fear not, Esarhaddon. I am Bel. (Even as) I speak to you, I watch over the beams of your heart. When your mother gave birth to you, sixty great gods stood with me and protected you[1]. Sin was at your right hand, Shamash at your left, sixty great gods were standing around you and girded your loins. Do not trust in man. Lift up your eyes, look to me! I am Ishtar of Arbela; I reconciled Ashur with you. When you were small, I took you to me. Do not fear; praise me! What enemy has attacked you while I remained silent? The future shall be like the past. I am Nabu, lord of the stylus. Praise me!'

(Parpola 1997, 6)

1   There is no question of divine conception and birth here, as so graphically represented in Egyptian and some Israelite evidence. But the king's birth was evidently attended by all the powers in heaven, who protected his person, and endowed him with their various qualities.

This passage graphically illustrates Parpola's view that the Assyrian cult of Ashur was to all intents monotheistic (though some scholars voice reservations). Even Marduk's title 'Bel' is appropriated. The other deities are agents of Ashur, rather like Yahweh's angels. More particularly, Parpola argued that Ishtar was to Ashur ('Aššur revealed in his mother aspect', p. xxvi) as the Holy Spirit is to the Christian god.

11(8) Prophecies from Assyria iii):
Esarhaddon's Victory granted by Ashur

The word of Ashur comes to Esarhaddon, in the form of an address to his people endorsing his policies.

[List]en, O Assyrians! [The king] has vanquished his enemy. [You]r [king] has put his enemy [under] his foot, [from] sun[se]t [to] sun[ris]e, [from] sun[ris]e [to] sun[se]t! I will destroy [Meli]d, I will destroy [   ], I will

[   ], I will deliver the Cimmerians into his hands and set the land of Ellipi on fire. Ashur has given the totality of the four regions[1] to him. From sunrise to sunset there is no king equal to him; he shines as brilliantly as the sun. This is the (oracle of) well-being placed before Bel-Tarbaṣi and the gods.

(Parpola 1997, 23)

1   On the notion of total cosmic rule cf. §3(22) n. 1. This is a classic statement of the king's role as cosmocrator ('world-ruler'). But he was merely the agent of the gods, putting their plans into execution. This is a classic account of how political ambition was given a theological gloss (the 'God on our side' principle, which has been a powerful force in world military history).

11(9) Prophecy in Egypt i): Oracle of Amun to Hatshepsut

The occasion of this oracle was undoubtedly a request for divine guidance concerning a planned commercial mission to Somalia (Punt).

The king himself[1], the King of Upper and Lower Egypt, Makere Hatshepsut. The majesty of the court made supplication at the steps of the lord of the gods; a command was heard from the great throne[2], an oracle of the god himself, that the ways of Punt should be searched out, that the highways to the myrrh-terraces should be penetrated: 'I will lead[3] the army on water and on land, to bring marvels from God's land[4] for this god, for the fashioner of her beauty[5].'

(*ARE* ii 116, §285)

1   Hatshepsut, widow of Tuthmosis II, mother of Tuthmosis III and his co-regent during his childhood, usurped the throne, and considered herself as 'king' in her own right, ruling *ca* 1490-69 BCE.

2   Sc. the shrine of the god in the cella of the Karnak temple of Amun.

3   That is, the image of the god, or some device symbolizing his presence, would be carried in procession with the army.

4   That is, land not yet controlled by Egypt. This is a trade delegation, but the presence of the army will guarantee favourable terms.

5   Amun-Ra was Hatshepsut's father. A narrative on the wall of her funerary temple (*ARE* ii 80, §196) narrates how the god impersonated her father (Tuthmosis I), slept with her mother and made her pregnant.

11(10) Prophecy in Egypt ii):
Tuthmosis IV consults the Oracle of Amun

The Konosso inscription of Tuthmosis IV (*ca* 1412-1403 BCE). It tells of rebellion in Nubia, of the king consulting the oracle (the present text), and then proceeding south to a conclusive victory, returning with spoil and captives.

The king proceeded in peace to the temple in the morning, to have a great oblation offered to his father, the fashioner of his beauty[1]. Behold, His Majesty, he himself, petitioned[2] in the presence of the ruler of the gods, that he might counsel him concerning the affair of his going, and inform him concerning that which would happen to him, leading him upon a goodly road to do that which his Ka desired[3]…

(*ARE* ii 328, §827)

1   Cf. §11(9) n. 5.

2   The king was the high priest. All other priests acted as his deputies. The account takes it as worthy of note that the king himself, and not a deputy, consulted the oracle of Amun.

3   The Ka (*k3*) was the divine element in the king (§2(7) n. 1). The term was originally used only of kings and gods, and denoted the supernatural power. The self-expression of the king's Ka had complete autonomy in an absolute monarchy. This could be interpreted as meaning that that whatever the king wanted was good in the sight of the gods. Cf. §11(8) n. 1. We see here, on a psychological account of some aspects of ancient religiosity, the principle of empowerment at work, religion providing the tools of decision-making. Cf. the mechanical procedures outlined below (§11(17-41)).

11(11) Prophecy in Israel and Judah i): the Oracle of Micaiah ben Imlah

There is a very large corpus of prophetic material in the Bible. It stands out from the materials illustrated above by its continued reworking over many centuries, ancient oracles being constantly redacted and reapplied to new situations. This has parallels in Mesopotamia, as in the Apišal oracle-series, discussed by Glassner 1993. A city called Apišal had been captured by Naram-Sin of Agade. Diviners noted that the name evoked the perforations (√*plš*) on sheeps' livers used in hepatoscopy (see §11(34) below), and thus reinterpreted the victory as achieved by mining operations (also √*plš*). Similar word-games occur in biblical prophecy, as in §§11(13, 14). The larger prophetic books in the Bible (*Isaiah, Jeremiah* and *Ezekiel*) in particular became anchors for all kinds of extraneous materials, so that isolating individual oracles can be tricky.

The first passage quoted here, §11(10), gives us a rare insight into the psychological experience of the prophet, who like a king, could experience an ascent to heaven and a direct encounter with the gods. It is to be compared to the account of Isaiah's inaugural vision in §7(18). On ascents to heaven in general see §7 *passim*.

Jehoshaphat of Judah and Ahab of Israel had formed an alliance to recapture territory in Gilead from the Aramaeans (*ca* 850 BCE). They consulted the oracle before joining battle. With the exception of Micaiah, all the prophets predicted victory. When Jehoshaphat asked if anyone thought differently, Micaiah came forward. At first he answered favourably, but Ahab recognized the irony in his voice, and demanded the truth.

'I see[1] all Israel scattered across the mountains like sheep with no shepherd. And Yahweh says, "These have no masters. Let them each return in peace to their own homes."'

Then the king of Israel said to Jehoshaphat, 'Did I not say to you that he never prophesies favourably concerning me, but only unfavourably?'

Then he (Micaiah) said to them, 'Now, listen to the word of Yahweh: I see[1] Yahweh seated upon his throne, and the entire host of heaven are around him, to right and left. And Yahweh says, "Who will trick Ahab into marching to his death at Ramoth Gilead?" Now one answers this way, and another answers that way. But now the spirit[2] comes forward, and stands in Yahweh's presence, and says, "I shall trick him!" And Yahweh says to him, "How?" And he replies, "I shall go and shall become a lying spirit in the mouths of all the prophets." And he (Yahweh) replies, "You shall trick him. You shall succeed. Now go and do it!" Now see how Yahweh puts a lying spirit in the mouths of all these prophets. But Yahweh has pronounced disaster on you!'

(*1 Kings* 22:17-23)

1   All the verbs in Micaiah's account are usually treated as past tense, as though he describes a vision he has had. It is more likely that he describes the vision as he still sees it in his mind's eye. Cf. §9(5) nn. 1 and 7.

2   Or, 'a certain spirit'. But the use of the article suggests a specific one. This appears to be the prototype of Satan (whose name, 'Adversary', means the prosecutor in a court of law: cf. §12(13b); on his later development see §3(11) n. 2). But he may be, more generally, 'the spirit of Yahweh' who performs his will, even when, as here, it involves deception. Cf. Ishtar's role above, §11(6). Yahweh was originally responsible for evil (e.g. *Isaiah* 45:7) before the 'dark' side was centred on Satan (§3(11) n. 2).

11(12) Prophecy in Israel and Judah ii): an Oracle of Isaiah

This passage is taken up in the New Testament (*Matthew* 1:23) as one of the great proof-texts of the coming of the Messiah. Its historical reality was indeed royal, and dealt with the expected birth of a divine king, though it anticipated an event actually unfolding while the prophet spoke rather than events some 700 years hence. The occasion was the alliance between Israel and Aram, which tried to force Judah to join in a war against Assyria (*ca* 735 BCE). The prophet advised the king to remain calm: before long, the threat would have evaporated. This example may have been prompted by the appearance of the queen's evident advanced state of pregnancy, which may have triggered off the oracle.

'So the Lord himself will give you a sign: Behold, the Sacred Bride[1] has conceived, and is about to give birth[2] to a son, and she will call him 'Immanuel'[3]. Curds and honey he will eat, when[4] he knows how to refuse evil and choose good. But before the prince knows how to refuse evil and choose good, the land before whose two kings you are trembling will be deserted.'

1   The Hebrew *ʿalmâ* denotes the female partner in sacred marriage rites. Here it will be Queen Hepzibah, pregnant with Ahaz's successor, Hezekiah. The Greek version was in the spirit of the ritual and ideological tradition when it translated it by παρθενος, 'virgin'.

2   Or perhaps, 'is giving birth'.

3   The Hebrew *ʿimmānûʾēl* means 'El (or: God) is with us'. The birth of a prince and heir was a sign of divine blessing.

4   Or, 'until'. The point is that the threat would not last as long as it took the child to reach the age of discretion. The reference to curds and honey seems to presuppose a land laid waste, in which normal crops were destroyed, and people survived on herding and foraging.

11(13) Prophecy in Israel and Judah iii): an Oracle of Amos

Here an everyday occurrence, a builder's plumb-line in use on a building site, evidently triggered off an association of ideas in Amos' mind.

'Thus he showed me. Lo, the Lord was standing by a wall, a plumb-line in his hand. And Yahweh said to me, "What do you see, Amos?" And I said, "a plumb-line". And the Lord said, "Look, I am setting a plumb-line among my people Israel. No longer am I going to overlook them[1].

Now the high places of Isaac will be laid waste,

and the sanctuaries of Israel will be put to the sword,

and I shall rise up against the house of Jeroboam with a sword.

(*Amos* 7:9)

1   The sense is 'overlook their sins'.

11(14) Prophecy in Israel and Judah iv): an Oracle of Jeremiah

This is not merely a clever word-play on Jeremiah's part, but a skilful application of an important symbol of the Jerusalem cult. The Menorah, the seven-branched lamp stand, of which there may have been two in the temple (because they later became symbols of the two Messiahs — §§6(12, 13)), was constructed, according to *Exodus* 25:31-9, 37:17-24, to resemble an almond tree (§6(9)). The Menorah also represented the divine light shining into the world, as it were the eye of God. Jeremiah may have seen an ordinary almond-tree, or perhaps the temple Menorah.

'Now the word of Yahweh came to me, saying "What do you see, Jeremiah?" And I replied, "I see the branch of an almond-tree[1]". Then Yahweh said to me, "You have seen well. For I am watching[2] over my word, in order to fulfil it."'

(*Jeremiah* 1:11-2)

1   Hebrew *šāqēd*.

2   Hebrew *šōqēd*. It is possible that originally the two forms were phonetically identical.

11(15) Consulting the Oracle by Mechanical Means: *Urim* and *Tummim*

In some respects the technique illustrated here belongs with the omens category (§11 IV). But it was essentially an extension of speech, since whatever the precise nature of the *'ūrîm* and *tummîm* (see Robertson 1964; van Dam 1997), it appears that they (inscribed or coloured stones or other tokens?) were read as equalling 'yes' or 'no' responses to the questions posed. A similar example is *1 Samuel* 23:1-12. Saul, king of Israel, had failed in his attempt to rout the Philistines, after vowing (see §11 II) to Yahweh that no one would eat until the battle was over. In such a situation, the first thing to be done was to find who had broken the terms of the vow.

Then Saul said to all Israel, 'Stand on one side, and I and my son Jonathan will stand on the other side.' And all the people replied, 'Do as you think fit.' Then Saul said to Yahweh, 'God of Israel, why did you not answer your servant today? If the fault is with me or my son Jonathan, give *Urim*; if the fault is with your people Israel, give *Tummim*.' Jonathan and Saul were identified, and the people were free. Then Saul said, 'Let the lot be cast[1] between me and Jonathan my son.' And Jonathan was identified.

(*1 Samuel* 14:40-2, Greek)

1   The different usage may appear to indicate a different technique. But *Urim* and *Tummim* are probably the means by which the lot was cast. On their possible royal background see §6(11) n. 4.

11(16) Consulting the Oracle by Necromancy: the 'Witch of Endor'

Saul, desperate for guidance concerning an approaching showdown with the Philistines, sought it as a last resort from Samuel's ghost.

Samuel consulted Yahweh, but Yahweh did not answer him, either in dreams, or oracles (*'ūrîm*) or by prophets. So Saul said to his servants, 'Seek for me a woman who is a medium (*baᶜⁱlat 'ôb*[1]), so that I may go and consult her.' And his servants replied, 'There is a medium at Endor.' So Saul disguised himself, changing his clothes, and went off with two men and came to the woman by night[2]. He said, 'Reveal the future to me by means of a ghost (*'ôb*), and conjure up for me the person whose name I shall give you...' Then the woman asked, 'Whom shall I conjure up for you?' He replied, 'Conjure up Samuel for me.'

The woman saw Samuel and gave a great cry, saying to Saul, 'Why have you deceived me? You are Saul!' The king said to her, 'Do not be frightened. What can you see?'[3] The woman said to Saul, 'I see a spirit (*'elōhîm*)[4] coming up from the underworld.' He said to her, 'What does he look like?'[3] And she replied, 'It is an old man coming up, and he is wrapped in a cloak.' Then Saul knew that it was Samuel, and he bowed his face to the ground and paid him homage. And Samuel said to Saul, 'Why have you disturbed me by conjuring me up?' And Saul said, 'I am very distressed. The Philistines have declared war on me, and God has abandoned me, and no longer answers me[5] through the prophets or dreams; so I have invoked you to tell me what to do.'

(1 Samuel 28:6-15, selected verses)

1	That is, 'the mistress of a ghost'. Sometimes the term *'ôb* was used of the medium him- or herself.
2	Night was the time for conjuring up the spirits of the dead.
3	Note that Saul had to ask for details from the medium. He could not see or hear the apparition himself. The ensuing conversation was probably carried on through the medium.
4	Or, 'a god'. In West Semitic thought, kings were divinized in life and remained divine after death. Samuel, as a *šōpēṭ* ('judge'), may have been conceived in royal ideological terms.
5	'God has abandoned me... answers': or, 'the gods have abandoned me... answer'. There is no reason to suppose that the 'historical Saul' even worshipped Yahweh, let alone was a monotheist.

This narrative may be compared with two famous examples from the classical world. In *The Odyssey* Book xi, the hero goes to the Ocean, the end of the world, on the command of Circe, and offers sacrifices to the dead. To drink the blood and converse with him, up come Teiresias the seer, Anticlea his mother, various other heroes and heroines, chief of whom was Achilles, who told him that he would rather live as a serf on earth than be king of all the dead underneath it. The account of Aeneas' descent in *The Aeneid* Book vi is clearly modelled on it.

II   Vows

The vow was an ancient and widespread practice, originating in the appeal to supernatural help to gain the desired end, which was very often a fairly ordinary matter like food, safety, or offspring.

Most vows known from the ancient world have a stereotyped formulation:
i) the address: the god is invoked; ii) the protasis (conditional proposition) formulated in a clause beginning 'if'; iii) the apodosis (conclusion), expressed in the form of the

desired outcome. Very often the offering to the deity, if the request was granted, was in the form of a gift to the temple, of gold or silver, or sacrifices, or a commemorative stela. Many stelae, uninscribed or otherwise, are probably votive gifts.

11(17) A Vow in Ugarit: King Keret's Vow

Keret was on his way to attack the kingdom of King Pabil, to force him to grant him his daughter in marriage, in accordance with an oracle of El. On the way, he stopped on his journey to invoke Athirat. This is a classic instance of the formula.

1   There Keret the votary vowed a gift:
     'O Athirat of Tyre,
        and goddess of Sidon,
     if I take Hurriy to my house,
5   and bring the sacred bride into my dwelling,
     twice her weight in silver shall I give,
        and three times her weight in gold.

(Wyatt 1998a, 200-1: KTU 1.14 iv 36-43)

There is an irony in the narrative: Keret had been instructed to fulfil El's command in order to gain a bride, and thus further offspring, after suffering a series of family catastrophes. In turning aside on his journey, he was, in the name of piety, committing a greater impiety. See Wyatt 1998a, 200 n. 111.

11(18) A Vow in Damascus: Votive stela of Barhadad

Barhadad was brother to the king of Damascus in the late 9th century BCE. The stela has a relief of the god Melqart of Tyre.

Stela which was set up by Barhadad, son of Idrishamash, father of the king of Aram, for his lord Melqart, because he (Barhadad) had made a vow and he (Melqart) had hearkened to his voice.

(Beyerlin 1978, 229)

11(19) A Vow in Cyprus: Votive Image of Yatonbaal

Inscription on pedestal of statue, Cyprus, *ca* 272 BCE.

Votive image of good fortune! This statue is a votive image. I am Yatonbaal, son of Gerashtart, governor, son of Abd[ashtart...] I have set up this statue in the sanctuary of Melqart as a monument to my name among the living to bring me good fortune... I set up the votive image of the face of my father in bronze in the sanctuary of Melqart... During the lifetime of my father, I offered and dedicated... many beasts to my lord Melqart... and I have been making burnt offerings of beasts to this day, and also made a model temple in silver, 102 *kars* in weight, and I have consecrated this to my lord Melqart... for the sake of my life and for the sake of the life of my seed... May authority and good fortune be secure for me and my seed. And may Melqart remember me [and establish] the good fortune of my stock.

(Beyerlin 1978, 233-4)

Yatonbaal lists a number of offerings: a steady stream of sacrificial offerings and a model temple made of silver, apparently as acts of general piety, and one or two votive gifts: a statue and, if it is not a description of the statue, a separate bronze portrait of his father. These are designed to bring good fortune to him and his descendants. The particular details of the vow(s) are not given.

11(20) Hittite Vows: Vows of Queen Puduhepa

Puduhepa was queen of Hattusilis III, who usurped the throne of Hatti (mid 13th century BCE). He appears to have suffered from some chronic disease, and she went to considerable lengths and expense in search of a cure. He reigned for about 30 years.

If you, Lelwani, my lady, relay the good word to the gods, grant life to your servant Hattusilis, and give him long years, months, and days, I will go and make for Lelwani my lady, a silver statue of Hattusilis — as tall as Hattusilis himself, with its head, its hands and its feet of gold...

If you, goddess, my lady, make His Majesty well again, and do not give him over to the evil, I shall make a statue of gold for Hebat and I shall make her a rosette of gold.

If you do thus for me and my husband remains alive, I shall give to the deity three *haršialli*-containers, one with oil, one with honey, and one with fruits.

If His Majesty's [disease] passes quickly, I shall make for Ningal ten oil-flasks of gold set with lapis lazuli.

If you, O goddess, my lady, preserve His Majesty alive and well for many years, so that he walks before you, goddess, for many years, then, goddess, I will give annually the years of silver and gold, the months of silver and gold, the days of silver and gold, a cup of silver and a cup of gold, a head of His Majesty of gold, [and] I will give you sheep annually, whether a hundred or fifty is of no matter.

(Parker 1989, 72-5, adapted)

Lelwani was a Hittite chthonian sun-goddess derived from Ereshkigal, the Mesopotamian goddess of the underworld (see §2(23)); Hebat was the Hurro-Hittite consort of the storm-god, assimilated in Hatti to the sun-goddess of Arinna; Ningal was a Sumerian goddess whose cult travelled as far as Ugarit.

11(21) Vows in Egypt i): Votive Stela of Neb-Ra

Votive stela from the New Kingdom period set up by the tomb-painter Neb-Ra, on the occasion of the healing of Nakht-Amun (his son, or a friend?) after some obscure affair concerning a cow (perhaps the theft of one from the temple herd?), which had made Nakht-Amun ill.

Amun-Ra, Lord of Karnak, the great god, the first one of Thebes, the holy god who hears prayers, who comes at the voice of the poor and the troubled, who gives breath to the one who is weak.

(a hymn follows)

Neb-Ra, painter of Amun in the necropolis of Thebes, son of Pay, painter of Amun in the necropolis of Thebes, has made this in the name of his lord Amun, Lord of Thebes, who comes at the voice of the poor.

What he has made for him were hymns to his name, because his power is so great. What he made for him were prayers to him, in the presence of the whole land, on behalf of the painter Nakht-Amun, when he was lying sick and likely to die, under the power of Amun because of his cow.

(a hymn follows)

He says: '"I will make this stela in your name and I shall immortalize this hymn on it as an inscription, if you save the scribe Nakht-Amun for me". So I said to you, and you heard me. Now see, I am doing what I said. You are the lord for the one who calls to him and acknowledges the truth, you, the lord of Thebes.'

(Beyerlin 1978, 33-4, adapted)

11(22) Vows in Israel i): Hannah's Vow

The following three examples illustrate the typical personal concerns of the votary, a childless woman, a warrior seeking victory in battle, and an exile seeking a safe return home.

The barren woman desperate for a child is a typical folklore motif, leading to the birth of a hero. Samuel, judge and ruler of Israel, will be the hoped-for child in the present narrative. So desperate is the childless Hannah that she is willing to give up her only son, if only Yahweh will grant her prayer.

'Yahweh of Hosts, if you will only see the wretchedness of your handmaid, and will remember me and not forget your handmaid, and will give your handmaid a male child, then I shall give him to Yahweh for the whole of his life, and no razor shall touch his head[1].'

(*1 Samuel* 1:11)

1   The Nazirite ('one under a vow') did not cut his hair (cf. the laws in *Numbers* 6:1-21, and the case of Samson in *Judges* 13:2-7).

11(23) Vows in Israel ii): Jephthah's Vow

Summoned to lead the army against an enemy, Jephthah vowed a holocaust to Yahweh if he returned safely. The irony of this rash vow is that it was his only daughter who came out to greet him... Cf. §12(12) and n. 5.

'If you will indeed put the Ammonites within my grasp, then whoever comes out of the doors of my house to greet me on my safe return from the Ammonites shall belong to Yahweh, and I shall offer him up as a holocaust.'

(*Judges* 11:30-1)

11(24) Vows in Israel iii): Jacob's Vow

Set in the context of the patriarchal narratives (see §7(22) for the previous part of this narrative), this appears at first sight to be an ancient tale of Israel before the settlement. It is more likely however that it is an exilic story, describing the aspiration of Diaspora Jews to return home. See Wyatt 1990c; Husser 1991.

'If God[1] will be with me and protect me on this journey on which I am going, giving me food to eat and clothes to wear, so that I return safely to my father's house, then Yahweh will be my god, and this stone which I have set up as a stela will be a temple of God[1], and of everything you give me I will give you a tenth part.'

(*Genesis* 28:20-2)

1   Since the narrative is about choosing Yahweh as personal deity, it is arguable that the narrative does not presuppose monotheism. In this case, perhaps read 'the gods'.

III   Curses

The word uttered in favour of someone, the blessing, operated on the principle that the power of the utterance would bring about the well-being of the recipient. Generally blessing involved material benefits, children, land, wealth, as graphically expressed in the blessings Yahweh offered Israel in *Deuteronomy* 27:11-3, 28:1-8, 15-20. The latter passages are significant, because they occur within the context of a treaty ritual (the 'covenant'), and, applying to an obedient Israel, are balanced by the corresponding curses on a disobedient Israel.

Curses therefore had an integral role in liturgical contexts. They invoked divine judgment on those who disregarded the laws, written or otherwise, of a just society. Presupposing the inherent power in the uttered word, they were frequently used, as in the following examples, to deal with secret malefactions, which escaped the sanction of the law. If human justice could not prevail, it was expected that divine justice could.

11(25) Curses from Egypt i): the Curses of Nenki, Meni, and Seti

These are typical tomb curses, invoking divine punishment on those who desecrated tombs.

(Nenki): 'As for this tomb, which I have made in the necropolis of the west, I made it in a clean and central place. As for any noble, any official or any man who shall rip out any stone or any brick from this tomb, I will be judged with him by the great god[1], I will seize his neck like a bird, and I will cause all the living who are upon the earth to be afraid of the spirits who are in the west.'

(*ANET* 327: Saqqara tomb of Nenki, 6th dynasty)

(Meni): The eldest of the house of Meni says this: 'The crocodile will be against him in the water, the snake against him on land — against him who may do a thing to this tomb! I never did a thing to him. It is the god[1] who will judge him.

(*ANET* 327: Giza tomb of Meni, 6th dynasty)

(Seti): As for anyone who shall avert the face from the command of Osiris, Osiris shall pursue him, Isis shall pursue his wife, Horus shall pursue his children, among all the princes of the necropolis, and they shall exercise their judgment on him.

(*ARE* iii 86, §194: Redesiyeh inscription of Seti I, 19th dynasty)

1   In the first two curses it is probably Osiris, who judges the dead, who is invoked. He is named in the third.

11(26) Curses from Egypt ii): Egyptian Execration Texts

The Egyptians performed a graphic ritual against their enemies in Middle Kingdom times. The names of various foreign powers and their rulers were inscribed on pots, which were then ritually smashed, thus annihilating the named foe. Every possible contingency seems to be covered in the second paragraph. A part of the efficacy of this ritual was no doubt on account of its link with the symbol of the forming of the king by Khnum on his potter's wheel. Here kings could be unmade by the effective word.

The ruler of Iy-Anaq, Erum, and all the retainers who are with him; the ruler of Iy-Anaq, Abi-Yamimu, and all the retainers who are with him; the fruler of Iy-Anaq, Akirum, and all the retainers who are with him...

The ruler of Shutu, Ayyabum, and all the retainers who are with him; the ruler of Jerusalem, Sety-Anu, and all the retainers who are with him...

All the Asiatics — of Byblos, of Ullaza, of Iy-Anaq, of Shutu, of Iy-Muaru, of Qehermu, of Rehob... their strong men, their swift runners, their allies, their associates and the Mentu in Asia, who may rebel, who may plot, who may fight, who may talk of fighting, or who may talk of rebelling, in this entire land. All men, all people, all folk, all males, all eunuchs, all women, and all officials, who may rebel, who may plot, who may fight, who may talk of fighting, or who may talk of rebelling, and every rebel who talks of rebelling, in this entire land. Every evil word, every evil speech, every evil slander, every evil thought, every evil plot, every evil fight, every evil quarrel, every evil plan, every evil thing, all evil dreams, and all evil slumber.

(*ANET* 328-9: selections)

11(27) Curses in Ugarit and Israel i): Testament and Curse of Arhalbu of Ugarit

It seems that Arhalbu was deposed by the Hittites, in favour of his brother Niqmepa. At any rate, he seems to have been childless. This text has been interpreted as an example of the levirate law. More probably it reflects the matrilineal system whereby the right to the throne passed through the female line, as appears to have been the case in both Egypt and Israel. So whoever married Kubaba would become king. He wished his brother to replace him, not an upstart. In addition to the selection here, see *CS* ii 154 (Hadad-Yith'i), 155 (Zakkur), 157-8 (Panamuwa). A slightly different translation by van Soldt 1985-6, may be understood as meaning that fellow kings who married the widow would be cursed.

Thus says Arhalbu, king of Ugarit: whoever after my death takes in marriage my wife Kubaba, daughter of Takanu, from my brother, may Baal crush him! May he not make great his throne! May he not dwell in a palace! May Baal of Saphon crush him!

(Tsevat 1958, 237, adapted: RS 16.144)

11(28) Curses in Ugarit and Israel ii): Danel curses the Land

Aqhat has been murdered by the goddess Anat and her henchman Yatipan. Danel, his father, half-guesses the news when his daughter tears his robe, a powerfully symbolic act. Until a culprit is found, the land itself is cursed. (Cf. *Deuteronomy* 21:1-9, which provides legislation for the unsolved murder.)

1   Then
    Danel the ruler of Rapha cursed the clouds,
      which rain on the dreadful heat,
    the clouds which rain on the summer-fruit,
5   the dew which falls on the grapes:
    'For seven years Baal shall fail,
      for eight, the Charioteer of the clouds!
    No dew,
      no rain,
10 no welling up of the deeps,[1]
    no goodness of Baal's voice[2]...!

(Wyatt 1998a, 295-6: KTU 1.19 i 38-46)

1   The curse will prevent life-giving water from three sources, which represent the three dimensions of the cosmos: no dew from the earth, no rain from the sky above, and no spring-water from the underworld below. There are two deeps. Cf. §§6(1, 32), 9(8) introduction and 11(29) n. 1.

2   Sc. the thunder, understood to be the voice of the storm-god. Cf. §3(5) introduction.

11(29) Curses in Ugarit and Israel iii): David curses Mount Gilboa

When Saul died in a battle against the Philistines, a messenger came to David with the news. It drew the following response.

1 'O mountains of Gilboa,
  let there be no dew,
    no shower upon you,
      no welling up of the (two) deeps[1]!
5 For there the shield of the mighty ones was dishonoured.

(2 Samuel 1:21)

1   Corrected text. The Masoretic Text reads 'nor Fields of Offering'. 'The Fields of Offering' were the ideal land in which the dead continued to live in Egypt, portrayed in idyllic scenes in the Egyptian *Book of the Dead.* So a kind of sense can be read. However, not only is the curse suspiciously like the Ugaritic example in §11(28), suggesting that the same formula is in use, but the text itself reads as though an original has been misread. This can be seen in transliteration and transcription:

        Reading adopted: *wsry thmt*   וסרי תהמת
        MT: *wsdy trwmt*   וסדי תרומת

The letters *r* [ר] and *d* [ד] in the first word look very similar, having the same overall number of strokes. Similarly with *h* [ה] and the letters *r, w* [ר, ו] in the second.

The similarity is even more striking in the palaeo-Hebrew script, where in the first word (*wsry, wsdy*), *r* and *d* were written identically (ᐊ, ᐊ), or very similarly (ᐊ, ᐱ), in some forms of the script, and could thus be read either way. Cf. §12(12) n. 4.

11(30) Curses in Ugarit and Israel iv):
Curses against Sins Committed in Secret in Israel

Certain crimes and sins, being perpetrated in secret, were not generally amenable to legal control. The curse was the means to threaten sanctions against them.

Cursed is the man who carves or casts an idol — an abomination to Yahweh! — the work of a craftsman's hands, and sets it up in secret...[1] Cursed is he who dishonours his father or his mother... Cursed is he who moves his neighbour's boundary mark...[2] Cursed is he who leads a blind man astray on the road... Cursed be he who denies justice to the resident alien[3], the orphan or the widow...[4] Cursed is he who sleeps with his father's wife, who removes his father's robe (from her)... Cursed is he who has intercourse with any kind of animal...[5]

(Deuteronomy 27:15-21)

1   Each curse ends with the antiphonal response 'and all the people said "Amen!"' or similar.

2   Examples of boundary-stones (*kudurru*) have been found in Mesopotamia, invoking the anger of the gods on those who interfered with them. See Seidl 1989.

3   The 'resident alien' did not have the legal rights of the citizens of the country, and so could be readily exploited.

4   Care for the widow and the orphan appears frequently in ancient Near Eastern literature as the duty of the righteous king.

5   The list continues with five further curses, making a dodecalogue.

When treaties were drawn up in the ancient world, the legal clauses were implemented by elaborate rites. The gods of the two parties were summoned as witnesses to the binding agreement. Should either side break the treaty, the gods would punish them.

11(31) Curses from Treaties i):
Suppululiumas I of Hatti and Kurtiwaza of Mittanni

The treaty dates from the early 14th century BCE. Copies were housed in the shrines of the chief gods.

If you, Kurtiwaza, the prince, and (you), the sons of the Hurri country do not fulfil the words of this treaty, may the gods, the lords of the oath[1], blot you out, Kurtiwaza and the Hurri men together with your country, your wives and all that you have... May they overturn your throne... May the oaths sworn in the presence of these gods break you like reeds, you, Kurtiwaza, together with your country. May they exterminate from the earth your name and your seed...

(ANET 206: from KBo 1.1)

1   All the gods are granted this title as witnesses. Among the Hurrian (Mittannian) gods listed are five Vedic gods (Mitra, Varuna, Indra and the Ashvins), representing all levels in society. The name Mitra specifically meant 'oath' or 'treaty'. He may have been worshipped at Shechem in Palestine as El (or Baal) Berit, 'the god (master) of the oath'.

11(32) Curses from Treaties ii):
Shaushgamuwa of Amurru and Ammithtamru II of Ugarit

The letter dates from the mid 13th century BCE. Tudhaliya IV of Hatti, the overlord, is obliging Shaushgamuwa to accept a ruling that his sister, the divorced wife of Ammithamru II, be handed back to him for punishment. (She was thrown overboard from a ship.)

If Shaushgamuwa commits violence against Ammithtamru... or commits violence against the ships or troops which are taking away the daughter of the Great Lady, Heaven and Earth will know of it, Hadad of the Curtain wall and Ishtar of Tunip, Hadad of Mount Hazzi (= Saphon) and Hebat of Ari, the Sun of heaven, Sin, Ishhara, the guardian of oaths, will know of it! Concerning Shaushgamuwa, king of Amurru, son of Benteshina... may the gods do violence to him! May they cause him to disappear from his father's house, from his father's land, and from the throne of his fathers!

(after J. Nougayrol, PRU 4:137-8: RS 18.06+17.365)

11(33) Curses from Treaties iii):
Ashurnirari V of Assyria and Mati-Ilu of Arpad

This vassal treaty dates from the mid-8th century BCE. The sacrificial language is a metaphor for the physical destruction of Mati-Ilu if he should break his word. The realities of the situation are evident: no such sanctions are threatened against the Assyrian overlord!

This spring lamb has been brought from its fold... to sanction the treaty between Ashurnirari and Mati-Ilu.   If Mati-Ilu sins against this treaty made under oath by the gods, then just as this spring lamb, brought from its fold, will not return to its fold, will not behold its fold again, alas, Mati-Ilu, together with his sons, daughters, officials and the people of his land will be ousted from his country, will not return to his country, and will not behold his country again. This head is not the head of a lamb; it is the head of Mati-Ilu, it is the head of his sons, his officials, and the people of his land. If Mati-Ilu sins against this treaty, so, just as the head of this spring lamb is torn off, and its knuckles placed in its mouth, may the head of Mati-Ilu be torn off, and his sons... This shoulder is not the shoulder of a spring lamb; it is the shoulder of Mati-Ilu...

(ANET 532-3: BM 79-7-7,195 fragment)

IV   Omens

In addition to oracular techniques, which had their origin in the recognition of the power of the human voice in world-construction and social management, ancient societies believed that the gods communicated through the processes of nature, 'in other languages', as it were. Any natural occurrence might, to those with eyes to see, contain warnings of what might happen if certain courses of action were followed. Thus all portentous events (e.g. battles, enthronements, treaties, house, palace or temple construction) were commonly preceded by consultation as to divine wishes and purposes. As well as the reading of cultic signs (§11(34)) and various manipulative techniques (see §§11(35-7), meteorological and celestial events were regarded as significant.

Some of the following accounts are apt to strike the modern reader as supreme examples of irrationality. This is to miss the point. The very fact that almost anything seems to have been able to provide guidance indicates that what was at issue was a decision-making system, and any external means, if the rules were followed, could allow a decision to be made and adhered to as authentically mediated from the gods. The modern practices of tossing a coin, or having palms, horoscopes, the *I Ching* or Tarot cards read, belong to the same field of thought, as do many modern traditional forms of divination. The distinctive feature of ancient thought was the absence of the concept of chance. Nothing occurred without a nod from on high.

11(34) Cultic Procedures controlled by the Priest i):
Hepatoscopy (Livers)

With the vast numbers of sacrificial victims passing through the temple cult-industrial process, the priests would notice that the internal organs of the victims were broadly similar, but with occasional variations. These variations were noted, and correlated with contemporary events. Over the centuries a science developed, based on observation and classification, so that significant markings could be interpreted as coded divine messages concerning future events. The main organ used was the liver. 'Reading the omens' (*omina*) was really a matter of 'reading the internal organs' (*omenta*).

If there is a cross drawn on the 'strong point' of the liver, an important person will kill his lord. If there are two 'roads' on the liver, a traveller will reach his goal. If the lobe is red on left and right, there will be a conflagration. If on the right of the liver there are two 'fingers', it is the omen 'Who is king?' Who is not king? — that is, of rival pretenders.

(Loewe and Blacker 1981, 148)

11(35) Cultic Procedures controlled by the Priest ii):
Lecanomancy (Oil)

Oil was poured into a bowl of water.

If the oil divides into two: for a campaign, the two camps will advance against each other; for treating a sick man: he will die. If from the middle of the oil two drops come out, one big, the other small: the man's wife will bear a son; for a sick man: he will recover.

(Loewe and Blacker 1981, 152)

11(36) Cultic Procedures controlled by the Priest iii):
Aleuromancy (Flour)

If the flour, in the east, takes the shape of a lion's face: the man is in the grip of a ghost of one who lies in the open country; the sun will consign it to the wind and he will get well.

(Loewe and Blacker 1981, 152)

11(37) Cultic Procedures controlled by the Priest iv):
Libanomancy (Smoke)

If the smoke bunches towards the east and disperses towards the thigh of the *bārû*[1]: you will prevail over your enemy. If the smoke moves to the right, not the left: your enemy will prevail over you.

(Loewe and Blacker 1981, 153)

---

1   The *bārû* priests specialized in reading omens.

11(38) Meteorological and Celestial Occurrences i):
Reading the Weather

If Adad roars[1] in Sivan: revolt in the land[2]. If it rains in Ulul on the eighth day[3]: widespread loss of life. If Adad in the middle of the day rains 'wheat': there will be flood[4].

(Loewe and Blacker 1981, 160)

1   That is, if it thunders. Adad was the storm-god.

2   Sivan (§2(39)) fell in May-June. Storms at this time would destroy ripening cereal crops, leading to threats to the food-supply.

3   The eighth day of the month was a day of ill omen. The month Ulul (§2(39)) occurring in August-September, there would be further disruption of later harvests. In addition, summer rainfall might well cause the rivers to be in spate, causing flooding.

4   'Wheat' is a reference to hail. Melting hailstones after a storm would also risk flooding.

11(39) Meteorological and Celestial Occurrences ii):
Atmospheric Effects

If in the days of the moon's invisibility the god does not promptly disappear from the sky, there will be a drought in the land. If the moon is surrounded by a halo and Jupiter stands in it, the king of Akkad will be imprisoned. If the sun rises in a cloudbank, the king will become angry and take up arms.

(Loewe and Blacker 1981, 160)

These examples are probably all based on extrapolations from actual correlations drawn between the heavenly and the earthly events.

11(40) Meteorological and Celestial Occurrences iii):
A Solar Eclipse at Ugarit

This text has been widely interpreted, though most scholars take it to be a solar eclipse, as I have done. Wyatt 1998a gives nine interpretations.

At the sixth (hour) of the first day of Hiyyar the sun set[1], her attendant being Mars[2]. Livers were examined: beware!

(Wyatt, 1998a, 366-7: KTU 1.78)

1   On this translation, it must be a description of a solar eclipse, which probably took place on 5 March 1223.

2   Mars was the god Reshef.

11(41) Animal Movements: Some Mesopotamian Omens

If on New Year's Day, before a man gets out of bed, a snake comes up out of a hole and looks at him before anyone has seen it, the man will die during the year. If he wants to stay alive, he must... (shave?) his head, and shave his cheeks. He will be afflicted for three months, then he will get well.

If a dog enters the palace and lies down on a bed, that palace will acquire a new possession. In order that so-and-so may carry out his undertakings with success, let either a *kudurranu*-bird or a 'broad-wing' or an *arabanu*-bird run from my right towards my left.

An *alliya*-bird came from beyond the river flying low, and it settled in a poplar tree, and while we watched it, another *alliya*-bird attacked it from beyond the river on the good side, and it went... but it did not go beyond the river. But the *alliya*-bird that was on the poplar rose up and came back... And from beyond the river it came back up from the good side and came across the river... Then an eagle came up from in front of the river...

(Loewe and Blacker 1981, 155)

V   Eschatology: Rituals of Death in Egypt

Four examples of Egyptian mortuary spells. Some spells of this kind were evidently connected directly with funerary rites and the subsequent maintenance of the well-being of the deceased, and of their cult as minor family deities. The present examples fall rather into the category of 'virtual rites'. The spells were provided for use by the deceased, as part of the process of equipping him or her with all the necessary technical detail to deal with the contingencies encountered in the underworld journey to the Fields of Offering (§9(8)). Another example is the provision of the names of the guardians of the gates (§2(22)).

11(42) A Shabti Spell

This first example deals with the provision of *shabtis* who will perform the routine tasks of the deceased. Presumably the pleasurable ones, like eating, drinking, copulation and other recreational activities, required no substitute.

Spell for causing shabtis to do work for their owner in the Realm of the Dead...

'O you shabtis which have been made for N, if N be detailed for his task, or an unpleasant duty in it be imposed on N as a man at his task:

'Here we are', you shall say[1].

If N be detailed to keep an eye on those who work there at turning over new fields, to plant the lands of the river-bank or to convey sand to the

West which was placed on the East — and *vice versa* — 'Here we are', you shall say.'

To be spoken over an image of the owner as he was on earth, made of tamarisk or zizyphus wood and placed in the chapel of the deceased.

(Faulkner 1977 ii 106: from CT 472)

1   Hence the name 'shabti': 'one who answers'.

11(43) Transformation into a Snake

The purpose of the following three spells was to transform the deceased into an alternative form. Each of these, and many others, was either a divine form or some other symbol of liberation from human limitations. They are generally accompanied by a vignette, in this instance a snake on two legs. Thus the snake itself is partially transformed. The vignette, given the psychology underlying Egyptian art, was as much a 'performative utterance' as the text was supposed to be. The very presence of the two in the *Book of the Dead* papyrus effected the desired transformation in principle.

Spell for being transformed into a snake:
1   'I am a long-lived snake;
       I pass the night and am reborn every day.
    I am a snake which is in the limits of the earth;
       I pass the night and am reborn,
5   renewed and rejuvenated every day.'

(Faulkner 1985, 84: BD 87)

11(44) Transformation into a Crocodile

The accompanying vignette shows the crocodile god Sebek on a shrine. The transformation into snake (previous example) and crocodile, here, are really the acting out of fantasies and phobias, part aversion-therapy, part appeal to the attractive features of their very different ways of life, free of usual human constraints.

Spell for being transformed into a crocodile:
    'I am a crocodile immersed in dread,
    I am a crocodile who takes by robbery,
    I am the great and mighty fish-like being who is in the Bitter Lakes.
    I am the Lord of those who bow down in Letopolis.

(Faulkner 1985, 84: BD 88)

11(45) Transformation into a Phoenix

The vignette shows a phoenix, clearly recognizable in the vignette in P. Ani (Faulkner 1985, 83) as the purple heron (*ardea purpurea*): cf. §5(1) introduction. Thus the deceased aspired to identification with the sun-god, which explains the further reference here to Khepri, the beetle-god of the dawn. But the deceased was also identified with Khonsu the moon-god of Thebes and with 'every god'.

Spell for being transformed into a phoenix:

1 'I have flown up like the primaeval ones,
    I have become Khepri,
  I have grown as a plant,
    I have clad myself as a tortoise,
5 I am the essence of every god...
    I have come on the day when I appear in glory
       with the strides of the gods,
    for I am Khonsu who subdued the lords.'

As for him who knows this pure spell, it means going out into the day after death and being transformed at will...

(Faulkner 1985, 80: *BD* 83)

Chapter 12

MYTH, HISTORY, AND THE FLOW OF TIME

Contrasts are frequently drawn between myth and history, as though they are entirely different literary genres. The reality is more complex and interesting.

Suggested Reading:

Albrektson 1967; Collingwood 1946; J. B. Curtis 1963; Evans 1997; Glassner 1993; Grabbe 1997; Halpern 1988; Lowenthal 1985; Marwick 1989; van de Mieroop 1999; van Seters 1983; id. 1992; Strenski 1987; Tonkin 1992; Wyatt 1996b, 373-424; id. 2001a.

12.1 Introduction

12.1.1 Myth and history have often been taken to be mutually exclusive, on grounds that history is 'true', and myth 'false'. This approach, once surprisingly common among Old Testament scholars, is simplistic. Firstly, let us note the problem of definitions.

12.1.2 What is 'myth'? 'Myths are fables'; 'myths are stories about gods'; 'myths are charters for society's values'; 'myths describe the ontologically true'... There are almost as many definitions as there are scholars discussing myth. I have tried to get away from endless paper-chasing by defining it as 'the religious mind-set' rather than a literary type (Wyatt 2001a). This also gets us off the 'myth *versus* history' hook.

12.1.3 What is 'history'? Is it what happened, or the way a historian says it happened? What if two or more historians disagree on what happened? Can historians lie? Is it the 'event', the telling (a narrative, a story with a beginning, a middle and an end), or the explaining (this was the result of that, history happens according to economic laws, etc.)?

12.1.4 We can in fact see mythical elements in history ('I saw an angel at Mons', 'the evacuation at Dunkirk was a miracle') as not uncommon in the modern experience, just as myths may containing germs of history, or be based on historical events. Any *theological* account of history (e.g. the history books in the Bible) is 'myth', simply because God is an actor, and it *functions* religiously in church and synagogue. This in no way impugns it.

12.1.5 Is time linear, spiral or circular (cyclical)? Israelite views have often been contrasted with those of other ancient Near Eastern cultures. Is the contrast warranted? See J. B. Curtis 1963 for an account of the cyclical aspects of Hebrew time-consciousness.

12.1.6 All societies have a collective memory of real or imagined events in the past, which constitute 'history'. In a precritical context, it may well contain mythical elements. For example, Livy's *History of Rome* begins with narratives that have close parallels in the mythology of other Indo-European societies. The modern concern with 'scientific accuracy' was unknown to the ancients, and all was grist to the mill, and increasingly so with remoteness in time. Some myths probably began as relatively trivial stories, others perhaps as accounts of real events. But the 'mythicization' of such material would grow, as its ideological and symbolic potential was able to incorporate into the narrative, even at a subliminal level, values, demands and prohibitions considered vital for the community's well-being. The process of increasing symbolization had been in continuous development from Palaeolithic times, and the evidence from the Bronze Age civilizations of the Near East was the culmination of a process lasting nearly 200,000 years, but in a vastly accelerated mode since the Neolithic (from *ca* 10000 BCE). It is fair to say that religious life was transformed in this period (Cauvin 1994), and the rise of the city was both a function and an impetus to the acceleration. The myths we encounter were therefore already of considerable age and sophistication. There is a direct link from collective memory expressed in mythic terms to the rise of a sense of history.

12.1.7 The invention of writing, usually traced back to a little before 3000 BCE, provided a very adaptable tool for the development of *external* memory. Records could now be kept, which had a powerful effect on agricultural and other economic activity. Royal decrees, law, divine messages all became memorable beyond the point of utterance and individual memory. Other media could also be means of remembering: see Renfrew and Scarre 1998. On the broad development of human culture see for example Donald 1991, Knight 1991, and Deacon 1997.

12.1.8 Even when history set out to be sober, it did of course have a perspective, a bias. There was frequently a theological component in ancient historiography, so that deities played active parts in affairs. A modern historian would tend to read an account saying that god X determined this or that historical outcome as meaning that the people living that history, or recording it later, believed this to be the case. Cf. Hobbes' famous dictum (*Leviathan*), that for a man to say that God appeared to him in a dream is to say no more than that he dreamt that God appeared to him. Different historians, either contemporaries or living at different times, would also have different perspectives. Historiography can never escape the bias of the particular viewpoint.

12.2   Egypt

Four examples of historical record are given (§§12(1-4)). They readily allow us to see the biases at work in Egyptian thought. The action of the gods behind the scenes is recognized as a matter of course. The palette (§12(1)) is the last of a series of predynastic pictorial historical records. Mace heads were also carved in commemoration of great events. While §12(2) is rather prosaic, merely recording 'facts', it already decides what is important. Selectivity is essential in historiography. §§12(3, 4) are blatant propaganda (as is much historiography down the ages!). The one exaggerates the religious decay now put right by the king. It is the perspective of the Amun priesthood. The other puts the appropriate spin on a usurpation of the throne, making it all seem divinely ordained.

12.3   Mesopotamia

Genealogies and lists played an important part in constructing mental conceptions of time. Laying claim to an ancient hero in one's lists lent prestige. Cf. the position of Didanu in §12(5) (and see n. 1 *ad loc.*), who was claimed as ancestor by Assyrians, East Syrians and Ugaritians. The Bible has numerous such genealogies (§12(8) below). In §12(6) we cite three Assyrian accounts of one event (among more such narratives), illustrating how the understanding of it alters with political and temporal perspective. In §12(6), we have Sennacherib's (704-681) account of his sack of Babylon. No religious slant is given. In §12(7), Sennacherib's son Esarhaddon (680-669) gives a theological account, in which Marduk punishes the Babylonians for impiety. The means (viz. the Assyrian army) is not even mentioned. In §12(8) this theological dimension is further heightened. Finally, in §12(9), we have a Babylonian reflection which merely says that the king was deported. The sub-text is 'the eternal city cannot be destroyed!' This may be compared with the biblical belief in the inviolability of Zion.

12.4   The West Semitic World: Moab and Israel

12.4.1 We have a selection of different West Semitic approaches.

12.4.2 The Mesha inscription (§12(10)) belongs to a genre of autobiographical votive inscriptions (cf. §11(19)) which give an account of recent history intended to play up the piety of the votary. Note how political action (the account of which becomes history) was actually motivated by religious concerns (and *vice versa*: see §11(10)). Mass-slaughter was an offering to a vengeful deity. This is abundantly echoed in biblical accounts.

12.4.3 §12(12) gives an Israelite account of the same period, now featuring Mesha as the enemy. This account is at first glance remarkably sober. (The uncited part, however, tells of a miracle wrought by Yahweh: water in the desert, seeming like blood to the Moabites.) It is the wrath of Chemosh, if anything, resulting from Mesha's ritual act, which forces the Israelite retreat.

12.4.4 §12(13) gives two accounts of David's taking of a census, reflecting developing theology. In §a, it is Yahweh, motivated by anger, who prompts David to do what seems routine to us, but an affront to Yahweh. §b, written perhaps a couple of centuries later, reflects the hiving off of the performance of evil to Satan, a member of the heavenly court.

12.4.5 §§12(14-7) offer various perspectives on the relationship of the past to the future, and raise issues of determinism.

12.5   The Problem of the Supposed Distinctiveness of Israelite Historiography

12.5.1 The history of scholarship requires the inclusion of some brief observations on this topic. 'The Hebrew Bible is a historical book.' Statements like this appear frequently in introductions. It is perfectly correct in the sense that it is a product of history. It is correct up to a point in that it contains, alongside poetry, hymnody, wisdom literature and ritual prescriptions, a number of historiographical compositions. It is correct, but rather less so, in so far as it is presented as giving us the history of Israel. At this point it requires serious qualification, in so far as all historiography is biased in various ways, and this corpus particularly so. This is not intended as any kind of rejection of its value. It is rather the recognition, firstly that this particular corpus has undergone radical redactional processing over a number of centuries, and secondly that the extraction of a history that will satisfy modern academic canons in history is a long and difficult exercise, and cannot always meet with unqualified success. But the statement is false in the way it has often been interpreted, that Israelite religion was by virtue of a supposedly unique historical awareness a 'historical religion', that is, a religion which took history seriously in a 'unique way'.

12.5.2 This conception of Israelite religious history and theology is essentially a modern construction, and is to be studied rather in the context of European cultural history than ancient Near Eastern cultural history. If we wish to undertake the latter exercise, then we are obliged to treat Israelite historiography and its theological awareness of time alongside the same matters in other parts of the ancient Near East. When this is honestly done, there are certainly distinctively Israelite biases, just as there are distinctive Egyptian or Mesopotamian ones, but we can no longer be satisfied with the claim that was once fashionable, that all Israel's neighbours lived in an ahistorical, myth-driven, cyclical time-process.

12.5.3 It was once fashionable to contrast Israelite historiography, with its allegedly unique linear view of time, and long-term conception of divine purpose, with the writings of the rest of the ancient Near East. See for instance G. E. Wright 1952. This approach was discredited by Albrektson 1967. For discussion of intention, method and achievement in ancient historiography see J. van Seters 1983, id. 1992, 1-103; Glassner 1993, and van der Mieroop 1999.

12.6   Theocratic History

12.6.1 'Theocratic History' is the expression of Collingwood 1946, 14, used to describe ancient historiography in which the gods play an active role. History nowadays, while it may be hijacked by ideologues, is essentially the interpretation and evaluation of evidence for cause and effect in the events we live through. A number of possible philosophical or practical stances (e.g. idealism, postmodernism) may influence motivation, selection and procedure. But the causes of events are people, economic pressures, environmental disasters, plagues, etc. In ancient history, apart from a few exceptions like Herodotus, Theucydides and later Hellenistic and Roman writers, these 'causes' are actually effects wrought by the gods as first causes, generally for the punishment of this nation, the aggrandizement of that nation, and above all the increase of their own prestige. It is as though the gods rival each other in heaven, and we fight their surrogate wars!

12.6.2 The whole of Israelite history is played out on two axes: the centralization of the cult in Jerusalem, and the 'sin of Jeroboam', meaning the political and religious secession of Israel from Judah *ca* 921 BCE. Every Israelite king is damned simply for ruling a secessionist kingdom (though Yahweh had himself engineered it! *1 Kings* 11:26-12:33) as can be seen from the regnal formulae (e.g. *1 Kings* 15:25-34; 16:29-34 etc.), while most of the kings of Judah fall foul of the centralization demand of *Deuteronomy* 12 (cf. e.g. *1 Kings* 14:21-4; 15:1-3; *2 Kings* 14:1-4; 18:1-8; 21:1-9). It is evident that the chief character in this drama is Yahweh himself. The other historical composition, *Chronicles*, simply writes Israel out of history, like the doctoring of a Soviet photograph.

12.7   The Conception of World Cycles

In the Epilogue, on pp. 325-6, we shall see evidence of the imposition of a 'world cycle' on biblical chronology, with regard to the ante-diluvian chronology of *Genesis*. This is difficult to treat simply: it involves the recognition of a widespread arithmetical pattern imposed on historiography from India to the Roman world. Much of this is attested only from the Hellenistic period, but is probably derived from much older antecedents. It causes embarrassment to the view that the biblical view of time and history is unique, since along with all the other versions of it, it betrays a debt to Babylonian theory.

I   Egyptian Historiography

12(1)   The Narmer Palette

Decorative palettes were in use from at least late predynastic times to the beginning of the Old Kingdom (third millennium BCE) to record important events. Writing was evidently in use, to judge from the Narmer palette, but the main 'message' was pictorial. Palettes were probably discontinued with the rise of more monumental art and the advent of writing. Decorated maceheads also appear.

The example given is perhaps the most important of the genre, dating from the time of the unification of Egypt under Narmer, king of Upper Egypt. He probably ruled from Hierakonpolis, where the palette was discovered. On the left (verso) he stands in the 'smiting posture', being about to kill his victim, the vanquished Washi of Lower Egypt, by offering him as a sacrifice to the gods. The lower scene represents a battlefield strewn with corpses. On the right (recto) he walks in procession behind four standards of royal gods (the royal Ka [see §12(4) n. 2)], Wepwawet, the 'Opener of the Ways', and two Horus gods) towards rows of bound and beheaded prisoners. Below, two lions, representing boundaries, intertwine as Egypt is united. Cf. Lewis 1996 for the motif. Below, the king, as a bull (also 'ka': *k3*) gores an enemy by a broken city-wall.

Narmer Palette Verso   Narmer Palette Recto

after W. B. Emery, *Archaic Egypt*, 44-5

12(2) The Palermo Stone

This fragmentary record lists reigns of early kings, from the late predynastic to the fifth dynasty (*ca* 3500-2350 BCE). Each regnal year is given, with important events. See Kemp 1989, fig. 5 for discussion. The record becomes more complete as the scribe approaches his own time. The measurements are the height of the Nile at its greatest flood-level.

(King 5 of Dynasty 1: Den [Udimu])

————— [born of Me]ret-[Neith].

Year x + 1   Station in the temple of Saw in Heka. 3 cubits, 1 palm, 2 fingers.

Year x + 2   Smiting of the troglodytes. 4 cubits, 1 span.

Year x + 3   Appearance of the king of Upper Egypt. Appearance of the king of Lower Egypt. Sed Jubilee¹. 8 cubits, 3 fingers.

Year x + 4   Numbering of all people of the Nomes of the west, north, and east. 3 cubits, 1 span.

Year x + 5   Second appearance of the Feast of Djet². 5 cubits, 2 palms.

Year x + 6   Design of the House called 'Thrones of the gods'. Feast of Sokar. 5 cubits, 1 palm, 2 fingers.

Year x + 7   Stretching of the cord[3] for the House called 'Thrones of the gods' by the priest of the goddess Seshat. Great door. 4 cubits, 2 palms.

Year x ╎ 8

etc.

(*ARE* i 59-60, §§103-10, adapted)

1   An important feast of renewal of the king's power, performed at intervals.

2   Djet was Den's predecessor. As kings were gods, a festival is not surprising.

3   A ritual performed by the king at the foundation of a new temple

12(3) The Abjuration Stela of Tutankhamun

This stela comes from the Karnak temple of Amun. In it Tutankhamun ('The Living Image of Amun'; originally he was named Tutankhaten, 'The Living Image of Aten') is represented as restoring true religion after the disastrous interlude of the Aten cult under Akhenaten (Amenhotpe IV). The style is propagandistic, and describes a complete breakdown in traditional religion, together with political and social breakdown, which is undoubtedly greatly exaggerated, for purposes of political rhetoric.

When his Person appeared as king, the temples and the cities of the gods and goddesses, starting from Elephantine as far as the Delta marshes… were fallen into decay and their shrines were fallen into ruin, having become mere mounds overgrown with grass. Their sanctuaries were like something that had not come into being and their buildings were a footpath — for the land was in rack and ruin. The gods were ignoring this land: if an army [was] sent to Djahy to broaden the boundaries of Egypt, no success of theirs came to pass; if one prayed to a god, to ask something from him, he did not come at all; and if one beseeched any goddess in the way, she did not come at all.

(Murnane 1995, 213)

12(4) The Coronation of King Haremhab

Haremhab, last king of the 18th dynasty, seized the throne *ca* 1350 BCE. The text's main purpose was to justify his action, nicely illustrating the point that history is generally written by the victors. He vigorously implemented a full return to the cult of Amun, which endeared him to the Theban priesthood. Thus theological developments in the ancient world were frequently motivated by, or at least related to, political events. The language is that of a drama, in which all the actors, including the king, were divine. (Priests wore masks to play the parts of the gods in the temple rituals.) It remains, however, a historiographical document.

Then did Horus of Henes proceed amid rejoicing to Thebes, the city of the Lord of eternity[1], his son in his embrace, to Luxor[2], in order to induct him into the presence of Amun for the handing over to him of the office of king...

Then did the majesty of this god (= Amun) see Horus, lord of Henes, his son with him in the king's induction in order to give him his office and his throne...   Thereupon he betook himself to this noble the Hereditary Prince, Chieftain over the Two lands, Haremhab. Then did he proceed to the king's house when he had placed him before himself to the *Per Wer*[3] of his noble daughter the Great-[of-Magic[4], her arms] in welcoming attitude, and she embraced his beauty and established herself on his forehead[5]...

(Gardiner 1953, 15, adapted)

1   Sc. Amun, to whom the Karnak temple was dedicated.

2   At Luxor, about two miles south of Karnak, was the temple of the holy family, Amun, Mut and Khonsu. This was dedicated to the cult of the royal Ka (the king's placenta *ḥ nsw*, identified with Khonsu, *ḫnsw*). It is the placenta that is represented on the standard nearest Narmer on the recto of the palette, §12(1).

3   'The Great House' (*pr wr*) was the shrine of the White Crown at Luxor, used in coronation rites.

4   Sc. the White Crown, identified as the goddess Nekhbet.

5   That is, the crown was placed on the king's head.

II   Mesopotamian Historiography

12(5) The Assyrian King-list

Various king-lists have survived from Mesopotamia, Sumerian (*ANET* 265), Babylonian (*ANET* 271-4, *CS* i 461-2) and Assyrian, the present one (*CS* i 463-5 and *ANET* 564-6), and a Seleucid one (§12(15)).

They are comparable to the Palermo Stone (§12(2)) and other Egyptian king-lists (Turin Papyrus, and Karnak, Abydos, Manetho, etc.), to the Ugaritic king-list (Wyatt 1998a, 401-3 and references), and to various biblical genealogies. All signify primarily the authentic chain of authority from primordial times, when, in the words of the Sumerian king-list, 'kingship was lowered from heaven'. A genealogy was, by definition, 'canonical', and asserted a legal identity.

Tudiya, Adamu, Yangi, Suhlamu, Harharu, Mandaru, Imsu, Harsu, Didanu', Hanu, Zuabu, Nuabu, Abazu, Belu, Azaeah, Ushpia, Apiashal. Total: 17 kings who lived in tents.

Aminu was the son of Ilu-kabkabu, Ilu-kabkabu of Yakur-el, Yakur-el of Yakmeni, Yakmeni of Yakmesi, Yakmesi of Ilu-Mer, Ilu-Mer of Hayani, Hayani of Samani, Samani of Hale, Hale of Apiashal, Apiashal of Ushpia. Total: 10 kings who are their ancestors.

Sulili son of Aminu; Kikkiya; Akiya; Puzur-Ashur (I); Ahalim-ahhe; Ilu-shuma. Total: 6 kings [named? on] brick…

Erishu (I), son of Ilu-shuma, [whose x?] ruled for 30/40 years. Ikanu, son of Erishu, ruled for [x years]. Sargon (I), son of Ikunu, ruled for [x years]. Puzur-Ashur (II), son of Sargon, ruled for [x years]. Naram-Sin, son of Puzur-Ashur, ruled for [x]4 years. Erishu (II), son of Naram-Sin, ruled for [x] years.

Shamshi-Adad (I)[2], son of Ilu-kabkabu, went to Karduniash[3] [in the t]ime of Naram-Sin. In the eponymate of Ibni-Adad, [Shamshi]-Adad [went up] from Karduniash. He took Ekallatum where he stayed three years. In the reign of Atamar-Ishtar, Shamshi-Adad went up from Ekallatum. He ousted Erishu (II), son of Naram-Sin, from the throne and took it. He ruled for 33 years…

(Millard, CS i 463-4: The Assyrian King-list excerpts)

1   Didanu (variant Ditanu) also appears several times in Ugaritic texts, both as a minor god, and as ancestor of the Ugaritian royal line, as well as that of King Keret. The name may belong to a tribe, along with others in the list of tent-dwelling 'kings'. In Wyatt 1999, 864 n. 30, I wondered whether the Greek Titans might also owe something to him, a question asked independently by Annus 1999.

2   The first 'real' Assyrian king. The ancestors are drawn together for prestige. They ruled in Agade, in southern Mesopotamia.

3   The name given to Babylon during the Kassite period.

4   The list, reconstructed from five versions, continues down to Shalmaneser V (726-22).

12(6) The Destruction of Babylon i): Sennacherib's Account

The following four accounts all deal with the same event, the destruction of Babylon by Sennacherib of Assyria in 689 BCE, written from different perspectives.

Sennacherib describes the event in terms of his motivation (bent on conquest), and military tactics. The only allusions to the supernatural are the recapture of Assyrian divine images, and the fear of Ashur which fell on those who saw the outcome.

At the time of my second campaign, bent on conquest, I promptly marched against Babylon. I advanced rapidly, like a violent storm, and enveloped (the city) like a fog. I laid siege to it and took possession of it by means of mines and ladders. [I delivered] over to pillage its powerful [   ]. Great or small, I spared no one. I filled the squares of the city with their corpses. I led away to my country, still alive, Mušēzib-Marduk, the king of Babylon, with his entire family [and] his [nobility]. I distributed to [my troops], who took possession of them, the riches of that city, the silver, the gold, the precious stones, the furniture and the property. My troops seized them, and smashed the gods who dwelt there, taking away their wealth and their riches. After 418 years I removed from Babylon and returned to their sanctuaries Adad and Šala, the gods of Ekallāte, which Marduk-nādin-aḫḫe, king of Babylon, had seized and carried off to Babylon in the time of Tukulti-Ninurta (I), king of Assyria. I destroyed, laid waste and burned the city and its houses, from the foundations to the tops of the walls. I tore (from the ground) and threw into (the waters of the) Araḫtu the interior and the exterior fortifications, the temples of the gods, the ziggurat of bricks and earth, as much as it contained. I excavated canals in the middle of that city, flooded its terrain and caused even its foundations to disappear. I arranged it so that the water level of my destruction surpassed that left by the Flood. In order to make it impossible in any future time for the location of that city or the temples of the gods to be identifiable, I destroyed it in the waters and annihilated it, (leaving the place) as a land under water.

After I had brought Babylon to ruin, smashed its gods, exterminated its population with steel, so that the very soil of that city could be carried away, I took away its soil and had it thrown into the Euphrates, and (then) into the sea. Its rubbish drifted as far as Dilmun. The Dilmunians saw it, and fear mingled with the respect inspired by the god Aššur seized them. They brought their gifts (...). I removed the debris of Babylon and heaped it up in (the) Temple of the Feast of the New Year in Aššur...

(after Glassner 1993, 42-3)

12(7) The Destruction of Babylon ii): Esarhaddon's Account

Writing some years later, in the context of his reconstruction of Babylon, Esarhaddon of Assyria gave a theological explanation of events: the citizens had sinned by neglecting the gods, lying, and blasphemously stealing temple treasures to pay off the Elamites. Thus divine wrath was visited on Babylon.

Formerly, in the reign of a former king, there were evil predictions in Sumer and Akkad. The populations dwelling there cried out to one another (saying) 'Yes!' (but meaning) 'No!' Thus they lied. They neglected the worship of the gods [ ] the goddesses [ ] and [ ] they laid hands on the treasure of Esagila, the palace of the gods, a place into which no one enters; and in payment (for its assistance), they gave away (its) silver, gold (and) precious stones to Elam. Filled with wrath and thinking evil thoughts, Marduk, the Enlil of the gods, decided on the destruction of the country and the extinction of (its) inhabitants. The Araḫtu, an abundant watercourse, (set in motion) in response to the flood, began to sweep downstream in a torrent unleashed, a violent deluge, a powerful inundation. It swept over the city, its dwellings and sacred places, and reduced them to rubble. The gods and goddesses living there flew away like birds, and rose into the skies. The population living there fled to other places and sought refuge in an [unknown] land. Having inscribed [on the tablet of destinies] seventy years as the duration of its abandonment, Marduk took pity, his heart being appeased and reversed the numbers, deciding that it should be reoccupied after eleven years"[1].

(after Glassner 1993, 43-4)

1   The number 70 was written ⟨cuneiform⟩; 11 as ⟨cuneiform⟩. For an explanation of this see Saggs 1988, 117.

12(8) The Destruction of Babylon iii): Esarhaddon's Second Account

Now a purely theological account is given. Marduk punishes his people, and the other gods (all subordinates) cower in fear at his anger. When it is appeased, he restores the city.

'Before my time, the great lord Marduk, was wroth, livid and filled with anger; with rage in his heart and his spirit incandescent, he lost his temper with Esagila and Babylon. Left fallow, they turned to desert. The gods and goddesses, in fear and trembling, abandoned their shrines and rose into the skies. The populations dwelling there, scattered among a strange people, went into, slavery. (...) When the great lord Marduk, his heart appeased and his spirit calmed, had become reconciled with Esagila and Babylon which he had punished (...)'

(after Glassner 1993, 44)

12(9) The Destruction of Babylon iv): From the Babylonian Chronicle

In this account the seriousness of the defeat of Babylon is played down from a Babylonian perspective.

On the first day of the month Kislev the city was captured. Mushezib-Marduk was taken prisoner and transported to Assyria. For four years Mushezib-Marduk ruled Babylon.

(Kuhrt 1995 ii 585)

III   West Semitic Historiography, from Moab and Israel

The setting together under this rubric of Moabite and Israelite material is deliberate. Most biblical scholars would insist on the quite distinctive qualities of Israelite material. Such a position is tenable, however, only from a confessional perspective. From the perspectives of genre, and of the general conception of the historical process and the nature of divine involvement in human events, they are not seriously to be distinguished. (As they are not, indeed, in principle, from Mesopotamian material. See Albrektson 1967.)

12(10) **The Moabite Stone**

This inscription was found in (Trans)Jordan in 1868, and describes events in *ca* 830 BCE, when Moab and Israel were at war. It is a votive stela, in the form of an autobiography of Mesha.

I am Mesha, son of Chemosh-[   ], king of Moab, the Dibonite... who made this high place for Chemosh in Qarhoh [   ] because he saved me from all the kings and caused me to triumph over all my adversaries. As for Omri, king of Israel, he humbled Moab many years, for Chemosh was angry with his land[1]. And his son[2] followed him, and he also said, 'I will humble Moab.' In my time he spoke (thus), but I have triumphed over him and over his house, while Israel has perished for ever!...

Now the men of Gad had always dwelt in the land of Ataroth, and the king of Israel had built Ataroth for them; but I fought against the town and took it and slew all the people of the town as satiation for Chemosh and Moab. And I brought back from there Ariel, its chieftain, dragging him before Chemosh in Kerioth, and I settled there men of Sharon and... Maharith. And Chemosh said to me, 'Go, take Nebo from Israel!'[3] So I went by night and fought against it from the break of dawn until noon, taking it and slaying all, seven thousand men, boys, women, girls and maid-servants, for I had devoted them to destruction[4] for the god Ashtar-Chemosh. And I took from there the [   ] of Yahweh, dragging them before Chemosh...

(*ANET* 320: Stela of Mesha)

1   The correlation between military defeat and divine anger is commonplace in the ancient world.

2   Ahab.

3   The words would have been given in an oracle.

4   This is the institution of *ḥerem*, 'devotion' (lit. 'setting apart'). It involves the complete destruction of the enemy: genocide with divine sanction.

12(11) **Israelite Genealogy**

The so-called historical books of the Hebrew Bible are often held up as the paradigm of ancient historiography, with an emphasis on its supposed linearity, its large-scale perspective, and its radical distinctiveness (particularly on the moral plane). Most of these claims are special pleading; the style and ethics of biblical accounts are widely paralleled in other ancient writings; and like them, it is also subject to a variety of ideological presuppositions. When eschatology enters the scene, its cyclicity is as pronounced as anything claimed for other traditions. The following selection illustrates material comparable to the passages above.

The 'table of nations' in *Genesis* contains considerable numbers of genealogies. Their strictly historical value is probably not great, but they are examples of the widespread practice of giving an account of perceived relationships, social, political and geographical, through the medium of personalities. In the present passage the individuals are the eponyms of various peoples on the fringe of the purview of Israel and Judah. They represent the imagined entire population of the world, following the catastrophe of the flood (§4(8)), and regarded as descendants of Noah. Where known equivalents can be given with reasonable confidence they are added in brackets. In the overall historiographical enterprise of biblical tradition, the point is the singling out of Shem, from whom the patriarchs and then the tribal eponyms of Israel descended. It is therefore the framework for the doctrine of election.

Now this is the genealogy of Noah's sons, Shem (Semites), Ham (Africans) and Japheth (Indo-Europeans), to whom sons were born after the flood.

Japheth's sons: Gomer (Cimmerians), Magog (Scythians), the Medes, Javan (Ionian Greeks), Tubal, Meshech, Tiras. And Gomer's sons: Ashkenaz, Riphath, Togarmah. Javan's sons: Elisha (Cyprus), Tarshish (Sardinia or Spain), the Kittim (Greeks), the Dodanites (Danaan Greeks or Rhodians). From these were peopled all the islands of the nations <. These were Japheth's sons,> according to their countries and each of their languages, their tribes and their nations.

Now the sons of Ham: Cush (Ethiopia), and Misraim (Egypt), and Put (Libya), and Canaan (Phoenicia). Cush's sons: Saba (Sabaean Arabs? or Meroe?), and Havilah (Gulf peoples), and Sabtah (Hadramaut?), and Raamah (also South Arabia), and Sabteca. Raamah's sons: Sheba (Somalia?), Dedan… Now Canaan fathered Sidon (on the Phoenician coast) his first-born and Heth (Hittites), and the Jebusites (Jerusalem), and the Amorites[1] and the Girgashites, and the Hivites (Hurrians) and the Arkites and the Sinites, and the Arvadites (Arwad the island off the Syrian coast?) and the Zemarites, and the Hamathites (central Syria)…

(Genesis 10:1-18, excerpts)

1   The Amorites (Akkadian *Amurru*, Sumerian MAR.TU, 'westerners') appear in early Mesopotamian documents as troublesome interlopers, who later constitute the Semitic-speaking peoples of the region. Mari ('West-(town)') was an important state in northwest Mesopotamia; Amurru appears as Ugarit's southern neighbour in the Late Bronze (*ca* 1500-1200 BCE), while the Amorites mentioned in the Hebrew Bible at times appear to be synonymous with the 'Canaanites' (a similarly elusive term), and the name comes to be a pejorative term for foreigners (van Seters 1972).

12(12) **Israel against Moab**

This belongs to a large historiographical work probably completed within or shortly after the exile (early sixth century BCE). The source goes back considerably earlier. Cf. §12(7). How far a synthetic account is to be constructed out of the two documents is uncertain.

Now Mesha king of Moab was a sheep-breeder[1], and supplied the king of Israel with 100,000 lambs and and 100,000 ram-fleeces (as tribute). But when Ahab died, the king of Moab rebelled against the king of Israel... Then they set out, the king of Israel and the king of Judah, and the king of Edom...

> (The army ends up in the desert with no water. On Elisha's intervention, water is miraculously supplied[2]. The country turns into a lake. Mesha musters his troops...)

When they shouldered arms in the morning, the sun was shining on the water, and the Moabites saw the water in front of them as red as blood. Then they said, 'This is blood! The kings must have fought among themselves and killed each other. So now for the spoils, Moab!' But when they reached the camp of Israel, the Israelites arose and attacked Moab. And they fled before them, and they (the Israelites) advanced and cut them to pieces. And they sacked the cities, and everyone threw rocks into the best farmland, blocked up all the wells and felled all the sound trees[3]... When the king of Moab saw that the battle had gone against him, he took seven hundred swordsmen, to break out to the king of Aram[4], but were unsuccessful. Then he took his eldest son, who was due to succeed him, and offered him up as a holocaust[5] on the (city-) wall. Then there was great anger against Israel, and they retreated, and returned to their country.

(2 Kings 3:4-27 excerpts)

1   Moabite *nqd* = Hebrew *nōqēd*. The term probably refers to the overseer of a temple herd. Cf. Amos and Ilimilku of Ugarit.

2   More correctly, perhaps, a miraculous gloss is put on an account of a common-sense solution to the problem, digging trenches to attract ground-water, and a convenient flash-flood from Edom. Accounts of miracles and divine interventions in ancient historiography belong not to the realm of sober history, but to the half-mythical world which characterizes all ancient Near Eastern material, often giving a theological rationale to natural events.

3   Note the general ecological depredation: a scorched earth policy. The trees are described as *ṭôb*, literally 'good'. This probably means that they were economically useful, such as fruit and nut trees. Their treatment is hardly in the spirit of *Deuteronomy* 20:19-20!

4   The text reads Edom, but this is one of the attacking states. Edom (אדם) and Aram (ארם) are written virtually identically in Hebrew, and identically in some forms of palaeo-Hebrew. Cf. §§11(29) n. 1.

5   The scope of child-sacrifice is disputed. Evidence from Carthage, a Phoenician colony, is at best uncertain. Evidence from Ugarit relies on one disputed reading (Wyatt 1998a, 422 n. 43). We are left with the present case,

and Israelite evidence: Jephthah's daughter, *Judges* 11:29-40 (cf. §11(23)); Ahaz's son, *2 Kings* 16:3; and general condemnations, *Jeremiah* 7:31, *Ezekiel* 20:25, 31, and *Isaiah* 57:5-6. Cf. also the curious myth of Kronos (= El) and his son Jedud, in which the 'beloved son' (*yedûd*) is sacrificed after being dressed in royal regalia, a tradition to be linked to the accounts of the passion of Jesus and perhaps *Genesis* 22 (§8(9)) (Eusebius, *Praeparatio Evangelica* 1.10.44, Beyerlin 1978, 267).

12(13) David's Census

The two accounts of the same episode that follows illustrate changing theological perspectives. Just the introductions are given. In the first, Yahweh is the author of all, good and evil. In the second, Yahweh is the author of good, but evil is laid at the door of the divine prosecutor (*haśśāṭān*) the prototype of Satan. Cf. §11(11). When David has completed the census, he is told that he will be punished for impiety (!), and is given a choice of punishments. On the punishments offered to him, and their ideological reference, see Wyatt 1990d.

a)   The Deuteronomistic Account

Again the anger of Yahweh burnt against Israel. And he incited David against them. 'Go on,' he said, 'take a census of Israel and Judah...

(*2 Samuel* 24:1)

b)   The Chronicler's Account

Now Satan[1] stood up against Israel[2], and incited[3] David to take a census of Israel.

(*1 Chronicles* 21:1)

1   The term *śāṭān* has no article here, and so is to be taken as a name. Cf. n. 2.

2   The image is probably that of the divine council, where Satan is a prosecutor, whose function is to accuse people of sin. Cf, the spirit in §11(11) and in *Job* 1-2, where he has developed an unhealthy pleasure in his work. In the latter passage, *śāṭān* has the article (*haśśāṭān*), and so retains the original meaning 'opponent'.

3   The same verb (√*nāsâ*) is used as in §a, but it has now taken on the more sinister sense of 'tempt'. There is an obvious word-play between this verb and the term *śāṭān*.

IV   The Past and the Future

One of the hallmarks of true historiography, over against mere chronicle or annal, has long been regarded as its openness to the future. In modern terms this may be described in terms of recognizable causality, where the recognition that this event was the outcome of that cause (understood as a direct causative foundation of what followed), and a consequent element of predictability (that if *a*, *b* and *c* happen in history, then we may expect outcomes *x*, *y* and *z*) is part of the agenda. We see just such thinking in economic forecasting, with the language of 'economic cycles' and so forth. The germs of this lie in the past. The beginnings of such thinking are already to be found in ancient writing.

12(14) From Babylonian Annals i): An Astronomical Diary

The following looks as though it merely deals in trivia. But the details are obviously of general interest in that matters of public health and economics could have far-reaching effects (they seem to dominate contemporary British politics!). Much modern historiography no longer deals with the *grandes gestes* of kings, but with economic matters such as the price of gold and the availability of copper, and their effect on the wider scene. Here all sorts of details are listed, because in the broader context they provided raw data for the interpretation of astronomical observations. If such and such a planetary or stellar feature was contemporaneous with any event listed, then its recurrence in the night sky could be used to predict the recurrence of a similar feature on earth. Nor were these mechanical and uncritical. The predictions of prophetic texts (e.g. Drews 1975, 49) often took the form of alternatives, alternative interpretations, or a choice of responses, just as we see in §§11(35, 41). That is, there is evidence of a serious concern with cause and effect (remembering that every sign in heaven was a 'heavenly sign', that is, a sign from the gods).

... Adar. In that month the general assembled the royal army which was in Akkad from its head to its... and in Nisan marched to Eber-nari[1] to assist the king.

In that year they paid current prices in Babylon and the cities in copper coins of Greece. In that year there was much scabies in the country.

In the 37th year, Antiochus and Seleucus. In the month of Adar on the ninth the governor of Akkad and the town magistrates of the king, who went to Sapardu in the 36th year to the king, returned to Seleucia, the royal city on the Tigris...

(Drews 1975, 46: quotation from Smith 1924)

1   'Beyond the river', or 'Trans-Euphrates', an Akkadian term denoting Syria to the west of the Euphrates. Cf. §12(16b) n. 1.

12(15) From Babylonian Annals ii): a Seleucid King-list

For earlier king-lists and genealogies see §§12(2, 5 and 11). The present Seleucid text, like the Palermo Stone (§12(2)), mentions events in the reigns of various kings. These provided data for prediction purposes as discussed in §12(13) introduction above.

[   ] Alexander the Great [   ]

Philip, the brother of Alexander, [did   ]

For [x] years there was no king in the country. Antigonus, the commander of the army, was [   ].

Alexander the son of Alexander (was reckoned as king) for six years.

Year 7 is the first of year (of Seleucus). Seleucus (I, Nicator) became king; he reigned for 25 years.

Year 31, month Elulu: King Seleucus (I) was killed in the West.

Year 32: Antiochus (I, Soter), son of Seleucus (I) became king. He ruled for 20 years.

Year 51, month Aiaru, 16th (day): Antiochus (I), the great king, died.

Year 52: Antiochus (II, Theos), son of Antiochus (I), became king. He ruled for 15 years.

Year 66, month Abu: the following (rumour) was he[ard] in Babylon: Antiochus (II) the great king [has died]…

(*ANET* 567)

12(16) From the Deuteronomic History

The product of its own complex compositional and redactional history, still much debated, the so-called '*Deuteronomistic History*' contains *Joshua*, *Judges*, *1* and *2 Samuel*, and *1* and *2 Kings*. The book of *Deuteronomy* serves, if not as actual prologue, then at least as theoretical basis for its treatment of historical events. Many events in the history are presented as the fulfilment of prophecies uttered previously in the narrative. In §12(7) a list is given. The present § gives one representative example of prophecy and fulfilment.

a)   Prophecy

Then Yahweh will raise up for himself a king over Israel, who will annihilate the dynasty of Jeroboam[1]… Then Yahweh will strike Israel as a reed is shaken in the sea, and uproot Israel from this fertile land which he gave to their forefathers, and will scatter them beyond the river[2], because they made their sacred poles[3], thus provoking Yahweh to anger.

(*1 Kings* 14:14-6)

1   Jeroboam had himself been proclaimed by an oracle of Yahweh, in *1 Kings* 11:26-40.

2   Hebrew *mē ʿēber lannāhār*, the equivalent of Akkadian *eber nari* above (§12(13) n. 1). The obvious meaning of this would be Syria west of the Euphrates, which was under Assyrian control. The fulfilment (passage b)) takes it to refer to territories *east* of the Euphrates.

3   See §6(8). The term used here, *ʾašērîm*, has become masculine.

b)   Fulfilment

This describes events in about 721 BCE. Only the leading citizens, the intelligentsia and officials, would be deported, and similar deportees from other Assyrian campaigns settled in Samaria in their place.

In the ninth year of Hoshea (king of Israel) the king of Assyria captured Samaria and deported Israel to Assyria, settling them in Halah on the Khabur, a river of Gozan[1], and in the cities of the Medes[2]. And this happened because the Israelites had sinned against Yahweh their god, who had brought them up out of the land of Egypt, from under the power of Pharaoh king of Egypt, and feared other gods.

(*2 Kings* 17:6-7)

1   The Khabur is a tributary of the Euphrates in eastern Syria, coming from the north.

2   The Medes lived in western Iran, presumably an area under Assyrian control.

12(17) The Programme

Here is a complete list of such related passages in the *Deuteronomistic History* (from Wyatt 1996b, 274 n. 107), each reference in parentheses being the fulfilment of the preceding oracle, with some duplicating others:

Deuteronomy 1:35 (1:46, 2:7, 14); 4:25-8 (*2 Kings* 24 and 25); 4:29-30 (*2 Kings* 25:27-30); 8:19-20 (*2 Kings* 24 and 25); 11:22-5 (*Joshua* 1-11); 18:18 (*passim*: summary of all oracles cited later); 28:7-14 (*Joshua* 1-11); 28:20-68 (*2 Kings* 24 and 25); 29:17-27 (*2 Kings* 24 and 25); 30:1-10 (*2 Kings* 25:27-30);

Joshua 6:26 (*1 Kings* 16:34);

Judges 4:9 (*Judges* 4:21, 5:26);

1 Samuel 2:31-4, 3:12-4 (*1 Samuel* 4:11, 18); 2:35-6 (*2 Samuel* 8:17, *1 Kings* 1:28-40, 2:26-7);

2 Samuel 7:9-12 (*1 Kings* 8:24-5); 7:13 (*1 Kings* 6:1-38, 8:17-21); 12:10-2 (*passim* in *2 Samuel* 13-30); 12:14 (*2 Samuel* 12:18);

1 Kings 8:46-51 (*2 Kings* 24 and 25, 25:27-30); 11:29-39 (*1 Kings* 12:20); 13:1-3 (*2 Kings* 23:16 — three hundred years later!); 14:6-11 (*1 Kings* 15:29); 14:12 (*1 Kings* 14:17-8); 14:14 (*1 Kings* 15:27-30); 14:14-6 (*2 Kings* 17:6); 16:1-4 (*1 Kings* 16:8-12); 17:1 (*1 Kings* 17:7, 18:2); 19:15-8 (*2 Kings* 8:9-15, 9:3-6); 20:13 (*1 Kings* 20:21); 20:22 (*1 Kings* 20:25-26); 20:28 (*1 Kings* 20:29-30); 20:35-6 (*1 Kings* 20:36); 20:38-42 (*1 Kings* 22:40, cf. 21:27-9); 21:21-2 (*1 Kings* 22:40); 21:23 (*2 Kings* 9:33-7); 21:24 (*2 Kings* 9:22, 10:1-17); 22:17 (*1 Kings* 22:29-38);

2 Kings 1:4, 6 (*2 Kings* 1:17); 3:17-9 (*2 Kings* 3:20, 24-7); 4:16 (4:17); 4:43 (4:44); 5:27 (5:27); 7:1-2 (7:16-20); 8:9-13 (8:14-5, 13:3, 22); 9:6-10 (9:22-9, 10:1-17, 9:33-7); 17:13-8, 23 (cf. 18:12); 19:6-7 (19:35-7); 19:20-34 (19:35-7); 20:1-6 (20:7); 20:8-10 (20:11); 20:16-8 (24 and 25); 21:10-5 (24 and 25); 22:16-20 (24 and 25; note 23:29-30!).

There is no formal statement of the programme in the *Deuteronomistic History* itself. The nearest we get to this is the summary of the demise of Israel, the northern kingdom, *ca* 721 BCE, when it was reorganized into an Assyrian province. A remarkable interpolation into the book of *Amos* does provide the programme in the briefest manner. Both passages are cited.

a)   The End of Israel

The force of this passage becomes clear when it is compared with §12(16b) above. It repeats the general historical and theological theme, but now emphasizes its fulfilment of all the prophetic oracles uttered in the kingdom's previous history.

Yahweh thrust Israel away from before his face[1], exactly as he had said through all his servants the prophets, and he deported Israel from its own territory to Assyria, right down to today[2].

(*2 Kings* 17:23)

1   The point of the phrase is the loss of communication between deity and his people. Cf. §6(11) n. 4.

2   That is, the time of writing, probably in the sixth or fifth century BCE.

b)   The Prophet's Duty and the Apocalyptic Scheme

This is a powerful poem about the compulsion by which the prophet is constrained. In vv. 3-6 (lines 1-14) a series of questions, each inviting the obvious answer 'No!' is asked, skilfully moving in vv. 5-6 (ll. 11-4) to the political world. In v. 8 (lines 17-20) the same unfolding works with two perfect forms ('past tense'), which demand a positive response, simply on the rhetorical force of the poem, from the prophet. He has no choice but to declare the word of Yahweh.

Into this has been thrust a small prose statement, verse 7, lines 15-6, which subverts the poem into an apocalyptic programme. All prophecy is to be seen, the writer appears to be saying, in terms of strict prediction concerning the future. All that Yahweh does (that is, everything involving Israel's history, and then the wider world history) he has revealed to his servants. It is now a matter of reading through the oracles to find what his plans are for the immediate future. The final editors of the *Deuteronomic History* have done just that in all the passages listed above. Thus the openness of history is transformed into a closed, logical world, in which *everything* is predicted. Absolutism in high places, an uncomfortable memory for those who have lived in the twentieth century world!

1   Do two men go walking together
      … unless they have planned to do so?
    Does the lion roar in the forest
      before he has captured his prey?
5   Does the lion-cub growl in his lair
      unless he has captured something?
    Does the bird fall into the snare on the ground
      if no trap has been set for it?
    Does the snare leap up from the ground
10   unless it has caught something?
    Or does the ram's horn sound in the city
      without the population becoming afraid?
    Or does evil befall a city
      if Yahweh has not done it?

15 For the lord Yahweh does not do a thing unless he
      has revealed his plan to his servants the prophets.
  The lion has roared!
    Who is not afraid?
  Lord Yahweh speaks!
20   Who can refuse to prophesy?

                                (*Amos* 3:3-8)

By way of bringing this varied material together, into an ordered whole, two further elements deserve brief consideration.

I   The Extent of Time and the Concept of World Ages

Firstly, we have seen eschatology emerging in various contexts. At times this appears to have been a council of despair, a radical response to a desperate situation, as though nothing further was to be done with the present corrupt world. It is certainly arguable that any kind of belief in *post-mortem* felicity, a serious case of 'jam tomorrow', was a means of committing a kind of spiritual or moral suicide. Rather the realism of the gloom of older beliefs! But religion, like every other human system, develops its own, often unforeseen, logic, and there was a general drift, which is sometimes traced back to the so-called 'axial age' of the sixth century BCE, towards the reification of better imagined futures, either this-worldly or other-worldly. Imagined worlds became seen as possible worlds, then as ideal worlds, and finally as 'real' worlds. One area of speculation in which this operated on the grand scale was that of sidereal time. The ancient world was awash with grand theories about the extent of time, and invariably it found expression in an overall sense of its cyclicity. Biblical and post-biblical conceptions were no exception.

Let us begin by considering some cosmic theories. The first is the Hindu conception, necessarily simplified to bring it within reasonable compass. I beg indulgence of my readers for another apparent departure at a tangent (the first being §1(9) above). It will shortly become apparent that India and the ancient Near East were in touch not only commercially and diplomatically, but intellectually too.

Historical time in Indian thought is constructed according to a proportionate form, in which from creation, the gradually increasing corruption leads to a decline from the first, perfect age, into a fourth, almost wholly corrupt age, which will eventually come to a cataclysmic end. The system may be set out as follows:

YUGA	MEANING	PROPORTION		TIME SPAN IN YEARS
Kṛta	'perfect'	4	lasting	1,728,000 years
Treta	'three parts'	3	lasting	1,296,000 years
Davāpara	'two part'	2	lasting	864,000 years
Kali	'strife'	1	lasting	432,000 years

the four *yugas* constituting 1 *Mahāyuga*

('great *yuga*')			lasting	4,320,000 years

The key element here is the figure of 432 and its multiples. We shall revert to this. But since the Hindu perception is fascinating in its own right, let us give a brief exposition of the overall system.

Except in the *Viṣṇu Purāṇa* 6.1, which has one, there is no *Pralaya* ('dissolution') at this point in other expositions of the system. We shall meet such a period below.

The following sums presuppose a day and a night, 360 such periods making up a year, and a divine lifetime of a hundred years, of Brahmā, the creator god, and the first person of the Hindu Trimurti (the triad Brahmā-Viṣṇu-Śiva). For every day of his life, there is also a night, which is a cosmic dissolution (*Pralaya*) of the same length (*Viṣṇu Purāṇa* 6.3, which takes no account of 6.1):

1,000 *Mahāyugas* constitute 1 *Kalpa*, one day in the life of Brahmā,	4,320,000,000 years
one night in the life of Brahmā,	4,320,000,000 years
Total length of Kalpa (Day + Night)	8,640,000,000 years
one year in the life of Brahmā,	3,110,400,000,000 years
one whole life of Brahmā (*Mahākalpa*),	311,040,000,000,000 years
followed by a Pralaya of equal length,	311,040,000,000,000 years
the entire cycle totalling	622,080,000,000,000 years

We need not pursue this; suffice to say that various texts fit this single lifetime of a god into ever-grander schemes[1]. The ultimate result is of

---

[1]   Cf. for instance the charming story of the parade of ants, in which the overweening Indra is put in his place on being told that every member of a huge column of ants passing through his palace had once been Indra (and he a god of no importance beside Brahmā!). See Zimmer 1962, 3-11. The systematization of the theory developed throughout the purāṇic literature, but

staggering proportions. All the *textual* evidence for the Hindu materials is mediaeval, however, though it undoubtedly preserves traditions (the meaning of the term *purāṇa*) already long in the shaping.

This is time-theory run riot. In the west, nothing quite so elaborate happened, but speculation was by no means absent. Let us note, by means of returning to our context, the time-span covered in the biblical narrative from creation to the flood.

Time and the Biblical Patriarchs

	PATRIARCH	REFERENCE	AGE AT FATHERING	AGE AT DEATH
1	Adam	*Genesis* 5:3-5	130	930
2	Seth	*Genesis* 5:6-8	105	912
3	Enosh	*Genesis* 5:9-11	90	905
4	Kenan	*Genesis* 5:12-14	70	910
5	Mahalalel	*Genesis* 5:15-17	65	895
6	Jared	*Genesis* 5:18-20	162	962
7	Enoch	*Genesis* 5:21-24	65	365
8	Methuselah	*Genesis* 5:25-27	187	969
9	Lamech	*Genesis* 5:28-31	182	777
10	Noah	*Genesis* 5:32	500	950
	Period to Flood	*Genesis* 7:6	(100	years from birth to flood)
	TOTAL	Creation to Flood		1,656 years

This is the biblical 'Priestly genealogy' of descendants from Adam through Seth, with figures according to the Hebrew text; Samaritan and Greek texts give 1,307 and 2,242 years respectively for the same total of ten generations. Cf. the 'Yahwist genealogy' of *Genesis* 4:17-22, with different descendants of Adam through Cain. This tradition knew no flood story, and had Yabal, Yubal and Tubal-Cain, metalworking and musical culture-heroes, the equivalents of Noah as the culture-hero who introduced the vine. The different enumerations betray a variety of attempts to fit

---

the classical statements are found in the *Laws of Manu* and the *Mahābhārata* (Bühler 1886, lxxxiii), as discussed by van der Waerden 1977-8, 361-4.

chronology into some grandiose scheme or other, with opinions apparently varying on the precise computations to be followed.[2]

But let us pursue the example given above. 1,656 years is 86,400 weeks (1,656 × 52 weeks), and this sum is one fifth of 432,000. (These figures are not strictly accurate, but the ancients had no decimal places.) This is probably no accident. The point is that there does appear to be a similarity of thought here, various ancient chronographers evidently playing about with cosmological figures with which they were acquainted. The Hebrew writer has evidently interpreted 5 years of the Babylonian chronology of Berossus as 1 week. This implies, of course, that Babylonian thinking has had some significant input. Weeks frequently appear in Hebrew thought as conventional 'cosmic periods', as in *Jubilees*.

Strikingly, one Hebrew theory of world time finding expression in *4 Ezra* 9:38-47, 10:45-6, Josephus *Antiquities* viii 61-2, x 147-8 and *Assumption of Moses* 1:2, 10:12, set the anti-diluvian and post-diluvian periods in a proportion of 4 : 1 (1,656 : 414 years), the same proportion as between the first and fourth *yugas* of Hindu thought above, thus confirming a connection, however remote, between the two systems.

This is also to be compared to the Babylonian system, in so far as it can be discerned in Berossus, a priest at the Marduk temple in Babylon during the Seleucid period, who moved to the Aegean island of Cos[3]. He composed a now lost work, the *Chaldaica*, which argued that a new world era (sc. section of time within a larger construct) had begun with the coming of Alexander the Great, (who died in Babylon in 323 BCE. There were according to Berossus ten kings before the flood (the same number as the ten patriarchs of *Genesis*), the length of whose reigns totalled 84,000 years. Another calculation (by Berossus) gave the time as 432,000 years, while the Sumerian king-list (dating from the 19th to the 17th centuries BCE) had eight antediluvian kings, and gave 241,200 (wrongly calculated as

---

[2]   See Hughes 1990 for a thorough survey of biblical chronological schemes and their mutual contradictions.

[3]   Many scholars distinguish the two, the islander being 'Pseudo-Berossus'. Drews 1975, 50-2, insisted on the identity of the two.

241,000) years[4]. The period of time from the flood to the capture of Babylon by Cyrus was computed at 36,000 years[5]. The match with the biblical scheme is not perfect. And it is again evident of a number of minds at work, all using different starting points for their calculations.

Jeremias (1908, 183) cited the following passage from Seneca (*Fragments of Greek History* ii 50):

> Beros[s]us [using a slightly different arithmetic] says that everything takes place according to the course of the planets, and he maintains this so confidently that he determines the times for the conflagration of the world and for the flood. He asserts that the world will burn when all the planets which now move in different courses come together in the Crab, so that they all stand in a straight line in the same sign, and that the future flood will take place when the same conjunction occurs in Capricorn. For the former is the constellation of the summer solstice, the latter of the winter solstice; they are the decisive signs of the zodiac, because the turning-points of the year lie in them.

This leads us to suppose that the Hindu system elaborated the simpler western one, adding the intermediate *yugas*. But Hinduism would scarcely have borrowed from biblical thought, and the common denominator appears to be Babylon, as represented by Berossus. Drews (1975, 51) quoted the same passage from Seneca, but was taken to task by Lambert (1976, 172-3), for inferring from it that Berossus, as distinct from Seneca, had believed in a doctrine of world-cycles. 'So far as the present writer has been able to ascertain,' he wrote, 'no cuneiform text expresses any such idea.' The same assessment had already been offered by Brandon (1965, 84). But so far as the Great Year (as distinct from a continuing series) the Babylonian input is clear. But Lambert's caution should warn us that the Great Year and successive Great Years are not necessarily the same, and nor does one necessarily imply the other.

The 360 days of a year of Brahmā corresponds to a 360-day year in Babylonia, which was also the basis of the Indian calendar, and the Egyptian calendar, to which five epagomenal days were added, to match (slightly inaccurately) the real solar year. The Babylonian week consisted of five days, so that 72 weeks ($72 \times 5 = 360$) made a complete year. The fact that 360 corresponded to the number of degrees in a circle in

---

[4]   Van der Waerden 1977-8, 360-1, cites several rival computations.

[5]   Note that 36,000 × 360 days gives a figure of 12,960,000 (a figure M. L. West 1971, 162 attributes to Plato in the *Republic*), which is 2,000 × 25,920.

Babylonian mathematics (from which the modern system is derived) was not lost on them, for nothing in nature happened by chance: everything was a sign from heaven to those with eyes to see. Indeed, if we look at the way in which the units of time of a day were calculated in Babylon, we find that it is a microcosm. We can present it in terms of time and space, the latter being degrees of a circle.

The smallest unit of time was a barleycorn, $1/72$ degree.

BARLEYCORNS		TIME	SPACE
18	=	1 min.	
72	=	4 mins	$1°$
432	=	24 mins	$6°$
2,160	=	2 hrs	$30°$
4,320	=	4 hrs	$60°$
25,920	=	24 hrs	$360°$

The year is the same principle on a larger scale, and of course this could lead to the same arithmetical form being imposed on yet larger units of time, with the following result. By a series of computations with these figures, we arrive at the following scheme. It should be noted that the figure of 432 and multiples applies throughout this material. India is hardly likely to be the sources, since its arithmetic goes right off the scale. The figure of 25,920 occurring here is not only more reasonable in principle (it is not designed to numb the mind, which is perhaps a motive in the Indian context), but actually corresponds roughly to the period taken for the entire cycle of the zodiac.

72 years × 360° (sc. a full circle of the zodiac)
= 25,920 years = 1 Great Year

Given Lambert's strictures above, we should be cautious about attributing a cyclical view to Babylonian thought, and thus the source of the specific doctrine of cycles over and above the Great Year remains uncertain. A feature of Mesopotamian historical thinking which is found in the *Sumerian king-list*, according to Glassner 1993, 84-7, was an elliptical process he described as 'sinusoidal'. It amounts to a species of 'double helix', in which the rise and fall of dynasties alternated in a striking pattern. This can only have been a deliberate systematization by the author(s), but did not imply cycles. It was a one-way, quasi-linear conception. So the view of G. E. Wright (see *1.8.1 n. 1) that everyone but the Israelites thought in cyclical terms, is doubly nonsensical.

As for the origin of the cyclical view, that Great Years succeeded one another *ad infinitum*, Brandon (1965, 96), assessing it as 'rather of the nature of an intellectual tour de force that doubtlessly intrigued those of a speculative turn of mind', while not making a specific commitment, appears to have associated it primarily with the Greek 'Orpheo-Platonic tradition'. M. L. West (1971, 155-6, 161-2) considered the first hard evidence to be that of Plato's *Timaeus* (39d, 22 c-d), while seeing Heraclitus and Pythagoras lurking in the background.

II Historical Process

Secondly, most of the foregoing material belongs within the ancient Near Eastern religious environment, though in some instances belonging to those traditions which visibly survived, to develop into the modern forms of Judaism and Christianity.

An obvious question to be asked is why did this (Christian and Jewish) material survive and even flourish, while other traditions, often obviously cognate, appear to have died completely, until recovered, but as dead artifacts, through the work of archaeology and decipherment. The kind of superficial answer that is sometimes given, and even by academic writers, who ought to know better, is that the ancient imperial systems of religion typified by Babylonia, Assyria, Anatolia and Egypt were somehow theologically, morally or spiritually bankrupt. They were simply outflanked by the more perceptive (or even 'true') systems we know today.

This answer will not do. If Judaism and Christianity (and to some extent Islam) do belong within a continuum of experience and intellection that can be traced back some five thousand years to the origins of writing, then it is arguable that it was the same impulses and imperatives which drove both. We must look to larger historical forces, rather than to the spiritual content of religious systems, to form an adequate judgment. (It is in any case rather premature to make any long-term historical judgments: our own era hardly bears much examination!)

I shall discuss one passage from Jonas (1963, 11-7), which provides a brilliant insight into the matter of historical flow and religious development. It makes what I think is a valid historical judgment on the great powers of the ancient Near East, with powerful explanatory force; that is, that it was the outcome of administrative policies of deportation and centralization which characterized some centuries of imperial history (it almost sounds like a dress rehearsal for the history of the twentieth century). But, very interestingly, it also offers an explanation of how religious systems could be transformed by their severance from ancient historico-political roots, which gave them the freedom to develop other aspects of their internal logic.

Jonas' argument ran as follows. The first matter is why Hellenism[6], spread as a cultural overlay by Alexander the Great and his successors, had such a profound effect on the cultures of the ancient Near East, which were all immeasurably older than Greek culture. One important factor Jonas identified was the political apathy that had been engendered in subject peoples for centuries by the vast imperial policies of Assyria, Babylon and Iran (under the Achaemenids). Many local cultures, each potentially as vibrant and dynamic as Greek culture, had been systematically crushed by one great military power after another, each great power mistakenly seen by subject populations as liberator from its predecessor. So political apathy was accompanied by cultural stagnation. Of Egypt and Mesopotamia, Jonas argued that 'only the inertia of formidable traditions was left'.

The long-term policy of the deportation and resettlement of the intelligentsia and political leadership of conquered peoples (e.g. §12(16b)), which had led to atrophy not only among the subject peoples, but their inevitable failure to fertilize the dominant culture — the imperial powers 'had as it were surrounded themselves with a desert', and all their gains in territory and resources led only to material enrichment — was accompanied by general spiritual and intellectual impoverishment.

But against this generally negative development, Jonas argued that the policy of deportation had an important positive effect:

> On the one hand, it favored the disengagement of cultural contents from their native soil, their abstraction into the transmissible form of teachings, and their consequently becoming available as elements in a cosmopolitan interchange of ideas — just as Hellenism could use them. On the other hand, it favored already a pre-Hellenistic syncretism, a merging of gods and cults of different and sometimes widely distant origins, which again anticipates an important feature of the ensuing Hellenistic development. Biblical history offers examples of both these processes.

---

6   It might have been preferable to write of 'Hellenisticism', being an attempt by Macedonians, a kind of barbarian, at copying 'Hellenism', the ethos of Greece; but no matter, the word has stuck.

He cited the foundations of Samaritanism, supposedly attested in *2 Kings* 17:24-41,[7] in which the biblical narrator (whether with historical accuracy is not at issue here) attributed the syncretism of his own day to the outcome of Assyrian policies in the eighth century.

An important development, and perhaps for the first time in human history, was the implication for a succession of religious forms of the removal of their political underpinnings. As each empire collapsed, subsumed under the heel of the next (Assyria, Babylon, Persia, Hellenism, Rome), the process led to 'the transformation of the substance of local cultures into ideologies'. Jonas cited the religion of Judah as an example:

> the Babylonian exile forced the Jews to develop that aspect of their religion whose validity transcended the particular Palestinian conditions and to oppose the creed thus extracted in its purity to the other religious principles of the world into which they had been cast. This meant a confrontation of ideas with ideas...

Similar developments were to be traced through other cases, such as the fall of Babylon:

> No longer connected with the institutions of a local power-system and enjoying the prestige of its authority, it was thrown back upon its inherent *theological* qualities, which had to be formulated as such if they were to hold their own against other religious systems which had similarly been set afloat and were now competing for the minds of men. Political uprooting thus led to a liberation of spiritual substance.

Babylonian astronomy and astrology flourished in the wider world. The eclipse of Persia gave a new lease of life to Zoroastrianism and Mazdaism; dualist systems resulted. From the loss of independence under Greek and then Roman rule, Egypt and Greece itself developed the mystery-cults. We see in all this a renewal and transformation of ancient religious forms.

If Jonas' assessment is correct, as I believe it to be in substance, we have a useful insight into the way historical experience shaped and reshaped religious beliefs and practice. The corollary to this was that the religious systems changed partly in response to events, and partly as an unconscious strategy for becoming proactive in the face of historical change. Thus its strategic role, discussed throughout this anthology, of coming to terms with the past, and using it as a means to face the future, is borne out, and

---

[7]   If we take this passage to refer to the origins of Samaritanism, it is anachronistic, since the sect began not at the time of the fall of Israel (721 BCE) but in or after the third century BCE. See Albertz 1994, 525-32.

continues to function.   This is as true of contemporary as of ancient religion. The explosion of cults in the twentieth century was an inevitable, and a thoroughly healthy, response to the recent history of the world: the brutal colonization of the Americas, the grand land seizure by the European powers in Africa, the swallowing up of tiny island nations in the Pacific Basin in the interests of western colonialist drives and military strategies, and the use of 'the little people' in the interests of global politics, all required a means for the victims of the system to deal with their predicament, and to find a way out of it. The process continues apace.

References and Selected Reading

Abusch, T.

1995   Marduk, cols. 1014-26 in *DDD* (= *DDD²*, 543-9).

Albertz, R.

1994   *A History of Israelite Religion in the Old Testament Period* 2 volumes (London: SCM).

Albrektson, B.

1967   *History and the Gods* (Horae Soderblomianae 5, Lund: Gleerup).

Albright, W. F.

1964   *Yahweh and the Gods of Canaan* (London: Athlone Press).

Alexander, P. S.

1997   Jerusalem as the Omphalos of the World: on the history of a Geographical Concept, *Judaism* 46:147-58.

Allen, T. G.

1974   *The Book of the Dead, or Going Forth by Day. Ideas of the ancient Egyptians concerning the Hereafter as expressed in their own Terms* (SAOC 37, Chicago Oriental Institute: Chicago University press).

Annus, A.

1999   Are there Greek Rephaim? On the etymology of Greek *Meropes* and *Titanes*, *UF* 31:13-30.

d'Aquili, E. and Newberg, A. B.

1998   The neuropsychological basis of religions, or why God won't go away, *Zygon* 33:187-201.

Astour, M.

1967   *Hellenosemitica* (Leiden: Brill²).

Aus, R. D.

1998   *'Caught in the Act', Walking on the Sea, and the Release of Barabbas Revisited* (SFSHJ 157, Atlanta GA: Scholars Press).

Bagrow, L.

1964   *History of cartography* (London: Watts).

Barker, M.

1987   *The Older Testament* (London: SPCK).

1991   *The Gate of Heaven* (London: SPCK).

2000   *The Revelation of Jesus Christ, which God gave to him to show his servants what must soon take place (Revelation 1.1)* (Edinburgh: T. & T. Clark).

Barton, G. A.

1909   Berosus, ii 533-5 in *ERE*.

Batto, B. F.

1983   The Reed Sea: *Requiescat in Pace*, *JBL* 102: 27-35.

1993   *Slaying the Dragon* (Louisville KY: Westminster-John Knox).

von Beckerath, J.

1984   *Handbuch der ägyptischen Königsnamen* (MÄS 20, Munich: Deutscher Kunstverlag).

Bell, C. M.

1992   *Ritual Theory, Ritual Practice* (Oxford: Oxford University Press).

Berger, P.

1973   *The Social Reality of Religion* (Harmondsworth: Penguin; first published as *The Sacred Canopy*, New York 1967).

Berger, P. and Luckmann, T.

1971   *The Social Construction of Reality* (Harmondsworth: Penguin; first published in USA 1966).

Bernal, M.

1991   *Black Athena. The Afroasiatic Roots of Classical Civilization.* Volume 2: *The Archaeological and documentary Evidence* (New Brunswick NJ: Rutgers University Press).

Bettelheim, B.

1978   *The Uses of Enchantment. The Meaning and Importance of Fairy Tales* (Harmondsworth: Penguin; London: Thames and Hudson 1976).

Beyerlin, W.

1978   *Near Eastern Religious Texts relating to the Old Testament* (London: SCM).

Blacker, C. and Loewe, M. (eds)

1975   *Ancient Cosmologies* (London: Allen and Unwin).

Blackman, A. M. and Fairman, H. W.

1941   A group of texts inscribed on the façade of the sanctuary in the temple of Horus of Edfu, *MG* 1941:397-428.

Blackmore, S.

1999   *The Meme Machine* (Oxford: Oxford University Press).

Blythin, I.

1970   Magic and methodology, *Numen* 17:45-59.

Bottéro, J.

1971   Syria before 2200 B.C., 315-62 in Edwards *et al.*, 1970-5.

Bourdillon, M. F. C. and Fortes, M. (eds)
1980   *Sacrifice* (London: Academic Press).

Boyer, P.

1993   *Cognitive Aspects of Religious Symbolism* (Cambridge: Cambridge University Press).

Boylan, P.

1922   *Thoth, the Hermes of Egypt* (London: Oxford University Press).

Brandon, S. G. F.

1962   *Man and his Destiny in the Great Religions*   (Manchester: Manchester University Press).

1963   *Creation legends of the Ancient Near East* (London: Hodder and Stoughton).

1965   *History, Time and Deity* (Manchester: Manchester University Press).

1967   *The Judgment of the Dead* (London: Weidenfeld and Nicolson).

Breasted, J.H.

1906   *Ancient Records of Egypt* 5 volumes (Chicago: University of Chicago Press).

Brody, A. J.

1998   'Each Man cried out to his God': the Specialized Religion of Canaanite and Phoenician Seafarers* (HSMP 58, Atlanta GA: Scholars).

Brooke, G. J. *et al.* (eds)

1994   *Ugarit and the Bible* (UBL 11, Münster: Ugarit-Verlag).

Bühler, G.

1886   *The Laws of Manu* (SBE 25, Oxford: Clarendon).

Burkert, W.

1983   *Homo Necans* (Berkeley CA: University of California Press).

1992   *The Orientalizing Revolution* (Revealing Antiquity 5, Cambridge MA: Harvard University Press).

Callender, D. E. Jr.

2000   *Adam in Myth and History: Ancient Israelite Perspectives on the Primal Human* (HSS 48; Winona Lake: Eisenbrauns).

Camille, M.

1996   *Gothic Art* (London: Weidenfeld and Nicolson; Calman and King).

Cauvin, J.

1994   *Naissance des Divinités, Naissance de l'Agriculture. La Révolution des Symboles au Néolithique* (Paris: CNRS).

Černy, J.

1952   *Ancient Egyptian Religion* (London: Hutchinson's University Library).

Charles, R. H. (ed.)

1913   *The Apocrypha and Pseudepigrapha of the Old Testament* 2 volumes (Oxford: Clarendon).

Charlesworth, J. H. (ed.)

1983-5   *Old Testament Pseudepigrapha* 2 volumes (New York: Doubleday).

Childs, B. S.

1961   *Myth and Reality in the Old Testament* (SBT 27, London: SCM[2]).

Clifford, R. J.

1972   *The Cosmic Mountain in Canaan and the Old Testament* (Cambridge MA: Harvard University Press).

1994   *Creation Accounts in the Ancient Near East and the Bible*   (CBQMS 26, Washington CD: Catholic Biblical Association of America).

Cohn, R. L.
1981   *The Shape of Sacred Space. Four Biblical Studies*   (AARSR 23, Chico CA: Scholars).

Collingwood, R. G.
1946   *The Idea of History* (Oxford: Clarendon).

Collins, A. Y.
1984   *Crisis and Catharsis: the Power of the Apocalypse* (Philadelphia: Westminster Press).

Collins, J. J.
1998   *The Apocalyptic Imagination. An Introduction to Jewish Apocalyptic Literature* (Grand Rapids: Eerdmans²).

Collins, J. J. and Fishbane, M.
1995   *Death, Ecstasy, and otherworldly Journeys* (Albany NY: State University of New York Press).

Cook, R.
1974   *The Tree of Life. Image for the Cosmos* (London: Thames and Hudson).

Cornelius, I.
1994   *The Iconography of the Canaanite Gods Reshef and Ba'al. Late Bronze and Iron Age I Periods (c. 1500-1000 BCE)* (OBO 140, Fribourg: Fribourg University Press; Göttingen: Vandenhoek & Ruprecht).

Craigie, P. C.
1983   *Ugarit and the Old Testament* (Grand Rapids MI: Eerdmans).

Curtis, A.
1985   *Ugarit* (London: Lutterworth).

Curtis, J. B.
1963   A suggested interpretation of the biblical philosophy of history, *HUCA* 34:115-23.

Dalley, S.
1989   *Myths from Mesopotamia* (Oxford: Oxford University Press).

van Dam, C.
1997   *The Urim and Thummim. A Means of Revelation in Ancient Israel* (Winona Lake IN: Eisenbrauns).

David, A. R.
1981   *A Guide to the Religious Rituals of Abydos* (Warminster: Aris and Phillips).
1982   *The Ancient Egyptians. Religious Beliefs and Practices* (London: Routledge).

Davies, D.

1977   An interpretation of sacrifice in Leviticus, *ZAW* 89:388-98 = 151-62 in Lang 1985.

Davila, J.

1995   The flood hero as king and priest, *JNES* 54:199-214.

Day, J.

1985   *God's Conflict with the Dragon and the Sea* (UCOP 35, Cambridge: Cambridge University Press).

2001   *Yahweh and the Gods and Goddesses of Israel* (JSOTS 265, Sheffield: Sheffield Academic Press).

Deacon, T.

1997   *The Symbolic Species. The Co-evolution of Language and the Human Brain* (London: Allen Lane).

Dick, M. B. (ed.)

1999   *Born in Heaven, made on Earth. The Making of the Cult Image in the Ancient Near East* (Winona Lake IN: Eisenbrauns).

Dijkstra, M.

1991   The weather-god on two mountains, *UF* 23:127-40.

Donald, M.

1991   *Origins of the Modern Mind* (Cambridge MA: Harvard University Press).

Douglas, M.

1970   *Purity and Danger* (Harmondsworth: Penguin; London: Routledge and Kegan Paul 1966).

1973   *Natural Symbols* (Harmondsworth: Penguin; London: Barrie and Rockliffe 1970).

Drews, R.

1975   The Babylonian Chronicle and Berossus, *Iraq* 37:39-55.

Driver, G. R.

1956   *Canaanite Myths and Legends* (Edinburgh: T & T Clark).

Driver, T. F.

1991   *The Magic of Ritual: our Need for Liberating Rites that Transform our Lives and our Communities* (San Francsico CA: Harper).

Dunne-Lardeau, B. (ed.)

1997   *Jacques de Voragine: La Légende Dorée* (Textes de la Renaissance 19, Paris: Honoré Champion).

Durand, J.-M.

1993   Le mythologème du combat entre le dieu de l'orage et la mer en Mésopotamie, *MARI* 7:41-61.

Edwards, I. E. S., *et al.*,

1970-5   *The Cambridge Ancient History* volumes I₁, I₂, II₁ and II₂ (Cambridge: Cambridge University Press³).

Eilberg-Schwartz, H.

1990   *The Savage in Judaism. An Anthropology of Israelite Religion and Ancient Judaism* (Bloomington, Indianapolis: Indiana University Press).

Eliade, M.

1954   *The Myth of the Eternal Return* (Princeton: Princeton University Press).

1958   *Patterns in Comparative Religion* (London: Sheed and Ward).

1964   *Myth and Reality* (London: Allen and Unwin).

1964   *Shamanism. Archaic Techniques of Ecstasy* (London: Routledge and Kegan Paul).

Emery, W. B.

1961   *Archaic Egypt* (Harmondsworth: Penguin).

Erikson, E. H.

1966   Ontogeny of ritualization, *RSPT* 63/251: 337-49.

Eslinger, L.

1995   The infinite in a finite organical perception (Isaiah vi 1-5), *VT* 35:145-73.

Evans, J.

1998   *The History and Practice of Ancient Astronomy* (Oxford: Oxford University Press).

Evans, R. J.

1997   *In Defence of History* (London: Granta).

Evelyn-White, H. G.

1914   *Hesiod, the Homeric Hymns and Homerica* (Loeb Classical Library, London: Heinemann; Cambridge MA: Harvard University Press).

Faulkner, R. O.

1969   *The Ancient Egyptian Pyramid Texts* (Oxford: Oxford University Press).

1973-8   *The Ancient Egyptian Coffin Texts* 3 volumes (Warminster: Aris and Phillips).

1985   *The Ancient Egyptian Book of the Dead* (London: British Museum²: first edition New York: Limited Editions Club, 1972).

Fawcett, T. R.

1970   *The Symbolic Language of Religion* (London: SCM).

Fenn, R. K.

1997   *The End of Time: Religion, Ritual, and the Forging of the Soul* (London: SPCK).

Fisher, L. R.

1965   Creation at Ugarit and in the Old Testament, *VT* 15:313-24.

Flanagan, J. W.

1995   Finding the arrow of time: constructs of ancient history and religion, *CR:BS* 3:37-80.

Fleming, D. E.

1992   *The Installation of Baal's High-Priestess at Emar. A Window on Ancient Syrian Religion* (HSS 42, Atlanta GA: Scholars Press).

2000   *Time at Emar. The Cultic Calendar and the Rituals from the Diviner's Archive* (Winona Lake IN: Eisenbrauns).

Fletcher-Lewis, C

1997   The High Priest as Divine Mediator in the Hebrew Bible: Dan 7:13 as a Test Case, 161-93 in *Society of Biblical Literature 1997 Seminar Papers* (Atlanta GA: Scholars Press).

Fohrer, G.

1973   *History of Israelite Religion* (London: SPCK).

Fontenrose, J. A.

1971   *The Ritual Theory of Myth* (Berkeley: California University Press).

Fox, M. V. (ed.)

1988   *Temple in Society* (Winona Lake IN: Eisenbrauns).

Frankfort, H. *et al*

1948   *Kingship and the Gods* (Chicago: Chicago University Press).

1949   *Before Philosophy. The Intellectual Adventure of Ancient Man* (Harmondsworth: Penguin; = *The Intellectual Adventure of Ancient Man*, Chicago University Press 1946).

1951   *The Problem of Similarity in Ancient Near Eastern Religions* (Frazer Lecture: Oxford).

1961   *Ancient Egyptian Religion* (San Francisco: Harper and Row; New York: Columbia University Press, 1948).

Frazer, J. G.

1921   *Apollodorus, the Library* 2 volumes (Loeb Classical Library, London: Heinemann).

Garbini, G.

1988   *History and Ideology in Ancient Israel* (London: SCM).

Gardiner, A. H.

1950   *Egyptian Grammar* (Oxford: Oxford University Press²).

1953   The Coronation of King Haremhab, *JEA* 39:13-31.

1961   *Egypt of the Pharaohs* (Oxford: Clarendon).

van Gennep, A.

1909   *Les Rites de Passage* (Paris: Librairie Critique).

George, A. R.

1993   *House Most High. The Temples of Ancient Mesopotamia* (Mesopotamian Civilizations 5, Winona Lake IN: Eisenbrauns).

1999   *The Gilgamesh Epic* (New York: Barnes and Noble).

Gibbs, L. W. and Stevenson, W. T. (eds)

1975   *Myth and the Crisis of Historical Consciousness* (Missoula MA: Scholars Press).

Gibson, J. C. L.

1978   *Canaanite Myths and Legends* (Edinburgh: T & T Clark).

Gifford, E. H.

1903   *Evangelicae Praeparationis Libri XV, ad Codices Manuscriptos denuo collatos recensuit, Anglice nunc primum reddidit, notis et indicibus instruxit* 4 volumes (Oxford: Oxford University Press).

Gilhus, I. S.

1997   *Laughing Gods, Weeping Virgins* (London: Routledge).

Girard, R.

1977   *Violence and the Sacred* (Baltimore MD: Johns Hopkins University Press).

Glassner, J.-J.

1993   *Chroniques Mésopotamiennes* (Paris, Les Belles Lettres 1993). (ET in preparation with Scholars Press: translations are mine for this edition.)

Godley, A. D.

1921-5 *Herodotus* 4 volumes (Loeb Classical Library, London: Heinemann; Cambridge MA: Harvard University Press).

Gordon, C. H.

1969   Vergil and the Near East, *Ugaritica* 6:267-88.

Grabbe, L. L.

1997   *Can a 'History of Israel' be Written?* (JSOTS 245, ESHM 1, Sheffield: Sheffield Academic Press).

Gray, J.

1965   *The Legacy of Canaan* (SVT 5, Leiden: Brill ²).

Griffith, J. G.

1960   *The Conflict of Horus and Seth* (Liverpool: Liverpool University Press)

Grimes, R. L.

1995   *Beginnings in Ritual Studies* (Columbia SC: University of South Carolina Press).

Guthrie, S. E.

1993   *Faces in the Clouds* (Oxford: Oxford University Press).

Habel, N. C.

1972   He who stretches out the heavens, *CBQ* 34:417-30.

Halevi, Z. ben Shimon,

1979   *Kabbalah. Tradition of Hidden Knowledge* (London: Thames and Hudson).

Hall, E. T.

1966   *The Hidden Dimension* (Garden City NY: Doubleday).

Hallo, W. W. (ed.)

1998-2001 *The Context of Scripture* 3 volumes (Leiden: Brill).

Halpern, B.

1988   *The First Historians. The Hebrew Bible and History* (San Francisco CA: Harper and Row).

Haran, M.

1985   *Temples and Temple Service in Ancient Israel* (Winona Lake IN: Eisenbrauns²; Oxford: Oxford University Press 1978).

Hastings, J. (ed.)

1908-26 *The Encyclopaedia of Religion and Ethics* (Edinburgh: T. & T. Clark).
        Calendars iii 61-141.
        Cosmogony and Cosmology iv 125-79 (excerpts).
        Time xii 334-45.

Hayman, A. P.

1986   The temple at the centre of the universe, *JJS* 37:176-82.

1998   The 'Man from the Sea' in 4 Ezra 13, *JJS* 49:1-16.

Heidel, A.

1942   *The Babylonian Genesis* (Chicago: Chicago Univerity Press). 1972 reprint.

1949   *The Gilgamesh Epic and Old Testament Parallels* (Chicago: Chicago Univerity Press²). 1963 reprint.

Heil, J. P.

1981   *Jesus Walking on the Sea. Meaning and Gospel Functions of Matt 14:22-33, Mark 6:45-52 and John 6:15b-21* (AnBib 87, Rome: Pontifical Biblical Institute).

Hendel, R.

1987   Of Demigods and the Deluge: toward an Interpretation of Genesis 6:1-4, *JBL* 106:13-26.

1995   The shape of Utnapishtim's ark, *ZAW* 107:128-9.

Himmelfarb, M.

1993   *Ascent to Heaven in Jewish and Christian Apocalypses* (Oxford: Oxford University Press).

Hinde, R. A.

1999   *Why Gods Persist. A Scientific Approach to Religion* (London: Routledge).

Holloway, S. W.

1991   What ship goes there: the flood narratives in the Gilgamesh epic and Genesis considered in light of ancient near eastern temple ideology, *ZAW* 103:328-55.

1998   The shape of Utnapishtim's ark: a Rejoinder, *ZAW* 110:617-26.

Holm, J. and Bowker, J. (eds)
1994   *Sacred place* (London: Pinter).

Hooke, S. H.

1953   *Babylonian and Assyrian Religion* (London: Hutchinson)

Hornung, E.

1983   *Conceptions of God in Ancient Egypt* (London: Routledge and Kegan Paul). Reprinted 1996.

1995   *Akhenaten and the Religion of Light* (New York: Cornell University Press).

Horowitz, W.

1998   *Mesopotamian Cosmic Geography* (Mesopotamian Civilizations 8, Winona Lake IN: Eisenbrauns).

Hughes, J.

1990   *Secrets of the Times. Myth and History in Biblical Chronology* (JSOTS 66, Sheffield: Sheffield Academic Press).

Hurowitz, V. A.

1992   *'I have built you an Exalted House.' Temple Building in the Bible in the Light of Mesopotamian and Nortwest Semitic Writings* (JSOTS 115, Sheffield: Sheffield Academic Press).

1999   Splitting the sacred mountain: Zechariah 14,4 and Gilgamesh V vii 4-5, *UF* 31:241-5.

Husser, J.-M.

1991   Les Métamorphoses d'un Songe. Critique littéraire de Genèse 28,10-22, *RB* 98:321-42.

1994   *Le Songe et la Parole. Etude sur le Rêve et sa Fonction dans l'ancien Israël* (BZAW 210, Berlin: de Gruyter).

1999   *Dreams and Dream Narratives in the Biblical World* (BS 63, Sheffield: Sheffield Academic Press).

Huxley, M.

1997   The shape of the cosmos according to cuneiform sources, *JRAS* series 3, 7:189-98.

Hyatt, J. P.

1971   *Exodus* (New Century Bible, London: Oliphants).

Jacobsen, T.

1976   *The Treasures of Darkness* (New Haven: Yale University Press).

1987   *The Harps that once... Sumerian Poetry in Translation* (New Haven: Yale University Press).

James, P. (ed.)

1991   *Centuries of Darkness. A Challenge to the conventional Chronology of Old World Archaeology* (London: Jonathan Cape).

Jaynes, J.

1976   *The Origin of Consciousness in the Breakdown of the Bicameral Mind* (Boston: Houghton Mifflin).

Jeremias, A.

1908   Ages of the World (Babylonian), i 183-7 in *ERE*.

Jonas, H.

1963   *The Gnostic Religion. The Message of the Alien God and the Beginnings of Christianity* (Boston MA: Beacon²).

Jones, H. L.

1917-32 *Strabo, Geography* 8 volumes (Loeb Classical Library, London: Heinemann; Cambridge MA: Harvard University Press).

Kaiser, O.

1974   *Isaiah 13-39, a Commentary* (London: SCM).

Kapelrud, A. S.

1963   Temple building, a task for Gods and Kings, *Orientalia* 32:56-62.

Keel, O.

1978   *The Symbolism of the Biblical World* (London: SPCK).

1998   *Goddesses and Trees, New Moon and Yahweh. Ancient Near Eastern Art and the Hebrew Bible* (JSOTS 261, Sheffield: Sheffield Academic Press).

Keel, O. and Uehlinger, C.

1998   *Gods, Goddesses, and Images of God in Ancient Israel* (Edinburgh: T. & T. Clark).

Kemp, B.

1989   *Egypt, Anatomy of a Civilization* (London: Routledge).

Kirk, G. S.

1970   *Myth, its Meaning and Function in Ancient and other Cultures* (SCL 40, Cambridge: Cambridge University Press).

Klimheit, H.-J.

1974-5 Spatial orientation in mythical thinking as exemplified in ancient Egypt: considerations towards a geography of religions, *HR* 14:266-81.

Kloos, C.

1986   *Yhwh's Combat with the Sea* (Leiden: Brill).

Knight, C.

1991   *Blood Relations. Menstruation and the Origins of Culture* (New Haven: Yale University Press).

Kramer, S. N.

1961   *Sumerian Mythology. A Study of Spiritual and Literary Achievement in the Third Millennium* B.C. (New York: Harper Row²).

Kuhrt, A.

1995   *The ancient Near East c. 3000-330 BC* 2 volumes (London: Routlege).

Kunin, S.

1998   *God's Place in the World. Sacred Space and Sacred Place in Judaism* (London: Cassell).

Kvanvig, H. S.

1988   *Roots of Apocalyptic: the Mesopotamian Background of the Enoch Figure and of the Son of Man* (WMANT 61, Neukirchen-Vluyn: Neukirchener Verlag).

Lambert, W. G.

1976   Berossus and Babylonian Eschatology, *Iraq* 38:171-3.

Lambert, W. G. and Millard, A. R.

1969   *Atra-Ḥasīs, the Babylonian Story of the Flood* (Oxford: Oxford University Press. Reprinted Winona Lake IN: Eisenbrauns, 1999, with additional section by M. Civil).

Lambert, W. G. and Walcot, P.

1965   A new Babylonian theogony and Hesiod, *Kadmos* 4:64-72.

Lambrou-Philippson, C.

1990   *Hellenorientalia: The Near Eastern Presence in the Bronze Age Aegean, ca 3000-1100 B.C.* (Göteborg: P. Astroms Förlag).

Landsberg, A.

1995   Prosthetic memory: *Total Recall* and *Blade Runner*, 175-89 in M. Featherstone and R. Burrows (eds), *Cyberspace/cyberbodies/cyberpunk: cultures of technological embodiment* (London: Sage).

Lang, B. (ed.)

1985   *Anthropological Approaches to the Old Testament* (London: SPCK).

Lévi-Strauss, C.

1968   *Structural Anthropology* (London: Allen Lane).

Lewis, T. J.

1996   *CT* 13.33-34 and Ezekiel 32: lion-dragon myths, *JAOS* 116:28-47.

Lewy, J.

1945-6 The late Assyro-Babylonian cult of the Moon and its Culmination in the time of Nabonidus, *HUCA* 19:405-89.

Lichtheim, M.

1976   *Ancient Egyptian Literature* 3 volumes (Berkeley CA: University of California Press).

Lindblom, J.

1962   *Prophecy in ancient Israel* (Oxford: Blackwell).

Lipiński, E. (ed.)

1992   *Dictionnaire de la Civilisation Phénicienne et Punique* (Turnhout: Brepols).

Loewe, M. and Blacker, C. (eds)

1981   *Divination and Oracles* (London: Allen and Unwin).

Lowenthal, D.

1985   *The Past is a Foreign Country* (Cambridge: Cambridge University Press).

Luckenbill, D. D.

1926   *Ancient Records of Assyria and Babylonia* 2 volumes (New York : Greenwood Press).

Luyster, R.

1981   Wind and water: cosmogonic symbolism in the Old Testament, *ZAW* 93:1-10.

Maccoby, H.

1982   *The Sacred Executioner. Human Sacrifice and the Legacy of Guilt* (London: Thames and Hudson).

Madden, P.

1997   *Jesus' Walking on the Sea. An Investigation of the Origin of the Narrative Account* (BZNW 81, Berlin: de Gruyter).

Maher, M.

1992   *Targum Pseudo-Jonathan: Genesis* (The Aramaic Bible 1b, Edinburgh: T. & T. Clark).

Malamat, A.

1989   *Mari and the early Israelite Experience* (Schweich Lectures; Oxford: Oxford University Press for the British Academy).

Mallowan, M. E. L.

1964   Noah's flood reconsidered, *Iraq* 26:62-82.

Marshack, A.

1996   A Middle Palaeolithic symbolic composition from the Golan Heights: the earliest known depictive image, *CA* 37:357-65.

1997   The Berekhat Ram figurine: a late Acheulian carving from the Middle east, *Antiquity* 71:327-37.

Marwick, A.

1989   *The Nature of History* (Badingstoke: MacMillan³; 1ˢᵗ edition 1970).

Maspero, G.

1894   *The Dawn of Civilization, Egypt and Chaldea* (London: SPCK).

McCurley F. R.

1983   *Ancient Myths and Biblical Faith. Scriptural Transformations* (Philadelphia: Fortress).

McCutcheon, R. T. (ed.)

1999   *The Insider/Outsider Problem in the Study of Religion: a Reader* (London: Cassell).

van de Mieroop, M.

1999   *Cuneiform Texts and the Writing of History* (London: Routledge).

Miller, F. J.

1956   *Ovid, Metamorphoses* 2 volumes (Loeb Classical Library, London: Heinemann).

Mol, H.

1976   *Identity and the Sacred* (Oxford: Blackwell).

Montgomery, J. A.

1938   *Yām Sûf* ('the Red Sea') = *Ultimum Mare? JAOS* 58:131-2.

de Moor, J. C.

1982   *An Anthology of Religious Texts from Ugarit* (Nisaba 16, Leiden: Brill).

1994   Ugarit and the origin of Job, 225-57 in Brooke 1994.

1997   *The Rise of Yahwism* (Leuven, Peeters²).

Morenz, S.

1973   *Egyptian Religion* (London: Methuen).

Moscati, S.

1968   *The World of the Phoenicians* (London: Weidenfeld and Nicolson).

Muchiki, Y.

1999   *Egyptian Proper Names and Loanwords in North-West Semitic* (SBLDS 173, Atlanta GA: Society of Biblical literature).

Munz, P.

1973   *When the Golden Bough breaks: Structuralism or Typology?* (London: Routledge and Kegan Paul).

Murnane, W. J.

1995   *Texts from the Amarna Period in Egypt* (WAW5, Atlanta GA: Scholars).

Murray, A. T.

1924   *Homer, the Iliad* 2 volumes (Loeb Classical Library, London: Heinemann; Cambridge MA: Harvard University Press).

Murray, M.

1977   *The Splendour that was Egypt* (London: Sidgwick and Jackson²).

Neiman, D.

1977   Gihôn and Pishôn: mythological antecedents of the two enigmatic rivers of Eden, 321-8 in A. Shinan (ed.), *Proceedings of the 6th Congress of Jewish Studies*, Jerusalem.

Neusner, J.

1988   *The Mishnah. A new Translation* (New Haven: Yale University Press).

Nissinen, M. (ed.)

2000   *Prophecy in its Ancient Near Eastern Context* (Williston VT: Society of Biblical Literature).

Noegel, S.

1998   The Aegean Ogygos of Boeotia and the Biblical Og of Bashan: Reflections of the same myth, *ZAW* 110:411-26.

Nougayrol, J.

1956   *Le Palais Royal d'Ugarit IV Textes Accadiens des Archives Suds* (Paris: Imprimerie Nationale).

Oden, R. A.

1979   'The contendings of Horus and Seth' (Chester Beatty Papyrus No. 1): a structural interpretation, *HR* 18:352-369.

O'Flaherty, W. D.

1975   *Hindu Myths* (Harmondsworth: Penguin).

del Olmo Lete, G.

1981   *Mitos y leyendas de Canaan* (FCB 1, Madrid: Cristiandad).

1999   *Canaanite Religion according to the Liturgical Texts of Ugarit* (Bethesda MD: CDL Press; ET of *La religión Cananea*, AuOrS 3, Barcelona: AUSA 1992).

Oppenheim, A. L.

1964   *Ancient Mesopotamia. Portrait of a Dead Civilization* (Chicago: Chicago University Press).

L'Orange, H. P.

1953   *Studies in the Iconography of Cosmic Kingship* (Oslo: H. Aschoug and Co.).

Otto, R.

1950   *The Idea of the Holy* (London: Oxford University Press²).

Page, H. R.

1996   *The Myth of Cosmic Rebellion. A Study of its Reflexes in Ugaritic and Biblical Literature* (SVT 65, Leiden: Brill).

Pardee, D.

2000a   Ugaritic Studies at the End of the Twentieth Century, *BASOR* 320:49-86.

2000b   *Les Textes Rituels* (RSO 12, Paris: ERC).

2001   *Ugaritic Ritual Texts* (Scholars Press, in press).

Parker, S. B.

1989   *The Prebiblical Narrative Tradition. Essays in the Ugaritic poems* Keret *and* Aqhat (SBL Resources for Biblical Study 24, Atlanta: Scholars Press).

Parkinson, R. B.

1997   *The Tale of Sinuhe and other Ancient Egyptian Poems 1940-1640 BC* (Oxford: Oxford University Press).

Parpola, S.

1993   The Assyrian tree of life: tracing the origins of Jewish monotheism and Greek philosophy, *JNES* 52:22-40.

1997   *Assyrian prophecies* (SAA 9, Helsinki: Helsinki University Press).

Patai, R.

1948   *Man and Temple* (London, Nelson).

Patton, L. E. and Doniger, W. (eds)

1996   *Myth and Method* (Charlottesville VA: University Press of Virginia).

Penglase, C.

1994   *Greek Myths and Mesopotamia. Parallels and Influence in the Homeric Hymns and Hesiod* (London: Routledge).

Pope, M. H.

1955   *El in the Ugaritic texts* (SVT 2, Leiden: Brill).

Postgate, N.

1992   *Early Mesopotamia. Society and Economy at the Dawn of History* (London: Routledge).

Pritchard, J. B. (ed.)

1969   *Ancient Near Eastern Texts relating to the Old Testament* (Princeton: Princeton University Press³; first edition 1950).

Quirke, S.

1992   *Ancient Egyptian Religion* (London: British Museum Publications).

Rappaport, R. A.

1992   Ritual, Time and Eternity, *Zygon* 27:5-30.

1999   *Ritual and Religion in the Making of Humanity* (Cambridge: Cambridge University Press).

Redford, D. B.

1992   *Egypt, Canaan and Israel in Ancient Times* (Princeton NJ: Princeton University Press).

Reiner, E.

1961   The etiological myth of the seven sages, *Orientalia* 30:1-11.

Renfrew, C. and Scarre, C. (eds)

1998   *Cognition and Material Culture: the Archaeology of Symbolic Storage* (Cambridge: McDonald Institute for Archaeological Research).

Reymond, P.

1958   *L'Eau, sa Vie et sa Signification dans l'Ancien Testament* (SVT 6, Leiden: Brill).

Richards, E. G.

1998   *Mapping Time* (Oxford: Oxford University Press).

Richardson, M. E. J.

2000   *Hammurabi's Law. Text, Translation and Glossary* (BS 73, STS 2, Sheffield: Sheffield Academic Press).

Ringgren, H.

1966   *Israelite Religion* (London: SPCK).

1973   *Religions of the Ancient Near East* (London: SPCK).

Roberts, A.

1995   *Hathor Rising* (Totnes: Northgate).

Robertson, E.

1964   The 'Urim and Tummim'; what were they? *VT* 14:67-74.

Rogerson, J.

1974   *Myth in Old Testament Interpretation* (BZAW 134, Berlin: de Gruyters).

Rohl, D.

1995   *A Test of Time* volume 1 *The Bible — from Myth to History* (London: Random House).

Roux, G.

1964   *Ancient Iraq* (London: Allen and Unwin).

Rowley, H. H.

1967   *Worship in ancient Israel* (London: SPCK).

Ryan, W. and Pitman, W.

1999   *Noah's Flood. The new Scientific Discoveries about the Event that changed History* (London: Simon and Schuster).

Saggs, H. W. F.

1978   *The Encounter with the Divine in Mesopotamia and Israel* (London: Athlone).

1984   *The Might that was Assyria* (London: Sidgwick and Jackson).

1988   *The Greatness that was Babylon* (London: Sidgwick and Jackson²).

Sandys, Sir J.

1915   *The Odes of Pindar* (Loeb Classical Library, London: Heinemann; Cambridge MA: Harvard University Press).

Segal, R. A. (ed.)

1998   *The Myth and Ritual Theory, an Anthology* (Oxford: Blackwell).

Seidl, U.

1989   *Die Babylonischen Kudurru-Reliefs. Symbole Mesopotamische Gottheiten* (OBO 87, Freiburg, Göttingen).

Semple, E. C.

1927   The Templed Promonotories of the Ancient Mediterranean, *GR* 17:352-86.

van Seters, J.

1972   The terms 'Amorite' and 'Hittite' in the Old Testament, *VT* 22:64-81.

1975   *Abraham in History and Tradition* (New Haven: Yale University Press).

1983   *In Search of History. Historiography in the Ancient world and the Origins of Biblical History* (New Haven CT: Yale University Press).

1992   *Prologue to History. The Yahwist as Historian in Genesis* (Louisville KY: Westminster-John Knox Press).

Shafer, B. F. (ed.)

1998   *Temples of ancient Egypt* (London: Tauris).

Simkins, R. A.

1994   *Creator and Creation. Nature of the Worldview of ancient Israel* (Peabody MA: Hendrickson).

Skinner, J.

1910   *A Critical and Exegetical Commentary on Genesis* (ICC, Edinburgh: T. and T. Clark).

Smith, J. Z.

1987   To take place : toward Theory in Ritual (Chicago : University of Chicago Press).

1999   The Devil in Mr Jones, 370-89 in McCutcheon 1999.

Smith, M.

1987   *Palestinian Parties and Politics that shaped the Old Testament* (London: SCM²).

Smith, M. S.

1990   *The Early History of God. Yahweh and other Deities in Early Israel* (San Francisco: Harper and Row).

Smith, S.

1924   *Babylonian historical texts relating to the capture and downfall of Babylon* (London: Methuen).

Snaith, N. H.

1965   ים־סוף: the Sea of Reeds: the Red Sea, *VT* 15:395-8.

Van Soldt, W. H.

1985-6 The queens of Ugarit, *JEOL* 29:68-73.

Spieser, C.

2000   *Les Noms du Pharaon comme Êtres Autonomes au Nouvel Empire* (OBO 174, Fribourg: Editions Universitaires; Göttingen: Vandenhoek & Ruprecht).

Spronk, K.

1995   Rahab, cols. 1292-5 in *DDD* (= 684-6 in *DDD* ² 1999).

Stadelmann, L. I. J.

1970   *The Hebrew Conception of the World* (AnBib 39, Rome: Pontifical Biblical Institute).

Starr, I.

1990   *Queries to the Sun-god: Divination and Politics in Sargonid Assyria* (SAA 4, Helsinki: Helsinki University Press).

Stevenson, J.
1965   *A New Eusebius. Documents illustrative of the History of the Church to A.D. 337*
         (London: SPCK).

Stoneman, R.
1991   *The Greek Alexander Romance* (Harmondsworth: Penguin).

Strenski, I.
1987   *Four Theories of Myth in twentieth-century History* (London: Macmillan).

Strong, H. A. and Garstang, J.
1913   *The Syrian Goddess* (London: Constable).

Swerdlow, N. M. (ed.)
1999   *Ancient Astronomy and Celestial Divination* (Dibner Institute studies in the
         history of science and technology, Cambridge MA, London: MIT Press).

Takács, G.
1999   *Etymological Dictionary of Egyptian* volume 1 (Leiden: Brill).

Terrien, S.
1970   The omphalos myth and Hebrew religion, *VT* 20:315-38.

Thomas, D. W.
1951   Mount Tabor: the meaning of the name, *VT* 1:229-30.
1958   *Documents from Old Testament Times* (Edinburgh: Nelson).

Thompson, T. L.
1974   *The Historicity of the Patriarchal Narratives* (BZAW 133, Berlin: de Gruyter).

Tobin, V. A.
1989   *Theological Principles of Egyptian Religion* (AUS VII 59, New York: Peter
         Lang).

Tonkin, E. (ed.)
1992   *Narrating our pasts: the Social Construction of Oral History* (Cambridge:
         Cambridge University Press).

van der Toorn, K.
1997   *The Image and the Book* (Leuven: Peeters),
1996   *Family Religion in Babylonia, Syria and Israel* (SHCANE 7, Leiden: Brill).

Tromp, N. J.
1969   *Primitive Conceptions of Death and the Nether World in the Old Testament*
         (BiOr 21, Rome: Pontifical Biblical Institute).

Tsevat, M.
1958   Marriage and monarchical legitimacy in Ugarit and Israel, *JSS* 3:237-43.

Tuan, Y-F.
1977   *Space and Place. The Perspective of Experience* (London: Arnold).

Ulansey, D.
1989   *The Origins of the Mithraic Mysteries* (Oxford: Oxford University Press).

Vanderkam, J. C.

1998   *Calendars in the Dead Sea Scrolls: Measuring Time* (London: Routledge).

de Vaux, R.

1961   *Ancient Israel* (London: Darton, Longman and Todd).

te Velde, H.

1977   *Seth, God of Confusion* (PÄ 6, Leiden: Brill).

van der Waerden, B. L.

1977-8   The Great Year in Greek, Persian and Hindu Thought, *AHES* 18:359-383.

Walcot, P.

1966   *Hesiod and the Near East* (Cardiff: Wales University Press).

Waltke, B. K. and O'Connor, M.

1990   *An Introduction to Biblical Hebrew Syntax* (Winona Lake IN: Eisenbrauns).

Wensinck, A. J.

1916   *The Ideas of the Western Semites concerning the Navel of the Earth* (Verhandelingen der Koniklijke Akademie van Wetenschappen te Amsterdam, Afdeeling Letterkunde NS xvii 1, Amsterdam: Müller).

1918   *The Ocean in the Literature of the Western Semites* (Verhandelingen der Koniklijke Akademie van Wetenschappen te Amsterdam, Afdeeling Letterkunde NS xix 2, Amsterdam: Müller).

West, D. R.

1995   *Some Cults of Greek Goddesses and Female Daemons of Oriental Origin especially in Relation to the Mythology of Goddesses and Daemons in the Semitic World* (AOAT 233, Kevelaer: Butzen and Bercker; Neukirchen-Vluyn: Neukirchener Verlag).

West, M. L.

1966   *Hesiod: Theogony* (Oxford: Oxford University Press).

1971   *Early Greek Philosophy and the Orient* (Oxford: Clarendon).

1988   *Hesiod: Theogony, Works and Days. A New Translation* (Oxford World's Classics, Oxford: Oxford University Press).

1997   *The East Face of Helicon: West Asiatic Elements in Greek Poetry and Myth* (Oxford: Clarendon Press).

Westenholz, A.

1974-7   Old Akkadian school texts, *AfO* 25:95-110.

Westermann, C.

1984   *Genesis 1-11, a Commentary* (London: SPCK).

Widengren, G.

1950   The Ascension of the Apostle and the Heavenly Book, *UUÅ* 1950.7.

1951   The King and the Tree of Life in ancient Near Eastern Religion, *UUÅ* 1951.4.

Wiggins, S. A.

1993   *A Reassessment of 'Asherah'. A Study of the Textual Sources of the First Two Millen[n]ia B.C.E.* (AOAT 235, Neukirchen-Vluyn: Neukirchener Verlag, and Kevelaer: Verlag Butzon und Bercker).

Wilkinson, R. H.

1992   *Reading Egyptian Art. A hieroglyphic guide to ancient Egyptian painting and sculpture* (London: Thames and Hudson).

Wilson, J. A.

1951   *The burden of Egypt. An Interpretation of Ancient Egyptian Culture* (Chicago: Chicago University Press).

Wintermute, O. S.

1985   Jubilees, ii 35-142 in Charlesworth 1983-5.

Woodward, D.

1987   *History of Cartography* (Chicago: University of Chicago Press).

Wright, G. E.

1950   *The Old Testament against its Environment* (SBT 2, London: SCM).

1952   *God who Acts* (SBT 8, London: SCM).

Wright, G. R. H.

1970   The mythology of pre-Israelite Shechem, *VT* 20:75-82.

Wyatt, N.

1979   The development of the tradition in Exodus 3, *ZAW* 91:437-442.

1981   Interpreting the creation and fall story in Genesis 2-3, *ZAW* 93:10-21.

1985a   Killing and cosmogony in Canaanite and biblical thought *UF* 17:375-81.

1985b   'Araunah the Jebusite' and the throne of David, *ST* 39:39-53.

1985   'Jedidiah' and cognate forms as a title of royal legitimation, *Biblica* 66:112-25.

1986   The hollow crown: ambivalent elements in West Semitic royal ideology, *UF* 18:421-36.

1987a   Sea and desert: symbolic geography in West Semitic religious thought, *UF* 19:375-89.

1987b   Who killed the dragon? *AuOr* 5:185-98.

1988a   When Adam delved: the meaning of Genesis III 23, *VT* 38:117-22.

1988b   The source of the Ugaritic myth of the conflict of Baal and Yam, *UF* 20:375-85 (Loretz FS).

1990a   There and back again: the significance of movement in the Priestly work, *SJOT* 1990.i:61-80.

1990b   'Supposing him to be the gardener' (*John* 20, 15): a study of the Paradise motif in John, *ZNW* 25:21-38.

1990c   Where did Jacob dream his dream? *SJOT* 1990.ii:44-57.

1990d   David's census and the tripartite theory, *VT* 40:352-60.

1992   Of calves and kings: the Canaanite dimension in the religion of Israel, *SJOT* 6:68-91.

1993   The darkness of Genesis i 2, *VT* 43:543-54.

1994   The theogony motif in Ugarit and the Bible, 395-419 in Brooke 1994.

1995   The significance of *ṣpn* in West Semitic thought, 213-37 in M. Dietrich and O. Loretz (eds) *Ugarit, ein ostmediterranes Kulturzentrum* (ALASP 7 i, Ugarit und seine altorientalistische Umwelt, Münster: Ugarit-Verlag).

1995b   The liturgical context of Psalm 19 and its mythical and ritual origins, *UF* 27:559-96.

1995c   Asherah, cols. 183-95 in *DDD* (= 99-105 in *DDD²*).

1996a   The vocabulary and neurology of orientation: the Ugaritic and Hebrew evidence, 351-80 in N. Wyatt, W. G. E. Watson and J. B. Lloyd eds. *Ugarit, Religion and Culture* (UBL 12, Münster: Ugarit-Verlag).

1996b   *Myths of Power* (UBL 13, Münster: Ugarit-Verlag).

1998a   *Religious Texts from Ugarit* (BS 53, Sheffield: Sheffield Academic Press).

1998b   Arms and the king, 833-82 in M. Dietrich and I. Kottsieper (eds) *'Und Mose schrieb dieses Lied auf...' Studien zum Alten Testament und zum alten Orient.* FS O. Loretz (AOAT 250, Münster: Ugarit-Verlag).

1999   Degrees of divinity: mythical and ritual aspects of West Semitic kingship, *UF* 31: 853-87.

2001a   The mythic mind, *SJOT* 15:3-56.

2001b   Ilimilku the theologian: the ideological roles of Athtar and Baal in KTU 1.1 and 1.6, 597-610 in O. Loretz, K. Metzler and H. Schaudig (eds) *Ex Oriente Lux.   Festschrift für Manfried Dietrich zu seinem 65. Geburtstag am 6.11.2000...* (AOAT 281, Münster: Ugarit-Verlag).

2001c   'Water, water everywhere...': Musings on the Aqueous Myths of the Near East, in *De la Tablilla a la Inteligencia Artificial. Homenaje al Prof. Jesús Luis Cunchillos en su 65 aniversario* (CD-ROM publication and WWW Site, Madrid). (In press.)

Zatelli, I.

1998   The origin of the biblical scapegoat ritual: the evidence of two Eblaite texts, *VT* 48:254-63.

Zevit, Z.

2001   *The Religions of Ancient Israel: a Synthesis of Parallactic Approaches* (Poole: Continuum).

Zimmer, H.

1962   *Myths and Symbols in Indian Art and Civilization* (New York: Harper and Row; Pantheon Books, Bollingen Foundation, Washington 1946).

ii) Biblical (New Testament)

iii) Post-Biblical (Apocryphal and Pseudepigrapha)

iv) RABBINICAL WRITINGS

v) WEST SEMITIC TEXTS

vi) AKKADIAN TEXTS

vii) ARABIC TEXTS

viii) EGYPTIAN TEXTS

ix) Greek Texts

II Authors